THE AMAZING VICT

Books by Mervyn Jones

NOVELS

A Survivor
Joseph
Holding On
Strangers
Lord Richard's Passion
Nobody's Fault
Today the Struggle
The Beautiful Words
A Short Time to Live
Two Women and their Man
Joanna's Luck
Coming Home
That Year in Paris

NON-FICTION

Chances: An Autobiography
A Radical Life: A Biography of Megan Lloyd George
Michael Foot

The Amazing Victorian
A LIFE OF GEORGE MEREDITH

Mervyn Jones

CONSTABLE • LONDON

First published in Great Britain 1999
by Constable and Company Limited
3 The Lanchesters, 162 Fulham Palace Road,
London w6 9ER
Copyright © 1999 Mervyn Jones
The right of Mervyn Jones to be identified as author
of this work has been asserted by him in accordance with
the Copyright, Designs and Patents Act 1988
ISBN 0 09 479810 7

Set in Monotype Baskerville 11pt by
Rowland Phototypesetting Ltd
Printed in Great Britain by
St Edmundsbury Press Ltd
both of Bury St Edmunds, Suffolk

A CIP catalogue record for this book is available from the British Library

Contents

1 A Veil of Reticence   1

2 Foundations   26

3 Born Again   39

4 Attempts and Failures   61

5 Through the Ordeal   79

6 The Best Years   98

7 The Faith of George Meredith   119

8 Champion of Women   139

9 Money Is Power   175

10 European and Cosmopolitan   197

11 Forgotten and Discovered   216

Plot Summaries   249

The Ordeal of Richard Feverel   249

Evan Harrington   252

Emilia in England   257

Rhoda Fleming   259

Vittoria   261

The Adventures of Harry Richmond   265

The Egoist   268

Beauchamp's Career   271

Diana of the Crossways   274

The Tragic Comedians   277

[5]

One of Our Conquerors 278
Lord Ormont and his Aminta 280
The Amazing Marriage 282
Celt and Saxon 285
References 287
Select Bibliography 296
Index 299

Illustrations

between pages 156 and 157

73, High Street, Portsmouth, George Meredith's childhood home
Thomas Love Peacock
George Meredith in 1860, portrait by D. G. Rossetti
W. C. Bonaparte Wyse, 1860
Sir William Hardman, the original of Blackburn Tuckham in
  Beauchamp's Career
George Meredith and his son Arthur, 1862
George Meredith, 1862
'Meredith destroying literary form' *Punch*, July 28th, 1894
Frederick Maxse, RN, the original of Nevil in *Beauchamp's Career*
Interior of the Chalet
Mary Ellen Meredith 1858. Drawing by Henry Wallis
Marie Vulliamy 1864. Drawing by Frederick Sandys
Leslie Stephen. The original of Vernon Whitford in *The Egoist*.
  Photograph by Julia Margaret Cameron
Virginia Woolf as a young girl
The last sketch of Meredith. By the French artist Noël Dorville
Flint Cottage. Photograph by Mervyn Jones

Author's Note

I am deeply grateful to Christine Fox, who has carried through the laborious task of preparing the notes to this book. Any lacunae in these notes should be attributed to my remissness in failing to do this work at an earlier stage. I am also grateful to Barbara Hardy and to Naomi Shepherd for constructive comments on my text.

In the book, I have discussed some of Meredith's novels in various contexts: for example, in relation to his humanist philosophy, to his attacks on class privilege, and to his sympathy for women. It would be tedious to recapitulate the plot of the novel in each context. Besides, Meredith's plots were often complex and intricate. I have therefore made summaries of the plot of each novel, to which the reader may refer when necessary.

1

A Veil of Reticence

In 1919, ten years after George Meredith's death, a book appeared which set out to be the first substantial biography, as distinct from the literary appreciations which had hitherto been published. The author was S. M. Ellis, Meredith's second cousin. As a member of the family, he was naturally well placed to record the personal as well as the public facts of Meredith's life. His opening paragraph was somewhat startling, yet undeniably true:

> During his lifetime an impenetrable veil of reticence, and, in consequence, of mystery also, hid the facts of George Meredith's origin and family history and his own early days from public knowledge . . . Various authors who produced appreciations of Meredith during his lifetime shied as they neared the danger zone of his origin, and slid warily over their thin ice with a few words of polite nebulosity.[1]

At the time when Ellis was at work, Meredith was generally regarded as a great writer, with a status equalled only by Thomas Hardy. In 1892 he was elected as President of the Society of Authors, a recognition of his eminence by his professional peers. He was awarded honorary degrees. In 1905 he became the first literary or cultural figure to hold the Order of Merit, otherwise given to political or military personalities. His eightieth birthday in 1908 and his death in 1909 evoked reverent tributes. Today, the entire life of such a writer would be exhaustively researched and publicized in newspaper and television profiles. Meredith preserved his reticence and his mystery. If he was asked where he came from, he replied vaguely: 'Hampshire.' Late in life, when a friend was helping him to complete the form for the 1901 census, he said that his place of birth was 'near Petersfield'. If this was true, the birth must have occurred when his mother was away from home on a visit. Ellis stated firmly that George Meredith was born at 73 High Street, Portsmouth, which was certainly his childhood home, and arranged for a plaque to be placed on the house. House and plaque were destroyed in the bombing of the Second World War, which might have pleased Meredith's ghost.

What was even more curious was that the truth about his family and youth had been told by Meredith himself, with very little disguise, in a novel, *Evan Harrington*, published in 1861 when he was thirty-three years old. George Meredith was the son of a tailor living and working in Portsmouth; Evan is the son of a tailor living and working in 'Lymport-on-the-Sea'. The outstanding figure in the Meredith family, dead before George was born but well remembered, was his grandfather, Melchizedek. The outstanding figure in the Harrington family, dying in the first chapter of the novel, is Evan's father, Melchisedec. Three of Melchizedek's daughters (George's aunts) were Louisa, married to a Consul in the Azores who rose to distinction in Portuguese society; Harriet, married to a brewer; and Catherine, married to an officer in the Royal Marines. Melchisedec Harrington's daughters are Louisa, married to a Portuguese Count; Harriet, married to a brewer; and Caroline, married to a Marines officer. Only one name is changed, and George did have an Aunt Caroline, who died young and whom he did not know. Some other characters in the novel are named as well as drawn from real life – for instance, an innkeeper with the unusual name of Kilne. One feels that Meredith was performing a double bluff and defying his readers to pierce the veil of reticence. *Evan Harrington* was accepted, and indeed criticized, as a work of pure fiction. The *Saturday Review* called it 'fresh, odd, a little extravagant, but noble and original'. The *Spectator* was nearer the mark, commenting: 'He thinks and speaks of what he has seen and known for himself.' But no one explicitly connected the Harringtons with the Merediths until the appearance of Ellis's biography almost sixty years later.

Dramatically, the mainspring of the novel is Evan's desire – supported by the frenetic stratagems of his sister Louisa, the Countess – to be accepted as a gentleman rather than merely the son of a tailor. Meredith, as we known from letters to his publisher, considered various titles, including *Gentle and Genteel, Gentility and a Gentleman,* and *All but a Gentleman.* In the end he settled for *Evan Harrington,* but with 'He Would be a Gentleman' as a subtitle. Ambiguity, or uncertain identity, is a central theme in the novel and in the young man's personality, just as in another novel of the period, Dickens's *Great Expectations*. But *Evan Harrington* gains greatly in resonance because Evan has inherited this ambiguity from Melchisedec, the dead man whose spirit pervades the young man's life – in fiction the young man's father, in reality the young novelist's grandfather.

Fact and fiction are, indeed, virtually inextricable. It is probably true that Meredith the tailor was known, like Harrington the tailor in the novel, as 'the Great Mel'. It seems to be true that he was the leading tailor in Portsmouth and made uniforms for some of the Admirals of his age, including Nelson; that he was an acceptable guest in the homes of the gentry; that he kept horses and hunted; that he was a prominent citizen and a churchwarden; that he was an officer in the militia yeomanry, a part-time force raised during the Napoleonic wars; that he had numerous love affairs, sometimes with ladies of high social ranking; that he spent money lavishly and left heavy debts when he died at the age of fifty-one. As Meredith wrote on the first page of the novel: 'This had been a grand man, despite his calling, and in the teeth of opprobrious epithets against his craft.' Lady Jocelyn, the wife of a baronet, says of him:

> He measures your husband in the morning: in the evening he makes love to you, through a series of pantomimic transformations . . . Though he was a snob, and an impostor, he could still make himself respected by his betters . . . I prefer him infinitely to your cowardly democrat, who barks for what he can't get, and is generally beastly. In fact, I'm not sure that I haven't a secret passion for the great tailor.

In the first chapter of *Evan Harrington*, a fellow-townsman tells the story of how the Great Mel, when staying at a hotel in Bath, was believed by the 'hotel people' to be a Marquis in disguise, and how the rumour spread until a lady at a dinner-party addressed him as 'my lord'. The Great Mel denies that he is a Marquis, but only after having some fun with the confusion and establishing that he could carry off the pretence if he chose. Whether this incident had actually occurred it is impossible to say, but Meredith was surely making use of a legend that had been attached to his grandfather.

As a boy, George Meredith was living in a house filled with memories of this remarkable ancestor. We can well understand the effect that being the grandson of 'the Great Mel' could have had on an imaginative child, and how he may have wondered what this greatness meant. At the same time, he had to be aware that he was living in a tailoring workshop. What, then, was his real social identity? It was in an uncertain zone somewhere between privileged wealth and abject poverty, both visible in the house or in the nearby streets. As. J. B. Priestley put it in his biography of Meredith, his position was 'between fish and fowl'.[2] The same can be said of most of the great Victorian novelists, and it gave them a sensitivity to nuances of social status that we recognize as an outstanding feature of their writing. Dickens – born, like Meredith, in Portsmouth – was the son of a clerk in the Navy pay office. Thackeray, born in Calcutta, was the son of an official in the service of the East India Company. Trollope's father was a lawyer, but an unsuccessful lawyer who ruined the family by ill-advised speculations.

The nineteenth century was an age of great social mobility – probably, although the point can hardly be proved statistically, greater than the twentieth. The thousands of new factories were, in most cases, the creation of men from humble homes who had the energy and ambition to seize the opportunities. The building of the railways was a bonanza in itself (though attended by failures and bankruptcies as well as successes.) Fortunes were to be made from industry, but also from supplying the market and pleasing the taste of the growing numbers of the wealthy – the wealthy being partly the established aristocracy, partly the newly rich themselves. Architects, builders and decorators, tailors for men and dress designers for women, entrepreneurs who launched hotels and restaurants could all find a place in the glittering scene. An army of clerks was needed to staff the banks and insurance companies, the head offices of all kinds of businesses, and the expanding bureaucracy of State and government. Those who rose to the surface of this bubbling cauldron might be rewarded with knighthoods or peerages and mingle with the descendants of genuine 'old families', but in moments of candour the realities were recognized. Louisa, in *Evan Harrington*, is a Countess and an outrageous snob; yet she asks: 'What does anybody's birth matter who's well off?' and declares: 'Half the aristocracy spring from shops.' She has discovered that Beckley Court, the mansion in which she has secured a foothold, was built by Lady Jocelyn's father 'from the proceeds of a successful oil speculation'. Oil as fuel was a thing of the future, and the oil in question would have been lamp or cooking oil, so Louisa comments cuttingly: 'That, I conceive, is grocery. So, you are all grocers on one side!'

All this mobility was incarnated in the figure of Jorrocks, the hero of R. S. Surtees' comic novel *Jorrocks' Jaunts and Jollities*, which was published in 1838 and became an instant best-seller. Jorrocks, who has indeed made his money from a chain of grocery shops, buys a country mansion, pushes his way into 'county' society, and becomes Master of the local hunt.

Although he transgresses every possible social convention, his breezy self-confidence is so potent that the landowning gentry have no option but to accept him. The Great Mel of *Evan Harrington* is a sort of Jorrocks, with the difference that he behaves so correctly that he can pass for a Marquis and make love to ladies. Sadly, there is another difference. Jorrocks, despite his vulgarity, has real money and can therefore surmount all the social barriers. Melchisedec, despite his gentlemanly manners and his commendable freedom from vulgarity, is nevertheless a tailor. At the dinner-table or in the hunting field, it may be difficult to remember this . . . difficult, but not impossible.

Genteel society in Victorian times maintained a rigorous attitude of superiority to what was called 'trade'. The element of hypocrisy, perceived by Louisa Harrington (or Meredith), only made it more vital to observe the distinctions. The professions – the Church, the law, medicine – occupied a borderland, clearly preferable to 'trade'; but one of Meredith's novels, *Diana of the Crossways*, contains a mordant portrait of a lawyer's wife who senses that she is rejected by 'society' although her husband has achieved a judgeship and a knighthood. The husband, Meredith noted, 'was by birth of a grade beneath his wife; he sprang (behind a curtain of horror) from tradesmen'. Of all the phrases that the writer might have chosen – 'curtain of snobbery' comes to mind – 'curtain of horror' has a peculiar emotional force.

If a taint of contaminating shame clung to 'trade' of any kind, there was something particularly degrading, and at the same time particularly ridiculous, about being a tailor. In relation to the gentleman who employed him, the tailor suggested a combination of subservience and personal – literally physical – intimacy. It was the tailor's function to measure the chest, the waist and the 'inner leg'. His role was akin to that of a servant – for instance, a valet – whose ability to overhear secrets and make shrewd observations had to be uneasily admitted, yet could not be overtly recognized. Above all, the tailor was ineradicably a tailor and could not, so long as he was a tailor, be a gentleman. The Great Mel's performance in an upper-class social milieu was admired, but only on the understanding that it was a performance, not a transformation. A revealing passage in one of Trollope's novels, *Lady Anna*, stated the rules:

Minnie loved her friend, but thought it to be a thing of horror that her friend should marry a tailor. It was almost as bad as the story of the Princess who had to marry a bear – worse indeed, for Minnie did

[15]

not at all believe that the tailor would ever turn out to be a gentleman, whereas she had been sure from the first that the bear would turn out to be a prince.

Trollope's tone is playfully mocking (although one notes, again, the word 'horror') but for Meredith – grandson of the Great Mel – the predicament was serious, and *Evan Harrington* is a serious novel. It must have been serious for the Great Mel himself, whether we think of him as Melchisedec Harrington or as Melchizedek Meredith. It was impossible for him not to feel the humiliation of being a tailor, and hence an object of contempt and ridicule. There had to be some escape; and he did find escape in his expansive social life, his indulgence in good food and wine, his love affairs. There was still a sense of alienation, of two aspects of his life that could not be reconciled. Riding to hounds, drilling with the militia, taking part in a ball at a great house, making love to a lady, he felt that he was truly himself. He was not simply happier but more alive when freed from the humdrum routine and the distasteful compulsions of the workshop.

Lady Jocelyn was unjust, or careless with her language, when she said that the Great Mel was an impostor. As the 'Marquis' episode shows, he made no deliberate pretence of being other than what he was. But when he sat at the dinner-table and received the respectful attentions of the lady who addressed him as 'my lord', he was certainly relishing a fantasy that he had already conjured up in his imagination. If he was not an impostor, he was nevertheless a fantasist – a Walter Mitty of his age.

As a writer, Meredith paid full attention to fantasy and never despised it. He understood the human need for it as a relief from the limitations of everyday real life. In a novella, *The House on the Beach*, the fantasist is a man called Tinman, who has the humble position of bailiff in a small town. His fantasy is that he is to be presented to the Queen; he has a Court suit made, dresses in it when he thinks himself unobserved, and practises the formal bow to be made at the Palace. Herbert Fellingham, a young journalist, penetrates Tinman's secret and regards it without sympathy. Meredith tells us:

Herbert's contempt for Tinman was intense; it was that of the young and ignorant who live in their imaginations like spendthrifts, unaware of the importance of them as the food of life, and of how necessary it is to seize upon the solider one among them for perpetual sustenance when the unsubstantial are vanishing . . . As cart or cab-horses, uncomplaining as a rule, show their view of the nature of harness when they

[16]

have release to frisk in a field, it is possible that existence was made tolerable to the jogging man by some minutes of excitement in his bailiff's Court suit.

Here, Meredith defines the function and the value of fantasy – to make existence tolerable. The theme of fantasy recurs often in his novels and is treated most elaborately in *The Adventures of Harry Richmond*, with the figure of Richmond Roy, whose life is an indulgence in fantasy. But this novel also warns of a danger – the danger of going too far, of surrendering entirely to fantasy and becoming incapable of distinguishing between fantasy and reality. The climactic scene, when Richmond Roy sacrifices his life by rushing into a blazing house to rescue a woman who is not there, is the ultimate *reductio ad absurdum*. Meredith would have agreed with Freud that the process of growing into maturity consists of replacing fantasy with reality. This advance is the laborious, sometimes painful, experience of the Meredithian young man: Richard Feverel, Harry Richmond, Nevil Beauchamp, Matthew Weyburn.

To return to the Great Mel: his escape into fantasy takes the form of reveries of a remote period of history, as a contrast to the materialistic nineteenth century. He has pictures of medieval knights in his room, and Evan recalls: 'I know he wished he had lived in those days of knights and battles.' Such nostalgic thoughts, evoking ideals of chivalry and heroism, occupied Meredith's imagination throughout his writing life. When he was commissioned, during the American Civil War, to write an account of a battle between a Union and a Confederate warship – a battle fought in the English Channel and visible to people in Cherbourg – he wrote: 'Never did knightly tournament boast a more eager multitude of spectators', and went on: 'The chivalrous give and take of battle was glorious.' The terminology was wildly inappropriate, considering that the battle was between ironclad, steam-powered ships, whose crews were seeking to smash the opponent with heavy guns firing explosive shells, and would have been very surprised to hear that they were involved in a chivalrous tournament. But in this sphere, too, Meredith was always conscious of the disparity between chivalrous ideals and everyday rationality – between fantasy and reality. One of the books that he most loved and often re-read was *Don Quixote*.

For Meredith – and for the Great Mel – fantasy took yet another form: that of imagining himself to be the illegitimate son of a mysterious, but certainly aristocratic, biological father. Louisa in *Evan Harrington* says: 'Had poor Papa been legitimised, he would have been a nobleman.' The theme is not elaborated, and of course Meredith has depicted Louisa as a champion fantasist. But it was sometimes suggested that Meredith himself was not the son of a tailor. The hidden father might have been, as Ellis put it, 'some aristocratic and amorous admiral ashore', or even possibly the notoriously dissolute Prince Regent, later King George IV. It would be hard to make the dates fit, since Meredith was born in 1828 and George IV lived from 1762 to 1830, but a dash of inventiveness and the name 'George' would be enough to set the story going. Ellis knew of it, which indicates that it was a family legend, and wrote reprovingly:

> Whatever the causes that prompted Meredith's reticence on the subject of his origin, he was singularly ill-advised in preserving that silence to the end; for the sake of his mother's reputation he should, presumably, have refuted the absurd rumours – if they ever reached his ears – that were current about his paternity. For, baulked of any authentic information, public curiosity was titillated, and speculation rife as to the causes or necessities for this strange and mysterious reserve.[3]

If speculation was indeed 'rife', it would be hard to believe that the rumours never reached Meredith's ears. What is certain is that the theme appealed to the novelist alert to the workings of fantasy. It is a theme amply developed in the character of Richmond Roy, who is convinced that he is the son of an actress and an aristocratic or royal personage, and who dedicates himself to gaining a 'rightful' social position, whether for himself or for his son, Harry. The 'absurd rumours' about Meredith's own parentage may well have contributed to this plot, for *The Adventures of Harry Richmond* is the only Meredith novel narrated in the first person.

In the days of 'knights and battles', personal combat – often to the death – was an accepted means of resolving a dispute on a point of honour. Shakespeare (Meredith was a devotee of Shakespeare) had made effective dramatic use of it in *Richard II* and in *Romeo and Juliet*. From the seventeenth century, such personal combat became formalized in the procedure of the duel, with its traditional ritual and its codified rules. In England, duelling flourished well into the Regency period, to which Meredith sometimes looks back nostalgically from his own unromantic Victorian age. His grandfather, Melchizedek (who lived from 1763 to 1814), was a Regency character – with the elegance, the financial extravagance, and the loose sexual morals of the period – and so is the Great Mel of *Evan Harrington*. Lady Jocelyn, in the panegyric quoted above, remarks approvingly: 'The fellow had some capital points. He fought two or three duels, and behaved like a man.' The duel, in fact, served more than one purpose. It resolved the actual dispute; it validated the personal courage of the duellist; it also validated his social status (Evan Harrington, the tailor's son, is deemed ineligible); and it earned him the admiration and perhaps the love of a desirable woman, or her tears if he did not survive.

Duels are described in *The Ordeal of Richard Feverel*, *Vittoria*, *The Adventures of Harry Richmond*, *Rhoda Fleming* and *The Tragic Comedians*. This recurrence is all the more remarkable when we bear in mind that duelling was never so prevalent in England as in some other countries, and by Meredith's time had become an anachronism. (George Smythe, who was credited with fighting the last duel in England in 1852, was a friend of Meredith's.) As a convention of upper-class behaviour, duelling was particularly dominant in Russia, where it brought about the deaths of Pushkin and Lermontov; in the southern states of the USA; and above all in Germany, where the visible scar was a badge of honour for students and the custom lingered into the twentieth century. All these societies could be defined as aristocratic, in contrast to bourgeois England, and retained the values – or the delusions and absurdities – of chivalry. The duel that is the climax of *The Tragic Comedians* is fully convincing because the novel is set in Germany and based on real events. The duel in *Rhoda Fleming* is fought between Army officers in India, and in *Vittoria* the champion duellist is an Austrian captain.

The conclusion must be that duelling held an irresistible fascination for Meredith. Fascination, however, is not the same as rational approval, and all the duels in the novels are unjustified or foolish. Richard Feverel's challenge to Lord Mountfalcon is the foolhardy act of an immature young man, and Mountfalcon is behaving sensibly when he tries to dissuade Richard from going through with it. Alvan in *The Tragic Comedians*, like Ferdinand Lassalle in real life, is driven by sheer pride into a course that Meredith depicts as both culpable and suicidal. We could, indeed, regard these duels, and the disasters that result from them, as in the nature of an awful warning.

Moreover, Meredith explicitly and repeatedly manifests his disapproval. Duelling is denounced in *Beauchamp's Career* as a 'sickening folly' and a 'foul custom'; in *Harry Richmond* as 'a silly business' and 'the pastime of brainless young men'. This last phrase is the verdict of Princess Ottilia, on whose behalf the duel is being fought. In *Diana of the Crossways*, Sullivan Smith, an impetuous Irishman who is in love with Diana, imagines that she has been insulted and decides to issue a challenge, only to be deterred by the more mature and reasonable Redworth with the words: 'You don't mean to say you're the donkey to provoke a duel?'

In his characteristic fashion, Meredith was involved in the contest within himself between fantasy and reality. The duels – whether they take place or not, and even when the results are extremely serious – have a quality of fantasy; we can imagine Alvan, for example, saying to himself: 'I can't believe I'm doing this.' Meredith touches the extremes of fantasy when Nevil Beauchamp, in a deluded paroxysm of patriotism, challenges the whole French Army. Once again, it is incumbent on the duellist – if only he can survive the duel – to regain a sense of reality. And yet, there is always a certain nobility and a certain heroism inherent in even the most foolish or absurd of challenges. Meredith did not create a scenario in which the villain, aiming to entrap or destroy the hero, makes the challenge. No: the challenge comes from the hero, or at least from the character with whom Meredith feels sympathy and makes identification.

Torn between fascination and aversion, Meredith found a solution. This was to endorse and praise the ability to fight without justifying the commitment to kill or be killed. Fencing or 'swordsmanship' is extolled, in *Vittoria* and again in *Lord Ormont and His Aminta*, as a praiseworthy skill. Thus, Vittoria asks Carlo, the man to whom she is becoming attracted, whether he is a good swordsman; he replies, to her satisfaction, that he fenced with his father for two hours a day. Another sublimation of lethal combat is boxing. Skepsey, a somewhat comical but attractive character in *One of Our Conquerors*, is an enthusiast for boxing and instructor at a boxing club, while a detailed description of a boxing match figures in *The Amazing Marriage*. In these novels, written in the 1880s when Meredith was concerned about the threat of attack by Germany and the defence-lessness of Britain, boxing is the symbol, made explicit by Skepsey, of an improvement in the standard of health and readiness for action. Meredith himself, for most of his life, was endowed with exuberant good health and surplus energy and took a great deal of exercise.

There was yet another strand in the complex texture of George Meredith's inheritance. Growing up in England – indeed, in the part of southern England that was conquered and settled by Saxons – he convinced himself that he was a Celt, Welsh on the paternal and Irish on the maternal side. In this, he was relying on the family names; he was patrilineally a Meredith and his mother's maiden surname was Macnamara.

Meredith is certainly a Welsh name, found most often in the border counties of Powys and Clwyd and also in Shropshire, an English border

county with a distinct Welsh cultural flavour. The original Welsh form
was Maredudd, but the 'u' should be pronounced like an English short
'i' and the final 'dd' like the English 'th'. Thanks to the arrival of scribes
from England, serving in feudal baronies or in the Church, the spelling
'Meredith' came into use soon after the first English conquest in the
Middle Ages, and it became official in later centuries when the old Welsh
patronymics were replaced by surnames. However, it is one of the names
– like Jones, Price and Powell – which in modern times can belong to
people in England who are quite unaware of a Welsh ancestry. George
Meredith's own family had been rooted in Hampshire for at least three
generations, and the men had doubtless married English women. Similarly, while Macnamara is certainly an Irish name, Meredith's mother
(she was Jane Macnamara, daughter of a Portsmouth innkeeper) came
from a family long settled in the south of England. To find someone in
the Meredith biography who was really as much as half Welsh, we must
wait until we meet Mary Ellen Peacock, whom George married. Her
mother had been Jane Gryffydh, from the truly Welsh town of Maentwrog. For George, that must have been part of the attraction.

Meredith created Welsh characters whenever he could, often when
their role in the novel would have been just the same had they been
English. In *Vittoria*, Merthyr Powys, who volunteers to fight for the liberation of Italy, is Welsh. In the novella *General Ople and Lady Camper*, the
high-spirited Lady Camper, who teaches the General a valuable moral
lesson, is 'of Welsh blood, and born among the mountains'. In another
novella, *A Tale of Chloe*, the noble and self-sacrificing Chloe is Welsh.
Victor Radnor, the central character in *One of Our Conquerors*, is a millionaire with a home in London and an estate in Surrey, but his descent from
'Welsh princes' is casually mentioned. In *The Amazing Marriage*, Gower
Woodseer tells us that his mother came from Glamorgan, and Owain
Wythan is a Welshman from the mining valleys, the setting for an important episode in the story. The names – Powys, Radnor, Gower – are
pointers. All these characters are men and women for whom the reader
must feel admiration or at least sympathy. Woodseer was in fact modelled
on a Scot, Meredith's friend Robert Louis Stevenson.

Meredith was positive that the Welsh were very different from the
English, and indeed from any other people. A sentence in *Emilia in England*
sums up his view: 'There is human nature and Welsh nature.' For him,
the Celtic peoples – Welsh, Irish and Scots – are imaginative, artistically
creative, emotionally spontaneous and impulsive, while the English are
dull and unimaginative, though efficient and reliable in practical matters.

In a letter written in 1881, he grumbled: 'The heart of the nation is Teuton and moral, and therewith intellectually obtuse, next to speechless.'[4] Earlier, in 1870, he had made this contrast the central theme in a novel entitled *Celt and Saxon* (though he never completed it and it was published in unfinished form after his death). A representative English character is Mr Adister, a landowner living in North Wales, blind to the qualities of his Welsh neighbours or his Irish guests. But another Englishman in this novel, while agreeing that 'Welsh blood is queer blood', points out: 'They have poetry in them, they are valiant, they are hospitable . . . Their life is their friend's at need.' English dominance has created an environment intolerable to Celts, who are therefore emigrating across the Atlantic: 'America has caught the imagination of the Cambrian Celt,' Meredith remarks.

In *Diana of the Crossways*, the fascinating but irresponsible Diana Warwick – although her main role is to illustrate the predicament of a woman in a male-dominated society – injects extra drama into the story because of her Irish origin and what Meredith saw as her Irish personality. Ultimately, however, it was impossible for Meredith – with his English memories, English home and English friends – to make a wholesale rejection of English values. Diana eventually accepts the reliable Redworth as a husband and hopes for a child 'of the marriage of the two noblest of human souls (Irishwoman and Englishman, be it noted)'.

Meredith's belief in his Welsh origins was not altogether a fantasy, but it tipped over into fantasy – and merged with the visions of 'knights and battles' – when he imagined himself as the descendant not merely of Welsh ancestors but of Welsh princes. In the shadowy history of Wales before the English conquest, there are records of Maredudd, ruler of Powys in the eleventh century, who extended his power to Gwynedd and expelled the Viking invaders. Serious historians can scarcely see Maredudd as more than a clan chieftain, and the title of 'prince' was unknown, but the imagination of George Meredith supplied what was lacking. Both the Great Mel in *Evan Harrington* and Radnor in *One of Our Conquerors* make brief but confident allusions to these princely forebears. In *The Ordeal of Richard Feverel*, the Feverel family trace their descent to a medieval knight who, 'having quarters on the Welsh frontier, mixed his blood with the royal blood of Gruffudh: from whose fair Princess the Welsh estates were inherited, and who must at the same time have endowed them with that Cymric tinge to their habits and mental cast observable in the fortunes of the race'. Although the Feverels of the novel live in the Thames Valley and could quite well, for narrative purposes, be thoroughly English,

Richard is given a grandfather called Sir Caradoc, who had a mystical belief in a hereditary curse.

Thus, it is clear that Meredith drew on family memories and family stories – on realities and on fantasies – in his novels, and particularly in *Evan Harrington*. We could, indeed, take *Evan Harrington* as a straightforward autobiographical novel, but for one remarkable omission. There are obvious portraits of Meredith's grandparents, the 'Great Mel' and the dignified, strong-minded woman who was known as 'Mrs Mel', but no portraits of his parents. Because he was identifying himself with Evan Harrington, he had to juggle with the generations, turning a grandfather into a father and aunts into sisters.

The real parents were Augustus Urmston Meredith, son of Melchizedek, and Jane (Macnamara) Meredith. Like Evan Harrington, Augustus was the youngest of the family, with older sisters. He was seventeen years old when Melchizedek died. It is possible (firm evidence is lacking) that he had, like Evan, spent some time in Lisbon with his sister Louisa and her husband and acquired gentlemanly manners. It is certain that, like Evan, he was sternly ordered by his mother to carry on the tailoring business and pay off the debts. Thereafter, the divergence begins. Unlike Evan, Augustus Meredith did spend his life as a tailor; he did not marry a baronet's daughter, come into possession of a country estate and a fortune, or lead the life of a gentleman. One sees, all too well, why there was no use for him in the novel.

In adult life Meredith, as Ellis put it, 'regarded his early life only with bitterness and pain', and therefore refused to talk about it. Only when he was an old man did he, occasionally and sparingly, allow friends or interviewers some glimpses behind the veil. One interviewer was told: 'I was a very timid and sensitive boy. I was frightened of everything; I could not endure to be left alone.' He described his mother as 'handsome, refined and witty' – which may or may or may not be an idealization, since we have no other accounts of her.[5] Of his father, he said tersely: 'He was a muddler and a fool.'[6] Actually, Augustus may have been a muddler if judged by his management of a small business, but he was not a fool, for he belonged to the Portsmouth Literary and Philosophical Society and was an outstanding chess-player. Whether through his limitations of character, or simply through unhappy circumstances for which he was not to blame, he was doomed to be a failure. The qualities of Melchizedek – the magnetic personality, the self-confidence, the fascinating line of talk, the ability to win popularity, and the soaring imagination – seem to have missed Augustus to pass on to George.

The Meredith home at 73 High Street was less than a hundred yards from the sea front and the historic defences of Portsmouth: the Round Tower, the Square Tower, the Eighteen-Gun Battery, the Sally Port. Here was rich material for the daydreams of a boy growing up when the threat of French invasion and the glories of Trafalgar were still remembered by old salts puffing their clay pipes on the ramparts. Anyone living near the harbour could watch the arrival of warships returning from distant overseas stations, and also the departure of transports taking convicts to Australia. (In a letter written when he revisited Portsmouth at the age of thirteen, Meredith noted that some convicts were 'of distinguished appearance' and one was a clergyman.) But this part of old Portsmouth was a warren of narrow, twisting streets – in our century, swept away by bombing and rebuilt in sedate modern style – thickly spattered with pubs and recognized or unrecognized brothels. As sailors swarmed ashore after long voyages, the 'timid and sensitive boy' could hear the noise of drunken shouting and singing, the echoes of street fights, and the screams of assaulted or terrified women.

When George was five years old, his mother died. He was an only child, and there was no one to comfort him except a father whom he could not love nor admire and who was preoccupied with the struggle for financial survival. Funds from the Macnamara side of the family enabled him to attend a school in nearby Southsea which was deemed to be socially superior to the local school where other High Street boys went. Inevitably, this removed him from the community in which he lived and increased his loneliness. Nevertheless, he did not come to terms with his new schoolfellows and, according to an account recorded by Ellis, got the nickname of 'Gentleman Georgy' because of his aloof attitude, his refusal to join in playground games, and his 'drawling, patronising' speech. Already, the hero of *Evan Harrington, or He Would be a Gentleman* was taking shape.

In 1838, when George was ten years old, the suppliers of cloth with whom Augustus dealt demanded overdue payments which he could not make, and he was declared bankrupt. He left Portsmouth, handing over his premises to a rival, and went to London to live in lodgings and work as a wage-earning tailor. As well as his son, he was supporting a woman named Matilda Buckett, who had been his housekeeper (whatever that actually meant). Six months after the move, Augustus and Matilda were married. George could not accept her presence in place of his lost mother, and emotionally he was permanently alienated from his father. A year later, father and son were officially separated. Anna Macnamara, a sister of George's mother, died and left money invested for the boy, providing an income of £66 a year, enough for the fees at a modest boarding-school. Legally, George became a ward in Chancery and the responsibilities of parenthood were renounced by his father, to be exercised by the solicitor for the Macnamara family. He was sent to a school, presumably selected by this solicitor, which biographers have been unable to identify or place geographically. If it was like the school described in *Harry Richmond* as Rippenger's (Harry was also an orphan) it was tough, unpleasant and educationally useless, and George must have been unhappy there.

In 1842, after spending only one year at this school, Meredith made another move. The move, this time, was to a school in a foreign country – Germany – run on unorthodox educational principles. So far as we know, the idea was Meredith's own and was merely approved by the lawyer who was his official guardian. At the age of fourteen, George Meredith – alone in the world, without a mother, without a legally responsible father, without a home – was becoming a man.

2

Foundations

THE school at Neuwied, a small town on the Rhine, belonged to the Moravian Brotherhood. Back in the fifteenth century, religious reformers in Moravia and Bohemia (now the Czech Republic) had created this *Unitas Fratrum* as a Church independent of Rome, with its own bishops elected by Church members. It was the first Protestant Church in Europe, decades before Luther. After the Battle of the White Mountain in 1620, when Protestant forces were crushed by the armies of Catholic Austria, the Brotherhood found a new home in Lutheran Saxony. Through centuries of persecution, while Protestants were harried by Catholics in France, Catholics by Protestants in Ireland, and Jews by everybody, the devout Moravians were distinguished by a spirit of tolerance. The motto of Bishop Comenius was: 'In things essential, unity; in things non-essential, liberty; in all things, charity.' Count Zinzendorf, a leading figure in the Brotherhood, coined the word 'ecumenical' and taught: 'The Saviour is a loving friend to all who open themselves to him, equally for man and woman, Count and peasant, black and white, young and old.'

Followers lived together in a *Gemeined*, or community, which in the early period (the rules were gradually modified) had some resemblance to a pioneering kibbutz. For example, children were cared for in a dormitory building from the age of eighteen months, and from the age of four they took part in the farm work or gardening. The Brotherhood put great emphasis on education, with adults teaching children anything from theology to mathematics and from horticulture to carpentry. There were no teachers, as a special profession; it was every adult's duty to pass on skill and knowledge. Here, too, tolerance was a guiding principle. Zinzendorf wrote: 'We should not command or forbid anything to our children, but should seek to awaken tender love for the Saviour in their hearts . . . No child should be punished unless he is convinced that he is wrong.'

In the eighteenth century the Brotherhood developed schools in the usual sense, partly for the children of the community, partly to train future missionaries, for the Brotherhood was spreading its version of the Christian faith to Africans, black slaves in the Caribbean, Native Americans on the Alleghany frontier, and even nomadic Inuit in Labrador and Alaska. Some of the schools accepted pupils from outside the community and began to charge modest fees. Neuwied was started, with six pupils and one teacher, in 1756. The environment was favourable, since the princes of the small independent state of Wied pursued a policy of toleration and equal citizenship for Protestants, Catholics and even Jews. The fiftieth anniversary found Neuwied with 406 pupils, many from other parts of Germany or from Switzerland.

With the coming of peace after the Napoleonic wars, the appeal of Neuwied reached Britain. Historians of Neuwied write of an 'English period', dating from about 1820 and going strong until about 1870. In the 1830s, out of 346 boys at the school, 150 were British. Others were Swiss, Dutch or French, so that Germans constituted a minority. Later, there were several years in which Neuwied had no German pupils at all. As the school boomed, applications from Britain were turned down because there were not enough teachers. When it closed down in 1913, the records showed that it had received 4,573 pupils, of whom 2,720 – more than half – had been British. Most of them came from 'good families', though not generally from the really rich or the aristocracy. Several achieved distinction in adult life, including a Chaplain to Queen Victoria, a President of the Royal College of Surgeons, and a Professor of English at University College, London. This was Henry Morley, who for a time ran a school in England on Moravian lines. He was a friend of George Meredith (though he should not be confused with John Morley, a much closer friend). Thus, although Meredith's decision to go to Neuwied can be called adventurous, it was less than extraordinary.

Neuwied certainly made a contrast with British boarding-schools. Even the most prestigious, such as Eton and Harrow, had distinctly unattractive features: brutal punishments such as regular and merciless caning, systematic bullying tolerated by the staff, the fagging system which made the younger boys the virtual slaves of the older, Spartan living conditions, inadequate and unhealthy food. Mothers wept, and some fathers had qualms, when boys pleaded not to be sent back after the holidays. Parents who looked for an alternative were a minority, but a minority that grew. Hence, Neuwied served the function that in a later age was fulfilled by 'progressive schools' such as Bedales or Dartington. Henry Morley's testimony, written in 1854, twenty years after his spell at Neuwied, must have had an influence on the next generation:

> The multitude of boys, living together in a sort of federal republic, was not only maintained in perfect discipline without an act of violence, but very few went away from among us whose minds had not been, to some degree, enriched, enlarged, and ennobled . . . A spirit of truth-fulness, of gentleness, of cordiality between the teachers and the taught, pervaded our whole body; punishments of the most nominal kind sufficed for the scholastic discipline . . . Every one of us was being humanized in the best way, and trained to become a thinker and a student for himself thereafter.[1]

At the same time, thinking parents were observing that boys were emerging from British schools in a state of what could only be called ignorance. Teaching was often entrusted to 'ushers' who had no training and no qualifications, who were themselves quite uneducated, who took on the job because they could get nothing else, and who gave satisfaction if they could merely keep order in the classroom. Meredith portrayed these ushers derisively in the characters of Boddy in *Harry Richmond* and Jack Raikes in *Evan Harrington*. Even in prestigious schools, the curriculum was narrow and antiquated and the demands made on the pupils were minimal. A boy who managed to construe Caesar and scan Virgil could get passable reports and find his way to Oxford or Cambridge – and there were anxieties about the standards of the universities too. Education was falling short of the requirements of a growing capitalist economy, which could not be properly served by men who knew practically nothing of the sciences, nor of a rapidly changing technology. In Germany, apparently, learning was taken more seriously, tuition was more effective, and standards were significantly higher. Concern about the contrast, which became acute in the latter half of the nineteenth century when German industry and technology were visibly forging ahead, was already felt in the first half. In *Lord Ormont and his Aminta*, written in 1894, Meredith gives these reflections to Matthew Weyburn:

> French boys and German, having passed a year or two at an English school, get the liking for our games, and do a lot of good when they

get home. The things we learn from them are to dance, to sing, and to study – they are more in earnest than we about study.

There was a particular point concerning the teaching of languages. Traditional British schools provided some tuition of French (a kind of French, travellers discovered, that was not understood in France) but gave much more attention to Latin and classical Greek. This was not good enough at a time when the expansion of British export trade, and therefore of salesmanship, required an effective command of French and German. At Neuwied all the teaching was in German, while French was a compulsory subject. After two years, Meredith came home fluent in both these languages. Throughout his life, his linguistic capacity added considerably to his intellectual range, as well as to his enjoyment when he travelled.

The moral and religious philosophy of the Moravian Brotherhood was another element in the appeal to middle-class, liberal-minded British families. Up to the dawn of the Victorian age, the traditional parson in the Church of England was a country gentleman who drank his port, prayed for the King, and took his congregation through the Sunday services as a matter of routine; his moral code coincided with social custom and his political allegiance was conventionally Tory. This kind of Church was more suited to the landowners of the shires than to the factory-owners and merchants of the growing industrial towns. There, the Rector or Vicar was likely to be a man of earnest piety, strict in his morality, a serious student of theological literature, and more inclined to a cup of tea than a bottle of port. In 1846, nine hundred clergymen and laymen of this type attended a conference to found the Evangelical Alliance. For them, the Church had a duty to instil true Christian faith and improved moral behaviour in the population at large, the poor of the cities, and the pagans of heathen lands overseas. The Evangelical movement spread fast and struck deep. In parishes where it took hold, services were simple and austere, old rituals were discarded, and sermons were didactic and long. Large sections of the middle class were devoutly Evangelical, or had moved out of the Established Church altogether to become Methodists, Baptists or Congregationalists. Their beliefs meshed easily with those of the Moravian Brotherhood, and the greatest benefit that they could confer on their children was an education at Neuwied.

Under the Brotherhood system, the community (*Gemeined*) was divided into choirs (*Chören*) of people who lived in the same building, prayed together, and worked together on productive tasks. With the development of schools such as Neuwied, the pupils were likewise grouped in choirs, each consisting of fifteen boys or fifteen girls. In charge of each choir were two adults: a *Lehrer*, who was a teacher in the straightforward sense, and an *Erzieher*, a supervisor with the duty of attending to the moral growth, the conduct and the religious faith of those in his or her care. The aim was to guide the youngsters into living a Christian life, which would ensure salvation through Christ. A German historian writes of 'the principle of constant supervision, a remnant of early pietist days' and comments that it 'was reassuring and comforting but also resulted in over-protectiveness'. There were many religious services, at choir level or for the whole school, and of course daily prayers. As in Evangelical churches and Nonconformist chapels in England, the doctrine was based on the direct relationship between the individual and God through Christ, the Saviour. Pupils of the Moravians heard nothing of intercession through saints nor of the cult of the Virgin Mary, as inculcated by the Catholic Church or the High Church wing of the Church of England.

To say whether Meredith was a dutiful Christian while at Neuwied is as impossible as it is to say whether Stalin was an Orthodox believer during his years in a seminary. In one of his reminiscences towards the end of his life, he told a friend:

> When I was quite a boy I had a spasm of religion which lasted about six weeks, during which I made myself a nuisance in asking everybody whether they were saved. But never since have I swallowed the Christian fable.[3]

The 'spasm' may have lasted longer than a mere six weeks, since Meredith wrote a letter to another boy adjuring him that 'true fellowship is not to be had without Christianity; not the name but the practice of it', and this letter dates from his last year at the school in 1844.[4] There is no record that young George was a rebel at Neuwied, and it is likely that he was impressed by the dedication and sincerity of the *Erzieher* and inclined to accept their guidance. Where he diverged – certainly after he left Neuwied and throughout the rest of his life – was in rejecting the concept of Christ as a divine being, which of course is central to Christianity. But to reject the 'Christian fable' is not the same as rejecting the idea of God as an invisible spirit pervading the universe, and there are recurrent references to God, thus envisaged, in his poems and in personal letters over the years. To this extent, the teachings of the Brotherhood had a lasting influence on him.

One more aspect of the Neuwied education that won approval among

British parents was the emphasis on physical health, outdoor exercise and sport. Neuwied had a gymnasium (a new one was built shortly after Meredith left) with equipment for exercises on the Swedish model, an activity not yet introduced into British schools. There were team games, athletic contests and races, and the boys from England introduced cricket and hockey. There was also a swimming-pool fed from the Rhine. Many references to swimming can be found in Meredith's novels, sometimes literally and sometimes as a descriptive metaphor ('she swam across the room to meet him'), and the episode in *Lord Ormont and his Aminta* when Matthew and Aminta swim for miles in the sea is written with ecstatic fervour. Walking in the countryside in groups was already a German custom, linked with the romantic spirit, and taken up later by the Socialist and also the Nazi youth movements. An enjoyable feature of the Neuwied year, nostalgically recalled by Henry Morley, was the annual 'long walk', lasting several days, when the walkers slept in barns or under the stars. Almost all the characters portrayed favourably in Meredith's novels lead a vigorous physical life and are to be found walking, riding, swimming, boating, playing cricket, boxing or fencing. Evan Harrington walks over-night from London to Portsmouth, and Carinthia Jane in *The Amazing Marriage*, when she leaves her girlhood home, insists on walking to her destination and rejects her brother's proposal to take a carriage. Meredith himself was a great walker from his young days until he was crippled by spinal trouble in his sixties. On one walking holiday in the Italian Alps, he covered thirty miles a day for a week. It all began at Neuwied.

Finally, liberal British parents favoured Neuwied because it offered an education for their daughters. There were hardly any girls' schools with a serious teaching curriculum until the foundation of Queen's College in Harley Street and North London Collegiate School in the 1850s. In general, girls stayed at home in the care of more or less competent – or incompetent, but in any case untrained – governesses. If they could sew, play the piano, sing and behave correctly in the drawing-room, that was considered sufficient to equip them for adult life – with reasonable luck, for an early and suitable marriage. As Alice Woods observed sharply in a book published in 1937: 'Talent or no talent, they had to perform on a piano at parties, and were escorted to the instrument on a man's arm ... They were not allowed to work unless they were fortunate enough to belong to parents who were poor, as many of the clergy were.'[5]

The title of Alice Woods's book was *George Meredith as Champion of Women and of Progressive Education*, and she was right to make the link. Women were caught in a trap from which, it can be argued, they have not altogether escaped to this day: because they were not educated, they could be seen as ignorant, stupid and inferior to men, and their inferiority was a reason why they should not be educated. The vicious circle could be broken only by providing them with proper education, and Neuwied was one of the few schools anywhere in which this was done.

Neuwied was not a co-educational school; no such thing existed in any country until the end of the century. For moral reasons, unmarried young men and women had always been carefully segregated in the Moravian communities. However, since the structure of the community implied that girls did not grow up under the parental roof, and since all youngsters – indeed, children – were expected to make an economic contribution, the girls as well as the boys were given an education which might be described as 'separate but equal'. As early as 1723, there are records of parallel schools for girls and boys. By the nineteenth century, girls' choirs and boys' choirs at Neuwied were being taught the same subjects and, it appears, expected to reach the same standards. The boys outnumbered the girls; in the 1850s Neuwied had about one hundred of the former and about fifty of the latter. But this was because parents abroad, especially in England, were more likely to send boys to Neuwied.

Beatrice Batty, an English girl who was at Neuwied in the 1850s, recorded in a later account that 'Moravian schools in Germany were far ahead of English girls' schools in the methods of instruction . . . On my return home my descriptions of the manner in which lessons were given excited surprise and admiration.' She had been learning geography, history and mathematics. She added that gymnastic exercises for girls were 'almost the same as those for boys – on the bars, the horse, the horizontal ladder'. Another pupil, Jane Pinder, remembered the high-level teaching in botany and natural history.[6]

It is difficult to establish how much time the boys and girls were able to spend together outside the classroom. They met, presumably, at meals, at religious services, at concerts and other cultural occasions, and as spectators (if not participants) at sporting events. They may have worked together, for instance at picking grapes, and they may have gone for walks together, although one doubts whether girls were free to join the boys for the 'long walk' and the camping out. As and when they did meet, they could naturally discuss what they had learned from their teachers, since they were studying the same subjects. It is not too much to say that they could become friends. At the least, the boys saw enough of the girls – and vice versa – not to regard them as a strange, mysterious species, a focus of mingled fascination and fear. In the earlier chapters of *Lord Ormont and His Aminta*, Meredith drew a derisive picture of rigorous segregation of boys and girls. Attending schools in the same neighbourhood, Matthew and Aminta exchange glances on Sunday walks, are attracted, and get as far as a clandestine exchange of letters on which the heads of the two schools firmly crack down. Meredith's point is that normal contact and friendship are a safeguard against, rather than an invitation to, sexual disaster. When they meet again as adults, Matthew explains to Aminta:

> All the – *passez-moi le mot* – devilry between the sexes begins at their separation. They're foreigners when they meet; and their alliances are not always binding. The chief object in life, if happiness be the aim, and the growing better than we are, is to teach men and women how to be one; for, if they're not, then each is a morsel for the other to prey on.

Meredith was happy at Neuwied. To appreciate how much this mattered to him, we should recall how many boys of his age and in his time – especially boys without a home and family, without money, without assured prospects – were miserably unhappy, and indeed how unhappy he had been in the years before Neuwied. The knowledge that happiness was achievable gave him the courage and self-confidence to confront the troubles that were ahead of him, and became an important theme in his writing. Some Meredith novels end tragically, but most have a happy ending, not artificially tacked on, but arising convincingly from the core of the story.

The Neuwied experience planted a seed that bore fruit fifteen years later in Meredith's first important novel, *The Ordeal of Richard Feverel*. This is a *Bildungsroman* – a German word that has gained international currency. The German *Bildung* and the French *formation* are terms without an exact equivalent in English. Broader than 'education', they denote the development of personality in youthful years. Thus conceived, *Bildung* was the concern of the Neuwied *Erzieher*. The pattern for the *Bildungsroman* was set by Goethe in his Wilhelm Meister novels, which were translated by Carlyle (both Goethe and Carlyle were strong early influences on Meredith). English literature is rich in examples of the genre, from *David Copperfield* to *Sons and Lovers*. Three of Meredith's novels have the structure of the *Bildungsroman*, although they branch out to other themes: *Richard Feverel*, *Harry Richmond* and *Beauchamp's Career*.

Richard Feverel is a boy who takes eager, though clumsy, steps towards manhood at the age of fourteen, Meredith's age when he went to Neu-

wied. His father, Sir Austin Feverel, is warned by the commonsensical
Dr Clifford: 'You have to learn that your son is no longer a child.' This
is bad news for Sir Austin: 'The boy had embarked, and was on the
waters of life in his own vessel . . . A sensation of infinite melancholy
overcame the poor gentleman.'

Sir Austin has worked out a System designed to control Richard's
development. In his notebook:

> The Youth's progressionary phases were mapped out in sections, from
> Simple Boyhood to the Blossoming Season, the Magnetic Age, the
> Period of Probation, from which, successfully passed through, he was
> to emerge into a Manhood Worthy of Paradise.

Meredith is satirizing a heavy pedantry which one can recognize as
characteristically German. Even the capital letters for words that would
not be capitalized in English are a German usage.

The rigidity and solemnity of the System are baffling to ordinary,
non-intellectual people such as Sir Austin's sister: 'She deemed the system
Nonsense . . . all experiments in education, Nonsense.' While Meredith,
like Sir Austin, certainly was an intellectual, he found it easy to sympathize
with this point of view. He could remember that his *Bildung* at Neuwied
had been guided by a system. Richard Feverel has to give his father an
account of every evening of his studies and his 'moral experiences'; this must
have corresponded closely to the practice in a Neuwied choir. However,
while the system of the Moravian Brotherhood was based on the Christian
faith, Sir Austin's was in tune with the up-to-date thinking of the Victorian
age, and Meredith was drawing on an article by Herbert Spencer in the
British Quarterly Review in 1858, the year when the novel was written.

As most critics have pointed out, Sir Austin loves his son and is honestly
trying to do his best for him. Far from being a harsh father, he keeps
Richard at home precisely because of the brutalities of boarding-schools.
When Richard is guilty of burning Farmer Blaize's ricks, there is no
punishment; Richard simply has to recognize his wrongdoing and apologize. Alice Woods goes so far as to say:

> Sir Austin's aims were high and good . . . He noted the corrupt tenden-
> cies of the public schools of his day, and the dangers of college life,
> and determined not to expose his son to them . . . It was part of Sir
> Austin's principle of education that Richard should be thoroughly
> joyous and happy in early life, so life was made very pleasant for him.[7]

Richard does indeed have a pleasant life, but only so long as he conforms to Sir Austin's plans. The 1960s term 'repressive tolerance' might have been coined for Sir Austin Feverel. As at Neuwied, 'constant supervision' was undoubtedly benevolent but 'resulted in over-protectiveness'. Richard is expected to develop in accordance with the phases of the System, not at his own pace. When an unsuitable book is found in his bedroom, he is judged to be too precocious; when he starts to write poems, he has to burn them to regain his father's approval; and his unauthorized sexuality, years ahead of Sir Austin's calculations, leads to the final tragedy. Sir Austin's regretful conclusion is that 'it is useless to base any system on a human being'. Richard is unworthy of the System; Meredith would have appreciated Brecht's sardonic suggestion that the government should dissolve the people and elect a new one. While he was grateful for the benefits of the Neuwied system and for the happiness that Neuwied had given him, he was ultimately convinced that theoretical principles should yield to the needs of infinitely varied individuals.

When he recreated Neuwied fifty years later as the school planned by Matthew Weyburn in *Lord Ormont*, it was the internationalism of such a school that he stressed at its greatest merit. Matthew tells Aminta enthusiastically:

> Catholics and Protestants are both welcome to us, according to our scheme. And Germans, French, English, Americans, Italians, if they will come; Spanish and Portuguese, and Scandinavians, Russians as well. And Jews; Mahomeddans too, if only they will come! The more mixed, the more it hits our object.

Unlike at Neuwied, the staff too would be international. 'Emile Granat, Adolf Fleischer, and an Italian, Vincentino Chiuse, are prepared to start with me,' Matthew says. Later, when the school is running successfully in Switzerland, an Italian has this to say:

> He works for Europe and America – all civilised people – to be one country. He is the comrade of his boys. Out of school hours, it is Christian names all round – Matthew, Emile, Adolf, Emilio, Giulio, Robert, Marcel, Franz, etcetera. Games or lessons, a boy can't help learning with him. He makes happy fellows and brave soldiers of them without drill.

It all sounds like Bedales or Abbotsholme, the progressive schools founded a few years before Meredith wrote *Lord Ormont*.

Meredith was grateful to Germany as well as to Neuwied. In the 1840s, Germany was divided among scores of independent states, of which only Prussia and Bavaria were of considerable size, while the others could barely match English counties. While some of these states, like Wied, were politically liberal, most were deeply conservative and totally undemocratic. In *Harry Richmond*, Meredith described the exclusiveness and the arrogant stiffness of the ruling family in a German princedom. The aspiration of good liberals, in Germany as in Italy, was to sweep away these petty autocracies and unite the whole country. Meanwhile, a disunited Germany posed no threat to anyone; it was France, still cherishing the Napoleonic spirit, which appeared as militarist and aggressive. Germany was the land of poets and musicians, of philosophers, of Europe's most distinguished universities, all breathing a spirit of generous idealism; it was a German poet who had written: ' *Alle Menschen werden Brüder/ Wo dein sanfte Flügel weilt'*, and a German composer who had set it to unforgettable music. All this was to change after 1870, and the change can be charted in Meredith's attitudes, but as a boy at Neuwied he was simply impressed by German culture and eager to learn from it. At the end of his life, replying to a German academic who had asked him about his formative reading, he listed: 'first the Arabian Nights, then Gibbon, Niebuhr, Walter Scott; then Molière, then the noble Goethe, the most enduring'.[8] With George Eliot, Meredith is exceptional among English writers in his ability to read and speak German and appreciation of German achievement.

An English boy at Neuwied may have felt, however, that the German assumption of cultural superiority could have been more tactfully expressed. When Harry Richmond meets Princess Ottilia, she remarks coolly: 'My Professor tells me it is strange for any of your countrymen to love books.' Harry is then introduced to the professor in question, Herr Professor Doctor Julius von Karsteg (British readers would smile at the pompous succession of titles). Karsteg launches a contemptuous attack: 'You English live for pleasure ... We strive on, while you remain in a past age and are proud of it.' Harry protests: 'Still I think we are the only people on earth who have shown mankind a representation of freedom.' But the Professor dismisses this, to demand: 'Have you a scheme of life consonant with the spirit of modern philosophy?' Meredith repeated this character (while half-admitting that it was a stereotype) in *One of Our Conquerors* with 'the indisputably learned, the very argumentative, crashing, arrogant, pedantic, dogmatic, philological German gentleman, Dr Gannius, reeking of the Teutonic Professor, as a library volume of its leather.'

Writing long after his boyhood at Neuwied, Meredith was smarting –
as Harry Richmond smarts – not only from the assertion of German
intellectual claims, which he recognized as having considerable validity,
but more acutely from German arrogance and ungraciousness. In 1882,
he wrote from Lugano during a holiday:

> . . . through the St Gothard artery all Germania is now pouring, like
> frothing beer through neck of bottle, all the hotels, all the steamboats,
> compact of her progeny, resolute to see, careless of being a sight . . .
> These are the conquerors.[9]

By 1903 he saw Germany simply as a menace and warned in a letter to
the *Daily Telegraph*:

> Germany, once foremost among the nations for intellectual achieve-
> ments, now spouts Pan-Germanism over Europe, and seeks to com-
> mand the North Sea . . . A slumbering England will offer it the chance
> it craves before the inevitable financial strain brings it to the ground.[10]

From Goethe's times through the age of Bismarck to the reign of Kaiser
Wilhelm II, Meredith's perception of Germany had been transformed,
as had that of many others in England. Respectful admiration had given
way to resentful anxiety. Yet the roots of these mixed feelings – of resent-
ment colouring the admiration – may have been planted in his Neuwied
years. England at Neuwied was represented, after all, by boys and girls;
Germany by adults in a position of gently exercised but unquestionable
authority.

What never changed was his feeling for the beauty and majesty of the
German landscape, in particular the Rhineland. The mighty river, the
soaring mountain peaks, the romantic setting for the legends of the Drach-
enfels and the Lorelei: these are eloquently evoked in *Farina*, in *Richard
Feverel*, and in *Harry Richmond*. This nocturnal scene from *Feverel* has all
the vividness of emotional memory:

> An oppressive slumber hung about the forest-branches . . . Yonder in
> a space of moonlight on lush grass, the beams were as white fire to
> sight and feeling. No haze spread around. The valleys were clear,
> defined to the shadows of their verges . . . On a barren corner of the
> wooded highland looking inland stood grey topless ruins set in nettles
> and rank grass-blades . . . When he again pursued his course with his

face to the Rhine, a huge mountain appeared to rise sheer over him, and he had it in his mind to scale it. He got no nearer to the base of it for all his vigorous outstepping. The ground began to dip; he lost sight of the sky.

Meredith was at Neuwied for a few months less than two years. He did not come home (not that, in any real sense, he had a home) in the holidays, since there was no difficulty about staying in a school that was also a community. It was an experience of total and undiluted immersion. It does not appear that he left Neuweld at the end of this period because he was tired of it, nor because the money ran out, nor because he wanted to make a start on a career. Apparently, it was normal for English boys to spend two years in the German school, as in the case of Henry Morley and others who came from prosperous homes. However, George Meredith was emerging from a secure and protective environment into what could only be a wider world of uncertainties.

3

Born Again

GEORGE MEREDITH returned to England in the spring or summer of 1844, at the age of sixteen. Given his habits of reticence, it is not surprising that we have no certain knowledge of what he did or where he lived for the next two years. He had no affection for his father and stepmother and cannot have been willing to live under their roof; besides, he was always averse to living in London. A tempting conjecture is that he spent some time in the country – perhaps in Hampshire, the setting for *Evan Harrington*. He could have earned a little money, or at least board and lodging, working on a farm. An early poem, 'Pastoral', has the ring of experience:

> Summer glows warm on the meadows, and speedwell, and
> gold-cups, and daisies
> Darken mid deepening masses of sorrel, and shadowy grasses
> Show the ripe hue to the farmer, and summon the scythe and the
> haymakers
> Down from the village; and now, even now, the air smells of the
> mowing,
> And the sharp song of the scythe whistles daily; fresh dawn, till the
> gloaming
> Wears its cool star; sweet and welcome to all flaming faces afield
> now.

In *Evan Harrington*, Meredith reproduces the talk at the village inn convincingly enough. Blaize in *Richard Feverel* and Fleming in *Rhoda Fleming* are portraits of the sturdy English farmer, limited in his outlook but unshakeable in his traditional moral principles. Lionel Stevenson, in his biography of Meredith, suggests the further speculation of a love affair between young George and a farmer's daughter. A recurring figure in three novels – Lucy in *Richard Feverel*, Mabel in *Harry Richmond*, Dahlia in *Rhoda Fleming* – is an innocent, unsophisticated country girl whom the young hero finds irresistible. All three are blondes, beauties of the authentic English type. Such a girl is the object of erotic fantasy in another early poem, 'Love in the Valley':

> When from bed she rises clothed from neck to ankle
> In her long nightgown, sweet as boughs of May,
> Beauteous she looks! like a tall garden lily
> Pure from the night and perfect for the day!

Stevenson was scrupulous in admitting that his theory was guesswork, based solely on inferences from the poems, and so it must remain. It is certain, however, that Meredith had strong sexual drives and a romantic susceptibility to falling in love, and his education alongside girls at Neuwied had freed him from the inhibitions of the shy, gauche product of an English public school.

Meanwhile, he had to earn a living, for he could aspire neither to a life of leisure nor to admission to a university. One project, which went as far as a tentative agreement, was apprenticeship to a bookseller who was opening a shop in Hong Kong, which had recently come under British control. But Meredith did not go to Hong Kong, and it may well be that he refused to go. In January 1846 he was articled to a solicitor named Richard Charnock. He had no inclination to devote his life to the law, and he never sat for Law Society examinations; at most, he may have done clerking work in Charnock's office. Luckily, Charnock himself gave no more time than he needed to legal work and was much more interested in the literary and intellectual sphere. He shared with Meredith an attraction to Germany and later took a PhD at Göttingen, and he moved in a social circle of young men (and some young women) drawn together by a love of literature, Radical political sympathies, and a taste for lively conversation. In this environment, there was a ready welcome for eighteen-year-old George Meredith.

He was well developed, tall and exceptionally handsome. His social manners were perfect, he appreciated wine and cigars, and his command of educated English was impeccable. When he talked – and he was always ready to talk – he gave proof of wide reading and serious thought, but also of lively wit and humour. He could produce apposite quotations in French, German and Latin as well as from the English classics. There was no trace now of the tailor's son who had grown up in the Portsmouth dockland. The new friends did not know where he came from and granted him the right to reserve on the subject; there was nothing extraordinary about a young man who might have distanced himself from his origins, or whose parents might be dead, or who might have quarrelled with them. In fact, this George Meredith was new-born, or born again, on the threshold of adult life. With less trouble than Evan Harrington, and without the need for evasion or deceit, Meredith had become a gentleman.

Augustus Meredith was still in London, but father and son saw nothing of each other. In 1849, Augustus emigrated to South Africa, where he was able to forget his bankruptcy and set up a viable, if modest, tailoring business. When he returned fourteen years later to spend his last years in his native Portsmouth, his son was an established author. The son paid a few rare visits to the father and attended his funeral in 1876.

While the young men of the Charnock group were chiefly interested in literary efforts and social pleasures, they were stirred and excited by the dramatic political events that made 1848 the most astounding year in European history since the great French Revolution. Within six weeks in February to April of that year, news of popular uprisings came from Paris, Vienna, Berlin, Prague, Budapest, Milan, Venice and Florence. As France became a republic, the King escaped to England under an assumed name and found a home at Claremont, near Esher, where Meredith sometimes saw the ex-royal family after he came to live in the neighbourhood in the 1850s. Metternich, the great minister whose name had been a symbol of the established order in Europe since Waterloo, was a refugee in Brighton. Generally the turmoil was over in a few hours, but Milan saw five days of ferocious street fighting before the Austrian occupation forces gave up their hold on the city – a struggle that Meredith followed with intense sympathy and chronicled later in his novel *Vittoria*. Even Britain was touched by a ripple from the storm. Supporters of the People's Charter, whose key demand was universal suffrage, mobilized on 10 April to bring their petition to Westminster; the authorities enlisted thousands of special constables and made no concessions.

The heroes of 1848, with ardent admirers in England, were the Italians Mazzini and Garibaldi, the Hungarians Kossuth and Petöfi. Meredith met Mazzini several times in later years and portrayed him reverently as 'the Chief' in *Vittoria*. While Kossuth was at the head of a liberated

Hungary during a year of warfare, Meredith tried to organize help for a group of freedom fighters who had somehow reached the English Channel, and also tried to interest a publisher in a topical biography of Kossuth.

The wave of rebellion died away gradually. In June 1848, working-class Parisians who had hoped for a 'social republic' were crushed by the National Guard; three thousand were summarily shot, a foretaste of the massacre that followed the suppression of the Commune in 1871. Louis Napoleon, nephew of the great Emperor, was elected President in December and took the imperial crown three years later. In Germany, the Frankfort Parliament which was called to unite the kingdoms and princedoms as a constitutional state wasted a year in abortive debate, leaving a vacuum that was eventually filled by Bismarck's creation of a German Empire. The sprawling Austrian Empire seemed for a time to be breaking apart, but forces loyal to the Emperor reconquered northern Italy in 1848, restored order in Vienna, and regained control of Hungary by August 1849. British liberals were outraged by the atrocities laid at the door of General Haynau, and he was renamed Hyena. When he visited London he was physically attacked by the workers of the Barclay and Perkins brewery in Greenwich, a borough that retains a reminder of the period in the name of Kossuth Street.

The emotions aroused in 1848 must surely have been reflected in Meredith's early writing, but the evidence is lacking. He did not publish a book of poems until 1851, and there is no way of establishing when a particular poem was written. The Charnock group produced a handwritten journal, the *Monthly Observer*, containing poems, essays and review. Infuriatingly, the first ten issues are lost. The content must have been political, at least to some extent, for in January 1849 the editor, Austin Daniel, urged 'a return to Literature for its own sake'. About the poems contributed by young Meredith, he commented that they were 'too unfinished', but was sufficiently impressed to add: 'He has genius, we think, and if he has that perseverance so indispensable to its development, there is no reason why, in time, his name should not rank high.'

Ironically, the first poem by Meredith that reached a wider audience was in praise of soldiers of a regular army – the British – in a battle against rebels striving for independence. Punjab had been ruled by the Sikhs since the eighteenth century but, as a result of enforced treaties, was regarded by the British as a protectorate. From 1845, the Sikhs took up arms to put an end to British control. On 13 January 1849, Sikh and British forces fought a battle at Chillianwala. Neither side won an outright

victory, but the heavy British losses – over two thousand killed or wounded
– were regarded as disastrous, since British policy was to hold down India
with economy in white manpower, and brought a severe shock when the
news came home. Meredith wrote a poem which was greeted by 'hearty
congratulations' in the *Monthly Observer* and – thanks to the influence of
an older member of the group, Richard Horne – was republished in
Chambers' Edinburgh Journal. The tone is perceptible from the first and last
of the six stanzas:

> Chillianwallah, Chillianwallah!
> Where our brothers fought and bled,
> O thy name is natural music
> And a dirge above the dead!
> Though we have not been defeated,
> Though we can't be overcome,
> Still, whene'er thou art repeated,
> I would fain that grief were dumb.

> Chillianwallah, Chillianwallah!
> Thou wilt be a doleful chord,
> And a mystic note of mourning
> That will need no chiming word;
> And that heart will leap with anguish
> Who may understand thee best;
> But the hopes of all will languish
> Till thy memory is at rest.

Siegfried Sassoon condemned 'Chillianwallah' as 'the worst that he
[Meredith] ever published'.[1] In his large output, Meredith wrote other
poems that might compete for this distinction, and Sassoon was under-
standably repelled by 'Chillianwallah' in the light of his own revolt against
the official patriotism of the First World War. It would be difficult to
mount a defence, especially of the allusion to the Sikhs as 'savage plun-
dering devils'. One may say that the Sikhs were not Italians or Hungarians
and Meredith was not ready to extend his vision to a non-European
people – although he did so later, for instance when he declared his
sympathy with the Zulus in 1879. One may say that, like Kipling in
another generation, he was roused to compassion for the British 'Tommy
Atkins' called on to sacrifice his life for a nation that offered him little
reward or respect. But the likely truth is that this ambitious young writer

was falling in with a popular mood and seizing an opportunity to achieve real publication for the first time.

It was, in any case, a quite different mood and a quite different outlook which inspired some other poems written in 1849 or 1850. While Meredith championed those who, with Kossuth or Garibaldi, were fighting for freedom from alien power, he hailed the awakening of 1848 as the promise of a world in which national distinctions and national prejudice would vanish along with national oppression, and the way to durable peace would be open. In 'The Olive Branch' (this was the name of a ship launched in 1845) he wrote:

> Come, read the meaning of the deep!
> The use of winds and waters learn!
> 'Tis not to make the mother weep
> For sons that never will return;
>
> 'Tis not to make the nations show
> Contempt for all whom seas divide;
> 'Tis not to pamper war and woe,
> Nor feed traditionary pride . . .
>
> It is to knit with loving lip
> The interests of land to land;
> To join in far-seen fellowship
> The tropic and the polar strand . . .
>
> O may her voice have power to say
> How soon the wrecking discords cease,
> When every wandering wave is gay
> With golden argosies of peace! . . .
>
> On strengthened wing for evermore,
> Let Science, swiftly as she can,
> Fly seaward on from shore to shore,
> And bind the links of man to man;
>
> And like that fair propitious Dove,
> Bless future fleets about to launch;
> Make every freight a freight of love,
> And every ship an Olive Branch.

The theme is worked out in a subtler and more emotionally complex manner in 'The Sleeping City', a poem in which a mythical princess walks through a city frozen in stillness:

> Yet as her thoughts dilating rose,
> Took glory in the great repose,
> And over every postured form
> Spread lava-like and brooded warm –
>
> And fixed on every frozen face,
> Behold the record of its race,
> And in each chiselled feature knew
> The stormy life that once blushed thro'; –
>
> The ever-present of the past
> There written; all that lightened last,
> Love, anguish, hope, disease, despair,
> Beauty and rage, all written there . . .
>
> While noble things in darkness grope,
> The Statesman's aim, the Poet's hope;
> The Patriot's impulse gathers fire,
> And germs of future fruits aspire; –
>
> Now while dumb nature owns its links,
> And from one common fountain drinks,
> Methinks in all around I see
> This Picture in Eternity.

The philosophic concept, as well as the rhythm and the rhyme-scheme, point to an unmistakable influence – that of Blake. Yet Blake, long out of fashion, was not a poet who would have been readily imitated by a young writer in the mid-nineteenth century.

In 1848 Meredith was living in rented rooms – or probably just one room – in Ranelagh Street, now named Ebury Street. London was fast spreading westward from Hyde Park Corner and the Duke of Wellington's name for Apsley House – 'Number One, London' – had already become an anachronism. Symbolizing Meredith's in-between social position, the street where he lived was in a borderland between the opulent mansions of Belgravia and the humble streets of Pimlico. It was within easy reach of Hyde Park and Kensington Gardens, where many characters in Meredith's novels are seen walking or riding. Ebury Street itself was later dismissed in the *Survey of London* compiled by Meredith's friend Sir Walter Besant as 'an uninteresting street of unpretending houses and shops' (still a fair description). In the 1840s, however, the western part of the street was a lane bordered by the surviving fields of what had been Ebury Farm. After passing through the village of Chelsea, an energetic walker like Meredith would soon be in open country. Kossuth, as an exile, lived a block away from Ebury Street in Eaton Place, but he arrived after Meredith had moved out of London.

London already had a good bus service, but Meredith must often have stretched his legs and saved his pennies by walking to Charnock's office in Godliman Street, close to St Paul's Cathedral. On his way home, he could call at the rooms near the British Museum occupied by Edward Peacock and his sister Mary Ellen, both friends of Charnock and contributors to the *Monthly Observer*. Their father, Thomas Love Peacock, was the first writer of known reputation whom Meredith had a chance to meet.

Whether as a man or as a writer, Peacock is difficult to describe and practically impossible to classify. Sixty-three years old in 1848, he preserved a personality and habits that belonged to the Regency age rather than to the staider Victorian period. He had been a close friend of Shelley and in 1858 he wrote his *Memoirs of Shelley* to rebut what he regarded as inaccuracies in other accounts. The friendship was a surprising one and perhaps an attraction of opposites; Peacock had a stock of practical common sense, was a Tory in his politics, and was tolerantly amused by Shelley's idealism. However, they never quarrelled, and when Peacock poked fun at Shelley as Scythrop Glowry, a character in his novel *Nightmare Abbey*, Shelley did not resent it. In his own way, Peacock was just as unconventional as his more famous – or, at the time, notorious – friend. Indifferent to his reception by reviewers or readers, he wrote as he pleased and when he pleased. After producing four novels in quick succession, he then allowed himself long intervals and wrote only three more in the rest of his life. In his fiction, he drew on a variety of genres: historical romance, love story, political satire, and interspersed dialogues or monologues reminiscent of the eighteenth-century French *conte philosophique*. His best-known novel, *Crotchet Castle*, consisted largely of dinner-table conversations in which the characters exhibited their 'crotchets' – hobbyhorses or obsessions. Dr Middleton in Meredith's *The Egoist* – with his dogmatic opinions, his orotund style, and his addiction to old port – is clearly based on Dr Folliott in *Crotchet Castle*, or maybe on Peacock himself.

Peacock's practical side led him into another career. Although he had a private income sufficient to support a middle-class standard of living, he took a job at East India House, head office of the Company which exploited and governed India. It seems that East India House was something of a haven for intellectuals, for James Mill, his son John Stuart Mill and Charles Lamb also worked there. Before Meredith made his acquaintance, Peacock had risen to the top position with the title of Examiner and a salary of £2,000 a year.

Three aspects of Peacock's outlook struck a chord with Meredith. He believed that ideas or theories had a place in fiction and that it was justifiable to build a narrative simply to exemplify them. Peacock and Meredith are among the few nineteenth-century novelists who were ready to trouble their readers with words like 'idea', 'thought' and even 'philosophy'.

Although Peacock was not Welsh, he had a passion for Wales, its landscape and its culture. It was at Maentwrog, a place where an English visitor was a rarity, that he met Jane Gryffydh, whom he married in 1819. Her thorough Welshness is attested by the spelling of her surname – not the anglicized Griffith or Griffiths. In *Crotchet Castle*, for no reason necessitated by the plot, all the characters suddenly take off for a tour of Wales. Another novel, *The Misfortunes of Elphin*, is set in an unspoiled Wales centuries before the English conquest. Peacock learned Welsh, edited an anthology of Welsh poems, and was an enthusiast for *pennillion*, a traditional form of poetic song. 'This *pennillion*-singing,' he wrote, 'long survived among the Welsh peasantry almost every other vestige of bardic custom, and may still be heard on the few occasions on which rack-renting, tax-collecting, common-enclosing, Methodist preaching and similar developments of the light of the age have left them either the means or the inclination of making merry.'[2] The sentence is redolent of the kind of attitude – nostalgic for a romanticized past, yet angrily sympathetic to the victims of heartless officials or landowners – that Peacock shared, for instance, with William Cobbett.

Just as emphatically, Peacock opposed the prejudices that relegated women to an inferior status and denied them the opportunities open to men. He had grown up in an age when some men, at least, could admire women like Fanny Burney and Mary Wollstonecraft; and, as a friend of Shelley, he was also a friend of Mary Shelley. Anthelia, the heroine of his novel *Melincourt*, is lucky enough to have a father who 'maintained the heretical notion that women are rational beings'. To an audience of emancipated men, Anthelia complains: 'To think is one of the most unpardonable errors a woman can commit in the eyes of society. In our

[47]

sex a taste for intellectual pleasures is almost equivalent to taking the veil.' With the background of Neuwied, Meredith was ready to applaud the author of these lines. Moreover, he found that Mary, Peacock's daughter in real life, had been brought up on the same principles as Athelia.

Mary, the eldest child of Thomas and Jane Peacock, was six years older than Meredith. Later, in explaining the breakdown of his relationship with Mary, Meredith stated the age difference as eight (or, on another occasion, nine) years, but researchers have established the right dates. Two more children, Margaret and Edward, were born in quick succession after Mary, but Margaret died at the age of three. The death of a child was by no means a rare event in the nineteenth century, and losing one child out of three was about the statistical average. But the effect on this child's mother was devastating. Jane Peacock – so it was said – went mad.

The word 'mad' was then used with a ruthless candour that would nowadays be impermissible. Secluded rooms in hundreds or thousands of English houses were occupied by women – far more often than men – who were stated to be mad, were never seen by visitors, and were cared for by servants rather than, as a rule, by trained nurses. The sentimentality of the age made these women into tragically, or mysteriously, romantic figures and added to the success of *Jane Eyre*, published in 1847. Just how mad a real-life Mrs Rochester, or in this case Mrs Peacock, actually was – there is the debatable question. Probably many of these women were suffering from depression, which could often have been caused by the death of a child. There was no counselling, no psychotherapy, and for that matter no Valium. A woman plunged into depression would not have felt equal to presiding over a dinner-party, or contributing to the piano-playing and singing that were expected on social occasions, and would have preferred to avoid such duties. She stayed upstairs, alone; as time passed, she became adjusted to her isolation, lost the courage to emerge from it, and indeed had no desire to do so. Perhaps she screamed or moaned, as in the novels, but perhaps not. We can well believe that she was miserably unhappy, but this does not mean that, in any definable sense, she was mad.

The evidence that Jane Peacock was mad (whatever that means) is slender. Mary Shelley wrote, in a letter, that she was 'quite mad'; but she was a friend to Peacock, whom she had known before his marriage, and probably never saw the secluded Jane. Meredith, years later, said that 'there was madness in the family', presumably alluding to Jane, but he was explaining the unacceptable behaviour of Jane's daughter. The hereditary, or as we now say genetic, element in the causation of an unstable personality was (one remembers Zola's *mauvais sang*) much exaggerated in the nineteenth century. Mary's daughter Edith wrote later that her grand-mother (Jane) was inconsolable after the child's death, lost her health, and became 'a complete invalid'. J. B. Priestley, in a reliable biography of Pea-cock, accepts this 'complete invalid' terminology. Surprisingly, Diane John-son, a feminist writer who championed Mary, takes the view that 'invalid' was a euphemism and Jane must have been truly mad – a word used by Johnson without inhibition or qualification.[3] But caution must arise, par-ticularly, from the fact that Jane gave birth to another child, Rosa, after Margaret's death. Sexual relations between Peacock and his wife might have been compatible with depression on her part, and indeed pursued to give relief from it, but surely not with anything like madness.

Many writers who lived before the modern understanding of mental illness – most notably, Shakespeare in *Hamlet, Macbeth* and *King Lear* – have sought to deal with it and have shown great intuitive insight. Mere-dith described breakdowns – those of Barrett in *Emilia in England* and Hackbut in *Rhoda Fleming* – with an accuracy that would guide a present-day psychiatrist to a quite confident diagnosis. With Harry Richmond's mother, he made use (unoriginally, it must be admitted) of a 'Mrs Roch-ester' scenario. But when he wanted to depict the total collapse of a personality, as with Dahlia Fleming or Victor Radnor, it was ascribed to hopeless grief. He knew about Jane Peacock.

By all accounts, Mary was beautiful, very intelligent, and gifted with a sharp and witty tongue. She was closely attached to her father and, in view of her mother's seclusion, managed the household when she was old enough. While she was in command of domestic skills, such as cooking, she was decidedly an Athelia, fully capable of taking part in conversations that might, in other homes, have been the monopoly of men. Meredith described her in a poem, 'Marian', which was written some years later (and, alas, published after her death) but which conveys his first admiring impression of her:

> She can be as wise as we,
> And wiser when she wishes;
> She can knit with cunning wit,
> And dress the homely dishes.
> She can flourish staff or pen,
> And deal a wound that lingers;
> She can talk the talk of men,
> And touch with thrilling fingers ...

Such a she who'll match with me?
    In flying or pursuing,
Subtle wiles are in her smiles
    To set the world a-wooing.
She is steadfast as a star,
    And yet the maddest maiden:
She can wage a gallant war,
    And give the peace of Eden.

Peacock had a house in Lower Halliford, a village on the left bank of
the Thames about twenty miles out of London, which was the family
home, and another house in London where he stayed from Monday to
Friday. Mary, as a girl in her teens, generally stayed in the village but
met her father's distinguished friends when they came to dinner at the
weekends. In the nineteenth century a girl regarded as a 'catch' was often
married at seventeen or eighteen, but Mary was evidently not in a hurry
to leave the parental home. However, at the age of twenty-two she married
a lieutenant in the Navy, Edward Nicolls. He was a son of a General in
the Royal Marines, known as 'Fighting Nicolls' because of his aggressive
leadership and his daring exploits. Hailed as a hero, 'Fighting Nicolls'
was wounded six times, and was rewarded with a sword of honour and
a KCB (Knight Commander of the Bath). Crossjay Patterne in *The Egoist*,
snobbishly cold-shouldered by Sir Willoughby, is an officer in the Marines
– 'the corps of the famous hard fighters' – and is credited with 'an act
of heroism'. On the other hand, the brutal and dishonest Major Strike
in *Evan Harrington* is also in the Marines; he corresponds in real life to
Major Ellis, husband of Meredith's Aunt Catherine. S. M. Ellis, biographer of Meredith and grandson of this Major, was at pains to make it
clear that his ancestor – who also ended up with the rank of General
and a KCB – was a man of irreproachable character. Ellis thought that
Meredith was 'actuated by petty and long-brooded animus against his
relatives'; but, since Meredith did not malign any other relatives, it is
more likely that the animus was directed against Mary's first husband
and the Nicolls family.

The marriage of Edward Nicolls and Mary Peacock lasted only two
months. She went with him to Tarbert, on the west coast of Ireland,
where he was in command of a ship. In a sudden storm, he tried to
rescue a sailor whose small boat had been overturned, was hit on the
head by a block swinging in the gale, and was thrown into the sea and
drowned. It was an 'act of heroism' in the Nicolls tradition. Mary was

pregnant and in due course gave birth to a daughter, Edith. The year was 1844 – the year in which George Meredith returned to England from Neuwied.

Mary went back to the Peacock family, dividing her time between the Lower Halliford house and rooms in London shared with her brother Edward. With him, she found a place in the Charnock literary circle and contributed to the *Monthly Observer*. When she had been a widow for two years, a self-confident young man with some poetic talent appeared in this circle. Soon, he was declaring his love for her and begging her to marry him.

For Meredith, the attraction that Mary presented needs little explanation. As many novels reveal, a young widow was an object of fascination for the Victorian male, uniting beauty with sexual experience and thus bypassing the guilt that went with the violation of innocent purity. Male desires were no longer focused solely on naïve girls from the schoolroom; Balzac had launched a new fashion with *La Femme de Trente Ans*, published in 1844. The extra years had enabled Mary to develop plenty of poise and sophistication; she would be a 'fitting mate' (another key Victorian concept, recurring in Meredith's novels from *Evan Harrington* to *One of our Conquerors*) for a young man reaching for an ambitious future. Specifically, she was the daughter of Thomas Love Peacock, and thus promised her suitor a guaranteed entrée into the literary world. There is no reason to doubt that Meredith was genuinely in love and no reason to accuse him of cold calculation, but it was a love reinforced by strong motives.

Mary was much more hesitant. According to accounts accepted by some biographers, she refused his proposals six times. Once she had recovered from the loss of Nicolls, firm and affectionate relationships with her father and brother gave her life a reasonably satisfying framework. Besides, she did not want to risk disturbing little Edith. There is a story that Edith came into a room to find Meredith kissing her mother and said: 'Mama, I don't like that man.' True or apocryphal, the story shows that there was a problem. While Mary may well have found Meredith a remarkable twenty-year-old, and been excited by his talents and ambitions, she may also have thought him immature. Perhaps it was to his persistence and his eloquence that she finally yielded.

It is unlikely that the marriage was welcomed either by the Nicolls family, with whom Mary had remained on good terms, or by her father. Though Peacock had presumably been shocked by Nicolls's death and grieved in sympathy with Mary, he could also have been glad to have her home again as the comfort of his declining years. If he was fond enough of little Edith, he may have been daunted by the prospect of a brood of grandchildren generated by his vigorous young son-in-law. At a practical level, it was easy to see that Mary would need financial help if she married a man without a job, without a supportive family of his own, and in short – to use the standard Victorian phrase – without expectations. As a writer, Peacock was well aware of the uncertainties of the literary life, and he would have preferred to see Mary stand at the altar with a barrister or a stockbroker than with a hopeful poet – and Meredith had, so far, just one published poem to his credit. However, he put the best possible face on the situation and gave his daughter away on 9 August 1849, in the highly respectable ambience of St George's, Hanover Square. Meredith was now twenty-one and there could be no objections by his legal guardian (his father was already in Cape Town), while Mary was fully old enough to make her own decisions. On coming of age, Meredith had gained control of his Macnamara aunt's legacy, so the couple had some capital to begin married life, but it would be exhausted before long if it was not replenished.

They departed for a honeymoon in Meredith's beloved Rhineland, and then came to live temporarily with Peacock in his London house in John Street, near Charing Cross. But, as Meredith no longer made even a formal pretence of working in Charnock's office, there was no reason to stay in the city. Mary presumably wished to be within each reach of her father, so they took lodgings in Weybridge, on the Surrey side of the Thames but only three miles from Lower Halliford. Their new home was congenial; it was in a large, comfortable house called The Limes, belonging to Mrs Elizabeth Macirone. The name was Italian; Mrs Macirone, herself English, was the widow of an Italian military man. She was an educated woman, with friends in the literary world and the arts. Her daughters, Emilia and Giulia, lived at home, and it is easy to recognize Emilia who had a fine singing voice and liked to sing for labourers on the nearby farms, as the model for the heroine of *Emilia in England*.

Not only at this stage, but in later years, Meredith wanted to be regarded primarily as a poet, and poetry was the form of expression nearest to his heart. As an old man, he told a friend: 'Chiefly by that in my poetry which emphasizes the unity of life, the soul that breathes through the universe, do I wish to be remembered ... I began with poetry and I shall finish with it.'[4] V. S. Pritchett judged that it was the poetic mode which shaped his prose style: 'the poet in Meredith made him concentrate on intensity, economy and the image in his prose.'[5] The irony was, as Priestley put it: 'He began and ended his literary career with poetry and preferred to be thought a poet, but it was his fiction that made him famous.'[6] At the outset of his career, he may have envisaged writing both poetry and fiction, like Scott and others, but quite possibly he did not intend to write novels at all. Gradually, it became clear that he could hope to earn a decent living as a novelist, while poetry would bring in no more than derisory sums of money.

At The Limes in 1849 and 1850, he worked steadily at his poetry and produced a substantial body of work – sixty-six poems, mostly short but some quite long. (This includes some that, as we have seen, may have been written in 1848 or even earlier.) He submitted the collection to John Parker, a publisher who was a friend of Peacock. Presumably Meredith had Peacock to thank for the contact, and he dedicated the book 'To Thomas Love Peacock, Esq., with the profound admiration and affection-ate respect of his son-in-law'. However, Parker agreed to publish this unknown writer's work only with a subsidy; Meredith invested £50, a quantity of his scanty capital that he could ill afford to lose. Sadly, he got none of it back. Five hundred copies were printed but only one hundred were bound, and some of these were given away rather than sold. Publication was in May 1851. The volume was entitled simply *Poems*.

Meredith was not discouraged by this lack of commercial success. He regarded *Poems* as the first step on a long road; partly as a venture to intro-duce his name to a small discerning public, partly as a learning process for himself. Letters to older men whose approval might be helpful were written with becoming modesty. To the poet Edmond Ollier, he explained:

> I prepared myself, when I published, to meet with injustice and slight – knowing that the little collection or rather selection in my volume was but the vanguard of a better work to come . . . The poems are all the work of extreme youth and, with some exceptions, of labour. They will not live, I think; but they will serve their purpose in making known my name . . . I trust that my next work will be a nearer advance to that aim.[7]

And to A. J. Scott, Professor of English at University College, London:

> . . . the contents of the volume are the work of extreme youth, and I desire them to be considered more as *indications* than accomplishments . . . I would have given forth no volume bearing the title of *Poems* without full belief (and such a consciousness may be felt in all humility) that I was a Poet . . . More concisely I may say it all reads too young.[8]

These were serious and honest statements; yet Mary may have reflected that Shelley and Byron had been not much older than Meredith was now when they produced what was far more than apprentice work, and Keats had been even younger.

As we read the poems today, it can be said that they are manifestly from the same hand as Meredith's six later volumes and bear out his claim to be a Poet (with a capital). Already, there was proof of power of expression, command of a variety of verse forms, emotional strength, and a choice of language that seldom seems forced or strained. There was also a considerable range of subject-matter. The poems of political idealism which have been quoted earlier contrast with the personal passion of 'Angelic Love':

> Angelic love that stoops with heavenly lips
>   To meet its earthly mate;
> Heroic love that to its sphere's eclipse,
> Can dare to join its fate
> With one beloved devoted human heart
> And share with it the passion and the smart.
>   The undying bliss
>   Of its most fleeting kiss;
>   The fading grace
>   Of its most sweet embrace . . .
> And creeping up deliriously entwine
>   Its dear delicious arms
>   Round the beloved being!
>   With fair unfolded charms,
>   All-trusting and all-seeing . . .

'Daphne' was a long narrative poem (over a hundred four-line verses) based on the myth of the river-nymph Daphne who, according to Apollodorus, was pursued by Apollo and was saved by being transformed into a laurel tree (hence the laurel wreath traditionally worn by Apollo and conferred on poets). Meredith's version was rich in the indulgent sexuality over which Victorian readers loved to linger:

> And about the maiden rapture
> Still the ruddy ripples play'd,
> Ebbing round in startled circlets
> When her arms began to wade.

Flowing in like tides attracted
To the glowing crescent shine!
Clasping her ambrosial whiteness
Like an Autumn-tinted vine! . . .

Trembling up with adoration
To the crimson daisy tip,
Budding from the snowy bosom –
Fainter than the rose-red lip! . . .

Gleaming in a whirl of eddies
Round her lucid throat and neck;
Eddying in a gleam of dimples
Up against her bloomy cheek . . .

Till at last delirious passion
Thrilled the god to wild excess,
And the fervour of a moment
Made divinity confess.

Revealing himself, Apollo makes some progress:

Love-suffused, she quivers, falters –
Falters, sighs, but never speaks
All her rosy blood up-gushing
Overflows her ripe young cheeks . . .

Ah! but lovelier, ever-lovelier
As more deep the colour glows,
And the honey-laden lily
Changes to the fragrant rose

While the god with meek embraces,
Whispering all his sacred charms,
Softly folds her, gently holds her
In his white encircling arms!

The poem moves on to what might be called the climax:

Thus he nears! and now she feels him
Breathing hot on every limb;
And he hears her own quick pantings –
Ah! that they might be for him! . . .

In the earth her feet are rooting! –
Breasts and limbs and lifted eyes,
Hair and lips and stretching fingers,
Fade away – and fadeless rise

And the god whose fervent rapture
Clasps her, finds his close embrace
Full of palpitating branches,
And new leaves that bud apace.

Meredith must surely have enjoyed writing 'Daphne'. However, he could paint a much grimmer and more realistic picture in 'London by Lamplight':

Those violated forms have been
The pride of many a flowering green;
And still the virgin bosom heaves
With daisy meads and dewy leaves

But Stygian darkness reigns within,
The river of death from founts of sin;
And one prophetic water rolls
Its gas-lit surface for their souls.

I will not hide the tragic sight –
Those drown'd black locks, those dead lips white,
Will rise from out the slimy flood
And cry before God's throne for blood!

Those stiffened limbs, that swollen face –
Pollution's last and best embrace,
Will call as such a picture can
For retribution upon man.

Hark! how their feeble laughter rings,
While still the ballad-monger sings,
And flatters their unhappy breasts
With poisonous words and pungent jests . . .

Proclaim this evil human page
Will ever blot the Golden Age,
That poets dreams and saints invite,
If it be unredeemed this night!

There were also descriptive landscape poems, including one that stemmed
from the honeymoon trip to the Rhineland:

The winding river freshening the sight
At intervals, the trees in leafy prime;
The distant village-roofs of blue and white,
With intersections of quaint-fashioned beams
All slanting crosswise, and the feudal gleams
Of ruined turrets, barren in the light . . .

The lark is up; the hills, the vines in sight;
The river broadens with his waking bliss
And throws up islands to behold the light;
Voices begin to rise, all hues to kiss –
    Was ever such a happy morn as this!
Birds sing, we shout, flowers breathe, trees shine with one delight!

With 'South-west Wind in the Woodland', Meredith evoked a scene
repeatedly described in his novels, and which evidently appealed to his
temperament: the excitement of a storm:

                          . . . and now the whole
Tumultuous concords, seized at once
With savage inspiration – pine,
And larch, and beech, and fir, and thorn,
And ash, and oak, and oakling rave
And shriek, and shout, and whirl, and toss,
And stretch their arms, and split, and crack,
And bend their stems, and bow their heads,
And grind, and groan, and lion-like

Roar to the echo-peopled hills
And ravenous wilds, and crake-like cry
With harsh delight, and cave-like call
With hollow mouth, and harp-like thrill
With mighty melodies, sublime,
From clumps of columb'd pines that wave
A lofty anthem to the sky.

The reviews were mixed. Some, while doubtless intended to be kindly and encouraging, adopted the patronizing tone that is so infuriating to a young writer. The *Athenaeum* wrote that the poems 'might almost be called beautiful' and concluded with this pronouncement: 'Where the "prentice hand" is so manifest as in this volume, we accept the signs of care and intention which it exhibits as indications of an artistic tendency in the "singer", and to a certain extent as pledges that one day he may become a poet.' The *Spectator* judged that the volume 'possesses considerable poetical feeling, and poetical faculty, but displays more of promise than perform- ance'. The review in *The Leader*, probably written by the editor, G. H. Lewes, gave moderate praise: 'A nice perception of nature, aided by a delicacy of expression, gives to these poems a certain charm not to be resisted.' The best review was in the *Critic*; it commended Meredith for 'warmth of emotion and to a certain extent of imagination' and concluded: 'We shall not cease to look for his renewed appearance with hope, and to hail it with extreme pleasure, so long as he may continue to produce poems equal to the best in this first volume.' This review was written by William Michael Rossetti (brother of Dante Gabriel), a young man just a year older than Meredith. They met at about this time and soon became friends.

In the prevailing moral climate, Meredith was asking for trouble with 'Daphne' and another poem based on mythology, 'The Rape of Aurora'. The *Spectator* review contained a mild reproof for his 'sensuous warmth of image and expression, which, though not passing propriety, might as well be tempered'. The *Guardian*, a religious weekly, granted him 'consider- able poetical capacity' but went on to deliver this lecture:

He must, however, mend his morals and his taste. Coarse sensuality is no proof of power, and passionateness and vigour may be attained without impurity. Ovid is bad enough, but 'Daphne' and 'The Rape of Aurora' in this volume are worse, from their studied and amplified voluptuousness, than anything in the *Metamorphoses*. Mr Meredith is mistaken if he thinks this either classical or manly.

[58]

Here was the first shot in the barrage that fell on Meredith's head when he published *Modern Love* and *Richard Feverel*.

The cool reviews and abysmal sales were balanced by praise from two men of literary influence. Charles Kingsley was the author of two best-selling novels, *Yeast* and *Alton Locke*, and an outstanding figure in the liberal wing of the Church. His status as a clergyman could give Meredith some protection from the strictures of the *Guardian*. Parker, Meredith's publisher, was also Kingsley's publisher, and was able to persuade Kingsley to review the *Poems* in *Fraser's Magazine* – owned by Parker. Kingsley met expectations by writing: 'There is very high promise in the unambitious little volume . . . Health and sweetness are two qualities which run through all these poems . . . They are all genuine, all melodiously conceived.' He even singled out 'Daphne' as 'a charming poem'.

Still more welcome, because it was unsolicited and completely unexpected, was a letter of congratulation from Alfred Tennyson. Twenty years older than Meredith, he was regarded as the poet qualified to fill the gap left by the passing of the great Romantics. Anyone who read poetry at all had read 'Morte d'Arthur', 'Locksley Hall' and 'In Memoriam'. When Wordsworth died in 1850, Tennyson was given the coveted title of Poet Laureate. He wrote to tell Meredith that he was going round his house reciting 'Love in the Valley' and wished he had written it, and added that he hoped for a visit from the young poet. Meredith replied: 'you may imagine what pride and pleasure your letter gave me . . . I can scarcely trust myself to express with how much delight I would wait upon you – a privilege I have long desired'.[9]

The meeting, at a country house where Tennyson was staying, was not a success. Encountered on a morning walk, Tennyson treated Meredith to an indignant tirade against a minor critic who had voiced the opinion that the Laureate was 'not a great poet'. Obsessed by this criticism, Tennyson had nothing else to talk about, and may have forgotten who Meredith was. Meredith decided that, great poet or not, Tennyson was pompous and conceited, and in later years he came to detest him. Proud of being an unpopular outsider, Meredith saw Tennyson as the incarnation of Establishment literature, complacent British patriotism, and smooth, facile sentimentality. But in 1851 Alfred Tennyson was not yet the sanctified Lord Tennyson, and Meredith could be sincerely grateful for his praise.

Thus far, Meredith had been favoured by fortune, had forged ahead through his own efforts and talents, and had consistently made the right decisions. In 1841, he was nothing more than the son of a bankrupt tailor.

In 1851, he was a published poet with a right to look forward to an expanding reputation, an accepted member of a lively literary circle, the husband of a beautiful and universally admired woman, and the son-in-law of a distinguished writer. The future could still hold uncertainty and disappointment; he was only twenty-three. But he could fairly say to himself: so far, so good.

4

Attempts and Failures

For George Meredith, the 1850s were a difficult decade. We see him searching for the right mode of literary expression, trying to lure the public but achieving no solid success, always short of money, and meeting with deepening unhappiness in his personal life. Yet we see him reflecting and learning, accumulating the intellectual resources that equipped him to write his first major novel at the end of the decade. Though marked by failure, these years are most truly understood as a period of transition and growth.

Transition and growth are the key-words, too, for the Britain of the 1850s. The defeat of Chartism had removed all threat to the established social order. The ruling class – that comprehensive merger, more effective than in any other country, of old aristocracy and new plutocracy – could feel more secure than ever before. The 'respectable working man', properly grateful for a modicum of home comforts, was emerging from the hardships of the past. The Queen and her serious, dutiful Consort set a pattern for family life. In 1851 they gave their blessing to the Great Exhibition, a triumphant shop-window for British achievement, housed in the Crystal Palace which was itself a masterpiece of advancing technology. No nation, before or since, has ever reached the industrial pre-eminence attained by 'the workshop of the world', the title claimed at this time. Britain was producing about three-quarters of the manufactured goods in the world, including practically all the railway engines and merchant ships in use anywhere. The export trade in Welsh coal reached a milestone in 1840 by securing the contract to fuel the French Navy; in several Meredith novels, wealth is derived from Welsh mines. British managers gave the orders, not only in India and the colonies, but also in politically independent countries such as Russia, China, Spain, Italy and Argentina. In America's Wild West, men armed with British-made guns held up British-made trains to steal money borrowed from British banks.

This economic supremacy was often ascribed to the innate or God-given superior qualities of 'the British race', as it was confidently and unscientifically called. Endowed with these qualities, the British (or the English) had nothing to learn from 'lesser breeds without the law' and could happily treat them with disdain. That was the attitude of Dickens's Mr Podsnap and of Meredith's Mr Adister, who spoke contemptuously of 'ridiculous Germans, capricious Frenchmen' and declared: 'We want nothing new in musical composition and abstract speculation of an indecent mythology.' But Dickens created Mr Podsnap and Meredith created Mr Adister precisely to satirize and puncture British narrowness, complacency and philistinism. For that matter, Kipling's poem 'Recessional', in which the much-quoted phrase about 'lesser breeds' can be found, was written as a warning against national hubris. Even in the 1850s – fifty years before 'Recessional' – examples of British complacency can be matched by many other examples of British anxiety.

In fact, there was glaring evidence that the vaunted prosperity was not the whole picture. The raging cholera epidemic of 1849 killed 53,000 people, including 14,000 in congested London. Capable reformers were available to put in hand an overhaul of the polluted water supply; but the lesson to be drawn was that material possessions in the homes of the contented did not offset the neglect of the environment. In his extremely anxious *Culture and Anarchy*, Matthew Arnold drew the contrast (he was citing a classical Roman phrase) between 'private affluence and public squalor'.

If the epidemic in the London slums was nearer home, it was less devastating than the famine which afflicted Ireland in 1845–47. Out of a population of eight million, two and a half million perished through sheer hunger, died of diseases (including cholera) or emigrated. The tragedy generated a fierce hatred of the Government which ordered a continuance of wheat exports from Ireland to England and of landowners who evicted penniless tenants. In 1848 there was an attempted uprising in the suffering West, and in 1858 the Fenian Brotherhood was formed with the aim of fighting for an Irish Republic.

For liberal, middle-class Englishmen, economic prosperity went together with peace abroad, but in 1853 Britain stumbled into war, with Russia as the enemy and the France of Napoleon III as the ally. The strategy decided on was an invasion of the Crimea, and troops were landed there, only to be immobilized for months by the ravages of – yet again – cholera. After that, efforts to capture Sebastopol were hampered by supply shortages, incompetent generalship, and muddles such as the suicidal charge of the Light Brigade, which even Tennyson's grandiloquent verse could not make into a cause for pride. Reports from a brilliant war correspondent, William Howard Russell, told readers of *The Times* that the British Army's tents and rations were pitiful by comparison with the French. A nurse from the civilian world, Florence Nightingale, had to take charge of the grossly mismanaged hospital. In the actual battles, the losses were on a scale not to be matched until 1914. Sebastopol was finally stormed in an assault that cost 10,000 lives. The war ended in 1856 without bringing any visible rewards for victory, and with a distinct feeling that it had been a mistake all along. In nineteenth-century warfare it was usual for deaths through sickness to exceed those attributable to sword or bullet, and the Crimean War was no exception. The Allies had sacrificed 252,000 men, of whom only 70,000 could be listed as killed in action.

Survivors of the Crimean War had been home for less than a year when British power faced a more unexpected emergency – the Indian Mutiny, or for Indian historians the great revolt against alien rule. British forces had to give up Delhi, where the Mogul Emperor was restored to his throne, and besiege it for three months before they recaptured it. It was the Indian rebels who besieged Lucknow; a year passed until the garrison could be relieved. With the prospect of losing control of such an enormous and lucrative possession, the British reaction was one of panic, which led to fury and ferocious repression. A shocked British witness in Benares recorded: 'Old men who had done us no harm, and helpless women with sucking infants at their breasts, felt the weight of our vengeance.' The Mutiny was finally crushed in 1858. But the system of government by the East India Company, theoretically a commercial enterprise, was completely discredited. In November 1858, the first Viceroy proclaimed that the ruler of India was Queen Victoria.

The decade began hopefully for Meredith. Mrs Macirone was able to introduce him to a number of literary men who either visited The Limes or took lodgings there for varying periods. One of the latter was Tom Taylor, a remarkable self-made man, of working-class origin and with a German mother, always referred to (even in the Dictionary of National Biography) as Tom, not Thomas. Thirty-three years old in 1850, Taylor had already been a Professor of Literature at London University, been called to the Bar, worked as an official in the Board of Health, and written leading articles for the *Daily News*. He went on to write about seventy plays, lightweight but commercially successful, including a dramatization of *A Tale of Two Cities* and the first stage versions of 'Dick Whittington and His Cat', 'Babes in the Wood' and 'Cinderella', and crowned his career as editor of *Punch*.

An acquaintance on a higher social level was Sir Alexander Duff Gordon, a Treasury official who later became Commissioner of Inland Revenue, but also a cultured man with literary tastes. His wife Lucie was the daughter of John Austin, who wrote books on jurisprudence and lived at Weybridge. Lucie, like her mother, Sarah Austin, translated from German (it is interesting how often the motif of German culture recurs in Meredith's life). She also knew Peacock and admired his novels. In 1850 the Duff Gordons, with their eight-year-old daughter Janet, stayed all summer with the Austins, and next year they bought a house at Esher. Janet, a bright child, found Meredith fascinating and called him 'my poet'. The Duff Gordons can be recognized as Sir Francks and Lady Jocelyn in *Evan Harrington*, while Janet – as a seventeen-year-old ready for marriage – is their daughter Rose. In her memoirs, she wrote proudly: '*Evan Harrington* was *my* novel, because Rose Jocelyn was myself.'[1]

There was every reason for George and Mary Meredith to be a popular couple. Both were strikingly good-looking, intelligent and well read, outgoing and talkative. At a dinner-party or a picnic, they presented a picture of happiness. Yet a perceptive observer like Lucie Duff Gordon must have seen that all was not well with them.

Two children were born in the first few years of the marriage, and both died as infants. The example of Mary's mother was there to show how grief over the death of a child could affect mental stability, and to give Meredith uneasy thoughts. It was only in June 1853 that a son was born and lived. He was named Arthur, perhaps to emphasize his Welsh ancestry on both sides, perhaps as a bow to Tennyson and the revival of the King Arthur legend. But he was a delicate child, and never grew to be as robust and lively as his half-sister, Edith Nicolls.

Sometimes, Mary had to nurse her husband as well as her child. Meredith was strong and vigorous, able to work tirelessly and walk for miles; but when he caught a cold it was a heavy cold and he had to stay in bed, fed by Mary on beef broth. Worse, he was often attacked by painful indigestion. A family friend, Jefferson Hogg, nicknamed him 'the dyspeptic'. These bouts of indigestion or constipation (bradypepsy was then the medical term) plagued him throughout his life and gave rise to resentful complaints in his letters; it is likely that he had a stomach ulcer, never diagnosed. Thanks to Victorian eating habits, indigestion was a common complaint among older people, but it was surprising in a man in his early twenties. Mary, who was something of a nutritionist, thought that indigestion was a risk to be ascribed to the pressures of modern life. Reviewing a cookery book for *Fraser's Magazine*, she referred to stomach diseases caused by 'commercial anxiety, literary irritation, and moral vexation'.

Meredith was working hard at his poetry. In addition to the long poetic sequence *Modern Love*, written later, twenty-three shorter poems were published in his next collection in 1862. This may seem to be a slender output for a decade, but surviving notebooks and manuscripts show many poems – or attempts at poems – which were discarded, or were rejected by magazines to which they were submitted, or which Meredith himself did not judge worthy of preservation. He was never a writer of facility and was his own severest critic.

Through Richard Horne, who had helped him in early days and secured the publication of 'Chillianwallah', or through other friends, Meredith made contact with two important editors. One was Dickens, then at the height of his fame, who started the popular weekly *Household Words* in 1850. Meredith probably met Dickens briefly at this time, but they were not really acquainted until the 1860s when both were established novelists and habitués of the Garrick Club. The other was G. H. Lewes, editor of another new magazine, *The Leader*. Unhappily married, he was starting a discreet relationship with Mary Ann Evans, who had come to London from Warwickshire to work on the *Westminster Review*; she had not yet begun to write fiction under the name of George Eliot. Meredith had poems accepted by both *Household Words* and *The Leader*, and also wrote reviews for the latter journal. Since it was then customary for all contributions to magazines to be unsigned, we cannot be certain how many were written by Meredith, except for a few poems that were in *Household Words* and also in the 1862 book. A researcher in 1911 claimed to find twenty-three Meredith poems in *Household Words*, and Stevenson in 1954 identified twelve for the year 1851 alone.

To complicate matters, Mary was involved in the poetry. Ellis gave this account: 'Meredith and his talented wife found a congenial link in their literary pursuits. They were both writing a good deal of poetry, and sometimes they collaborated.' Mary had written a poem, 'The Blackbird', for the *Monthly Observer*, and Meredith took up the sentimental theme of the caged blackbird for a poem that appeared in *Household Words*. Mary also tried to help the family finances by writing a cookery book, which was never published although a publisher came up with an advance of £30. In her outline, she pointed out that 'Economy in a Wife is the most certain Charm to ensure the affection and industry of a husband'. With an eye to healthy nutrition, she announced: 'I have written for those who make Nourishment the chief end of Eating, and do not desire to provoke Appetite beyond the powers and necessities of Nature.'[2] The subject inspired an article on 'Gastronomy and Civilisation' for *Fraser's Magazine*, written by Mary in collaboration either with her husband or with her father (accounts vary). Peacock was a gourmet and a good cook, but by no means a health expert.

With all these efforts, the Merediths were failing to make ends meet. Their income in 1851 was about £60, including the £30 for the projected cookbook, and in 1852 it was probably less. Peacock had a solution: he could find a job for his son-in-law at East India House. Meredith turned down this offer. He felt, evidently, that an office job would divert him fatally from the pursuit of a literary career, and he was now planning a prose work that would demand all his time and all his concentration. Possibly, too, he glimpsed the approach of an Indian uprising and guessed that the days of the Company were numbered. In any case, the young man's rejection of the opportunity did not make him more popular with the father-in-law who was also the Examiner.

However, Peacock was aware of his daughter's unhappiness and prepared – if not keen – to do whatever he could to help. Jane died in 1852, after twenty-six years of seclusion and 'madness'. There was space in the house, which had been converted from two adjoining cottages. George and Mary were having real difficulty in paying the rent at The Limes, and made a prolonged visit to Mary's brother Edward and his wife, who lived at Southend-on-Sea, but in reality they had become homeless. Peacock invited – or at least allowed – them to move in.

Sadly but predictably, the arrangement was a disaster. Arthur was born soon after the move; a baby's cries were an unbearable irritation for the old gentleman (Peacock was now sixty-eight). Mealtimes and evenings were tense, with Meredith talking incessantly and annoying the Tory Peacock with his Radical opinions. Edith, an observant child of nine, recorded later that her grandfather 'could not stand him'. For a last straw, Meredith was a cigar smoker and Peacock loathed the smell of tobacco. Twenty years later, Meredith indulged himself in *Beauchamp's Career* with a portrait of Everard Romfrey as a dogmatic, intolerant anti-smoker. This battle, too, did not begin with the twentieth century.

Still, Peacock could not throw the young couple into the street. He loved his daughter, he wanted to keep her near by, and he had money. He rented a little house called Vine Cottage, on the other side of the village green of Lower Halliford. It was home for George and Mary as long as they stayed together.

Meredith was still visiting the Duff Gordons. One day at their house in Esher, he met a gentleman called Monsieur de Haxthausen, or Herr von Haxthausen (his antecedents are mysterious). This person had travelled adventurously in remote parts of Asia and had a repertoire of extraordinary stories, in which it was never clear just where fact melted into invention; he seems to have been a sort of Baron von Munchhausen, but rather more credible. On this occasion, he told the company that he had fought with the Queen of the Serpents. 'She called her subjects to her aid with loud, shrill hisses, and the earth became alive with snakes.' Asserting that he had killed quantities of snakes to make his escape, Haxthausen produced a silk bag containing, he said, the serpent crown. A doctor who was present identified it as 'a bony excrescence from a reptile and probably from the head'. Such was the account written later by Janet Duff Gordon, who remembered: 'Meredith never took his eyes off M. de Haxthausen while he told his weird tale, and when next he brought me home he told me a marvellous story about the Queen of the Serpents.'[3]

The marvellous story became *The Shaving of Shagpat*, Meredith's first work of fiction. The book contains a novella, *Bhanavar the Beautiful*, interpolated in the main story, and probably written first. In this novella, Bhanavar persuades her lover to steal a jewel that adorns the Serpent Queen. He obeys, and dies of the venom in the jewel, while Bhanavar is pursued by snake-spirits. There is, thus, a sinister connection between seductive feminine beauty and the malevolent serpent. The theme recurs in *Richard Feverel* (despite its surface realism) when Sir Austin reflects: 'We are pretty secure from the Serpent till Eve sides with him.' Richard is indeed ensnared by beautiful, immoral Bella Mount, who has 'sorcery in her hair'. In a vivid phrase, 'the ends of it stung him like little snakes'.

The villain of the main story is Shagpat, originally a clothier, who has gained absolute power in his city and can defy any challenge unless he is shaved, or rather shorn. He is escorted everywhere by slaves who support 'the masses of hair that spread bushily before and behind, and to right and left of him'. His strength is vested in all this hair and particularly in a single hair called 'the Identical'. Strength through hair is a theme in traditions from various cultures; the Samson story in the Bible is an obvious example. Perhaps it is not irrelevant that Meredith himself had a good head of hair and by this time had stopped shaving to grow a full beard. However, the magical single hair can be traced to the Welsh legends in the Mabinogion, translated in 1838 by Lady Charlotte Guest.

Barbers are forbidden to enter the city, but a young barber named Shibli Bagarag makes his way there. Noorna, whom he sees at first as an old hag but who is transformed into a beautiful woman, reveals to him that he is 'a youth destined to great things' and guides him towards the objective of shaving Shagpat. He is three times seized by Shagpat's minions and 'thwacked' – the slang word was presumably a memory of Meredith's schooldays. The rest of the book is filled with his adventures as he goes through all kinds of ordeals, wanderings and setbacks until he triumphantly severs the 'Identical' and takes power in Shagpat's place. He has to find three protective talismans – a phial of water from a magic well, a lily, and hairs (again) from the tail of an elusive horse – to outwit and finally kill the evil genie Karaz, and to arm himself with the magic sword of Aklis. Throughout, he is guided and advised by Noorna and it emerges that her father, Vizier in the Shagpat regime, is secretly opposed to Shagpat and willing to help Shibli. The book is replete with spells and curses, animals and birds with human properties, disguises, pursuits, imprisonments and escapes, duels and battles, and all the paraphernalia of exotic fantasy.

The inspiration for *Shagpat* clearly derives from the tales of the *Arabian Nights*, or *The Thousand and One Nights* (though the landscape descriptions, and the names of characters and places, are more Persian than Arabian). A translation had appeared in 1839 and swiftly become popular. It was heavily bowdlerized to eliminate the luxuriant sexuality of the Arabic original – there was no full translation until 1882 – but Meredith may have had access to franker eighteenth-century versions in English and French. However, he happily threw every possible ingredient into his casserole. The sword of Aklis, for instance, recalls the sword Excalibur in Arthurian legend. The theme of the young hero dedicated to an arduous and dangerous quest is traditional all over the world. At Neuwied, Meredith could have read of Parsifal in the medieval German romances that later gave Wagner his material.

If Shibli is the hero, Noorna is more emphatically the heroine. Although Shibli is brave and sincere, he is also naïve, easily fooled, and simply not very bright. There is something of Candide in Shibli, too. It is Noorna, markedly more mature and wiser, who gives him his mission in the first place, warns him of dangers that he fails to see, saves him when he makes a near-fatal blunder, and strengthens his morale when he is tempted to give up. Depicting Noorna in this way, Meredith was paying tribute to Mary, his worldly-wise (and older) wife – or, it would be truer to say, to an always loyal and supportive Mary as he wished her to be. While Noorna is faithful to Shibli, Shibli slips helplessly into unfaithfulness; he falls for the cunning Queen Rubesqurat and is even tempted by the 'plump girls' who are clearly vulgar tarts. Meredith's attitude to women, at this stage of his life, was ambivalent. They can be protective, trust-worthy and altogether admirable, like Noorna; or they can be selfish and treacherous, like Rubesqurat. Ambivalence, indeed, was developing in his feelings about Mary, for the possibility of estrangement appeared some time in the mid-1850s. He loved Mary and was proud of her; she was, as he said later, 'very clever'; but perhaps she was too clever to be reliable. From this angle, we can find in *Shagpat* a plea to Mary to be a Noorna and not a Rubesqurat.

What is *Shagpat* really about (a simplistic question, no doubt), or what was Meredith seeking to achieve by writing it? There are many uncer-tainties. The romantic and mysterious Arab world, then scarcely pene-trated, was exerting much fascination since the appearance of *Arabian Nights*; we cannot know whether Meredith genuinely admired the genre, or whether he was exploiting it in search of a much-needed success, or whether, conceivably, he was satirizing it by pushing it to an extreme of absurdity. The twists and turns of the story can be interpreted in various ways, but it is hard to believe that Meredith was pursuing any logical plan. One feels that he was writing intuitively, giving free rein to his power of imaginative invention, and, since he was not bound by any laws of probability, making it up as he went along. This does not mean, however, that the happenings in the story do not stem from his vision of the real world and cast light on his ideas and beliefs. It is best to read *Shagpat* as a precursor of what we now call magic realism, readily accessible to anyone who responds to Gabriel García Márquez, Isabel Allende or Salman Rushdie. The magic, after all, does not negate the realism.

In this sense, the confrontation between Shibli and Shagpat mirrors an antagonism between aspirations to an ideal world capable of liberating human potentialities, and on the other hand a restrictive domination of blind power. For Lionel Stevenson, 'it portrays the conflict of instinct and reason, the story of the human race in its painful struggle to overcome the heritage of animalism and develop the full power of mind'.[4] For the Marxist writer Jack Lindsay:

> The Identical is the egoist basis of personality, the false notion of
> Identity that rests on power and privilege, on a world organised in
> hierarchical exploitations ... This notion of Identity is the Illusion
> overthrown in the successful movement into reason and brotherhood.[5]

A 'movement into reason and brotherhood' had indeed been the aim
of the revolutionaries of 1848, with whom Meredith had passionately
sympathized, and he refused to accept that this aim could never be
achieved, or that the restoration of the old repressive regimes was irrevers-
ible. The Shagpat autocracy was a forceful representation of the spiritual
nullity, as well as the harshness, of Metternich's Austria, King Bomba's
Naples, or monarchist (and now, in the 1850s, Napoleonic) France. The
'thwackings' inflicted on Shibli can be equated with the brutality of police
repression, as it had been angrily depicted by Stendhal.

Shagpat, however, is not a king or emperor with a title validated by
ancient descent, but a dictator lacking any moral claim to respect. Minor
characters whom Shibli meets as he enters the city – a confectioner, for
instance – represent the narrow-minded bourgeois society on which the
regime is based. Shagpat himself is a clothier; although Meredith was
making a nod to Carlyle's *Sartor Resartus*, a book he had read attentively,
he must also have recalled the background of the Merediths as tailors
and asked what this commercial status could have to do with political
authority. Derisively, Shibli exclaims: 'A clothier to control the Vizier
and demand his daughter!' If Shagpat presages any figures in later history,
he presages Hitler and Mussolini. In fact, there is a powerless king in
Shagpat's city, just as there was a powerless King of Italy in Mussolini's
time.

Striking, too, is the complete passivity with which Shagpat reacts to
the final assault by Shibli, making no effort whatever to defend himself.
Devoid of any moral dynamic, entitled to no real loyalty, the regime had
endured solely through the hollow strength of illusion and the absence
of opposition. When the challenge comes, the immediate effect is collapse
– as it was in Paris and Vienna in 1848, or indeed in East Berlin and
Prague in 1989.

Since his aesthetic method was imaginative, Meredith chose to adopt
a literary style distinct from that of conventional, easily readable fiction.
Some of his devices – for instance, the inversions in a sentence such as
'Then loosed they him' – are admittedly irritating. (As sometimes with
Carlyle, we feel that we are reading German rather than English.) How-
ever, deliberate archaism in vocabulary and sentence structure was a

technique favoured by other writers in the nineteenth century: Kingsley in *Westward Ho!*, Stevenson in *The Black Arrow*, Morris in his versions of the Icelandic sagas. Meredith was writing – as, to a greater or lesser extent, he always did – as a poet. His mode of expression was heightened above the level of everyday prose, emotionally coloured, sometimes ruth-lessly violent and sometimes lyrical. The style had to conform to the content, and he would have argued that one cannot write about a woman being transformed into an antelope as one writes about a lady buying a new hat. At its best, the style did successfully match the mood:

> When the sun was red and the dews were blushing with new light, they struggled from a wilderness of barren broken ground, and saw beneath them, in the warm beams, green, peaceful, deep, the meadows of Melistan. They were meadows dancing with flowers, as it had been fresh damsels of the mountain, fair with variety of colours that were so many gleams of changing light as the breezes of the morn swept over them; lavish of hues, of sweetness, of pleasantness, fit garden for the souls of the blest.

In December 1855 (the date on the title-page was 1856) *Shagpat* was published by Chapman and Hall. This was something to celebrate that Christmas, for Chapman and Hall (Dickens's publisher) was a leading, perhaps *the* leading, firm. Meredith became personally friendly with Edward Chapman, the senior partner, and the firm published his books until they parted company much later. Instead of subsidizing the publi-cation, as with *Poems*, Meredith received an advance of £70. He did not, however, get magazine serialization, which was the best way to make money. He could claim professional status, but he was still far from earning the £300 a year which, it was reckoned, was the minimum needed for a man to keep himself, a wife and two children at a middle-class standard.

Some of the reviews were of the kind that fulfil a writer's dreams. Lewes wrote in the *Saturday Review*: 'George Meredith, hitherto known to us as a writer of graceful but not very remarkable verse, now becomes the name of a man of genius.' Mary Ann Evans – agreeing, not surpris-ingly, with Lewes – wrote in *The Leader* that *Shagpat* was 'a work of genius, and of poetical genius' and went on to praise its 'exuberance of imagery, picturesque wildness of incident, significant humour, aphoristic wisdom'. Exerting herself beyond the line of duty, she reviewed the book in the *Westminster Review* as well. The *New Quarterly Review* declared: 'We have in every line proof of a gorgeous imagination, literary skill of a high order and considerable dramatic power.' The *Sun* chimed in: 'We at once recognise a writer of real genius, of a genius large, true and original.' It is true that the word 'genius' was then used more readily than it is today; a critic of our times might have said 'talent'. But there was no doubt of the tone of enthusiastic approval. Privately, Mary Ann Evans thought the book rather lightweight, for she wrote to a friend: 'If you want some idle reading get *The Shaving of Shagpat.*' The reviews, however, were what mattered.

Some reviews were unfavourable, but even these were sympathetic. The *Spectator*'s verdict was: 'A mistaken undertaking by an able man . . . The story wants power to carry the reader along.' The *Critic* also considered *Shagpat* to be 'a mistake', arguing that 'an Englishman cannot think Eastern thoughts', and gave Meredith this advice: 'If he would write an English story in the English manner, laying his scenes among places familiar to him, and making his personages of those whom he has met in the actual world about him, he would, we believe, be entirely successful.' Within a few years, Meredith did just this.

Meredith had the unfortunate gift (like many other writers) of remembering his bad reviews and forgetting the good ones. Towards the end of his life, he said: 'When I was young, had there been given me a little sunshine of encouragement, what an impetus to better work would have been mine. I had thoughts, ideas, ravishment; but all fell on a frosty soil.'[6] In reality, the record of encouragement is clear enough.

If Meredith had counted on good reviews, Mary had not. In a letter of thanks to the reviewer in the *Sun*, she wrote: 'I am as much surprised as gratified to find the book so well received, for the work is so unlike modern literature that I expected it would not be understood.' She then voiced her anger at the *Spectator* review, which she called – perhaps quoting her husband – 'flippant, disparaging, ignorant and assuming'.[7]

The question of how *Shagpat* should be understood was indeed the stumbling-block. Reviewers suspected that it was designed as an allegory, but fought shy of this aspect. 'Our imagination', Mary Ann Evans wrote in *The Leader*, 'is never chilled by a sense of allegorical intention predominating over poetic creation.' The *Sun* reassured readers that the book could be read 'without regard to any hidden significance', and the *New Quarterly Review* dismissed the notion of an allegory as 'a supposition not entertained by us'. Meredith himself wrote a disclaimer in a preface to the second edition, published ten years later:

It has been suggested to me by one who has no fear of Allegories on the banks of the Nile, that the hairy Shagpat must stand to mean umbrageous Humbug ... while my heroic Shibli Bagarag is actually to be taken for Circumstance, which works under their changeful guidance towards our ultimate release from bondage ... Though a story-teller should be flattered to have it supposed that anything very distinct was intended by him, the Allegory must be rejected altogether ... He attempted to give a larger embrace to time than is possible to the profound dispenser of Allegories, which are mortal.

The search for allegories persisted, however, and in 1892 Meredith, now thoroughly tired of the subject, had to deal with an enquiry from a lady living in his neighbourhood. He told her:

I suppose he does wear a sort of allegory. But it is not as a dress-suit; rather as a dressing-gown, very loosely. And they say it signifies Humbug, and its attractiveness; while Noorna is the spiritual truth. Poor Bagarag being the ball between the two. I think I once knew more about them and the meaning, but have forgotten, and am glad to forget, seeing how abused I have been for having written the book.[8]

His attitude was, in fact, that of Browning, who, when asked to explain the meaning of one of his poems, replied: 'Ask the Browning Society.'

Finally, in 1906, an admirer called James McKechnie produced a whole book as a guide to *Shagpat*. For McKechnie, it was in the tradition of the supreme allegory of English literature, Bunyan's *Pilgrim's Progress*. All that was necessary was to read *Shagpat* in this spirit: 'So rich is it in the magical qualities of Allegory that fresh meanings and beauties will reveal themselves to every competent seeker.' He explained that Rubesqrat stood for 'life in its frivolous, superficial aspect'; Shagpatism for 'life in its institutional aspect, full of errors, superstitions and wrongs'; Shibli's quest for 'life in its aspiring and disciplinary aspect, a school wherein men may learn wisdom'. As for the three spells, the magical water was a symbol of Insight, the lily of 'the soul's vision', and the hairs from the horse's tail of Enthusiasm. The sword that provided Shibli with a triumphant weapon was the Sword of Christ – an interpretation that certainly cannot have appealed to Meredith. Impressed by McKechnie's laborious effort, Meredith wrote to him: 'You have done as much as could be done with the adventurous barber', but added that the effort was fairly pointless now that hardly anyone was interested. Contradicting his earlier disclaimer, he assured McKechnie that *Shagpat* really was an allegory and the fault lay with readers who failed to appreciate it: 'An Allegory is hateful to the English, and I gave it clothing to conceal its frame. But neither that nor the signification availed.'[9]

Despite the good reviews, *Shagpat* did not succeed with the reading public. Copies languished in the warehouse and were eventually remaindered. The successes of 1855 were Dickens's *Little Dorrit* and Trollope's *The Warden*, both firmly set in 'the actual world'. In another century and with a different public, *Shagpat* might have become a cult book like *Lord of the Rings*. (Could a present-day publisher test the wind with a reprint, one wonders?) But, although Meredith had established a reputation by the time of the second edition, this too failed. He was now able to look at the book with self-critical objectivity and wrote cheerfully to his friend Frederick Maxse: 'It is ten to one against your being able to read it. I have known kindly persistent people defeated very early in the opening pages. And in truth the main story is much too much spun out.'[10] In 1877, when the editor of the *Dublin University Magazine* asked for permission to reprint an extract from *Shagpat*, the author replied: 'I express my regret that I cannot suffer work of mine of that period to see the light.'

At the time, however, Meredith was badly bruised by the disappointment, and decided to make one more attempt to lure the public with a bouquet of magic and fantasy: *Farina*, published in 1857. The record for this period is difficult to piece together with any certainty. He spent several months of 1856 – without Mary – at Seaford, on the Sussex coast a few miles from Newhaven. He wrote to Edward Chapman that 'the dulness is something frightful', but for just this reason Seaford was a good place for hard work. It was not unusual, throughout his life, for Meredith to work on two books at the same time, and in 1856 he may well have been writing *Farina*, a short novel, while drafting passages of the substantial *Richard Feverel*. (Events in Meredith's life, as we shall see, show that *Feverel* cannot have been completed until 1858.) He referred in his letters to a book called *The Fair Frankincense*, a projected title that can be interpreted to apply to either *Farina* or *Feverel*. Chapman, while remaining on good terms with Meredith and welcoming him as a guest at his own house on the Channel coast, declined to publish *Farina*, presumably reckoning that it would sell no better than *Shagpat*, and chose to wait for the big realistic novel. So *Farina* was published by Smith, Elder and Co., also a leading firm (Charlotte Brontë had been their best-known author).

The subtitle of *Farina* is 'A Legend of Cologne'. Meredith made use of his memories of the romantic Rhineland scenery and of facts about

Cologne, a town that he had seen on his way to Neuwied and again on his honeymoon. While Cologne was a cathedral city with a long history, it was also an industrial centre trading, among other commodities, in dyes, chemicals, leather and hides. Given the production methods of the time, these generated noxious smells, but an antidote was available in the form of the perfume called eau de Cologne, first manufactured in the eighteenth century by an Italian who settled in the city, Giovanni Maria Farina. The Farina family, still managing this profitable business, had become Germanized by Meredith's time; Meredith made the Farina of his novel a German and pushed the creation of eau de Cologne back to the medieval age, when feudal barons dominated the Rhineland from the castles that he had seen on his boyhood walks. His first sentence set the tone of romance, or perhaps one should say of pastiche:

> In those lusty ages when the Kaisers lifted high the golden goblet of Aachen, and drank, elbow upwards, the green-eyed wine of old romance, there lived, a bow-shot from the bones of the Eleven Thousand Virgins and the Three Holy Kings, a prosperous Rhinelander, by name Gottlieb Groschen, or, as it was sometimes ennobled, Gottlieb von Groschen . . .

Gottlieb has a daughter, Margarita, so beautiful that she is adored by all the young men in Cologne. Farina, bravest and most handsome of these young men, loves Margarita and she loves him. Farina is busy with 'the extraction of essences'; when Margarita goes to his room, she finds it full of 'bottles, and vases, and pipes, and cylinders'.

While Cologne is expecting a visit by the Kaiser, it is invaded by the undisciplined private army of Baron Werner von Eck – 'godless, virgin-hunting devourers', in the words of Margarita's anxious Aunt Lisbeth. Farina saves her from the embraces of one of these men, but then she is kidnapped by the gang and carried off to the Baron's castle. Farina goes to the rescue with the aid of a jovial English soldier of fortune, Guy the Goshawk. Making a direct assault on the castle, Guy is captured, but Farina gets in through a secret passage thanks to the guidance of a supernatural being, the Water-Lady – she rises from a river – whose role parallels that of Noorna in *Shagpat*. The Baron is defeated in combat by Farina, Guy and Margarita, who wields a sword usefully, but also by the wiles of the Water-Lady. 'She slid to the Baron, and put her arms about him, and sang to him' (Meredith is drawing on the legend of the Lorelei). Encapsulated in this story is a contest between a monk, Father Gregory, and the Devil. The good monk is on Farina's side, and the Devil is a protector of the Baron. While the monk tries to guide Farina on his rescue mission, they are impeded by a storm aroused by the Devil. Meredith's description of the storm was vivid:

> Huge blocks and boulders were loosened and came bowling from above: trees torn by their roots from the fissures whizzed on the eddies of the wind: torrents of rain foamed down the iron flanks of rock, and flew off in hoar feathers against the short pauses of darkness; the mountain heaved, and quaked, and yawned, a succession of hideous chasms.

Pleased with his description of a Rhineland storm, Meredith used it again in *Richard Feverel.*

Gregory threatens the Devil with an all-out confrontation, but the Devil evades the challenge. Meredith's Devil, like some others in literature, is cynical, debonair and witty:

> 'Come!' said the Demon with easy raillery. 'You know your game – I mine! I really want the good people to be happy; dancing, kissing, propagating, what you will. We quite agree. You can have no objection to me, but a foolish old prejudice – not personal, but class; an antipathy of the cowl, for which I pardon you.

The Devil withdraws his protection from Werner, whose soldiers are paralysed during the crucial fight. In the contest between monk and Devil, Gregory is the winner on points and is rewarded by becoming a saint. Historically, St Gregory was a monk who became Pope, but Meredith may have confused (or conflated) him with a later Pope, Gregory VII, who waged a struggle against the German Kaiser, Heinrich III, and finally excommunicated him. Meredith's Kaiser in *Farina* is named Heinrich.

Though the Devil cannot prevent the defeat of Werner, he is not without further resources. Flying over Cologne, he blankets the city with the famous smells. For six days, the Kaiser's procession through the city has to be postponed. But Farina solves the problem:

> The Kaiser and the youth at his right hand were cheery ... Great was the wonderment of the people of Cologne to behold Kaiser Heinrich riding in perfect stateliness up the main street toward the Cathedral, while right and left of him bishops and electors were drop-

ping incapable . . . Men now pervaded Cologne with flasks, purifying the atmosphere. It became possible to breathe freely.

By comparison with *Shagpat*, *Farina* is relatively more realistic and less magical; medieval Cologne was a real city and was accurately described, whereas Shagpat's city was quite imaginary. However, *Farina* too is full of marvels and McKechnie could have interpreted it allegorically. As a young man faced with dangers and difficulties but sustained by a woman's love, Farina can be bracketed with Shibli. The lily, which we met as a precious talisman in *Shagpat* – and, earlier, in the poem 'Love in the Valley' – reappears as a symbol of purity. When Farina and Guy are first attacked by nasty smells, Guy finds relief by seizing a lily, calling it 'the breath of a fresh lass-like flower'. Later, the Water-Lady rises from her pool as a water-lily before revealing herself as a woman:

> No fairer figure of woman had Farina seen. Her visage had the lustrous white of moonlight, and all her shape undulated in a dress of flashing silver-white . . . As he retreated on the meadow grass, she swam towards him, and taking his hand, pressed it to her.

A dozen years later, Harry Richmond is saying: 'I came on the smell of salt air, and had that other spirit of woman around me, of whom the controlled sea-deeps were an image, who spoke to my soul like starlight.' Twenty years later again, Matthew and Aminta are realizing their love while they swim.

In keeping with his medieval setting, Meredith flavoured his pages with archaisms such as 'perchance', 'for the nonce', 'an' in the sense of 'if', and 'Avaunt, Fiend!' And, as in *Shagpat*, there were German-sounding inversions; Guy is made to exclaim: 'Out of this I'll get!' Touches of humour, generally rather facetious, added to the mixture; characters were given the names of German or Austrian coins – Groschen, Heller, Pfennig.

The reviews were again mixed, but none were as enthusiastically favourable as they had been for *Shagpat*. George Eliot – as we should now call her, as her first book had been published – confessed to 'something like disappointment' and considered that in some passages Meredith had 'sacrificed euphony, and almost sense, to novelty and force of expression'. She relented, however, to conclude that *Farina* was 'an original and an entertaining book'. The *Athenaeum* praised *Farina* as 'a real, lively, audacious piece of extravagance'. On the other hand, the *Saturday Review* dismissed it as 'flat and dull', while the *Spectator* found fault with its 'forced quaintness and facetiousness'.

Once again, the sales were very small, proving the correctness of Chapman's commercial judgement. By this yardstick, it was Meredith's third failure; yet it may not have been such a depressing event as could be assumed. Reading *Farina*, one has a feeling that he did not take it altogether seriously and, towards the end, that he was writing to polish it off and get it out of the way. His mind may well have been elsewhere —with the big novel that he was starting to write, and with the painful problems of real life.

In the later months of 1856, while Meredith was at Seaford, Mary was at Blackheath staying with General and Lady Nicolls, the parents of her first husband. It is not always clear where the children were, but Arthur went with his father on the visit to Chapman's seaside house. There was a tacit assumption that Arthur should be regarded as Meredith's child and Edith as Mary's.

In the summer of 1857, when *Farina* was published, Meredith was still at Seaford and Mary was in North Wales with her lover. George and Mary Meredith never lived together at Vine Cottage again. At the end of the year, Meredith took lodgings for himself and Arthur at 7 Hobury Street, Chelsea.

5

Through the Ordeal

WITH hindsight, it is safe to say that the marriage of George and Mary was a mistake from the start. The birth of Arthur, and George's affection for the child, served to postpone a break, but not to avert it. In writing his biography, Ellis was able to draw on the testimony of Edith, who was an observant girl in her teens and lived to be an old woman; thus, Ellis's judgement can be taken as sound:

> Husband and wife were too much alike in temperament and character and gifts to find permanent happiness together; if one partner . . . could have submitted to the stronger will of the other, final catastrophe might have been avoided. But Meredith and his wife were equally strong-willed, equally talented. Both were highly-strung, nervous, emotional, restless in mind and body. Both were hot in temper, satirical and violent in argument and dispute, quick to imagine offence. Consequently, peace was never of long continuance . . . Terrible scenes and quarrels took place.[1]

By 1857 at latest, the marriage had reached what the law now calls 'irretrievable breakdown', but divorce was not a feasible option. Separation was; Charles and Catherine Dickens separated in 1858 and the situation was accepted by his friends and his public (who knew nothing of his liaison with Ellen Ternan). Following a separation, Mary might have lived respectably with her father or with the Nicolls family, while Meredith lived in bachelor style. But this is not what happened, because Mary fell in love with Henry Wallis.

Wallis was an artist, with connections to the Pre-Raphaelite Brotherhood though not actually a member. He was two years younger than Meredith and could be seen by Mary, like Meredith in 1849, as a young man at the outset of a hopeful creative career. Like Meredith then, he was brought into her social circle by her brother, Edward Peacock. Welcomed in this circle, and accepted as a friend by George and Mary, he was commissioned to paint a portrait of Mary's father, which is now in the National Portrait Gallery.

His next work, exhibited at the Royal Academy in 1856, was 'The Death of Chatterton'. The subject was guaranteed to strike a chord. In 1769, at the age of sixteen, Thomas Chatterton had appeared in London with manuscripts of poems attributed to medieval monks. They were detected as a forgery by Thomas Gray (of the *Elegy*) and, after further unsuccessful attempts to break into the literary world, Chatterton committed suicide by taking arsenic. Despite his fraudulence and lack of real achievement – although he was remembered for his physical beauty – he won posthumous fame. Wordsworth immortalized him as 'the marvellous boy/The sleepless soul that perished in his pride'; Alfred de Vigny wrote a play about him; and Wallis was the sixth of the artists who portrayed him. The model for the dead or dying Chatterton, recumbent on a couch with one arm trailing gracefully to the floor, was George Meredith.

Whether Wallis and Mary were already lovers when the picture was painted; whether Wallis, sardonically or otherwise, asked Meredith to pose; whether the suggestion came from Mary, or whether Meredith volunteered – these are intriguing questions that cannot be answered.

Ruskin praised the picture, calling it 'faultless and wonderful' and commending it for 'the entire placing before your eyes of an actual fact – and that a solemn one'. A different view can be taken. The sentimental appeal is ludicrous; the calmness of the body disguises the agonies of someone genuinely dying of arsenic poisoning; and Chatterton's red hair is a false colour, reminding us of the dye of a 1980s punk. Meredith, after he realized that Wallis was Mary's lover, put him into *Richard Feverel* as Diaper Sandoe, the seducer of Lady Feverel, contemptuously describing him as 'some sort of poet', and made up lines from Sandoe's poems which placed him in a class with Wallis. However, 'The Death of Chatterton' was such a success that there was a lawsuit over unauthorized reproductions. It was bought by Augustus Egg, another artist then held in high esteem, and now hangs in the Tate Gallery.

After the summer exhibition at the Royal Academy, Wallis and Mary went to Wales together. Peacock, who evidently did not disapprove, wrote to her recommending 'the finest waterfalls' (they were near Maentwrog, where he had met her mother). She became pregnant; for her, this had never involved any delay. With a sister to care for her, she spent the winter in a rented cottage at Clifton, then on the outskirts of Bristol. In April 1858 a boy was born and named Harold. On the birth certificate, George Meredith was stated to be the father, an acceptable fiction. Wallis was submitting another picture, 'The Dead Stone-Breaker', to the Royal Academy. Though life was favouring him, he seems to have been drawn towards images of death. The appeal to sentiment was again apparent, though free of the blatant falsity of the Chatterton painting. It was another success, singled out by Ruskin as 'Picture of the Year', and can be seen in the Birmingham Art Gallery.

In the autumn, Wallis and Mary went to Italy, staying in Capri until the spring of 1859. Given that her marriage was clearly at an end, this was a reasonable course of action and her best chance of happiness. In a country where she and her lover were unknown and could appear as husband and wife if they chose, there was no risk of being recognized by friends or acquaintances from earlier days. Besides, Mary was in bad health; in a letter, she spoke of being 'very weak' and of 'dragging pains in my limbs'. Victorians, including Victorian doctors, had great faith in the benefits of a mild climate, whatever the ailment. It was not yet clear that Mary was suffering from kidney failure.

When they returned to England, Wallis and Mary ceased to live together. In most accounts, he has been blamed for breaking off the relationship and his conduct – considering that Mary was ill, was responsible for a twelve-month-old child, and was short of money – has been seen as heartless. A 1982 article in *History Today* states flatly that he 'abandoned her'. But he may well have been the sort of man who preferred to live without a woman, a preference that in his time was not considered extraordinary; he is not known to have had any other relationships and never married. Mary, for her part, had an independent and self-reliant personality. It is at least possible that they had committed themselves only to a love affair which was not necessarily expected to last, and which might have been still briefer had it not led to parenthood – like, for instance, the love affair between H. G. Wells and Rebecca West.

There is no doubt that Meredith was hard hit. Mary had left him, preferring another man, while there is no evidence that he had ever been unfaithful. A proud and sensitive man could well feel himself humiliated, and more so in the 1850s than today. The 'erring wife' was automatically condemned, and his reaction was to blame Mary. He explained later: 'The separation was her own doing, though not regretted by me, save for my boy's sake. It was not a formal separation, and was not considered to be final, until I had reason for knowing that it must be so.'[2] He also stated that:

> incompatibility of temper separated two people, of whom the man was eight years the junior, the woman very clever ... To say that she approached near madness without being quite mad is to express her mental and moral character. She dallied with responsibility, played with passions; rose suddenly to a height of exaltation, sank to a terrible level. And was very clever.[3]

However, this statement was designed for the eyes of Justin Vulliamy, whose daughter Meredith was courting as a second wife in 1864. Vulliamy, a strict moralist, had to be assured that the collapse of the first marriage was Meredith's misfortune and in no way his fault. Meredith revealed no self-examination to Vulliamy, nor to his friends; but it would be wrong to conclude that he was incapable of it.

While Mary was with Wallis, Meredith was working on his first long novel, *Richard Feverel*. Presumably the task helped him to keep his balance, but the novel illustrated his reaction to the blow he suffered. It was published by Chapman and Hall in October 1859. He had probably conceived the idea and started writing (while also completing *Farina*) before it was irrevocably clear that Mary was leaving him, but he must have gone back to the beginning when he put the manuscript into final shape, for the reader is told on the first page of the breakdown of Sir Austin Feverel's marriage. Tersely, Sir Austin says that he can forgive his treacherous friend, Sandoe, with a feeling of sheer contempt, but cannot forgive his wife. At one level, this reflects Meredith's attitude to Wallis and Mary.

Meredith was writing a rich and complex novel, dealing with a variety of themes: the conflict of father and son, principles of education, English class relationships, the morality of truth and lying, sexuality and innocence. Yet it was, very significantly, a novel about betrayal and desertion. Lady Feverel, before the story begins, has deserted Sir Austin. Lord Mountfalcon has deserted his wife, Bella, who then calls herself 'Mrs Mount'. Berry has deserted Mrs Berry. Richard, after marrying Lucy, betrays her by his night with Bella. (If Meredith had wanted to write a wholesale attack on disloyal women, he would have made Lucy, not

Richard, the unfaithful partner.) The saturnine butler, Benson, has been through an unspecified 'calamity' and prevents Sir Austin from being alone with Lady Blandish. Lady Blandish herself, a widow, was unhappily married, 'given to an ogre instead of a true knight'. Austin Wentworth's unsuitable marriage to a housemaid has ended in separation. Adrian Harley, Algernon Feverel and Hippias Feverel are all unmarried. In fact, the whole novel with its large cast of characters contains no example of a normal, successful marriage.

To gain a full understanding of the novel, one must read the passages that Meredith cut when he prepared a new edition in 1878. (These passages can be found in a separate volume of the 1910 Memorial Edition, but readers today are unlikely to be aware of them.) In a key passage in the original edition, Sir Austin as a young man has a conversation with his father, Sir Caradoc, who 'spoke of a special Ordeal for their race'. Austin's reaction is dramatic:

> Sir Caradoc's words smote him like a revelation. He believed that a curse was in his blood; a poison of Retribution, which no life of purity could expel; and grew, perhaps, more morbidly credulous on the point than his predecessor; speaking of the Ordeal of the Feverels, with sonorous solemnity, as a thing incontrovertibly foredecreed to them.

The Ordeal, it is made clear, has to do with women. Sir Austin is terrified of women and writes in his 'Pilgrim's Scrip': 'To withstand them, must we first annihilate our Mothers within us: die half!' The 'Scrip' is full of sexist dicta: 'Woman will be the last thing civilised by Man'; woman is 'the inferior creature'; 'women are born Pagans', and more in this vein. Sir Austin, like Sir Willoughby in *The Egoist*, is an utter misogynist. But, unlike Sir Willoughby, he is aware of it. 'It is the rank misogynist, who flees them, whom they hunt down,' he notes unhappily.

Meredith appears to be saying that, for a man, relationships with women are inevitably an ordeal. This, however, is a misinterpretation. The ordeal is the struggle to establish an honest, harmonious relationship in which the rights of both man and woman are recognized. Because of the misogynistic prejudice passed on by Sir Austin, and because of his own naïve blundering, Richard fails the ordeal and the novel ends tragically. Yet some of Meredith's other young men – Harry Richmond, Nevil Beauchamp – though almost equally prone to blundering, do in the end come through the ordeal with moral credit.

The literary landmarks of 1859, in addition to *Richard Feverel*, were

George Eliot's *Adam Bede* – an immediate success, placing her sales in the Dickens bracket – and Edward Fitzgerald's translation of *The Rubaiyat of Omar Khayyam*. However, in intellectual history the supreme event of 1859 was the publication of Darwin's *The Origin of Species*. If we can take any date as Year One of what we call the modern world, that date is 1859.

Of this modern world – or of 'modernism', the intellectual outlook which came to dominance in the late nineteenth and early twentieth centuries – the essential quality was the consciousness of instability. Previously, there had indeed been dramatic upheavals, most notably the democratic revolutions – American and then French – spurred by ideological impulses. However, the aim of these revolutions was to build a new stability, more solid and durable than the stability of the *ancien régime* because it would be based on more viable foundations of humanity and justice. One can hardly imagine a more confident statement of belief than a declaration that begins: 'We hold these truths to be self-evident.' If the truths could be transmuted into beneficent social structures, further change would be unnecessary and, for that matter, unthinkable. Such was the spirit of the rationalist, philosophical eighteenth century.

By 1859, a very different spirit prevailed. The world (that is, the world of western Europe and North America) had certainly changed; but it had changed in an unpredictable manner, governed by no philosophical blueprint, no collective purpose, no controlling plan. The dominating process was the industrial revolution – so called, though it had none of the coherence or compactness of a political revolution. New patterns of industry and trade had emerged, aggregate wealth had rapidly increased, and the lives of millions had been transformed; yet this transformation was accompanied by a remorseless infliction of human suffering, physical and psychological. Just as no apparent volition, human or divine, had set the process in motion, so it was impossible to foresee where it would end. And, at the political level, France in 1859 was a reactionary empire, while America was on the verge of civil war.

Scientists and intellectuals, too (both these words date from the nineteenth century), were denied the blessings of certainty. They had assumed that developing knowledge could make a permanent classification of plants, animals and 'the races of mankind'. Christian doctrine taught that God, on the sixth day of creation, had stocked the world with useful cattle, edible fish and beautiful birds, all in perfected form, and given mankind dominion over them. Then came *The Origin of Species*. The biblical account had already been heavily undermined by the geologists, but Darwin now showed that these plants and animals – and, by implication, human beings too, though he did not make this explicit until he published *The Descent of Man* in 1871 – had slowly evolved from the most primitive forms through a blind, ineluctable process, never to be deflected or reversed, and neutral between good and evil. In this bleak, friendless universe, it was no longer possible to rely for favour or protection on any benevolent power. Neither good behaviour nor prayer could decide whether any form of life would prosper, survive or perish. The only hope was in adaptation to external conditions, and that necessarily in the very long term. There was something chilling about Darwin's expression, 'natural selection', and even more so about 'the survival of the fittest', the phrase coined in 1860 by Herbert Spencer and soon endorsed by Darwin. Spencer went on to advance the social philosophy that he called Individualism, maintaining that attempts to benefit the population at large by collective measures were doomed to futility. Those who were already favourably placed, and thus defined as among 'the fittest', naturally found the argument convincing.

While some were appalled by the uncertainties of the times, others were delighted. Surveying the scene in 1848 in *The Communist Manifesto*, Marx and Engels exclaimed gleefully: 'All that is solid melts into air!' Marx appreciated *The Origin of Species* as a revolutionary work, and when he produced his own revolutionary work, *Capital*, he offered to dedicate it to Darwin (who, modestly or prudently, declined the honour). The first volume of *Capital* did not appear until 1867, and then only in German; but in 1859 Marx was ready with a short version of his theories, published as *A Critique of Political Economy*. One sentence in this book had the potential to reverberate: 'It is not the consciousness of men that determines their social being but, on the contrary, their social being that determines their consciousness.' The eighteenth-century *philosophes* had assumed that intellectually evolved ideas would shape a new social order; for Marx, it was the other way round.

With all these new thoughts in the air, there was space for a new kind of novel. Curiously, it was in the 1920s, when Meredith's stock was low and he had few readers, that other writers and critics appreciated his place in literature. Virginia Woolf, describing him as a 'great innovator', noted in her discussion of *Richard Feverel*: 'He has been, it is plain, at great pains to destroy the conventional form of the novel.'[4] J. B. Priestley declared: 'The modern novel began with the publication of *The Ordeal of Richard Feverel* in 1859.'[5] Arthur Bennett concurred, ranking Meredith as 'not the last of the Victorian novelists, but the first of the modern school'.[6] What these commentators perceived was that Meredith was a writer who did not limit himself to the traditional skills of story-telling and character depiction, but drew on intellectual concepts to sustain an interpretation of reality. Meredith himself once said sweepingly: 'Narrative is nothing. It is the mere vehicle of philosophy. The interest is in the idea which action serves to illustrate.'[7] This was a view that would have had little meaning for Defoe or Fielding, and not much for Thackeray or Dickens.

If we need proof that *Richard Feverel* was a new kind of novel, we can find it in the baffled tone of the reviews. For *The Times*, 'there is such purity mingled with its laxness, such sound and firm truth in the midst of its fantastic subtleties, that we hesitate whether to approve or condemn; and we have a difficulty even in forming a judgement'. Hedging its bets in similar vein, the *Critic* commented: 'It has great merits and great defects, and we believe that they are very evenly balanced.' Most of the reviewers evaded genuine literary judgement by turning their attention to the moral defects of the novel, or of the characters in it. We can only guess what it was that they found most shocking: perhaps the sexual feelings clearly shown by women (Lucy, Clare, Bella and Lady Blandish); perhaps Meredith's sympathy for the sinning woman, Bella (a 'spirited, dauntless, eager-looking creature' with 'eyes not afraid of men'); or perhaps the cross-dressing episode, an example of behaviour practised widely enough, historians know, but not admitted.

The *Athenaeum* stigmatized the novel as 'about as painful a book as any reader ever felt himself inexorably compelled to read through' and concluded: 'We hope the author will use his great ability to produce something pleasanter next time.' The *Critic* found that the scenes with Bella 'are dwelt upon by Mr Meredith with too much minuteness'. Only *The Times* defended Meredith, if rather nervously:

> This book has been charged with impurity, and tabooed, as we hear, in some quarters by the over-fastidious. It certainly touches a delicate theme, and includes some equivocal situations, but of impurity, in the sense of any corrupting tendency, we see not a trace, and we will not endorse the imputation. It is a novel, in short, which may be read by men and women with perfect impunity if they have no corrupt imagination of their own to pervert the pure purpose of the author.

The hints and suspicions were enough to lead to disaster. Mudie's, the big lending library whose purchases were vital to a fiction publisher, had ordered three hundred copies, but cancelled the order before delivery. Protests by Chapman were met with the explanation that Mr Mudie had received 'urgent remonstrances of several respectable families who objected to it as dangerous and wicked and damnable'. (The adjectives may have been chosen by Mudie with some irony, or perhaps dictated by his lawyer.) Meredith lamented in a letter to a friend: 'I find I have offended Mudie . . . O canting age!'[8] There was nothing to be done; like all his books so far, *Richard Feverel* was a commercial failure.

Fortunately, it was in this painful period of Meredith's life that three new sources of income came his way. All were unexpected. A man named Thomas Foakes, whom Meredith had known for several years, acquired the ownership of the *Ipswich Journal* by marrying the widow of the previous proprietor. He needed a writer to contribute a weekly leading article and two columns of notes on the news, and offered Meredith the job. The *Journal* was a Tory paper and Meredith was a self-proclaimed Radical, but he wrote anonymously and, in the unchanging tradition of journalism, saw no hypocrisy in doing a competent hack job, yielding a useful £200 a year. He did not have to go to Ipswich, but did the work on Thursdays in the paper's London office. It was a tedious chore; in his letters, Meredith referred to Thursday as 'Foakesday' or sometimes as 'Black Foakesday'. But he stuck to the job for about ten years, until he no longer needed the money.

Then, in 1860, Edward Chapman – perhaps as a consolation for the failure of *Richard Feverel* – gave Meredith the position of publisher's reader. He had to read and report on manuscripts submitted to Chapman and Hall, mostly working at home, but sometimes going to the office to meet authors and give them advice. To a degree, he filled the role of editor, a job that did not yet exist. He liked this work and applied himself to it conscientiously, as a service to literature, and he stuck to it for about thirty years, until he became physically incapable of going to the office.

The third job was more peculiar. An elderly widow named Mrs Benjamin Wood, who led a secluded and somewhat Miss Havisham-like life in a big house called Eltham Lodge, enlisted him to read aloud to her once a week. After finishing his stint on 'Foakesday', he took the train from Charing Cross to Eltham. It is not clear how he got the job, nor exactly when he started it, but he had known Mrs Wood's brother-in-law, an earlier Chapman and Hall reader. This too was a chore; but he enjoyed reading plays or poetry in a dramatic and expressive manner, and Mrs Wood was a well-educated woman with whom he could have interesting literary conversations. She has a place, incidentally, in political history. She was an aunt of Kitty O'Shea, Charles Stewart Parnell's mistress, and bought the little house in Eltham where they met; it was her death at the age of ninety-three which led to the O'Shea divorce suit and Parnell's downfall (a good subject for a novel that Meredith might have written).

After a year or so in Chelsea, Meredith – with little Arthur – returned to the Thames Valley and took lodgings in a former coaching inn at Esher. One day, Arthur fell over in the road trying to avoid a horse that was coming at high speed. The rider was Janet Duff Gordon, now sixteen years old. She took the child home and was confronted by Meredith, who exclaimed: 'Oh, my Janet, don't you know me? I'm your poet.' Her parents were living in Esher and invited Meredith to dinner the same evening. Soon, the deserted husband of Mary Meredith was in love with the charming girl.

Mary was leading a pathetically unhappy life. Ellis recorded: 'All those who remember Mrs Meredith in the last years of her life state that she was always sad and constantly in tears. Her warm, vehement nature could not meet sorrow with resignation . . .'[9] She moved from one lodging to another, in Twickenham, Richmond and finally Weybridge once more – always the remembered territory, always near her father, and always near the husband whom she no longer saw. She ended up in Grotto Cottage, a tiny house in the grounds of a stately home converted into a hotel, near an ornamental grotto surrounded by battered statues of nymphs supporting funeral urns. Victorian pathos could go no further. Her condition deteriorated through 1859 and 1860; she must have known that it was terminal.

There is no record of Mary receiving any money from either her husband, her lover or her father; it is impossible to say how she paid doctors, if she did pay them. In July 1860 she wrote to Edward Chapman: 'Can you lend me £10 until Michaelmas [29 September]? In the event of my death between this and that Papa will repay it to you . . . Moving spare things from Richmond has taken up my loose cash and I never get into debt.'[10]

Little Harold was being cared for by a kindly woman (it appears) called Mrs Bennet, at his father's expense. Edith, sixteen by now, was at boarding-school or with the Nicholls family. Arthur was with Meredith. Under the law at that time, in the event of a separation, formal or effective, a father had an unqualified right to possession of children of the marriage – more emphatically so if the wife was the 'sinner'. Trollope attacked this provision in his remarkable novel *He Knew He Was Right* (published 1869), but it was generally accepted by contemporary opinion.

The saddest aspect of the situation was that, until a late stage in Mary's illness, Meredith did not allow her to see Arthur. One can readily imagine how distressing it was for her to know that the child was in the neighbourhood, yet barred from her. Meredith may have felt – Victorian attitudes are distant from those of today – that the boy was best protected from knowledge that would disturb him and that he would forget a mother whom he had not seen since he was four years old. Still, even in 1860 the ban could have appeared harsh or even vindictive. It was Janet, now Meredith's regular companion, who eventually persuaded him to relent, and in the last months of Mary's life Arthur was taken by a nursemaid to see her every day.

Meredith was now living at Copsham Cottage, his home until 1864. He could walk from his front door on to Copsham Common (Esher Common on official maps), a stretch of heath and woodland which is still unspoilt today despite being bisected by the A3. Often, Janet was with him. 'He lives in my memory,' she wrote after he died, 'as the lithe, active companion who so often strode along by the side of my cob over Copsham Common, brandishing his stick and talking so brilliantly.'[11]

Youthful, high-spirited Janet attracted him exactly as her prototype, Rose Jocelyn, attracted Evan Harrington. He could not ask her to marry him, however, so long as Mary was alive. Divorce through the civil (as distinct from ecclesiastical) courts had only just become feasible with the new law of 1857, and would be associated with scandal and disgrace for almost another century. Besides, to divorce a dying woman by bringing her adultery into the public record would be intolerably selfish and punitive. To begin living with Janet without marriage would involve endless guilt and secrecy – the unhappy theme, eventually, of his novel *One of Our Conquerors*. The rational, if distasteful or indeed gruesome, course was to wait for Mary to die. But since Meredith was not seeing Mary, he did not know how much longer she might live or even whether she might recover. Whether he and Janet talked about these possibilities we do not know. If so, the strain and unpleasantness can well be imagined.

It was Janet, in the autumn of 1860, who cut the Gordian knot. Although in later years she enjoyed telling people that 'Rose Jocelyn was myself', she was not in reality the Rose Jocelyn who bravely and recklessly gave her hand to the tailor's son with uncertain prospects. 'I don't think she's one for a poor man,' a friend of Meredith's confided to an acquaintance.[12] Through the charm and impulsiveness that colour descriptions of Janet – not least in her own memoirs – one can perceive a distinctly cool customer, with limited inclinations to romantic love. Meredith was informed that she was to marry Henry Ross, a man twenty-three years older than her. A banker with a job in Egypt, he could offer a life of adventurous travel based on ample comfort. 'I was impressed', she explained in her memoirs, 'by his admirable riding, his pleasant conversation, and his kindly ways. The result was that I promised to marry him.' When Ross died in 1900, Janet regretted the loss of 'my dear friend and companion'.[13]

As the English winter set in and Meredith faced a lonely Christmas, Janet sailed for Alexandria. The firm of Willis and Sotheran were less than helpful about packing books for her; Meredith reminded her: 'Yes, but, my dear Janet, Willis & What's his name aren't in love with you.' He wrote on a photograph: 'Behind it lies her free youth.' Letters went at intervals from Copsham to Alexandria: 'I pray fervently that you may be happy'[14] . . . 'Here I have waited silently thinking much of you'[15] . . . 'It is my punishment that I have to tell you what I never prove, that I love you and shall do so constantly.'[16] They met again when she visited England in 1862 and 1864, and then in 1866 in Venice. Janet recalled: 'Suddenly I heard my name, Janet, called from the crowd, and turning round saw to my infinite joy my Poet . . . We made several excursions together . . . I tried to persuade him to come with me to Egypt, but, alas, he could not.' After 1870, when Ross retired, Janet lived near Florence. She and her Poet stayed friends and she went to see him for the last time in 1904, noting: 'He had aged and his deafness had increased, but the old fire and brilliancy were there.' He said to her: 'You have something of Rose in you still, my dear.'[17]

In 1861, while Meredith made a stimulating trip to the Alps and Italy, Mary drifted towards death. Peacock wrote in August: 'She seems to grow rapidly worse. But while there is life, there is hope.' This platitude was of no avail; she died in October. Meredith was on a visit to Suffolk and out of contact. He told a friend later: 'When I entered the world again I found that one had quitted it who bore my name; and this filled my mind with old melancholy recollections which I rarely give way to.'[18] Her funeral at Weybridge was attended neither by Meredith (he might have gone if he had known in time, but it is doubtful) nor by Wallis, nor by Edith, nor by Peacock.

There was bitterness in the lines by Tennyson that she had chosen to be carved on her tombstone:

> Come not, when I am dead,
> To drop thy foolish tears upon my grave,
> To trample round my fallen head,
> And vex the unhappy dust thou wouldst not save.
> There let the wind sweep and the plover cry;
> But thou go by.

However, there was no tombstone, for there was no money.

Wallis, although with Ruskin's backing he had prospects of a successful career, painted nothing after Mary's death that gained attention. He gradually gave up painting to become a collector of ceramics, and in time a respected authority with a number of books and monographs to his credit. Outliving Meredith, he reached the age of eighty-six.

He paid the school fees for his son, whose name was changed from Harold Meredith to Felix Wallis. At the age of twenty Felix joined the staff of the Bank of England, to work there for forty years and retire as Manager of the Dividend Department.

It was during this emotionally testing period of Meredith's life, while Mary was in her last illness and while he was frustratingly in love with Janet, that he wrote *Evan Harrington*. In career terms, he needed to establish himself firmly as a novelist and to make up for the disappointment with *Richard Feverel* – which, after all, might have achieved a reasonable measure of success but for the Mudie's ban. Also, he had begun a friendly relationship with Samuel Lucas, editor of the new (and, it turned out, short-lived) magazine *Once a Week*. Lucas published a number of poems and a couple of short stories by Meredith and then agreed to run his new novel as a serial. It appeared between January and October 1860, with Meredith racing to hand in each instalment by the press deadline, a system that did not come so easily to him as it did to Dickens. He was paid £400, by far the largest sum he had yet earned; with the odd jobs, he was freed from money worries. In book form, it was published in 1861 – not by Chapman, though Meredith remained on good terms with him, but by Bradbury and Evans, the firm that owned *Once a Week*.

Psychologically, *Evan Harrington* served two functions for Meredith. It enabled him to settle accounts with the miseries of his childhood and youth and the embarrassment of being a tailor's son, and to put that phase of his life behind him, without revealing to readers that the story was his own. In this sense, the book was a kind of auto-therapy. He was also creating a love story in which George (as Evan) triumphantly won Janet (as Rose) – a wish-fulfilment of which he could not be confident in reality. However, he knew that the novel lacked the imaginative power and intellectual complexity of *Richard Feverel*, and ranked well below it in literary terms. When he found that he had lost Janet and his happy ending was a fantasy, the book went sour for him. In a letter to William Rossetti, he declared that 'the writing is atrocious', and he was so disgusted with the book that he could not bring himself to revise it for the hardback publication.

With *Evan Harrington* out of the way, Meredith nerved himself to confront the searing emotional experience that had dominated the whole of his adult life: his marriage and its breakdown. He did this, not in a novel, but in a poetic sequence of fifty stanzas (each stanza has the form of an enlarged sonnet, with the traditional length of line and scansion but with sixteen lines instead of the standard fourteen). His first title was 'A Love Match', with the ambiguous interpretation of contract and contest; a marriage between well-suited people is a match but so is, for instance, a tennis match. However, he changed this title to the still more significant 'Modern Love', implying a relationship between a man and a woman characteristic of the 'modern world' that was taking shape as he wrote. Startling to Victorians, the poem is extraordinarily prescient; there can be few readers today who could not recognize – in their own experience, in the lives of friends or family members, or at least in newspaper-reading – the situation that Meredith analysed. If *Richard Feverel* can be called the first modern novel, there is an equally strong case for calling 'Modern Love' the first modern poem.

'Modern Love' may have been started or at least contemplated in the last months of Mary's life, but was more probably written after her death. To make up a volume, Meredith supplemented it with shorter poems which had appeared in *Once a Week*. These were mostly 'portrait pieces' of the type that we associate with Browning, whom Meredith admired; 'The Old Chartist' is an example. Set alongside 'Modern Love', they are relatively superficial and unimportant. The volume, *Modern Love and Other Poems*, was published in 1862.

To summarize the content at a surface level: a husband and wife (nameless) are unhappy together but are desperately trying to make the marriage work. They cannot live satisfactorily with each other, and cannot live without each other. That one can use such a phrase as 'trying to make the marriage work' – everyday speech today, but certainly not in 1862 – is an indication of the modernity that Meredith achieved. The wife has a relationship with another man and the husband with another woman. Attempts at reconciliation are earnest but unsuccessful. Suffering beyond endurance, the wife poisons herself.

It is a difficult poem by a difficult writer. Biographers and critics have tried, in a spirit of helpfulness, to explain what actually happens in a narrative sense. But 'Modern Love' is only partly a narrative; it is also an analysis, a meditation, and above all a work of the imagination. Some of the apparent incidents or events may be dreams, hypothetical possibilities, real or false memories, bright or dark fantasies. If Meredith had chosen to deal with the experience in primarily narrative terms, he would have written a novel rather than a poem (not that it is always quite certain what 'actually happens' in a Meredith novel). The only event that we must take literally is the wife's suicide, conveyed in the line: 'Lethe had passed those lips, and he knew all'. Suicide by poison had a significance for Meredith reinforced by the Chatterton picture, by reading *Madame Bovary* (it had appeared in 1857 and he read French easily) and by his own description of Clare Forey's suicide in *Richard Feverel*. He may have felt Mary's death as a suicide, or as a fatality for which he was responsible.

Two well-known passages in 'Modern Love' can be read as keynotes. One is:

> The wrong is mix'd. In tragic life, God wot,
> No villain need be! Passions spin the plot;
> We are betrayed by what is false within.

And the other:

> Ah, what a dusty answer gets the soul
> When hot for certainties in this our life.

With these reflections, Meredith expresses his understanding of the complexity of the situation that he had encountered in life and recalled in his poem, and the futility of imposing a simple, conventional moral judgement on it. There had been no comparable study of possessive jealousy since *Othello*, to which Meredith made an allusion with the line: 'The Poet's black stage-lion of wronged love'. And Desdemona was innocent, while the wife in 'Modern Love' was not.

For the outward record – although we can cite only a few sentences in letters and a few reluctant remarks elicited by questioning years later – Meredith blamed Mary for betrayal and desertion and could not forgive her. In the poem, drawn from a deeper self-scrutiny, he did not condemn her, nor absolve himself, so easily. With deliberate even-handedness, he charged the husband as well as the wife with adultery. He had not in real life, so far as is known, been sexually unfaithful; but, in the years since Mary left him, he must have been attracted by other women (Bella Mount strikes one as drawn from life) and his love for Janet was a kind of infidelity. For those who could read the poem as a *roman-à-clef*, Mary's affair with Wallis was a known fact, while Meredith was in no way obliged to reveal (or invent) a transgression to balance it. He wrote as he did in order to show that 'no villain (nor villainess) need be', and to repudiate the ruling assumptions about the treacherous wife and the offended husband. For almost any other Victorian male, the effect of Meredith's experience would have been to induce a righteous misogyny worthy of Sir Austin Feverel. Remarkably – let us say, astonishingly – the effect on Meredith was to deepen the sympathy for women that resounds as a *leitmotiv* through all his novels.

Victorian readers were accustomed to the sentimental euphemisms of poets like Tennyson. Love could be passionate, but not sensual; a kiss was its boldest expression. Meredith was frank about the furious possessiveness of the male sex drive: 'Shouldst thou wake/The passion of a demon, be not afraid' . . . The imperious/desire speaks out' . . . 'I feel the promptings of Satanic power'. No lines since Shakespeare had been so unmistakably physical as:

> He felt the wild beast in him betweenwhiles
> So masterfully rude, that he would grieve
> To see the helpless delicate thing receive
> His guardianship through certain dark defiles

– recalling, surely, the 'dark and secret place' of *King Lear*.

When the husband makes love with the 'other woman' (referred to as the Lady) there is guilt, but also unabashed sexual pride:

> She yields: my Lady in her noblest mood
> Has yielded: she, my golden-crownéd rose!
> The bride of every sense! more sweet than those
> Who breathe the violet breath of maidenhood.

But the excitement of sex is no remedy for the misery of a failed marriage, as Meredith had experienced it with Mary. The deep sadness of a fatal disharmony is first evoked in the opening stanza:

> They from head to feet
> Were moveless, looking thro' their dead black years,
> By vain regret scrawl'd over the blank wall.
> Like sculptured effigies they might be seen
> Upon their marriage-tomb, the sword between.

Then comes the husband's reaction to knowing that his wife has a lover:

> I bleed, but she who wounds I will not blame.
> Have I not felt her heart as 'twere my own,
> Beat thro' me? could I hurt her? Heaven and Hell!
> But I could hurt her cruelly!

The poignancy of compulsive, yet hopeless, efforts at reconciliation is summed up in the line: 'Her lost moist hand clings mortally to mine'.

As in the fantasies of *Shagpat*, snakes provide a recurrent metaphor for sexual guilt: the wife's sobs are 'like little gaping snakes/Dreadfully venomous to him' . . . 'A subtle serpent then has love become' . . . 'Who seeks the asp/For serpents' bites?' . . . 'Our eyes dart scrutinizing snakes'.

Both husband and wife yearn for a reconciliation that always eludes them: 'She will not speak. I will not ask. We are/League-sunder'd by the silent gulf between'. When he kisses her during a game, he exclaims to himself: 'Save her? What for? To act this wedded lie!' He recalls that, in earlier days, he had warned her: 'Love dies' and she 'yearned to me that sentence to unsay'. A vivid, if confusing, scene is set in a visit to a country house; they have separate rooms, but the husband blunders into the room given to his wife:

> I enter, and lie couched upon the floor.
> Passing, I caught the cover-lid's quick beat: –
> Come, Shame, burn to my soul! And Pride, and Pain –
> Foul demons that have tortured me, sustain! . . .
> I know not how, but, shuddering as I slept,
> I dream'd a banished Angel to me crept.

Towards the end of the poem, when they realize that there can be no more hope, they take a walk by the sea: 'Here is a fitting spot to dig Love's grave'. It brings a return, not of happiness, but of melancholy calm:

> Love that had robb'd us of immortal things
> This little moment mercifully gave,
> And still I see across the twilight wave
> The swan sail with her young beneath her wings.

This image leads to the suicide, and to this summing-up:

[95]

> Thus piteously Love closed what he begat:
> The union of this ever-diverse pair.

By implication, 'Modern Love' makes a protest against the society that inhibited an open recognition of the realities that provided its content. An ironic stanza begins: 'You like not that French novel? Tell me why'. Meredith may have been reading Flaubert, but he cites a typical novel acceptable in France:

> The actors are, it seems, the usual three:
> Husband, and wife, and lover. She – but fie!
> In England we'll not hear of it.

Having indicated the story of a love affair that does not fatally imperil the marriage, Meredith comments:

> Unnatural? My dear, these things are life:
> And life, they say, is worthy of the Muse.

He was making a direct challenge to the reviewers who had rebuked him for the unpleasantness of *Richard Feverel*, to would-be censors, and to all the guardians of British official morality. The *Spectator* took up the challenge in a review that denounced 'Modern Love' as a whole but singled out the stanza about the French novel – 'wretched jocularity, as pointless as it is coarse'. Readers were told:

> Mr George Meredith is a clever man, without literary genius, taste or judgment ... who likes writing about human passions, but does not bring either imaginative power or true sentiment to the task ... without any vestige of original thought or purpose which could excuse so unpleasant a subject ... Mr Meredith evidently thinks mud picturesque, as, indeed, it may be, but all picturesqueness is not poetry.

The *Athenaeum*, rather more temperately, wrote:

> Few readers, we think, will deny the poetic feeling and the truth of observation which our extract reveals. But if these gifts are to produce a lasting result, Mr Meredith must add to them a healthier purpose, a purer taste and a clearer style.

The *Westminster Review*, while praising Meredith's 'freshness and vigour', commented: 'It is unfortunate that many of these poems are tales of guilt and sin, of women's temptation and fall.'

A defence of Meredith came from Algernon Swinburne – a courageous defence, considering that Swinburne was a young man of twenty-five who had received little attention for his own first book of poems. In a letter to the *Spectator*, he wrote:

> Praise or blame should be thoughtful, serious, careful, when applied to a work of such subtle strength, such depth of delicate power, such passionate and various beauty, as the leading poem of Mr Meredith's volume ... There are pulpits enough for all preachers in prose; the business of verse-writing is hardly to express convictions; and if some poetry, not without merit of its kind, has at times dealt in dogmatic morality, it is the worse and all the weaker for that ... We have not too many poets capable of duly handling a subject worth the serious interest of man.

Meredith and Swinburne had met, through William Rossetti, at about this time, and they were soon friends. Four years later, Swinburne was the target of a yet more furious critical onslaught for his *Poems and Ballads*.

Meredith did not publish another book of poems until 1883, twenty-one years after 'Modern Love'. It may be that he was deterred by the attacks, but more probably he made up his mind that his profession was to be that of a novelist. Poetry became an occasional and spontaneous mode of expression, produced for his own satisfaction. He expected no income for his later collections, and asked his publisher not to send them out for review. Nevertheless, the later poems have much to tell us about his thoughts and feelings, and indeed add up to a considerable achievement. If Meredith the novelist has been neglected by the twentieth century, this is more emphatically true of Meredith the poet. But the writing of 'Modern Love' had been necessary to ensure his emergence from the painful experiences of the 1850s. By 1862, he had passed through his ordeal.

6

The Best Years

FRIENDSHIP was valuable for Meredith, as it generally was for men – and, less often, for women – in the nineteenth century. Over the claret and the port, the cigars and the pipes, these men argued, threshed out their ideas, gossiped and joked. Such sessions were supplemeted, for Meredith and some of his friends, by day-long walks in the English countryside and, every couple of years, walking holidays abroad. Between meetings, friendships were sustained by letters; before the telephone, it was customary to dash off a letter to a friend who lived a few miles away, writing when the day's work was over and catching the late post. Meredith wrote often, giving news, asking for news, and sometimes using a friend as a sounding-board for his literary or philosophical opinions. Of almost three thousand Meredith letters that have been preserved, only about forty date from earlier than 1859, but there are hundreds from the 1860s. It was in this decade that, producing one novel after another, he established a settled way of life, and it was also in this decade that he made a dozen firm and enduring friendships.

Most of his friends, as one would expect, were of roughly his own age, though John Morley was ten years younger. Some were married; others were unmarried when the friendship began but married – as Meredith himself married for the second time – during the decade. He was friendly with the wives, often flavouring letters with compliments and flirtatious jokes, but essentially the relationships were between men. With some exceptions, these men belonged to the literary world, but generally as publishers, journalists or editors of the bulky reviews – fortnightly, monthly or quarterly – that were the life-blood of thought and debate. Meredith's closer friends did not include the most outstanding novelists or poets of the century, for no particular reason except that they did not quite belong to his generation. Dickens, Thackeray, Browning and Tennyson were older than Meredith; Hardy, Henry James and Gerard Manley Hopkins were younger. George Eliot, only nine years older than Meredith, might have been a friend had she not secluded herself from social life.

Meredith's best friend, over a span of forty years, was Frederick Maxse. The surname was originally German, but the family was thoroughly English; Maxse's father was a wealthy merchant from Bristol and his mother was a daughter of the Earl of Berkeley (whose home was the picturesque Berkeley Castle, where King Edward II was murdered in 1327). As a young officer in the Navy, Maxse showed outstanding bravery in the Crimean War and was rapidly promoted to the rank of Captain. Revolted by the incompetence of the aristocratic commanders and the needless loss of life, he developed uncompromising Radical views and twice stood as a Radical candidate for Parliament. Maxse's career was clearly the model for *Beauchamp's Career*, published in 1875. Although he did not see active service after his early years, he kept his commission in the Navy and was eventually made a Rear-Admiral. Meredith, who had been addressing letters to 'Dear Fred' for years, took to starting them with 'Dear Admiral'.

The two men first came into contact when Maxse attempted to learn the writing craft and received criticism from Meredith as reader for Chapman and Hall. When Maxse took a cottage at Molesey, near Esher, he was able to join Meredith for walks on the Common. In 1862 Maxse married Cecilia Steel (Nevil Beauchamp is loved by Cecilia Halkett) and bought Ploverfield House in Bursledon, near Southampton. He owned a yacht, moored on Southampton Water, and Meredith was his guest on several trips in the Channel or across to France. Yachts and sailing expeditions figure repeatedly in *Beauchamp's Career*. When Meredith married in 1864, Maxse lent him Ploverfield House for the honeymoon. Later, after separating from his wife – for the marriage was not a success – Maxse lived at Effingham Hill, within walking distance of Meredith's home at Box Hill.

While the friends shared a basic outlook of opposition to privilege and authority, they had disagreements on current issues. Maxse supported the Union side in the American Civil War but Meredith sympathized with the South; he felt that the seceding states had a right to run their own affairs, and apparently had no views on slavery. Maxse – an attractive personality, liked by everyone who knew him – was noted for the fervour of his convictions rather than for their durability. At one period he gave up meat-eating and alcohol, but not for long. Violently opposed to religious dogma and indeed to Christianity, he refused in 1865 to be godfather to Meredith's son, who was to be christened with the names of William Maxse. Meredith wrote gently:

> I do wish the boy to have some little link with you, such as your name will give him. We differ in our spirit of objection to the dominant creed: but I suppose that twenty years hence we shall not differ . . . I think you altogether too impetuous: 500 years too fast for the human race: I think that where the Christian Ministers are guilty of little more than boredom, you have got them in a state of perfection and at least owe them your tolerance for theirs: – And so I shall continue to think until next I go to Church.[1]

In 1866, Meredith sent Maxse a joke letter criticizing him for going about dressed as a priest: 'when I see you walk from Holly Hill to Bursledon in stole and cope and biretta I cannot but feel at times that you undoubtedly have what I confess I have thought once or twice before – a tendency towards extremes'. Alluding to Maxse's temporary renunciation of fermented drink, he went on: 'I bear in mind your late extraordinary oration against One who turned the Water into Wine – in which you so violently denounced him for having done so.' For good measure, Maxse was reproached for favouring 'the admission of Great Britain among the States of the Union'. Actually written in 1866, the letter was dated 'Christmas 1870'.[2] The spoof fooled the first editor of Meredith's letters, who was none other than William Maxse Meredith. Meredith was shrewd in seeing his friend's 'tendency towards extremes' and his volatility, for Maxse ended up as a Tory.

The effect of friendship with Maxse was to bring out Meredith's sense of humour and his tolerance, of which there had been little evidence in earlier years. He was (unlike Maxse) a Radical to the end of his life, but a Radical for whom scepticism and free debate were essential values. While most of his friends were Radicals and agnostics, they were not his friends because they shared these values. James Cotter Morison was a leading figure in the Positivist Society, adhering to the philosophy of Auguste Comte. John Morley became editor of the *Fortnightly Review*, which published essays by John Stuart Mill, Thomas Huxley, Walter Bagehot and Matthew Arnold and was regarded as the organ of progressive thought. In later life, he was a Cabinet minister under Gladstone, entrusted with pursuing the policy of Irish Home Rule, and in 1914 he resigned from the Liberal government as a protest against war. Frederick Greenwood edited a left-of-centre newspaper, the *St James's Gazette*. On the other hand, one of Meredith's closest friends, William Hardman, was a staunch Tory. Distinctly an Establishment figure, he edited the *Morning Post*, was a barrister and Recorder, became Mayor of his home town, Kingston-on-Thames, and earned a knighthood. He was also a jovial, amiable man; Meredith, who did not take him very seriously, called him 'Friar Tuck' and signed his own letters 'Robin'. Hardman appears in *Beauchamp's Career* as Blackburn Tuckham, a socially acceptable husband for the languishing Cecilia.

Frank Burnand founded a magazine called *Fun*, which was a popular success, and went on to become editor of *Punch*. Lionel Robinson was a pleasant individual whom Meredith always called 'Pococurante' – that is, a man with few cares. William Charles Bonaparte Wyse, who walked with Meredith in Italy and spent much of his life in France, devoted himself to the study of the Provençal language and Provençal poetry. His father was an eccentric Irish baronet and his mother was a daughter of Lucien Bonaparte, the only one of Napoleon's brothers who declined to become a puppet king and stayed a lifelong republican. Lucien, incidentally, was also a direct ancestor of Marie Bonaparte, psychoanalyst and friend of Freud.

Augustus Jessopp, the only one of the friends who was older than Meredith, was a Church of England clergyman, but a clergyman of undogmatic views and mainly interested in education. He was headmaster of King Edward VI School in Norwich, which he ran in a benevolent, enlightened spirit reminiscent of Neuwied. Meredith's elder son, Arthur, was sent to this school from the age of nine to the age of thirteen. He was unhappy there and did not do well, but Meredith considered that Jessopp had done his best and was warmly grateful to him.

In Vienna in 1866, Meredith became friendly with another traveller, Leslie Stephen. A Positivist like Morison, Stephen had given up a Cambridge fellowship because the post required him to subscribe to the Christian faith, and was seeking a future in literary journalism. Five years later, he became editor of the prestigious *Cornhill Magazine*; he went on to create and edit the Dictionary of National Biography, a vast compilation for which he wrote over four hundred entries himself. Stephen was a keen mountain walker, like Meredith, and indeed a pioneering Alpine climber. In the 1880s he was the leading spirit of the Sunday Tramps, who often started on their walks from Meredith's house, although Meredith by that time was unable to go the distance with them. In 1887, ailing and a widower, Meredith spent the summer with Leslie Stephen and his family at St Ives. He became a sort of uncle, or great-uncle, to the talented Stephen children, and in 1892 he wrote to Mrs Stephen: 'I have to confess that my heart is fast going to Virginia' – who was ten years old. Today, Leslie Stephen is best remembered as Virginia Woolf's father and the original of Mr Ramsay in *To the Lighthouse*. Her heart never went to Meredith, but she became one of his most perceptive critics.

There were limits, Meredith discovered, to the advisability of these friendships. In 1862 he undertook to share a house in Chelsea with Swinburne, William Rossetti and the latter's brother, Dante Gabriel. In practical terms, the arrangement made sense. With his commitments to Chapman and Hall and to the *Ipswich Journal*, it was convenient to have a London *pied-à-terre* where he could sleep for two nights in the week without the expense of staying at a hotel. The house, 16 Cheyne Walk, was large and beautiful; it was called Tudor House and was believed to have been the home of Thomas More, though in fact it was an eighteenth-century building. Swinburne had chivalrously defended 'Modern Love' and had stayed at Copsham Cottage, where he introduced Meredith to the *Rubaiyat* and wrote 'Laus Veneris', the poem that made him famous. Dante Gabriel Rossetti, the founder of the Pre-Raphaelite Brotherhood, was admired both as an artist and as a poet. With all these talents in residence, there were prospects of enjoyable, exciting days and evenings.

The excitement turned out to be more than Meredith had bargained for. Dante Gabriel, temperamental and neurotic to a high degree, was in deep distress after the suicide of his wife, Lizzie Siddal. He dosed himself heavily with laudanum, but also disrupted the household routine with enormous late breakfasts – 'five poached eggs that had slowly bled to death on five slabs of bacon', Meredith complained to another friend, Wilfrid Scawen Blunt. Swinburne was an uncontrolled drinker and, according to Lionel Stevenson, 'was apt to fly into ferocious tantrums or to take off all his clothes and caper wildly through the house or slide down the banisters'. This sort of behaviour was alien to Meredith, who prided himself on being a serious, hard-working writer, as well as on his generally good health and reasonable habits. Stories have been handed down of bizarre incidents strongly flavoured with farce. Meredith's boots were stolen when he left them out to be cleaned; Dante Gabriel threw a cup of tea in Meredith's face; there were quarrels over contributions to the rent, paid late by Meredith or recklessly squandered by Dante Gabriel. Whatever the truth in legendary accounts of the ménage, Meredith withdrew from Tudor House after six months to the peace of Copsham Cottage.

Victorian men were classified as 'the marrying type' or 'the non-marrying type', and Meredith was decidedly a marrying man. His reaction to the failure of his marriage was to yearn for a second chance, although the experience had made him cautious and he enquired rhetorically in a letter to Bonaparte Wyse: 'Was there ever such a gambler's stake as that we fling for a woman in giving ourselves for her whom we know not, and haply shall not know when twenty years have run?'[3] The problem was to find a woman who was right for him (unlike Mary) and would commit herself to him (unlike Janet). 'Every desirable woman in the world is engaged,' he complained after a glance at a possible candidate. But physical attraction was not enough without the prospect of emotional satisfaction, as he half-regretfully explained to Maxse:

> I can't love a woman if I do not feel her soul . . . But I envy those who are attracted to what is given to the eye; – yes, even those who have a special taste for woman flesh, and this or that particular little tit-bit – I envy them! It lasts not beyond an hour with me.[4]

One of Meredith's favourite walks was through the valley of the River Mole, bypassing Leatherhead by a path across the fields, and on to the pretty village of Mickleham. A mile or so south of Mickleham, a narrower valley with a little stream passed between the steep slopes of Juniper Hill and Box Hill, even then a destination for outings from London. In 1861 Meredith wrote to Wyse: 'Yesterday I marched me to the vale of Mickleham. An English Tempe! Was ever such delicious greenery? The nightingale saluted me entering and departing. The walk has made of me a new man.'[5] A year later, Meredith and Hardman walked from Copsham Cottage to Mickleham in the evening, stayed at the Running Horse inn, and rose at half past five to start on the next day's walk, which took them by way of the North Downs escarpment and Guildford to Milford. Setting out from Mickleham, Meredith promised his friend: 'Here may be obtained one of the most perfect bits of rustic scenery in this country, and consequently in any other.'[6]

The neighbourhood was rich, too, in literary associations. John Evelyn, the seventeenth-century diarist, had planted the trees round the Mickleham churchyard. Fanny Burney had met her husband, General d'Arblay, at Juniper Hall, which was a centre for French liberals avoiding the most dangerous period of the Revolution. Keats had written *Endymion* when staying at the Fox and Hounds, which by Meredith's time had been renamed the Burford Bridge Inn.

The most imposing house in Mickleham, built in 1636 and known as the Old House, was the home of Justin Vulliamy and his three daughters. Vulliamy, a Frenchman with an English wife, had owned a wool business in Normandy. When he retired in 1857 his wife persuaded him to live in England and they settled at Mickleham; however, she died soon afterwards. Their sons stayed in Normandy, where Meredith later visited them and found the setting for the Château de Tourdestelle in *Beauchamp's Career*. The daughters at Mickleham (there was an elder daughter married in France) were Betty, Kitty and Marie. They had a cousin, presumably on the English side, married to a British Museum librarian who was a friend of Morison and Hardman; this cousin, Mrs Hamilton, introduced Meredith at Mickleham in the autumn of 1863. Apparently Kitty was the one who first attracted him but, like 'every desirable woman', she was already engaged. Marie, the youngest daughter, was still available – surprisingly, since she was attractive enough, her musical talent was outstanding, and at twenty-four she had passed what was then the standard marriage age. It may be that her father, a stern Huguenot with high moral standards, had vetoed one or more suitors.

In April 1864 Marie went to stay with friends in Norwich, and Meredith – probably not by coincidence – was in the same town to visit the Jessopps and see how Arthur was getting on at school. They took the train back to London together and were able, Meredith cheerfully reported to Jessopp, to find a carriage with no other passengers. Either in the course of the train journey or soon afterwards, he asked Marie to marry him and she accepted, subject to her father's approval.

It was less than a whirlwind romance, and his references to Marie in letters to his friends were less than ecstatic. He complained touchily to Jessopp: 'I still wonder why both of you *won't* think her very handsome . . . I mean, handsome, of that style. Some vitality being wanted; but the lack of it partially compensated by so very much sweetness.'[8] Sending Maxse a photograph which he called 'Libellous', he gave this description: 'The hair is perfect: – fair, with a golden line just over the forehead: the eyes blue, the lips red, soft, and full. Her figure is ample, but plastic, and the carriage of the bust full of grace and ease.'[9] Wyse was told: 'She is a very handsome person, fair, with a noble pose, and full figure, and a naturally high bred style and manner.' Marie, one deduces not unfairly, was not a beauty and was on the plump side.

If the friends suspected that Meredith was eager for marriage rather than passionate about Marie, they were reassured. He told Wyse: 'I have been for months, and I am now, desperately in love.'[10] Maxse received this effusion: 'I write with my beloved beside me; my thrice darling – of my body, my soul, my song! I have never loved a woman and felt love grow in me. This clear and lovely nature doubles mine.'[11] Reading this letter as Maxse read it, one would not guess that Meredith had ever been in love with Mary, nor with Janet.

There was still one obstacle on the way to the altar: though Marie was old enough to marry legally without her father's consent, in practice it was out of the question. A literary man whose previous essay in marriage had ended disastrously was not Vulliamy's idea of a well-qualified son-in-law. The exacting wool merchant required the applicant to submit a list of character references. Meredith was able to produce a senior Treasury official (Duff Gordon), a leading publisher (Chapman), the editor of the *Ipswich Journal* and the Rev. Augustus Jessopp, but Vulliamy was still suspicious. The most respectable among Meredith's close friends was Hardman, and Meredith appealed to him: 'I have an immense deal to tell you and something to ask you to do.'[12] Hardman duly went to see Vulliamy, armed with a statement (quoted earlier) explaining the collapse of Meredith's marriage. Vulliamy, however, required written answers by Meredith to eight questions, such as: 'the mode of your separation' and 'whether after the separation you both continued to reside in the same village, town, or place'. Beyond this, Meredith had to supply information about his income – which he put at £550 from paid work, in addition to literary earnings – and even about property belonging to a great-uncle which Meredith could possibly inherit (though he never did). All these enquiries and negotiations dragged on for six weeks; one can well imagine how infuriating Meredith must have found them. It was only at the end of August that he was able to tell Maxse: 'The old man is changed, and makes the best of the bad business for him.'[13] Vulliamy agreed to the marriage and promised Marie an allowance of £200 a year – perhaps to supplement Meredith's income, perhaps as an insurance in case anything went wrong.

The wedding was on 20 September at Mickleham Church, with Jessopp officiating and bringing Arthur from Norwich. Sir Alexander Duff Gordon came from Weybridge with his daughter Janet, who was in England at the time. At the last moment, it was discovered that the bride was named in the licence as Mary instead of Marie, and she had to sign the register accordingly. No one, it must be hoped, made any untoward comment.

After the honeymoon, the couple lived for six months in a rented house in Esher. Copsham Cottage, much though Meredith loved it, was too small, especially as Marie soon became pregnant. Hardman, helpful as ever, introduced the Merediths to a house called Kingston Lodge, directly opposite his own residence, Norbiton Hall. Although Kingston in those days was not regarded as a suburb, let alone a London borough, the environment was too urban for Meredith. 'No country around – brick, brick, brick,' he complained to Jessopp, 'but a middling pretty little house and Marie likes it, so I submit.' He took a three-year lease on Kingston Lodge, but looked forward to finding a home where he could walk out into real countryside and where children would be able to play in the woods and fields. George and Marie did not, however, have a large family. Will was born in 1865; a daughter, Marie Eveleen – known as Mariette, or sometimes as Riette – was born in 1871.

Meredith, meanwhile, had recurrent worries about Arthur. In 1863 the boy, then ten years old, survived what might have been a fatal accident when he fell off a horse and, with one leg entangled in the stirrup, was dragged over the furze of Copsham Common. Luckily, his boot came off, so there was no serious injury and no broken bones, but he was carried home unconscious and Meredith was anxious about the effects of concussion. '[My] darling is returned to me out of the jaws of death,' he wrote to Hardman two days after the accident, and the 'poor little fellow is very weak and somewhat shaky'. It was only after a week that he reported: 'My darling boy is going on all right. His head though bruised, and blue behind the ear, is sound.'[14] Though he had not been at the scene of the accident (a man called Wyndowe, presumably a groom or riding teacher, was held responsible), he may have felt that he was to blame, and Arthur may, unconsciously at least, have blamed the father who had kept him away from his mother in her last illness and had then despatched him to a boarding-school. A year later, this father inflicted another blow by presenting Arthur with a strange stepmother. Meredith, for his part, had cause to be troubled by this uncanny repetition of the story of his own boyhood.

Marie first met Arthur at Norwich when Meredith was courting her, and evidently realized the importance that the boy had for him. Tactfully, she asked for a photograph of Arthur during the crucial conversation in the train to London. Despite her good intentions, however, she never achieved any intimacy with Arthur, and naturally her emotional attachment was to her own son.

There was, indeed, no real intimacy between Meredith and Arthur. Meredith found it hard to accept that Arthur, although both his parents were strong personalities with creative talents, was at best a quite ordinary youngster. In 1865 he admitted to Jessopp: 'My son does not promise . . . He's a good fellow – which must content me.' Arthur ought to have

developed an interest in history, he complained, but he was merely swal-
lowing 'sensation novels'.[15] Perhaps Jessopp and the other teachers at
Norwich were not pushing the boy. When Arthur was twelve, he was
removed from Norwich and sent to a school at Hofwyl, in Switzerland,
which was run on the principles of Pestalozzi and was the prototype for
Weyburn's school in *Lord Ormont*. After visiting him there, Meredith told
Jessopp: 'He seems to be much the same style of boy . . . very quaint,
very thoughtful, not brilliant.'[16] Within less than two years, Arthur was
moved again, this time to the more orthodox and academic Gymnasium in
Stuttgart. The Professor informed Meredith 'that he has made astonishing
strides and is both a diligent and comprehensive student, besides being
a most polite, mannerly fellow'. But at the age of eighteen he was seen
by his father as 'a middling clear thinker, sensible, brilliant in nothing,
tending in no direction'. In a tone of objectivity, but clearly of disappointment, Meredith summed up: 'Though he seems never likely to be intellectually an athlete, one may hope he will be manful . . . In a competitive
examination of fifty he would be about the twenty-fifth.'[17]

Meredith had hoped that this education would benefit Arthur as he
had himself been benefited by Neuwied, but Arthur merely felt that he
had been sent into exile. Visiting him at Stuttgart, Meredith found: 'With
me he was scarcely civil though I believe he had no ill feeling.' Reserved
and uncommunicative, Arthur did not respond to his father's affection,
which he found – the word necessarily recurs – over-protective. In fact,
by prescribing what Arthur ought to be learning and how he ought to
be developing at a given age, Meredith was making just the error that
he had so keenly analysed in *Richard Feverel*. In letters, he inflicted on
Arthur a brand of moralistic preaching worthy of Sir Austin:

The Christian teaching is sound and good; the ecclesiastical dogma is
an instance of the poverty of humanity's mind hitherto . . . Belief in
the religion has done and does this good to the young; it floats them
through the perilous sensual period when the animal appetites most
need control and transmutation. If you have not the belief, set yourself
to love virtue . . . Pray attend to my words on this subject. You know
how Socrates loved Truth. Virtue and Truth are one.[18]

Arthur was nineteen when he received this screed. He may have reflected
that his father at nineteen had been charting the course of his own life
and working out his own ideas, free from any obligation to take advice
from *his* father.

Despite the disappointment with Arthur, these were good years for Meredith. His marriage proved happy and harmonious; his friendships gave him pleasure; his earnings were sufficient for his chosen way of life. Above all, he was productive. In the ten years between his thirtieth and fortieth birthdays, he published six books: *Richard Feverel*, *Evan Harrington*, *Modern Love and Other Poems*, *Emilia in England* (1864), *Rhoda Fleming* (1865) and *Vittoria* (1867).

Publishing conditions in the nineteenth century were difficult, favouring the guaranteed best-seller rather than a writer like Meredith who never made things easy for himself or for his readers. To bring in good money, a novel had to be accepted twice: first by a magazine which ran it as a serial, then by a book publisher. It was the heyday of the three-volume novel, running to 150,000 or often 200,000 words. The volumes were handsomely bound, printed in large type on thick white paper. They were meant to look impressive and to last – like Victorian four-storey houses, Victorian furniture, Victorian monuments, Victorian tweed suits and leather boots. Inevitably, they were expensive; the usual price was thirty shillings, a weekly wage for a clerk or a teacher. Most readers could only borrow them, so the favour of Mudie's and other lending libraries was vital to a writer. It was only in the 1890s that new, enterprising publishers made drastic price cuts and offered novels at six shillings.

In an age when there were no typewriters, let alone computers, writers groaned under the sheer toil of producing these long novels, revising them, and finally making a fair copy – though that task might fall on the shoulders of a wife or daughter. (Sonya Tolstoy is said to have copied out *War and Peace* seven times.) Moreover, novels were stretched beyond the length that would have been artistically desirable, as their authors were sometimes aware. Meredith could have rounded off *Evan Harrington* in Chapter 25, when Rose tells Evan that she loves him and is willing to marry him despite his humble origins, but he had to devise new obstacles to defer the happy ending to Chapter 47. Reardon, the unhappy novelist in Gissing's *New Grub Street*, laments: 'The three volumes lie before me like an interminable desert.' Shorter, one-volume novels did appear (Trollope was a specialist), but they were still costly to produce and publishers were not keen on them. Meredith hoped to make *Rhoda Fleming*, with its straightforward moral story, a one-volume novel, but in vain. Thoroughly weary of it, he wrote to Jessopp that he had tried 'to finish off *Rhoda Fleming* in one volume, now swollen to two – and Oh, will it be three?'[19] Another pressure came from magazine editors, who wanted to string out the novel if it was good for circulation or bring it to a close if it was not. Readers today, bored with sub-plots, digressions, indulgence in low comedy and the adventures of minor characters, may not realize that the writer who added them to reach his target was probably bored too.

As though to complicate his literary life further – and, no doubt, to exasperate his publishers – Meredith sometimes worked on two novels at the same time, or shelved a novel when he could not see the way ahead clearly. The weakness and shallowness of *Farina* can be ascribed to the fact that his mind was already with *Richard Feverel*. *Rhoda Fleming* was written by fits and starts over three years while he was also busy with *Emilia in England* and then *Vittoria*. In 1864 he submitted an outline and specimen chapters of a novel called *Richmond Roy*, which eventually appeared as *Harry Richmond* in 1871. The novella *The House on the Beach*, set in Seaford and mostly written in 1861, was put aside until a storm on the Sussex coast suggested an effective ending in 1877. *The Amazing Marriage* was started in 1878, resumed in 1889, and published in 1895. As for *Celt and Saxon*, which might be thought of as Meredith's last work because it was unfinished and the half-novel was published in 1910 after his death, it had actually been written in 1870. This tricky chronology should warn us against thinking easily of 'early Meredith' or 'late Meredith'. If we leave aside *The Shaving of Shagpat* and *Farina* as experiments that led nowhere, consistency is the hallmark of his work.

We can, however, see the 1860s as Meredith's Italian decade. In historical fact, it was the decade in which Italy achieved the unity and the liberation – from Austrian rule in the north, from petty despots elsewhere – which had been the goal of unsuccessful uprisings in 1821, 1831 and 1848. The base for the struggle was Piedmont, whose politically skilful Prime Minister, Cavour, forged an alliance in 1858 with the France of Napoleon III. Within the next few years, French and Piedmontese forces defeated the Austrians and pushed them out of Lombardy; Garibaldi and his 'Red shirt' volunteers liberated Sicily and Naples; and a kingdom of Italy was established, uniting the whole country except for Rome and territory belonging to the Pope, and except for the Venetian provinces, still held by Austria. As a by-product of the Prussian victory, Austria gave up Venice, only retaining South Tyrol and Trieste until 1918. In 1870, the so-called Papal States and the city of Rome merged with the rest of Italy, leaving the Pope to rule only over the Vatican.

Meredith went to Italy for the first time in the summer of 1861, travelling with his friend Wyse and his son Arthur. From Germany and Switzerland, they went to Merano (then an Austrian town called Meran), Venice,

Milan and Como, where Wyse's mother had a villa. He was entranced by everything he saw: first of all, by the Alps.

> My first sight of the Alps has raised odd feelings. Here at last seems something more than earth, and visible, if not tangible. They have the whiteness, the silence, the beauty and mystery of thoughts seldom unveiled within us, but which conquer Earth when once they are.[20]

Italy exerted on him the same emotional attraction as Germany, the only other foreign country he yet knew. Like Germany, Italy was rich in poetry, in music, and in visual art as well as in scenic beauty. Like Germany, Italy was carved up into outdated sovereignties – the Duchy of Oldenburg, the Duchy of Parma – and striving for nationhood. But in Italy more than in Germany, the struggle for freedom was a cause that aroused fervent sympathy in England. It was for the 1860s what Greece had been in the 1820s, or what anti-fascist Spain would be in the 1930s.

In the provinces under Austrian occupation, Meredith observed the patriotic boycott of the white-uniformed Austrians: 'Charming are the Venetian women! . . . Should one smile on a Whitecoat, she has the prospect of a patriotic dagger smiting her fair bosom.' In Verona:

> The soldiers have to keep to themselves, the officers are cut, and nothing so miserable and menacing can be fancied. Even the girls won't be spoken to. I saw an amusing scene of a couple of officers after two . . . They began chattering, wouldn't let Mr Oberlieutenant get in a word; suddenly they turned round, fired a volley of contempt and virtuous indignation and retired into the applauding crowd.[21]

There was no more Whitecoats in Milan, but memories of Austrian rule and of the bitter fighting in 1848 were still fresh. Meredith listened, learned, and prepared himself for the novel, or rather the sequence of two novels, that was taking shape in his mind. In 1863 he made another trip to Italy, this time with 'Poco' Robinson, who was a sturdier walker than Wyse. He stayed in Turin, capital of Piedmont and, pending the liberation of Rome, provisional capital of Italy.

The Italian novel sequence is thick with Meredithian complexities. The first novel was published in 1864 as *Emilia in England*, but the title was changed to *Sandra Belloni* for the new edition of 1886. The heroine's name, in fact, is Emilia Sandra Belloni. When she returns to Milan to become a prima donna at La Scala, she is called Vittoria. Meredith had intended to call the second novel *Emilia in Italy*, which would have rung a bell for readers, but the name change forced him to change the title to *Vittoria*. More important, the character undergoes a transformation; in the first novel she is naïve and innocent to an almost childish degree, and easily fooled by the first man who claims to be in love with her, but in the second she plays a responsible political role and marries a leader in the national struggle. The first novel is firmly English in its setting and focuses on the falsity of English social conventions; the second is an Italian drama. One could easily suppose that *Emilia in England* was designed to be complete in itself and Meredith subsequently decided to write a sequel, but there is conclusive evidence that he planned the whole work from the outset. While *Emilia* is a relatively simple novel (by Meredith's standards), *Vittoria* has a huge cast of characters and one of the most intricate plots of any novel ever written.

These novels gave Meredith a great deal of trouble. In January 1863 he told Wyse: 'I hope to finish this dreadful work [*Emilia in England*] in six weeks'[22]; but this was wildly optimistic. In March he confessed: 'Emilia has been bothering me. The gestation of this young woman is laborious.' In January 1864: 'I am not all right. Emilia Belloni is not all right. She has worried me beyond measure and couldn't expect to be all right. She will be, when she's in Italy.'[23] When the book was finally ready for publication in April, he was still not satisfied with it: 'The novel has good points . . . and some of my worst ones.'[24]

It was the same story with *Vittoria*. In July 1864, it 'goes on swimmingly'[25]; in November, '*Vittoria* lags.'[26] The project appealed to G. H. Lewes, editor of the *Fortnightly Review*, and he agreed to publish it as a serial, but in September 1865 Meredith was complaining that he had 'Lewes at me to get up steam for *Vittoria*'. It was only in June 1866 that he could claim: 'I am now finishing *Vittoria*.'[27] The serial was appearing in the magazine while the later chapters had yet to be written, a situation that Dickens took in his stride but which plunged Meredith into anxiety. In book form, *Vittoria* was published in January 1867.

It was fortunate that Meredith did finish it in June 1866, for in that very month he was off to Italy again, this time not as a tourist but as a war correspondent for the *Morning Post*. The choice of Meredith for this job reflects considerable credit on the editor, Sir Algernon Borthwick: firstly because the novelist had never worked as a reporter and was known for his difficulty – some critics said 'unreadable' – style; secondly because Meredith was a passionate partisan of the Italian side in the war, while the British government was friendly to Austria. But Borthwick cheerfully printed all Meredith's despatches, although they were sometimes more like editorials than reports – for example, when he wrote:

> [The British government] now find themselves, without rudder or compass, tossed to and fro on a shoreless sea. That comes of linking the fortunes of a party – and striving to link the fortunes of the nation – with the obstinacy and bigotry, with the senselessness and super-stition, of a decadent empire – of an empire with dry rot in its timbers.

Meredith proved to be an excellent war reporter – largely, no doubt, thanks to his personal commitment. He managed to write a vivid, racy prose, sometimes addressing the reader directly ('you must imagine . . .'). He marched with the troops, once through a pitch-black, stormy night which he described as 'like Dante's hell'. When he could not observe for himself he quoted what he was told by soldiers straight from the scene of action, but carefully warned of what might be rumour or exaggeration. Above all, he was stirred by examples of outstanding bravery:

> Talking of heroic, of inimitable endurance, what do you think of a man who has his arm entirely carried away by a grenade, and yet keeps on his horse, firm as a rock, and still directs his battery until hemorrhage strikes him down at last, *dead*!

In the run-up to the war, Meredith had been pessimistic. 'I mourn for the Italians. Their army is not yet fit to cope with the Austrian,' he had told Maxse.[28] He arrived in time for the Battle of Custozza, when the Italians tried to advance into the Austrian fortified zone, known as the Quadrilateral. This frontal attack was reckless, as Meredith pointed out:

> The Italian generals, in a spirit almost akin to that which dictated the charge of the 600 at Balaclava, chose to open the campaign of 1866 by leading their forces right into the jaws of the Quadrilateral and expose them to imminent danger.

The casualties were heavy, though they were shrugged off by a wounded Italian general who said to Meredith: 'You can't make an omelette without breaking eggs.' Meredith reported the remark in the *Morning Post*; this seems to be the first appearance in print of what has become a familiar cliché. The attack was repelled and Custozza was generally recorded as an Austrian victory, but Meredith saw it as an indecisive battle. His reports concentrated on the bravery of the Italian soldiers:

> Young recruits exposed to so severe a trial showed the nerve and steadiness of veterans and when cannonaded and sabred on all sides and compelled to fall back, did so with the calmness of the Old Guard . . .
>
> The engagement of last Sunday will always be ranked, as far as regards the valour displayed by all ranks of the combatants, amongst the most honourable events in the national history . . .
>
> The Italians fought from three in the morning to nine in the evening like lions, showing . . . that they are worthy of the noble enterprise they have undertaken.

As it turned out, this was the only battle of the short war. Crushingly defeated by the Prussians in Bohemia, the Austrians hastened to cut their losses, offered an armistice on the Italian front, and signed an agreement to give up Venice and Venetia. However, the agreement was negotiated, not with the King of Italy, but with the French Emperor, who had not this time participated in the war but assumed the role of arbiter. The Italians, or some of them, regarded this as an insult and wanted to reject the armistice and renew the offensive, in the hope of a battle that would wipe out the dubious memory of Custozza. Meredith strongly supported this view: 'There are high considerations of honour which no soldier or general would ever think of putting aside for humanitarian or political reasons.'

Thanks to French pressure, the armistice came into effect and the war was over. The Italians peacefully entered Venice, accompanied by Meredith. He had the pleasure of staying at the Hotel Vittoria, together with the other British correspondents, who included the veteran journalist George Augustus Sala, G. A. Henty and H. M. Hyndman. Henty became the author of a flood of successful books for boys, such as *Beric the Briton*, *With Clive in India*, and *The Lion of St Mark's*. Hyndman became the founder of the Social Democratic Federation, but always an advocate of a stronger British army. With these companions, and with an unexpected reunion with Janet Ross, Meredith was happy to spend several weeks in Venice.

It is in the light of Meredith's identification with the Italian cause that we can appreciate the significance that the 'Emilia' novels had for him. The novels were difficult to write because he was aiming, as he had not aimed hitherto, at a fusion of personal and political themes. Italy – a 'geographical expression', in Metternich's contemptuous phrase – was becoming a nation. The process was a self-realization, achieved through courage and self-sacrifice, through the growing maturity of 'young recruits' who showed the 'steadiness of veterans', and – a point that Meredith repeatedly stressed in his despatches – through the unity and comradeship of men who came from the hitherto divided regions of Piedmont, Tuscany, Naples and so forth. The argument for rejecting the armistice and winning Venice through an undeniable Italian victory was that it would set the seal on this national self-realization.

The other thread in the texture of the novel sequence is the self-realization of Emilia as a woman. Her immaturity in the first novel is designed to throw her later development, as Vittoria, into high relief. As a girl in England, she is the victim of what Meredith called Sentimentalism, the outlook of the Pole family who annex and patronize her. This term – not identical with what we commonly call sentimentality, though there are affinities – denotes an adherence to artificially conceived emotional attitudes, as distinct from those that equip a person for the real world. It is Sentimentalism which generates the shallowness and selfishness of the brand of love offered to Emilia by Wilfrid Pole (and to Dahlia by Edward Blancove in *Rhoda Fleming*, the novel that Meredith was writing at the same time). The second novel in the sequence showed Emilia – now Vittoria – achieving full self-realization, both through her love for Carlo and her role in the Milan uprising. But, like Italy in this historical period, she must do so by fighting her own battles and by leaving the past behind. When she inadvertently betrays the secret of the revolt, the source of the blunder is a reversion to the world of the Pole family.

In 1867, George and Marie Meredith left Kingston Lodge. He had never been fond of the house, the lease was running out, and Marie found it depressing when her baby niece (a child of her sister Kitty) died there. They stayed for a couple of months with Marie's father at Micklesham, and found a new home in the neighbourhood. It was a house about a mile from the village, standing in open country on a south-facing slope and with a splendid view towards Box Hill. They moved in November; Ellis, who knew the house well in later years, wrote that the landscape was most beautiful 'when the woods put on their autumn robes of russet, red, and innumerable shades of dark green, and the clouds are broken at close of day by bars of blood-red fire as the sun sets behind the hills'. However, Meredith's bedroom was on the east side of the house, so that he could see the sunrise.

The house is built of brick with a facing of flint, like many others in

Surrey and Sussex. In letters informing friends of the move, Meredith referred to it as 'Flint House' or 'Flinthouse'. For some reason, although it is a good deal larger than the average cottage – especially a nineteenth-century farm cottage – it became known as Flint Cottage, the name used by Ellis and subsequent biographers and also by the National Trust, which now owns the house. It is uncertain what Meredith himself called it, as the printed heading on his writing-paper was simply 'Box Hill, Dorking' (the postal address).

Cottage or house, it is a square-built structure with the simple plan of four rooms downstairs and four rooms upstairs, divided by a steep, narrow staircase. Each room is approximately the same size, about twelve feet by twelve. Large windows, reaching down almost to the floor and up to the ceiling, give an amount of daylight that is unusual for a house of the period. There were cellars, but no accommodation for servants; they came in from the village for the day's work. The house was not really big enough for a writer who needed a study, had a wife and two children, and a habit of hospitality. In 1876 Meredith built a two-room wooden chalet in Swiss style, higher up the slope above the spacious garden, where he wrote and slept during intensive spells of work. The guest-room in the house was adequate for a single person, but when a couple or a family came to visit, Meredith arranged for them to stay at the Burford Bridge Inn.

The closest neighbour was Charles Mackay, who wrote popular songs such as 'There's a good time coming, Be it never so far away'. His daughter, a child when the Merediths arrived, grew up to write best-selling romantic novels under the name of Marie Corelli – perhaps a tribute to Marie Meredith and to the Meredith Italophilia. Another neighbour was the elderly Dr Gordon, who sometimes had his teenage grandchildren, Jim Gordon and Jim's cousin Alice Brandreth, staying with him. In a book written many years later, *Memories of George Meredith*, Alice recalled that she and Jim woke him up early on a summer morning by throwing stones at his window and enticed him to walk up Box Hill with them in his slippers. Other walks followed, and she recorded:

His enthusiasm, his personality, so one with Nature, the summer, and the morning, startled and bewildered me, and for the first time in my spoilt only-child life I was awake and interested in something outside myself . . . his laughter, rhymes, and jokes were constant, but he was ever a master of exquisite chaff . . .[29]

The cousins were subsequently married, and it was Jim, an electrical engineer, who gave Will Meredith his first job. Left a widow when Jim was killed in a riding accident, Alice was a regular visitor at Flint Cottage in later years.

Flint Cottage was Meredith's home for the rest of his life. It suited him ideally, for he could walk through the unspoiled countryside of Box Hill and Ranmore Common, but could also reach London easily from the station in the nearby village of West Humble. He gave up 'Foakesday' at about the time when he moved from Kingston, but still went to the Chapman and Hall office at 193 Piccadilly. Visitors were instructed on how to reach Box Hill from either Charing Cross or London Bridge and given an early dinner if they were not staying overnight.

Although 'unspoiled countryside' was – and, thanks to the National Trust, still is – an accurate description of Meredith's immediate surroundings, Surrey as a county had changed a good deal since he had walked from London to Portsmouth in the 1840s. The building of the railways enabled successful businessmen to live within reach of their City offices and yet to adopt the habits of the landowning gentry. Victor Radnor in *One of Our Conquerors* gives ostentatious parties at his country home, which bears the typical name of Lakelands, but is first seen walking across London Bridge from the station. Anyone who knows Surrey has observed the quantity of opulent houses along the lanes or in the woods, whose architecture dates them to the period between 1850 and 1914, well before the curb of planning regulations. Alice Brandreth heard Meredith teasing the plutocrats about 'their French cooks, orchid houses, and well-filled stables', and observed:

> I do not think Mr Meredith liked the company of very rich people, and I remember well as a child how puzzled I was . . . when I heard him say that in many cases the vision of rich people was limited to their personal possessions, and that their mental horizon was bounded by their own park gates.[30]

The reviews of *Vittoria*, the novel in which Meredith had invested so much emotional capital, were mostly discouraging and the sales were poor. He wrote sadly to Swinburne: '*Vittoria* passes to the limbo where the rest of my works repose.'[31] However, he was working steadily on another big novel, *The Adventures of Harry Richmond*. The word 'adventures' – the titles of his last four novels had been simply the names of the central characters – indicated that he was placing this book in the tradition of the English eighteenth-century picaresque novel, like Smollett's *Adventures of Peregrine Pickle*. But this was only one element, for *Harry Richmond* is a complex and many-sided novel, mingling the 'adventures' with a *Bildungsroman*, with a passionate love story, with fantasy (some of the incidents, if taken literally, are far from realistic), with imagery and symbolism, and with social criticism into the bargain. If it can hardly be claimed as an integrated artistic success, it can be regarded as Meredith's most ambitious venture. In fact, his reaction to the poor reception of *Vittoria* was that he would write just as he chose to write.

For two months in the autumn of 1868, he left his desk and Flint Cottage to take part in an election campaign. Just as the stint as war correspondent was the only appearance of Meredith as reporter, this was his only direct intervention in politics. Far from contemplating any kind of political career, he was acting out of friendship for Fred Maxse, who was standing as Radical candidate for Southampton, the constituency nearest to his home at Ploverfield House. After the election, Meredith wrote to Arthur: 'My two months down with Captain Maxse was a dead loss of time to me.'[32]

The general election of 1868 was the first since the Second Reform Act, passed in the preceding year. While this measure did not enfranchise the whole adult male (let alone female) population, it did give the vote to considerable numbers of better-paid workers, craftsmen and shop-keepers. But, since there was as yet no secret ballot, these voters were vulnerable to intimidation; if they voted the wrong way, employees could be sacked or shopkeepers could lose custom. Predictably, too, the voters were open to bribery and some openly sold their votes to the highest bidder. Glaring evidence of bribery led to the introduction of the secret ballot before the next election in 1874.

Maxse refused to pay bribes but spent about two thousand pounds (there was no legal limit) on his campaign. As Meredith went round canvassing for his friend and chatting in the pubs, he became convinced that the Tories were spending much more and that a great deal of their expenditure was sheer bribery. In any case, Radicalism – or even Liberalism – did not have the support in Southampton that it found in northern industrial towns. Cautious voters did not know what to make of a candidate who was a naval officer and an earl's grandson, and who nevertheless made uncompromisingly Radical speeches and never went to church. To nobody's surprise – certainly not to Meredith's – Maxse was decisively defeated. In the same general election, Anthony Trollope was defeated at Beverley, also thanks to bribery.

In his letter to Arthur, Meredith linked the defeat to bribery, but also to political backwardness:

> We were badly beaten at Southampton, but I think it will be proved that bribery was done there. We on our side were not guilty of it, I know. It is a very corrupt place. It has been found by experience of the enlarged franchise that where there are large labouring populations depending upon hire (especially in a corrupt and languishing town like Southampton) they will be thrown into the hands of the unscrupulous rich. At all events this is one of the evils we have to contend against until the poor fellows know by enlightenment where their own interests lie and the necessity for their acting in unison and making sacrifices. Old Toryism has still a long spell of life in this country where the vitality has need to be strong in the centre of thick decay.[33]

Meredith's pessimism was not wholly justified; it must be remembered that the England he knew was limited to the southern counties and the West End of London. At a national level, the Liberals won the 1868 election, and were in power more often than not through the half-century from that date to 1918. Still, his impressions on the Southampton doorstep were emphatically of the dishonesty and the exploitation of ingrained prejudice that barred the way to fundamental social change. He made forceful use of these impressions when he described the election at 'Bevisham' in *Beauchamp's Career*.

Meredith was now forty years old. Reading his letters of the fourth decade of his life, one perceives a sense that these were his best years: years of happiness, years of good health and energy, years of satisfying work. From an arduous and testing ascent, he had reached a plateau. Yet he was only midway through a life that took him to the age of eighty, and his creative powers were very far from exhausted. *Beauchamp's Career*, *The Egoist*, *Diana of the Crossways*, *The Amazing Marriage*, scores of poems – all these were still to come.

7

The Faith of George Meredith

'NARRATIVE is nothing. It is the mere vehicle of philosophy.'[1] This conception is fundamental to Meredith's purpose as a novelist - and indeed as a poet too, for in many of his poems philosophy is mediated through a narrative, often taken from Greco-Roman mythology. The purpose is made explicit in a short chapter abruptly interpolated in *Emilia in England*. Here, Meredith contrasts the Philosopher (capital P) with the Hippogriff, a creature embodying conventional narrative and the 'sentimentalism' that he loathed. The reader is told: 'Let him, the Philosopher, repeat that souls harmonious to Nature, of whom there are few, do not mount this animal.'

Meredith admitted, or rather proudly asserted, that he was defying traditional assumptions about novel-writing. In doing so, he was willing to accept a limited readership, hostile reviews and general incomprehension. This Chapter 51 of *Emilia* continues:

All attestation favours the critical dictum, that a novel is to give us copious sugar and no cane. My Philosopher's error is to deem the sugar, born of the cane, inseparate from it. The which is naturally resented, and away flies my book at the heads of the librarians, hitting me behind them a far more grievous blow . . . Such is the construction of my story, however, that to entirely deny the Philosopher the privilege he stipulated for when with his assistance I conceived it, would render our performance unintelligible to that acute and honourable minority which consents to be thwacked with aphorisms . . . We are indeed in a sort of partnership, and it is useless for me to tell him that he is not popular and destroys my chance.

Twenty years later, the public was confronted with another manifesto, this time in Chapter I of *Diana of the Crossways*:

> If we do not speedily embrace philosophy in fiction, the Art is doomed to extinction under the shining multitude of its professors. They are fast capping the candle. Instead, therefore, of objurgating the timid intrusions of philosophy, invoke her presence, I pray you. History without her is the skeleton-map of events; Fiction a picture of figures modelled on no skeleton-anatomy. But each, with philosophy in aid, blooms, and is humanly shapely. To demand of us truth to nature, excluding philosophy, is really to bid a pumpkin caper. As much as legs are wanted for the dance, philosophy is required to make our human nature credible and acceptable . . . Philosophy bids us to see that we are not so pretty as rose-pink, not so repulsive as dirty-drab; and that, instead of everlastingly shifting those barren aspects, the sight of ourselves is wholesome, bearable, fructifying, finally a delight.

Diana Warwick writes novels and, of course, shares Meredith's ideas. She declares: 'The art of the pen (we write on darkness) is to rouse the inward vision.' When she is at work on a novel, her creator tells us:

> No hair's-breadth 'scapes, perils by sea and land, heroisms of the hero, fine shrieks of the heroine . . . She did not appeal to the senses nor to a superficial discernment. So she had the anticipatory sense of its failure; and she wrote her best, in perverseness; of course she wrote slowly; she wrote more and more realistically of the characters and the downright human emotions, less of the wooden supernumaries of her story, labelled for broad guffaw or deluge tears – the grappling natural links between our public and an author.

In 1862, when he was writing *Emilia in England*, Meredith explained to Augustus Jessopp:

> Between realism and idealism, there is no natural conflict. This completes that . . . Idealism is as an atmosphere whose effects of grandeur are wrought out through a series of illusions, that are illusions to the sense within us only when divorced from the groundwork of the Real . . . Men to whom I bow my head (Shakespeare, Goëthe; and in their way, Molière, Cervantes) are Realists *au fond*. But they have the broad arms of Idealism at command.[2]

In later years, he made occasional statements about his literary method, generally as a brief and, one feels, rather weary response to enquiries. He wrote in 1887:

> I have never started on a novel to pursue the theory it developed. The dominant idea in my mind took up the characters and the story midway. Concerning style, thought is tough, and dealing with thought produces toughness. Or when strong emotion is in tide against the active mind, there is perforce confusion.[3]

Also in 1887, he stated: 'I do not make a plot. If my characters, as I have them at heart before I begin on them, were boxed in a plot, they would soon lose the lines of their features.'[4]

He was a novelist, handling the novelist's concerns of characterization, human experience, emotion, dilemma and conflict. Had he been a simple story-teller, he would not have pondered on philosophy; but, had he been entirely a philosopher, he would have written essays, not novels. In practice, the narrative was never 'a mere vehicle'. For him, as for other novelists for whom philosophy was important – Hardy, Tolstoy, Mann – the relationship was reciprocal. The philosophy, it is true, inspires and guides the narrative; yet the narrative enlivens and enriches the philosophy, rather than merely illustrating it. This is what Meredith meant by his reconciliation of realism and idealism.

However, philosophy itself – or the search for philosophy – plays a genuinely dramatic role in some of the novels. Sir Austin Feverel's System is wrong-headed, but it arises from the labours of his earnest, reflective mind and confers dignity on a character who would otherwise be only a tactless blunderer. In *The Egoist*, Vernon Whitford's studious bookishness is the quality that impresses Clara and finally wins her love. Victor Radnor in *One of Our Conquerors* is haunted by the quest for an Idea that always eludes him. In *The Amazing Marriage*, a transforming experience for the rich, arrogant Lord Fleetwood in his encounter with Gower Woodseer, a man who is indifferent to money and comfort and cares only for philosophy. Each of these novels has a strong narrative line and we can imagine it written, perhaps more successfully in the obvious sense, by a writer of the traditional kind; but without philosophy, it could not be a Meredith novel.

As Meredith expected, his insistence on philosophy – and the authorial digressions which readers may well have skipped – gave him a daunting reputation which he still retains. Still, there was always an 'acute and

honourable minority' that understood his aims and his special contribution to the art of the novel, and as time passed this minority came to
include younger writers. Robert Louis Stevenson, whose *Prince Otto* was
a deliberately Meredithian novel (and did not attract the public that had
enjoyed *Treasure Island* and *Kidnapped*), echoed Meredith with the dictum:
'All representative art, which can be said to live, is both realistic and
ideal.' Oscar Wilde paid this tribute:

> One incomparable novelist we have now in England, Mr George
> Meredith. There are better artists in France, but France has no one
> whose view of life is so large, so varied, so imaginatively true . . . to
> him belongs philosophy in fiction. His people not merely live, but they
> live in thought . . . They are interpretative and symbolic.[5]

It is easier to illustrate Meredith's belief in the significance of philosophy
than to elucidate his own philosophy. In the strict or academic sense, he
was never a philosopher. It is more accurate to speak of his outlook on
life – in the comprehensive German term, his *Weltanschauung*. This outlook
was imaginative rather than analytical, and at various times it related in
different ways to personal, social or political problems. But his fundamental beliefs, by comparison with those of most other writers, remained
remarkably consistent throughout his life.

He was always a humanist, for whom human life was a value in its
own right, subservient to no extraneous purpose. He was never (except,
as we have seen, briefly in his Neuwied days) attracted by religion in the
form maintained by the Christian Churches. He rejected 'the Christian
fable' – the concept of Jesus Christ as a manifestation of divinity and a
saviour. This rejection was already taking shape at Neuwied or even,
perhaps, at his first school at Southsea. It can be traced to an innate
aversion to believing what he was ordered to believe and to a bright boy's
impatient boredom when subjected to lengthy services and sermons. As
a grown man and a father, he recalled this tedium in a letter pleading
with Jessopp, for Arthur's sake, to cut down the length of the three Sunday
services at the Norwich school:

> I remember, at that age, how all love of the Apostles was belaboured
> out of me by three Sunday services of prodigious length and dreariness.
> Corinthians will forever be associated in my mind with rows of wax
> candles and a holy drone over-head, combined with the sensation that
> those who did not choose the road to Heaven, enjoyed by far the

pleasantest way ... I have known subsequent horrors of ennui: but nothing to be compared with those early ones.[6]

Years later, he grumbled about a Sunday social engagement in London:

... gloom is before my sight. I have to traverse the livid streets of a London Sabbath and be drenched in the Stygian Springs of English Puritanism. Why have I been asked for a Sunday! ... It is the characteristic of the Seventh Day in your city that the more mundane are generally to be found attending to things eternal – dull sermons, for example.[7]

In other letters, he expressed his unflinching antagonism to orthodox religion, varied by a philosophical expectation that it would lose ground among intelligent people. In mid-century, the worshipped Christ was being displaced by biographies of Jesus as a human, historical figure, of which the first was translated from German by George Eliot. In 1874, he teased a clergyman who tried to score a point by asking if there was an extant portrait of Jesus. In the same year, he was delighted by Professor Tyndall's outspoken defence of evolution in the presidential address to the British Association. To his irreligious friend Maxse, Meredith wrote:

It has roused the Clergy, Fred ... They affirm that Tyndall is an atheist, and would dare to say he is already damned if the age were in a mood to hear that language. The man or the country that fights priestcraft and priests is to my mind striking deeper for freedom than can be struck anywhere at present. I foresee a perilous struggle with them.[8]

But, in an 1866 letter, he had cautioned Maxse that attacks on revealed religion must be intellectually solid, not merely abusive:

Will bawlings in the street avail, save to disturb and annoy the lieges? They irritate the slumbering dominant party, without strengthening the insurgent ... Let Philosophy sap the structure and work its way. What we have to anticipate is this: There is, and will further be, a falling off of the educated young men in seeking an establishment as Churchmen. These are highly educated, and in their nature tolerant. They are beginning to think for themselves and they give their lives to other matters. The Church will have to be recruited from a lower, a more illiterate, necessarily a more intolerant class. These will find themselves at variance with their intellectual superiors and in self-defence will attempt to wield the Dogma and knock us down with a club . . . If in the meantime we alarm such placid fellows as we see in the clerical robes, we are really doing Truth no service.[9]

In his novels, Meredith portrayed the clergy in unflattering terms, stressing their lack of the supposed Christian virtues. Dr Middleton in *The Egoist* is devoted only to money and old port, and mercilessly bullies his daughter. The Rev. Septimus Barmby in *One of Our Conquerors* repels Nesta, whom he hopes to marry, by his unctuousness (could the word 'smarmy' have been in Meredith's mind?), and there is a clear hint that the Rev. Abram Posterley is infected with venereal disease. But the most derisive portrait of a Christian believer is that of the crazy Captain Welsh in *Harry Richmond*, whose intolerant fanaticism is contrasted with the commonsense scepticism of his crew.

The Catholic Church was the ultimate in everything that was antipathetic to Meredith, representing blind obedience to dogma in place of liberated thought and myth-making in place of discoverable truth. Meredith's hostility was reinforced by his political sympathies, since the Vatican under Pope Pius IX was the stronghold of resistance to Italian freedom and nationhood. In *Evan Harrington*, it is the shallow and dishonest Louisa who is tempted by Catholicism, to the alarm of her sober-minded sisters. For Constance Asper in *Diana of the Crossways*, the Catholic faith offers a refuge from personal unhappiness and unrequited love. Father Boyle, the Irish priest in *Celt and Saxon*, is a likeable character but a captive of the most simplistic kind of dogma. When Lord Fleetwood in *The Amazing Marriage* embraces Catholicism, and actually becomes a monk, he deserves credit for renouncing a life of selfish pleasure, but is also retreating from the real moral challenges that have become too much for him. While Meredith was never a Protestant any more than he was a Catholic, and could deride the narrow-minded austerities of Puritanism, he continued to feel some respect for the sincere piety of the Neuwied teachers, and probably for the Huguenot beliefs of his wife, Marie, and her family.

All this seems straightforward enough; yet to see Meredith simply as a non-religious rationalist would be to miss a vital aspect of his outlook. Even the convenient word 'agnostic', invented by Huxley in 1869 and much in vogue in Meredith's time, does not altogether fit him, for he was temperamentally averse to setting fundamental problems aside as beyond the range of enquiry. Such words as 'belief' and 'faith', generally employed by adherents of a religion, recur time and again in Meredith's poems, which – rather than his novels – were his chosen vehicle for abstract speculation. The title of one highly significant poem, 'A Faith on Trial', tells us that, to his mind, his philosophy was a faith – or his faith was a philosophy. Indeed, 'religion' itself was not entirely absent from his vocabulary. In a poem entitled 'Creed' (published only after his death) he wrote:

> Religion should be universal love,
> And not a coop for blind Enthusiasts,
> Who cannot sympathise with natural life,
> And all the sweet desires of human being.

In 1884, he conveyed his deeper beliefs in a letter to Maxse:

> . . . it is quite certain that the best of us is in the state of survival. We live in what we have done – in the idea: which seems to me the parent fountain of life, as opposed to that of perishable blood. I see all around me how much Idea governs; and therein see the Creator; that other life to which we are drawn: not conscious, as our sensations demand, but possibly cognizant, as the brain may now sometimes, when the blood is not too forcefully pressing on it, dimly apprehend.[10]

The allusion to 'the Creator' may surprise some readers, and probably surprised Maxse. But Darwin, on the last page of *The Descent of Man*, had made clear his belief that evolution presupposed, rather than eliminated, an ultimate creation. It was only the naïve myth of creation in seven days that Darwin – and Meredith – rejected.

In 1900, Meredith advised Lady Ulrica Duncombe:

> Never attempt to dissociate your ideal from the real of life. It weakens the soul; and besides it cannot be done – and again it is a cowardly temporary escape into delusion, clouding the mind, through which is our only chance of seeing God, the God so much obscured by churchmen supplicating the Divinity's interposition . . . Be sure that the Spiritual God is accessible at all moments to the soul desiring him . . .[11]

However, Christian believers would have been unwise to draw sustenance from such a reference to God. Various spiritual leaders who gave allegiance to no particular religion, and certainly not to Christianity – Gandhi, for one – have spoken of 'God' as a kind of shorthand term for a beneficent force offering guidance in human life. Moreover, Meredith was inclined to recommend God to young people – to Arthur when a boy, and much later to the beautiful and intelligent Lady Ulrica – as, one would say, a supernatural guardian. This was, clearly, far from postulating a personal deity.

When we look for the essence of Meredith's philosophy (or faith), we find it in three words that recur many times – far more often than God – in the poems and letters. These words are Nature, Earth and Mother. They overlap, if not in their exact definition, then certainly in their emotional significance. Nature is of course a theme of poets across the centuries, and particularly of Wordsworth, who was still alive and enormously influential when the young Meredith was embarking on what he intended as a poetic career. The pronoun for Nature is sometimes 'it', never 'he', and most frequently 'she', for Nature personifies the helping, nurturing force that ensures the preservation and continuance of life. Earth is the natural environment wherein life grows. Meredith twice used the word as a title for a collection of poems – *Poems and Lyrics of the Joy of Earth* in 1883, and *A Reading of Earth* in 1888. One poem, 'Earth and a Wedded Woman', describes a woman who is waiting for conception while the earth waits for fructifying rain. As for the word Mother, it can stand for Mother Nature, Mother Earth, or in the literal sense a human mother. Thus, the three concepts merge into what Meredith felt as a unity.

From the beginning, Meredith's view was optimistic. As he saw it, human beings could only benefit from being in accord with the force of Nature. In 'South-west Wind in the Woodland', a poem that can be dated to 1851, he wrote:

> The voice of nature is abroad
> This night; she fills the air with balm;
> Her mystery is o'er the land;
> And who that hears her now and yields
> His being to the yearning tones,
> And seats his soul upon her wings,
> And broadens o'er the wind-swept world
> With her, will gather in the flight
> More knowledge of her secret, more
> Delight in her beneficence
> Than hours of musing, or the lore
> That lives with men could ever give! . . .

For every elemental power
Is kindred to our hearts, and once
Acknowledged, wedded, once embraced,
Once taken to the unfettered sense,
Once claspt into the naked life,
The union is eternal.

Eight years later, when Meredith had turned from poetry to the novel, Darwin opened a new epoch in thought with *The Origin of Species*. He too wrote of Nature as a pervasive and commanding force. He explained that he was using a metaphor, as when physicists wrote of 'the attraction of gravity'; that the single word, Nature, was a shorthand for 'the aggregate action and product of many natural laws'. But for him, as much as for any poet, Nature was 'she'. In an often cited phrase, he wrote: 'Man selects only for his own good: Nature only for that of the being which she tends.'

Thanks to Darwin more than to any other single man of the age, science swiftly became a dominant force – we can also say a philosophy, or indeed a creed – in intellectual life. A woman who grew up under this influence, Beatrice Webb, vividly described in her memoirs the role that the scientists assumed:

It was they who were routing the theologians, confounding the mystics, imposing their theories on philosophers, their inventions on capitalists, and their discoveries on medical men; whilst they were at the same time snubbing the artists, ignoring the poets and even casting doubts on the capacity of the politicians.[12]

The poets, however, could not ignore the scientists. They reacted in widely divergent ways to the Darwinian doctrine of evolution and the Darwinian conception of Nature. Among the poets of the period, the best prepared was undoubtedly Meredith. To say that he quickly and fully accepted evolution would be true; to say that he came under Darwin's influence would not be quite accurate. Rather, he had already arrived at beliefs that dovetailed perfectly with the lessons of Darwin, as we can see from his welcome to 'the voice of nature' and his 'delight in her beneficence'. His advantage was that he did not need to free himself from the religious dogmas that he had easily discarded. As J. B. Priestley commented:

Meredith escapes the Science-Religion, materialism-idealism trap because he is by temperament something different from all his contemporaries; he is a pure pagan ... One feels with him that if Evolution had not been there he would have had to invent it ... With Meredith, who appeared to take Evolution in his stride and was never happy unless he was talking about Nature, we feel that the sun is shining and the great winds blowing for the first time in Victorian literature.[13]

Other factors contributed to Meredith's rapport with the great scientist, and they also go far towards explaining the powerful position that Darwin achieved in the world of the 1860s and 1870s. Darwin wrote with effortless lucidity, in admirably readable English; his books could be understood, with a reasonable degree of application, by any educated person. His ideas were transmitted through the widely read journals of the time, notably the *Fortnightly Review*. He had an aesthetic sense that appealed to the imagination. 'Endless forms most beautiful and most wonderful have been and are being evolved,' he wrote persuasively. It was difficult not to respond to the rhetoric of a passage like this:

> How fleeting are the wishes and efforts of man! how short his time! and consequently how poor will be his results, compared with those accumulated by Nature during whole geological periods! Can we wonder, then, that Nature's productions should be far 'truer' in character than man's productions, that they should ... plainly bear the stamp of far higher workmanship?

Meredith never met Darwin, who confined himself to the company of other scientists; but two of the leading Darwinian popularizers, Grant Allen and Edward Clodd, were Meredith's friends and could enlighten him on any points that he did not readily grasp. In one novel, *The Egoist*, he drew on his understanding of sexual selection to show why the handsome Sir Willoughby Patterne gained favour with Clara Middleton:

> We now scientifically know that in this department of the universal struggle, success is awarded to the bettermost ... Thus did Miss Middleton acquiesce in the principle of selection ... He looked the fittest; he justified the dictum of Science.

The passage shows how ready Meredith was to adopt Darwinian theory and apply it to individual human behaviour. Darwin himself had been cautious in pursuing his conclusions; natural selection was expounded in *The Origin of Species*, but sexual selection was reserved for *The Descent of Man*, published twelve years later in 1871. All the evidence for evolution in *The Origin of Species* is drawn from what were then called 'lower forms of life', to the exclusion of the human species. In the later book, Darwin explained candidly: 'During many years I collected notes on the origin or descent of man, without any intention of publishing on the subject, but rather with the determination not to publish, as I thought I should thus only add to the prejudices against my views.' The twelve-year interval had an effect that Darwin had not intended. A school of thought arose which accepted evolution in principle, but maintained that mankind must have been a distinct creation because of the moral and intellectual qualities possessed by no other animal. Darwin dealt with this belief in *The Descent of Man* by showing that there was a wider gulf between a primitive insect and an ant than between a dog and a man. With some sharpness, he wrote: 'It is only our natural prejudice, and that arrogance which made our forefathers declare that they were descended from demigods, which leads us to demur to this conclusion.' And: 'If man had not been his own classifier, he would never have thought of founding a separate order for his own reception.' Meredith must have applauded as he read.

For men imbued with this arrogance, the medicine was hard to swallow. Dismay, even horror, was the reaction to Darwin's insistence that natural selection depended on fecundity, on the survival of only the fittest, and thus on lavish waste. Darwin wrote bluntly:

Heavy destruction inevitably falls either on the young or old, during each generation or at recurrent intervals. Lighten any check, mitigate the destruction ever so little, and the number of the species will almost instantaneously increase.

In his long and unhappy poem 'In Memoriam', Tennyson protested:

Are God and Nature then at strife
That Nature tends such evil dreams?
So careful of the type she seems,
So careless of the single life.

True, Darwin offered some reassurance:

We may console ourselves with the full belief, that the war of nature is not incessant, that no fear is felt, that death is generally prompt, and that the vigorous, the healthy and the happy survive and multiply.

But this was in *The Origin of Species*. 'Heavy destruction' was acceptable when the picture was of a mouse killed by a hawk; but when Darwin extended his doctrine in *The Descent of Man*, it could no longer be claimed that no fear was felt or that death was prompt. Many a Victorian had watched a beloved child fight a losing battle against consumption. Tennyson, although scientifically educated, aligned himself with those who exempted humanity from the Darwinian rules. 'No evolutionist', he wrote, 'is able to explain the mind of man.' Man was admittedly the product of Nature, but Nature failed to protect him:

> Man, her last work, who seem'd so fair,
> Such splendid purpose in his eyes,
> Who roll'd the psalm to wintry skies
> Who built him fanes of fruitless prayer
>
> Who trusted God was loved indeed
> And love Creation's final law –
> Tho' Nature, red in tooth and claw
> With ravine, shriek'd against his creed.

'Red in tooth and claw' . . . With his talent for the memorable, quotable line, Tennyson had encapsulated the pessimistic view of Nature. If Nature was an enemy, then harmony with Nature must be an illusion. Another poet, Matthew Arnold, viewed the notion with contempt:

> 'In harmony with Nature'? Restless fool . . .
> Man must begin, know this, where Nature ends;
> Nature and man can never be fast friends.
> Fool, if thou canst not pass her, rest her slave!

Meredith struck an entirely different note – not of Tennyson's shocked dismay, nor yet of facile cheerfulness, but of serene acceptance of the inevitable. He took from Darwin a sense of the infinite persistence of life, far beyond the limits of individual existence. 'O life as futile, then, as frail!' was Tennyson's despairing conclusion. For Meredith life could not be futile, since it progressed through endless stages of evolution, nor was it frail, since its durability was a sign of innate strength. Beyond 'life' in the everyday sense, there was an element which he sometimes called 'the mind' or 'the brain', sometimes 'the idea', sometimes 'the spirit'. This he perceived, or felt, as he gazed at the stars in the first minutes of a new year, that of 1878. He took up his pen to write to John Morley:

> I thought of you and how it might be with you this year: hoped for good: saw beyond good and evil to great stillness, another form of moving for you and me. It seems to me that Spirit is – how, where, and by what means involving us, none can say. But in this life there is no life save in spirit.[14]

There is truth in Priestley's remark that Meredith 'was never happy unless he was talking about Nature'. In the poems, which can be taken as Meredith's way of thinking aloud, Nature in the intangible or philosophic sense merges with the 'nature' that we have in mind when we speak of nature poetry. Meredith's poems are full of descriptions of landscape, trees, flowers and changing weather, which he observed with attentive scrutiny. But, in accordance with Darwinian theory, he bore in mind that Nature is destructive as well as creative. He exulted in storms, vividly described in set-pieces in *Richard Feverel, Harry Beauchamp* and the novella *The House on the Beach* (in which a storm that destroys half a town is recorded as an interesting event, not lamented as a tragedy). There are storms, too, in the early poem 'South-west Wind in the Woodland' (quoted in Chapter 3) and the later 'Hard Weather'. That poem moves from a description of the storm to a consideration of its value:

> Behold the life at ease; it drifts,
> The sharpened life commands its course.
> She winnows, winnows roughly; sifts,
> To dip her chosen in her source:
> Contention is the vital force,
> When pluck they brain, her prize of gifts,
> Sky of the senses! on which height,
> Not disconnected, yet released,
> They see how spirit comes to light.

'She' is of course Nature. In *Emilia in England*, a leading theme is Emilia's rapport with Nature, contrasted with artificiality and the emotional inhibitions of the Pole sisters. It was in 1862, while he was writing this novel, that Meredith made the clearest statement of his philosophy in 'Ode to the Spirit of Earth in Autumn':

> Great Mother Nature! teach me, like thee,
> To kiss the season and shun regrets.
> And am I more than the mother who bore,
> Mock me not with thy harmony!
>   Teach me to blot regrets,
>   Great Mother! me inspire
>   With faith that forward sets
>   But feeds the living fire . . .
>
> And O, green bounteous Earth!
> Bacchante Mother! stern to those
> Who live not in thy heart of mirth;
> Death shall I shrink from, loving thee?
> Into the breast that gives the rose,
> Shall I with shuddering fall?
>   Earth, the mother of all
>   Moves on her stedfast way,
>   Gathering, flinging, sowing.
>   Mortals, we live in her day,
>   She in her children is growing. . . .
> Behold, in yon stripped Autumn, shivering grey,
>   Earth knows no desolation.
>   She smells regeneration
>   In the moist breath of decay.

Meredith wrote few important poems in the next thirty years, devoting himself to novels. But in 1883 he produced a long poem (300 lines), 'The Woods of Westermain'. Although Westermain cannot be found on a map, the inspiration seems to have come from a dense woodland a few miles from his home, a part of which bears the name of Druids' Grove. The belief in woods or forests inhabited by magical, mysterious spirits is ancient and profound, both in Greek mythology and in Celtic folklore. The opening lines of the poem, recurrent as a refrain until the end, are: 'Enter these enchanted woods/You who dare'. The woods are the domain of a goddess, who extends to 'those who dare' the promise of love and reconciliation:

Here her splendid beast she leads
Silken-leashed and decked with weeds
Wild as he, but breathing faint
Sweetness of unfelt constraint.
Love, the great volcano, flings
Fires of lower Earth to sky;
Love, the sole permitted, sings
Sovereignly of Me and I.

The vision leads into what may be called a pagan sermon:

You must love the light so well
That no darkness will seem fell . . .
Light to light sees little strange,
Only features heavenly new;
Then you touch the nerve of Change,
Then of Earth you have the clue;
Then her two-sexed meanings melt
Through you, wed the thought and felt.

In another section, Meredith sees life as a unity of 'blood and brain and spirit':

Earth that Triad is: she hides
Joy from him who that divides;
Showers it when the three are one
Glassing her in union.
Earth your haven, Earth your helm,
You command a double realm.

Another poem in the *Joy of Earth* collection, 'The Day of the Daughter of Hades', sees a young man responding to the song of Earth:

                    . . . that song
Of the sowing and reaping, and cheer
Of the husbandman's heart made strong
Through droughts and deluging rains
With his faith in the Great Mother's love;
O the joy of the breath she sustains,
And the lyre of the light above,

[133]

And the first rapt vision of Good,
And the fresh young sense of Sweet.

A poem that was singled out for praise by Siegfried Sassoon, 'The Lark Ascending', repeats the theme of the song immanent in nature – this time the song of the lark, a favourite bird with poets:

> For singing till his heaven fills,
> 'Tis love of earth that he instils . . .
> Was never voice of ours could say
> Our inmost in the sweetest way,
> Like yonder voice aloft, and link
> All hearers in the song they drink.
> Our wisdom speaks from failing blood,
> Our passion is too full in flood,
> We want the key of his wild note
> Of truthful in a tuneful throat,
> The song seraphically free
> Of taint of personality,
> So pure that it salutes the suns
> The voice of one for millions,
> In whom the millions rejoice
> For giving their one spirit voice.

It is a reasonable conjecture that Meredith was echoing Schiller's 'An die Freude' and the music of the Ninth Symphony.

The 1883 collection also contained an extended new version of Meredith's early 'Love in the Valley'. Its appealing lyricism made it his most popular poem, often featuring as a recitation piece in the literary-musical soirées that followed Victorian dinner-parties.

The mood of the collection was one of happiness – a happiness that Meredith felt himself to have attained through the embrace of Nature, the Great Mother, and through the working out of his philosophy. But this happiness did not last much longer. Marie fell ill, attacked by what was soon diagnosed as cancer of the throat. She underwent two operations, in June 1884 and January 1885. Through the spring and summer months of that year, she was in constant severe pain and became unable to speak. In September, she died. She was forty-five years old; Mary, Meredith's first wife, had been thirty-nine at the time of her death. He had loved them both – Mary with a youthful passion destroyed by disillusion, Marie with a tranquil affection deepened by years of companionship.

Death – especially death long before old age, and death preceded by suffering – posed hard questions for Christians who believed in a loving, caring God. For Meredith, the believer in Nature's beneficence, the questions were just as hard. He had to ask himself whether his humanist faith, which had supplied him with strength and confidence as he went through life, was still valid. Writing at the time when he realized that Marie's illness was terminal, he wrestled with the problem in a poem courageously entitled 'A Faith on Trial'.

The poem opens with a tender reminiscence:

> Sweet was her voice with the tongue,
> The speechful tongue of her France,
> Soon at ripple about us, like rills
> Ever busy with little: away
> Through her Normandy, down where the mills
> Dot at length a rivercourse, grey
> As its bordering poplars bent
> To gusts off the plains above.
> Old stone château and farms,
> Home of her birth and her love!

But Meredith goes on to confront the experience of finding that beneficent Nature can be ruthless:

> I champed the sensations that make
> Of a ruffled philosophy rags.
> For them was no meaning too blunt,
> Nor aspect too cutting of steel.
> This Earth of the beautiful breasts,
> Shining up in all colours aflame,
> To them had visions of hags:
> A Mother of aches and jests:
> Soulless, heading a hunt
> Aimless except for the meal.

Then, with spring, 'the pure wild-cherry in bloom' is a symbol of 'a conquest of coward despair', and he sees

How a shaft of the blossoming tree
Was shot from the yew-wood's core.
I stood to the touch of a key
Turned in a fast-shut door.

So, he is able to reaffirm his faith with deeper understanding:

Harsh wisdom gives Earth, no more;
In one the spur and the curb . . .
Yet we have but to see and hear,
Crave we her medical herb.
For the road to her soul is the Real:
The root of the growth of man:
And the senses must traverse it fresh
With a love that no scourge can abate,
To reach the lone heights where we scan
In the mind's rarer vision this flesh;
In the charge of the Mother our fate;
Her law as the one common weal.

Hence the conclusion:

By Death, as by life, are we fed:
The two are one spring; our bond
With the numbers; with whom to unite
Here feathers wings for beyond:
Only they can waft us in flight.
For they are Reality's flower.
Of them, and the contact with them,
Issues Earth's dearest daughter, the firm
In footing, the stately of stem;
Unshaken, though elements lour;
A warrior heart unquelled.

'By Death, as by Life, we are fed' is a statement grounded in Meredith's understanding of Darwin. As a philosophy it is stoical, yet ultimately consoling. Three years after Marie's death, he wrote to a woman whose husband had died:

Death and Life are really one, each to feed the other; and nature has
no unkindness for us when we have comprehended this. She attaches

no more importance to the day's life than to the rise and fall of a wave. She presses to produce; our task is to hew and shape, lift, and leave behind us a race having more grip of the elements composing us. Thus at least the mind has an immortality.[15]

Meredith's nature poems – if, again, we use the term in both a descriptive and a philosophical sense – repeatedly illustrated this concept of death and renewal. He rarely set his scene in high summer nor in the eventless depth of winter, but rather in spring or autumn, seeing in these seasons an alternation that embodied a unity. A myth that held great significance for him, retold in 'The Day of the Daughter of Hades', was that of Persephone, forced to spend the dead winter months in the underworld but rescued each spring by her mother Demeter (the Roman Ceres, from whom we derive the word 'cereal'), who thus ensures a renewal of fruitful life. In 'Seed-Time', one of the poems in *A Reading of Earth*, Meredith wrote:

> Verily now is our season of seed,
> Now in our Autumn; and Earth discerns
> Them that have served her in them that can read,
> Glassing, where under the surface she burns,
> Quick at her wheel, while the fuel, decay,
> Brightens the fire of renewal: and we?
> Death is the word of a bovine day,
> Know you the breast of the springing To-be.

The idea that decay – even death – was a precondition of renewal was one that Darwin's contemporaries, even when they gave assent to the doctrine of evolution, found it difficult to assimilate emotionally. As Peter Morton has noted in his book *The Vital Science*: 'Evolutionary theory emphasised extinction and annihilation equally with transformation – and this was one of its most disturbing elements.' Tennyson and Arnold, as we have seen, recoiled. Winwood Reade, in his widely read novel *The Martyrdom of Man*, admitted that evolution was intellectually incontestable but found only gloom in its truths; a character says: 'Life is one long tragedy; creation is one great crime.' For Hardy, the implications of human suffering are either ironic or tragic, and in any case devoid of rational explanation. His most moving novel could only end with the bleak conclusion that the President of the Immortals 'had ended his sport with Tess'. Meredith was alone in putting Darwinian knowledge to positive, creative use, and in evolving a philosophy that saved him both from a relapse into traditional religion and from a surrender to hopeless pessimism.

While Meredith's poems give direct expression to his belief in the beneficence of Nature, his novels illustrate Darwin's dictum that 'the vigorous, the healthy and the happy survive and multiply'. In *Rhoda Fleming*, the tough and resolute Rhoda (though we cannot like her) is distinctly a survivor, while the weak and pathetic Dahlia is not. Whenever he can, Meredith ends his story with the union of a man and a woman who are vigorous, healthy and capable of overcoming obstacles in the way of happiness: Evan and Rose in *Evan Harrington*, Harry and Janet in *Harry Richmond*, Dartrey and Nesta in *One of Our Conquerors*, Matthew and Aminta in *Lord Ormont*. Moreover, Nature is ensuring the renewal of life in the next generation. Carlo is dead by the end of *Vittoria*, but the closing pages show Vittoria as the proud mother of a young Carlo. By the end of *Beauchamp's Career*, Jenny's baby by Nevil is thriving, but Rosamund's baby by the declining Lord Romfrey survives for only an hour. Carinthia in *The Amazing Marriage* not only demonstrates her fertility by conceiving after a single act of intercourse with Fleetwood, but goes on after Fleetwood's death to marry Owain Wythan, whose first wife (conveniently dead too by this time) was barren. Thus, Nature has weeded out both Fleetwood and the unfortunate Rebecca Wythan, to select Owain and Carinthia for her purposes.

Meredith took risks, as he well knew, by using the novel as a 'vehicle of philosophy'. At their weakest, the novels can be awkwardly didactic and events can be glaringly implausible. However, even these unlikely events are not really arbitrary or accidental, because they are informed by the philosophy. If we are to appreciate the full stature of Meredith as a novelist, we must respond to his faith.

8

Champion of Women

GEORGE MEREDITH's most remarkable quality as a novelist, and his most persuasive claim on the attention of today's readers, is his understanding of women. He had much to say on other subjects, but it is on this theme that his insights were most penetrating, most distinctive, and most challenging in relation to conventional assumptions.

This achievement is neglected, or relegated to minor significance, in most biographies of Meredith – for instance, by S. M. Ellis, J. B. Priestley, Lionel Stevenson, Siegfried Sassoon and Norman Kelvin. Jack Lindsay, writing as a Marxist, was most alert to whatever was revolutionary or innovative in Meredith, and hence to his sympathy for oppressed and downtrodden women. However, Lindsay's gaze was focused on the outrageousness of the oppressor rather than on the experience of the oppressed. In his discussion of *The Egoist*, he concentrated on the exposure of Sir Willoughby Patterne, not on Clara Middleton's battle for freedom and her growth in stature.

The two books that placed Meredith's women at the centre of the picture were both written, not surprisingly, by women. The first was Hannah Lynch, an Irish literary journalist who met Meredith in his later years and produced her book, *George Meredith: A Study*, in 1891. She wrote enthusiastically:

Apart from any other claim he may have upon his generation, Mr Meredith's greatest and most original will ever remain his marvellous knowledge of women. All young girls upon the verge of womanhood should be recommended an exhaustive study of him upon this subject, as a healthy antidote against the nauseous and abominable travesties of themselves and their species circulated by the libraries.[1]

[139]

While Lynch, in her opening pages, paid tribute to Meredith as 'a giant', she put her finger unequivocally on the reason:

> Woman is his study, especially young militant womanhood, and what a study he has made of her! Upon this theme not a single male writer, living or dead, since Shakespeare, can approach him, and to it he brings modern subtle penetration added to Shakespeare's purely natural instinct ... Women reading him gasp at his revelations, such as they would never dare to make or dream, so completely hedged round are they by the conventionalities of fiction.

Dealing with *The Egoist*, she saw that the egoism analysed by Meredith was not a mere character defect, but a weapon of domination. Male egoism, she wrote, 'makes straight for the whole race of women, mercilessly potent by reason of physical force, and backed by all the laws, written and unwritten, of its own making'.[2]

Alice Woods, writing about Meredith in 1937, was equally enthused and astonished: 'As we read we marvel that any man could have probed the depths of women's experience and grasped her possibilities as he has done.' Her book (quoted in Chapter 2) traced the inequality from which women suffered to the inadequacy of the education they were given. Of the women in Meredith's novel, she observed: 'Far from being the ideal heroines of romance, they are full of faults and failings as well as virtues ... They are terribly cramped by the defects of their education and tied by convention and custom.'[3]

Meredith had, in fact, explicitly made the link that Woods noted. In *Harry Richmond*, the thoughtful Janet Ilchester finds herself admitting that 'absolute freedom could be the worst of perils'. Harry asks: 'For women?' Janet prefers to say 'for girls', but adds: 'Yes, for women, as they are educated at present.' In *Lord Ormont*, he urged that girls should be educated together with boys and to the same standards, as 'the only way for them to learn to know and respect one another'.

He supported the cause of votes for women, but pointed out that the inadequacies of education left women unprepared to use their votes intelligently, as well as providing men with an argument against equal suffrage. Writing to Mrs Leslie Stephen n 1889, he explained:

> We have played fast and loose with them, until now they are encouraged to demand what they know not how to use, but have a just right to claim. If the avenues of the professions had been thrown open to

them, they might have learnt the business of the world, to be competent to help in governing. But these were closed, women were commanded to continue their reliance upon their poor attractions.[4]

As an old man, he was happy to see the cause near to success, thanks to the campaigners who had faced male violence and prison. He took a firm line in a letter to *The Times* after women, in 1906, had been jailed for invading the House of Commons:

> Until men have been well shaken at home, and taught that woman is a force to be reckoned with, they will not only more resolutely bar the fortress they hold against feminine assailants, they will punish offenders sharply . . . [But] the cause for which these imprisoned women are suffering is on its way to be realized. Men have only to improve their knowledge of women, and it will be granted speedily. Sentimental prattle of the mother, the wife, the sister is not needed when we see, as the choicer spirits of men do now see, that women have brains, and can be helpful to the hitherto entirely dominant muscular creature who has allowed them some degree of influence in return for servile flatteries . . . Women must have brains to have emerged from so long a bondage.[5]

Meredith's delineation of female experience begins with the approach to marriage. In his time, it was considered desirable for girls to be married as early as possible, if only to forestall unsuitable entanglements. The criteria for a good match could be dynastic (Prince Hermann for Princess Ottilia in *Harry Richmond*), social (Lord Laxley for Rose in *Evan Harrington*) or nakedly financial. As Meredith put it in a poem, 'The Three Singers to Young Blood':

> Mates are chosen marketwise:
> Coolest bargainer best buys.

This metaphor – if a statement so close to truth can be called a metaphor – is employed repeatedly in the novels. In *Richard Feverel*, the son and heir of Sir Austin is an obvious catch:

> Lady Attenbury of Longford House had brought her highly-polished specimen of market-ware, the Lady Juliana Jaye, for a first introduction

to him, thinking that he had arrived at an age to estimate and pine for her black eyes and pretty pert mouth.

In *Beauchamp's Career*, Cecilia Halkett reflects:

> She was one of the artificial creatures called women (with the accent) who dare not be spontaneous, and cannot act independently if they would continue to be admirable in the world's eye, and who for that object must remain fixed on shelves, like other marketable wares, avoiding motion to avoid shattering or tarnishing.

In *The Egoist*, when Clara realizes how she has been sold to Sir Willoughby, she asks herself: 'Was she much better than purchaseable stuff that has nothing to say to the bargain?'

In *Rhoda Fleming*, the operation of the market is undisguised. Fleming is ready to marry Rhoda to Algernon Blancove in order to raise money and save his farm, and to sell the disgraced Dahlia to an odious man for a cash payment at the church door.

Once she had given her consent – with the single word 'Yes', with the man's face hovering above hers and his hand applying a physical pressure, with awareness of the risks of rejecting an offer that carried social approval – the young woman was virtually committed. She was not free to break the engagement unilaterally, but had to persuade the man to release her. Just as much as in conservative Asian and Arab cultures today, the engagement was considered to be as binding as the marriage. A woman who broke it was condemned with the epithet 'jilt', which tarnished her reputation and imperilled her future chances. In her struggle to escape from Willoughby, Clara has to confront not only his determination to hold his possession, but also a whole framework of tradition and custom.

The pressure on the young woman is exerted by people for whom she feels, or by social assumption ought to feel, respect. Clara is heavily leant on by her father, Dr Middleton, but also by the experienced and worldly-wise Mrs Mountstuart Jenkinson. In *Beauchamp's Career*, Renée de Croisnel feels compelled to marry the repulsive Marquis de Rouaillout and turn away from the romantic attraction of Nevil, not only because her father deploys his authority, but also because it is endorsed by her brother Roland, who is of her own generation. Renée is emotionally close to Roland, and Carinthia in *The Amazing Marriage* is similarly close to her brother Chillon, whose need for money places an obligation on her:

'And how can I help being a burden on my brother?' she inquired, in distress.

'Marry, and be a blessing to a husband,' he said lightly.

In *Lord Ormont*, Aminta Farrell is dependent as soon as she leaves school on her aunt, Mrs Pagnell, who loses no time in engineering her marriage to Lord Ormont. His heroic military reputation leaves Aminta dazed so long as she knows nothing of his real character. Moreover, her experience is limited to a tentative flirtation at school, speedily terminated by the aunt.

Of all the unhappy situations brought about in this way, the most poignant is that of Renée, who falls in love with Nevil just too late to escape from the Marquis. Nevil hopes in vain to save her from 'the deadly iniquity of the marriage'. Roland warns him that the iron rules of the aristocracy cannot be overcome, but has no illusions about what the marriage will mean for Renée – 'a bud of a rose in an old man's button-hole'. His bitter comment is: 'In India they sacrifice the widows, in France the virgins.'

Meredith's point is that a sexually experienced man with no capacity for genuine love can only treat a wife as yet another plaything. Sure enough, the Marquis is soon neglecting Renée to spend his time with one or another mistress. Her fate is akin to that of Louise in the story 'The Gentleman of Fifty and the Damsel of Nineteen': 'M. de Riverolles, her father, gave her to the Marquis de Marzardouin, a roué young nobleman, immensely rich, and shockingly dissipated. And she married him.' Adiante in *Celt and Saxon* is married to Prince Nikolas Schinder-hannes, an elderly libertine and gambler, who forces her to sell her inherited land in Wales and finance a dynastic lawsuit in which he is engaged. Aminta realizes that her husband, Lord Ormont, 'had no under-standing of how to treat a woman, or belief in her having equal life with him on earth'. In his *Essay on Comedy*, Meredith extolled comedy, taking his examples from Molière and Congreve, as 'the fountain of sound sense', and pointed out: 'Comedy lifts women to a station offering them free play for their wit, as they usually show it, when they have it, on the side of sound sense. The higher the Comedy, the more prominent the part they enjoy in it.' He remarked: 'The poor voice allowed to women in German domestic life will account for the absence of comic dialogues reflecting upon life in that land.' For him, the tales in the *Arabian Nights*, very popular in his time, were devoid of true comedy: 'Where the veil is over women's faces, you cannot have society, without which the senses

X are barbarous and the Comic spirit is driven to the gutters of grossness.'

Meredith's young women seldom have mothers to protect them from being sacrificed. Lucy, Diana and Aminta – and Carinthia from her entry into adult life – are orphans. Emilia, the Fleming sisters, Renée and also Cecilia Halkett in *Beauchamp's Career*, Princess Ottilia, Clara Middleton and also Laetitia Dale in *The Egoist* – all are motherless, and have fathers who are either tyrannical or else ineffective and unhelpful. The picture strains credulity, since there were undoubtedly more widows than widowers in Meredith's time, but it enabled him to highlight the predicament of girls deprived of sympathy or good advice. The only mother who is alive and able to play a positive role is the tolerant and broad-minded Lady Jocelyn, whose support helps Rose to resist marriage to Lord Laxley and finds happiness with Evan. In real life, both Meredith's wives were motherless, since Mary's mother was classified as mad and Marie's was dead, and had fathers reluctant to accept the writer as a son-in-law. Meredith himself, from the age of five, was motherless, like Richard Feverel, Harry Richmond and Nevil Beauchamp. His devotion to the maternal power in Nature, or Earth, had a personal as well as a philosophical meaning.

As he showed time and again in the novels and poems, Meredith responded strongly to feminine beauty. Readers are left in no doubt that Lucy, Rose, Dahlia Fleming, Renée, Diana and Henrietta (in *The Amazing Marriage*) are very beautiful. In *Celt and Saxon*, Patrick does not even need to see Adiante, but is overwhelmed by a portrait:

> Adiante illumined an expanded world for him, miraculous, yet the real one . . . She lifted it out of darkness with swift throbs of her heavenliness as she swam to his eyelids . . . She was bugle, banner, sunrise, of his inmost ambition and rapture.

However, the most beautiful women were not necessarily Meredith's heroines, in the true sense of being heroic. He made it clear that Carinthia was far from being a beauty by the governing standards of the period (and of 'library' fiction). The sophisticated Lady Livia immediately judges that 'no young man would look at her'. If she is sexually attractive, as indeed she is, it is thanks to her readiness to give herself whole-heartedly to the physical aspect of life. Aminta, nicknamed 'Browny' from her complexion, is seen by men as beautiful, but not in a conventional style. What is important in these heroines is that they are strong; their physical strength – exhibited by Carinthia in walking long distances and climbing trees, by Aminta in a marathon feat of swimming – goes together with strength of character. Meredith is reflecting Darwin's belief in 'the vigorous, the healthy and the happy'. These young women are certainly vigorous and healthy, and are destined to be happy when their qualities of self-confidence and courage enable them to break free from the bonds in which they have been confined.

When Meredith described the ecstasies of romantic love, he wrote with zest and evident enjoyment, and was sometimes in danger of slipping into the conventions of 'library' fiction – although another possible reading is that he was parodying that genre. The most notable passage is the love scene between Richard and Lucy:

> 'My own! my own for ever! You are pledged to me? Whisper!'
> He hears the delicious music.
> 'And you are mine?'
> A soft beam travels to the fern-covert under the pine-wood where they sit, and for answer he has her eyes; turned to him an instant, timidly fluttering over the depths of his, and then downcast; for through her eyes her soul is naked to him.
> 'Lucy! my bride! my life!' . . .
> The soft beam travels round them, and listens to their hearts. Their lips are locked.

A dialogue in *Harry Richmond* is in the same vein:

> 'Tell me you love me,' said Heriot.
> 'I do, I do, only don't go,' she answered.
> 'Will you love me faithfully?'
> 'I will; I do.'
> 'Say "I love you, Walter."'
> 'I love you, Walter.'
> 'For ever.'
> 'For ever!'

And here is Wilfrid Pole appealing to Emilia:

> 'I love you now! I wake up in the night, thinking I hear your voice. You haunt me . . . I would do any madness, waste all my blood for you, die for you' . . .
> 'Oh! what can I do for you?' she cried.

'Nothing, if you do not love me,' he was replying mournfully, when 'Yes! yes!' rushed to his lips; 'marry me: marry me tomorrow.'

Yet Meredith is always aware that romantic love can be a trap. The language of 'sentimentalism' was not the language of authentic emotion. Even a reader who is reading *Richard Feverel* for the first time, and does not know how the plot will develop, is likely to sense that something will go wrong and Richard will not be able to sustain his devotion to Lucy. In the second passage quoted above, it is easier to guess that Walter Heriot will drop Julia Rippenger as soon as her admission of love has satisfied his vanity. In the third of these extracts, we can hardly believe that Wilfrid will keep his promise to give up his commission in the Austrian Army for Emilia's sake, and indeed he breaks it. Meredith has already, in an earlier scene between them, given a sardonic pointer to Wilfrid's incapacity for real feeling:

'Whatever you are, you are my dear girl; my own love; mine!' Having said it, he was screwed up to feel it as nearly as possible.

A sceptical attitude to romantic love is summed up in Mrs Berry's terse line in *Richard Feverel*: 'Kissing don't last, cookery do.' When Richard loses the wedding-ring on his way to the wedding, Mrs Berry intuitively discerns a presage of unfaithfulness and she exclaims: 'It's like a divorce, that it is!'

Meredith saw, too, that Victorian sentimentality over romantic love masked a hard-headed grasp of what was socially acceptable and what was not. Austin Wentworth, in *Feverel*, might have been forgiven for yielding to the charms of a housemaid and indulging in an affair with her, but not for marrying her. In a passage cut from later editions, Sir Austin Feverel takes a stern view:

To ally oneself randomly was to be guilty of a crime before Heaven, greater than the offence it sought to extinguish; and he had heard that his nephew was the one seduced. Wherefore he was doubly foolish; a thing in Sir Austin's opinion, he said, almost equal to depravity.

Wentworth has behaved scrupulously, indeed honourably, but this is no excuse. Sir Austin sums up: 'The nobler he, the worse his folly.'

Meredith never wrote more tenderly than when he invoked compassion for a woman who, not being endowed with beauty, is doomed to love in vain. Clare in *Richard Feverel* is hopelessly in love with Richard, her cousin, but she is whisked away from Raynham Abbey with orders to forget about it, and by the time she returns she has lost him to Lucy. Later, she is forced into an arranged marriage with an older, considerably shop-soiled man. On the eve of the wedding, Richard kisses her goodbye:

> He bent his head to meet her mouth, and she threw her arms wildly round him, and kissed him convulsively, and clung to his lips, shutting her eyes, her face suffused with a burning red. Then he left her, unaware of the meaning of those passionate kisses.

She treasures Richard's ring, which she picked up when he carelessly dropped it. Unable to endure life without him, she takes poison and dies, asking in her farewell note to be buried with the ring.

Juliana Bonner in *Evan Harrington* is just as hopelessly in love with Evan, but she is crippled and in delicate health as well as being unattractive. She has no chance of competing with beautiful, healthy, strong-minded Rose; but when Evan is the victim of a false accusation it is Juliana, not Rose, who believes in his innocence. While Rose's love for Evan is real, Juliana's is more completely proof against any wavering. Juliana too dies young. Although she does not literally kill herself like Clare, her resignation in the throes of illness, after making a will that benefits Evan and Rose, is a kind of suicide.

Writing these novels early in his career, Meredith was challenging the convention of virginal innocence by showing that a girl could feel erotic desire which had not been aroused by a man's advances. This, as much as anything else, gave him his reputation as a 'shocking' writer, unsuitable for family reading. And there was another cause for uneasiness. Richard and Evan are, in conventional romantic terms, the heroes of the novels, and one can hardly miss seeing their insensitivity to the feelings of Clare and Juliana.

Implicitly, Meredith was warning young women of the dangers of uncritical devotion. The extreme case of naïveté is Emilia's surrender to Wilfrid, but Emilia is saved by her perception of his dishonesty and by her own growth towards emotional maturity. In Meredith's view, women have a perfect right to make a shrewd judgement of men, and are well advised to do so, while men have no right to complain when their insincerity is detected. In *Richard Feverel*, they are treated to a salutary lecture:

If you fall below the common height of men, you must make up your mind to see her rustle her gown, spy at the looking-glass, and transfer her allegiance. The moral of which is, that if we pretend to be what we are not, women, for whose amusement the farce is performed, will find us out and punish us for it. And it is usually the end of a sentimental dalliance.

More clearly than any other male novelist of his century – though Thackeray and Trollope had comparable insights – Meredith was able to look at men as they were seen by women. 'A man is a savage,' Mrs Berry warns Lucy. Sir Willoughby Patterne wants his betrothed to treat him 'as an original savage'. The word recurs when Carinthia reflects that Fleetwood is blaming her for confronting him with his cruelty to her: 'She bore the blame for forcing him to an examination of his conduct at this point and that, where an ancestral savage in his lineaments cocked a strange eye.' Henrietta, finding the same predatory ruthlessness in Fleetwood and in Lord Brailstone, says: 'There's no mighty difference between one beast of prey and another.' When Fleetwood begins to understand the pain he inflicted on Carinthia, he exclaims: 'How can I describe the man I was! possessed! sort of werewolf.' Darwin had observed in *The Descent of Man*: 'Almost all civilised nations still retain traces of such rude habits as the forcible capture of wives.' In *The Egoist*, Meredith followed Darwin in his description of Sir Willoughby's capture of Clara:

Earlier or later they [women] see that they have been victims of the singular Egoist ... suffered themselves to be dragged ages back in playing upon the fleshly innocence of happy accident to gratify his jealous greed of possession ... The devouring Egoist prefers them as inanimate overwrought polished pure-metal precious vessels, fresh from the hands of the artificer, for him to walk away with hugging, call all his own, drink of, and fill and drink of, and forget that he stole them.

Willoughby is Meredith's most elaborate study in egoism, but there are others: Sir Austin Feverel, Richmond Roy, Percy Dacier in *Diana of the Crossways*, Alvan in *The Tragic Comedians*, Lord Ormont, and finally Fleetwood. Dacier and Alvan exemplify the egoism of the strong, while Willoughby and Wilfrid Pole represent the egoism of the fundamentally weak. Meredith reverted to this theme so often because he recognized egoism as an innate characteristic of the male. Ellis relates a significant incident. When someone complained to Meredith: 'Willoughby is me', Meredith replied: 'No, my dear fellow, he is all of us.'[6]

The obvious signs of egoism are vanity and selfishness; Willoughby and Wilfrid exhibit plenty of both these qualities. When Emilia sheds her illusions about Wilfrid, 'her heart gave her sharp eyes to see into his selfishness'. But egoism has a grimmer aspect, which we now call sadism. When Willoughby sees that Clara is escaping from him, 'desire to do her intolerable hurt became an ecstasy in his veins'. He has fantasies of her suffering through 'an illness, fever, fire, runaway horses, personal disfigurement, a laming'. Woodseer makes a penetrating observation about Fleetwood: 'He coveted beauty in women hungrily, and seemed born to be hostile to them.' Fleetwood, who might in the hands of a lesser novelist have been a one-dimensional villain, is one of Meredith's most complex and contradictory characters. Dame Gossip, a narrative voice in *The Amazing Marriage*, says: 'No one did ever comprehend the Earl of Fleetwood; he was bad, he was good . . . often a devil, sometimes the humanest of creatures.' He is indeed, as he says himself in a flash of introspection, a 'sort of werewolf'.

This depiction of egoism was strong medicine at a time when masculine superiority was taken for granted by all but an exceptional minority of men, along with the right to enforce it. Nevil Beauchamp, though he is the hero of *Beauchamp's Career* and is genuinely in love with Renée, says when he believes that he has captured her: 'She has no wish that is not mine.' Hannah Lynch was interpreting Meredith accurately when she defined male egoism as a weapon of domination. When Fleetwood realizes that he is on the verge of feeling real love for Carinthia and appreciating her qualities, his reaction is to seek a strategy to deal with this new situation: 'He would have to impress his own mysteriously deep character on her portion of understanding. The battle for domination would then begin.'

A Meredith novel is at the same time an illustration of his philosophy, a serious drama, and also a comedy. The first sentence of *The Egoist* begins: 'Comedy is a game played to throw reflections upon social life'. The novel contains scenes – such as Dr Middleton's befuddlement with old port – which are simply very funny; but the test of true comedy, Meredith said in the lecture published as *Essay on Comedy*, 'is that it shall awaken thoughtful laughter'. For Meredith, Molière was the supreme master of comedy because the laughter he awakened was thoughtful. This concept explains the apparently curious title of *The Tragic Comedians*; Alvan and Clotilde are caught up in a drama that ends in tragedy, but the irrationality of their behaviour makes them figures in a comedy. In the lecture, which Meredith gave when he was writing *The Egoist*, he said:

> Whenever they [men] wax out of proportion, overblown, affected, pretentious, bombastical, hypocritical, pedantic, fantastically delicate ... whenever they offend sound reason, fair justice; are false in humility or mined with conceit ... the Spirit overhead will look humanely malign and cast an oblique light on them, followed by volleys of silvery laughter. That is the Comic Spirit.

Willoughby's determination to enforce his will on Clara, regardless of her wishes and at the cost of her happiness, is no laughing matter – for her. But the comic side of his egoism is his ridiculous vanity, developed in his boyhood years:

> He had been once a young Prince in popularity: the world had been his possession ... He had been educated in the belief that Fortune had specially prized and cherished little Willoughby.

Unable to free himself from what can be called, in Freudian language, illusions of omnipotence, Willoughby reaches adult life unequipped to come to terms with the difficulties and disappointments of reality. His vanity is buffeted by one blow after another. Constantia Durham, his first fiancée, runs away to give herself to another man. Then Clara, apparently innocent and submissive, rebels. Compelled to release her, he falls back on Laetitia, the less attractive woman whom he had previously rejected. When even Laetitia will not come to heel, he is so blankly uncomprehending that he can only ask: 'Are you quite well, Laetitia?' Humiliated and panicking, he exclaims: 'I have sacrificed my pride for nothing.' Finally, she agrees to marry him on her own exacting terms, and he must be grateful for what he is allowed. Read as comedy, the downfall of Willoughby is matched only by the downfall of Malvolio, which Meredith may well have had in mind.

'Are you quite well?' ... Willoughby can regain his self-esteem only by assuming that Laetitia is behaving with the foolishness to which women are inherently liable. Masculine contempt for women, especially for their mental capacity, is another recurrent theme in the novels. Clara comes to see that the ideal to which she is expected to conform is 'the common male Egoist ideal of a waxwork sex'. Her father pompously explains to Willoughby (in Clara's presence) that girls 'have neither organs nor arteries, nor brains, nor membranes'. Alvan in *The Tragic Comedians* is desperately keen to marry Clothilde, but is capable of remarking to an older woman: 'After all, it's only a girl.' Wilfrid Pole reproaches himself for taking Emilia seriously: 'Here he was, running after a little unformed girl, who had no care to conceal the fact that she was an animal.' Lord Ormont considers that unconventional ideas are 'womanish, i.e. flighty, gossamer'; and Meredith comments: 'To the host of males, all ideas are female until they are made facts.' Edward Blancove, having made Dahlia Fleming emotionally dependent on him, makes no attempt to conceal his contempt when he writes to her:

> Pray discontinue that talk about the alteration in your looks. You must learn that you are no longer a child. Cease to write like a child . . . Buy nice picture-books, if the papers are too matter-of-fact for you . . . Read poetry, if it makes up for my absence, as you say. Repeat it aloud, minding the pulsation of feet . . . Be an obedient girl and please me.

From Meredith's work, a picture emerges of arrogant men insistent on their authority – sexist men, we say today – who are both shaped by and representative of Victorian upper-class and middle-class society. But Meredith had observed, and occasionally presented, another side to the picture; there were men whose insecurity was so acute that they were afraid of women. Domination had its obverse in the desire to be dominated, and sadism in masochism. In the novella entitled *The Case of General Ople and Lady Camper* (and there may be significance in the word 'case') the relationship of 'a simple man and a complex woman' leads the author to comment:

> Some are captivated by hands that can wield the rod . . . You hear old gentlemen speak fondly of the swish; and they are not attached to pain, but the instrument revives their feeling of youth . . . In the distance, the whip's-end may look like a clinging caress instead of a stinging flick.

Another 'case' is that of Sir Austin Feverel, who recoils from any intimacy with women, as Lady Blandish finds:

> As she spoke she slid down to his feet and pressed his hand to her bosom. The baronet was startled. In very dread of the soft fit that

wooed him, he pushed back his chair, and rose, and went to the window ... From that moment she grew critical of him, and began to study her idol – a process dangerous to idols.

Generally, however, Meredith was concerned with the 'normal man' – as conventionally seen – and with an attitude to women freely voiced over the brandy and cigars. Colonel de Craye in *The Egoist*, 'a sportive gentleman of easy life', classifies women simply: 'Some are flyers and some are runners; these birds are wild on the wing, those expose their bosoms to the shot.' Victor Radnor in *One of Our Conquerors* has a variant on this metaphor: 'There they are, stationary; women the flowers, we the bee; and we are faithful in our seeming volatility; faithful to the hive!' As Meredith comments: 'Victor's opinions were those of the entrenched majority.' Lord Ormont gives his view of women with a guiltless air of stating the obvious: 'She was created to attract the man, for an excellent purpose in the main ... To subdue and bid her minister to our satisfaction is therefore a right employment of man's unperverted superior strength.' Fleetwood, even after he has recognized the enormity of his violent assault on Carinthia, is able to say to her: 'You will overlook, I am sure – well, men are men! – or try to. Perhaps I'm not worse than – we'll say, some.'

Young men were expected to indulge their natural appetites, generally at the expense of girls of inferior social position. When Lady Blandish takes issue with Sir Austin Feverel over his objection to Richard's marriage to Lucy, she asks: 'Say: would you have had him act as young men in his position generally do to young women beneath them?' Yet there was a conflict, which Victorian society never managed to resolve, between an understanding of the impulses of the young men and the value placed on the virginity and purity of girls in danger of being 'ruined'. Dahlia Fleming's father sees irredeemable disaster when she has, as he puts it, 'gone to harlotry in London', and indeed she never recovers from the psychological injury of her seduction by Edward Blancove and his abandonment of her. But Robert Eccles sees the male hypocrisy inherent in a condemnation of Dahlia:

All these false sensations, peculiar to men, concerning the soiled purity of women, the lost innocence, the brand of shame upon her, which are commonly the foul sentimentalism of such as can be too eager in the chase of corruption when occasion suits, and are another side of pruriency, not absolutely foreign to the best of us in our youth – all passed away from him in Dahlia's presence.

[152]

Meredith well understood the force of an erotic passion in transgression of society's rules. The mainspring of *One of Our Conquerors* is the irresistible desire that Victor, as a young married man, felt for Nataly, his wife's companion, which has led him to spend his life with her in a pretended marriage. H. G. Wells, whose desires were just as irrepressible, recalled in his semi-autobiographical novel *The New Macchiavelli* that *One of Our Conquerors* was 'one of the books that have made me' and drew the lesson: 'A people that will not valiantly face and understand and admit love and passion can understand nothing whatever.'

Committed to Nataly, Victor manages to remain faithful to her even when strongly tempted by Lady Grace Halley. Meredith made a clear distinction between the fallible lover of women and the shallow, calculating collector of female flesh. He was inflexible in his denunciation of – and his contempt for – the seducer. From the woman's point of view, the insatiable seducer was the plague of Victorian England, and Meredith's novels are full of angry, mordant portraits: Lord Mountfalcon in *Richard Feverel*, Harry Jocelyn and Drummond Forth in *Evan Harrington*, Captain Gambier in *Emilia*, Walter Heriot in *Harry Richmond*, Comte d'Henriel in *Beauchamp's Career*, Morsfield in *Lord Ormont*, Lord Brailstone in *The Amazing Marriage*. Meredith's attack is directed at their heartlessness, their egoism and their cowardice. Harry Jocelyn is the father of Susan Wheedle's baby, but he takes no responsibility and the truth emerges only when he needs to borrow money to pay her off. Heriot moves on from Julia Rippenger to Mabel Sweetwinter, whom he transfers to Lord Edbury. Meeting him after a number of years, Harry Richmond notes: 'His talk of women still suggested the hawk with the downy feathers of the last little plucked bird sticking to his beak.' Harry is particularly disgusted by Heriot's habit of claiming to be the prey of women, not the predator:

> It was Cissy this, Trichy that, and the wiles of a Florence, the spites of an Agatha, duperies, innocent-seemings, witcheries, reptile-tricks of the fairest of women, all through his conversation . . . He saw the whole of women running or only waiting for a suitable partner to run the giddy ring to perdition and an atoning pathos.

Heriot is the nastiest of the seducers in Meredith's gallery, but others are not entirely devoid of conscience or compassion, and sometimes the lust for possession can be transmuted into love. Lord Mountfalcon gives up his pursuit of Lucy when he sees how gravely he might injure her. Gambier develops an admiring respect for Emilia when he rediscovers her as Vittoria. Blancove, finding that his feelings for Dahlia are deeper than he had imagined, eventually offers to marry her, and after her death he never marries anyone else.

Yet, in the sexual jungle a woman was never safe from the beasts of prey. Sir Lukin Dunstane in *Diana of the Crossways* is no worse than an average upper-class Englishman; having given up his Army career for the sake of his wife, Emma, he is at a loose end and bored; moreover, he is sexually frustrated because of Emma's fragile health. He cannot help being attracted to Diana although she is Emma's best friend, but she is appalled when he makes a pass:

> She found her hand seized – her waist . . . He stammered, pleading across her flying shoulder – Oh! horrible, loathsome, pitiable to hear! 'A momentary aberration . . . her beauty . . . he deserved to be shot! . . . could not help admiring . . . quite lost his head . . . on his honour! never again.'

As Sir Lukin spends much of his time in London while Emma is at their home in Surrey, doubtless this is not his only transgression. When Emma's life is in danger during a serious operation, he bursts out to his friends:

> 'I've been the biggest scoundrel of a husband unhung, and married to a saint; and if she's only saved to me, I'll swear to serve her faithfully . . . Take a warning from me. I've had my lesson.'

Later, when he hears that another man has pestered Diana, he forgets his own behaviour to exclaim: 'When you come to consider the scoundrels men can be, it stirs a fellow's bile.' Then he remembers: 'Oh! I'm a sinner, I know.' Sir Lukin is a comic character, or rather a character in comedy; but the laughter he evokes should be thoughtful.

Women – at least, attractive women – were always under attack, and sometimes they suffered severely; but Meredith does not imply that they are helpless or without resources. Victimized by Fleetwood, Carinthia is sustained by the support of Madge Winch when they leave the prize-fight (a symbol of male brutality) on her wedding day. Fleetwood begins his re-education when reminded of this by Woodseer:

> A thrill of compassionateness traversed him and shot a remorseful sting with the vision of those two young women on the coach at the scene

of the fight. He had sentience of their voices, nigh to hearing them. The forlorn bride's hand given to the anxious girl behind her flashed an image of the sisterhood binding women under the pangs they suffer from men.

The sisterhood of women is, indeed, another of Meredith's recurrent themes. It links Carinthia with Madge (across the class barrier, too) and also with Henrietta; Diana with Emma; Vittoria with Laura Paviani; Aminta with Selina Collett. Sometimes it links women who are supposed to be rivals for a man: Clara and Laetitia in *The Egoist*, Ottilia and Janet in *Harry Richmond*.

Since marriage was the only sexual relationship given the stamp of social approval, the women who are unhappily or naïvely driven into it are balanced in the novels by women who decide on it and get what they want, or rather whom they want. Lady Camper's schemes are aimed at ensuring that General Opie will marry her, and Meredith sums up: 'It came to pass that a simple man and a complex woman fell to union after the strangest division.' When Constance Asper secures a proposal from Percy Dacier, she writes smugly to her ally, Lady Wathin: 'Your prophecy is confirmed.' Meredith's sardonic chapter heading is: 'Reveals how the True Heroine of Romance comes Finally to her Time of Triumph'. Dacier does not love Constance, but at least he has made up his mind to marry her, whereas Wilfrid Pole is thoroughly outmanoeuvred by Lady Charlotte Chillingworth:

He heard the words like the shooting of dungeon-bolts, thinking: 'Oh, heaven! if at the first I had only told the woman I do not love her!' ... The game was now in Lady Charlotte's hands.

Margaret Lovell, the beautiful young widow in *Rhoda Fleming*, would be acting like a 'true heroine of romance' if she agreed to marry Major Waring, who has devotedly loved her for years. But Waring has no serious money, so she prefers Sir William Blancove and announces abruptly: 'I marry the banker.' As a shrewd, sensible woman, she is choosing security and comfort with a husband of the older generation – the choice that, in real life, Janet Duff Gordon made when she married the banker Henry Ross. Writing *Rhoda Fleming* four years after he had lost Janet, Meredith was conceding the woman's right to look after herself and take the best terms that are on offer.

In one way or another, the nineteenth-century woman had to find a survival strategy. One option was to go through life without marriage, and Meredith did not accept the conventional view that a woman who made this choice was necessarily a pitiable 'old maid'. Georgiana Powys in *Vittoria*, who works as a wartime nurse, opts deliberately for a non-sexual way of life that allows her freedom for friendships with men. Aunt Bel in *Evan Harrington*, too, has made a cool decision to remain single and has never regretted it; this is not a matter of lack of opportunity, for she was a beauty when young, nor is it a case of that favourite Victorian cliché, a broken heart. Rose is frankly intrigued:

> 'Aunt Bel! I want to ask you something. We've been making bets about you. Now, answer honestly, we're all friends. Why did you refuse all your offers?'
> 'Quite simple, child,' replied the unabashed ex-beauty. 'A matter of taste. I liked twenty shillings better than a sovereign.'
> Rose looked puzzled, but the men laughed, and Rose exclaimed:
> 'Now I see! How stupid I am! You mean, you may have friends when you are not married.'

Rose is being naïve, but the men can easily see that Aunt Bel has a history of discreet affairs. Discretion was vital; it is permissible for the 'ex-beauty', speaking in retrospect, to drop broad hints, but for a young woman to give an opening to gossip would be far more dangerous. Women who valued their reputation had to be extremely careful, especially if they were engaged or married. When Ottilia travels from Germany to the Isle of Wight to see Harry Richmond, respectable people are horrified at the idea that she is irresistibly drawn to him and relieved to find that she has been tricked into believing that he is dying. When Renée appears unexpectedly in the London house where Nevil is staying, he hastens to find a chaperone for her and goes to spend the night in a hotel. The conventions are perhaps rather difficult for today's readers to grasp. It would be understandable for Renée and Nevil to go off to Greece or Italy – or for Diana and Percy Dacier to go abroad – although they would have burned their boats and excluded themselves from 'society'. But a night together on British ground, if detected, would be judged more harshly.

While Renée can, if careful, preserve her virtuous reputation, Meredith also portrayed women who had forfeited theirs – and acquired a reputation of another kind. He was describing the 'loose women', the 'shameless women', who had such a compelling grip on the Victorian

73, High Street, Portsmouth,
George Meredith's childhood home

Thomas Love Peacock

George Meredith in 1860,
portrait by D G Rossetti

W C Bonaparte Wyse, 1860

Sir William Hardman, the original
of Blackburn Tuckham in
Beauchamp's Career

George Meredith and his son
Arthur, 1862

George Meredith, 1862

'Meredith destroying literary form',
Punch, July 28th, 1894

Frederick Maxse, RN, the original of
Nevil in *Beauchamp's Career*

Interior of the Chalet, showing also the communicating room
where Meredith slept. Meredith by J Thomson on wall, centre

Mary Ellen Meredith 1858.
Drawing by Henry Wallis

1858

Marie Vulliamy 1864.
Drawing by Frederick Sandys

Leslie Stephen. The original of Vernon
Whitford in *The Egoist*. Photograph by
Julia Margaret Cameron

Virginia Woolf
as a young girl

The last sketch of Meredith. By the French artist Noël Dorville

Flint Cottage. Photograph by Mervyn Jones

imagination. Generally they were married, though unhappily so and living apart from their husbands; unlike the victims of seduction, such as poor Mabel Sweetwinter, they came from a middle-class or even upper-class background; they formed a society or sisterhood of their own, distinct from 'society' as officially defined. In Meredith's accounts, the transgressions of the wives are a reaction to – perhaps even a retaliation for – those of the husbands. Lord Mountfalcon has behaved quite as badly as his estranged wife, who calls herself Mrs Mount; in *Lord Ormont*, Mrs Lawrence Finchley and Mrs Amy May are the unfaithful wives of unfaithful husbands. As the law then stood, a husband could divorce a wife if he could prove adultery, while wives had no such recourse. It is Lord Ormont, always tolerant of the misdemeanours of an attractive woman (except, of course, his own wife), who provides a defence of Mrs Lawrence Finchley:

> She concealed what it was decent to conceal, without pouting hypocritical pretences; she had merely dispensed with idle legal formalities, in the prettiest curvetting airy wanton way, to divorce the man who tried to divorce her.

Bella Mount's frank sexuality, free of 'hypocritical pretences', is shown as a contrast to Lucy Feverel's innocence. Helplessly succumbing to Bella, Richard persuades himself that he is trying to reclaim her for virtue; Meredith presumably knew about Mr Gladstone's strange prowls round the West End streets. Bella is naturally amused and plays games that soon have him out of his depth. But Bella, capable of real affection as well as sexual skill, winds up out of her depth too:

> Various as the Serpent of old Nile, she acted fallen beauty, humorous indifference, reckless daring, arrogance in ruin. And acting thus, what think you? – She did it so well because she was growing half in earnest.

Soon it is more serious for her than for him:

> Lost, Richard! Lost for ever! give me up!'
> He cried 'I never will!' and strained her in his arms, and kissed her passionately on the lips. She was not acting now as she sidled and slunk her half-averted head with a kind of maiden shame under his arm, sighing heavily, weeping, clinging to him. It was wicked truth.

By refusing to go away to Sussex and plunge into living with Richard, Bella saves his marriage. Richard is a dubious hero, but the novel has two heroines – Lucy and Bella.

Judith Marsett, too, tries to safeguard an innocent young woman, writing to Nesta Radnor: 'I entreat you not to notice me, if you pass me on the road again. Let me drop, never mind how low I go. I was born to be wretched.' But Nesta – repudiating innocence to claim a place as a 'new woman', of the type emerging when Meredith wrote *One of Our Conquerors* in 1890 – offers Judith her friendship.

Over the span of Meredith's career, attitudes were changing. Mrs Lawrence Finchley could be described as 'an example to the English of the punishment they get for their stupid Puritanic tyranny'. When Matthew Weyburn and Aminta decide to live together without marriage, he can reassure her: 'There are hints of humaner opinions; it's not all a huge rolling block of a Juggernaut. Our case could be pleaded before it. I don't think the just would condemn us heavily.' *Lord Ormont* was published in the same year as *The Woman Who Did*, by Meredith's friend Grant Allen, a challenging defence of a woman who lives openly with her lover and bears his child. Hardy's *Jude the Obscure* followed in the next year, 1896. The way was being cleared for Wells and Forster, even for Lawrence.

The change was connected with the gradual recognition that a woman could possess an intellectual capacity equal to that of a man. By the closing decades of the century, men who patronized women in the style of Sir Willoughby Patterne or Lord Ormont were coming to be regarded as survivors from a benighted past. There were now women doctors (a few), women graduates (especially from the pioneering University College, London) and women like Octavia Hill and Lady Burdett-Coutts who had shown their ability in the sphere of philanthropy and social reform. Welcoming this change, Meredith notably advanced it by drawing portraits of intelligent, serious-minded women, such as Laetitia Dale in *The Egoist*, Jenny Denham and Cecilia Halkett in *Beauchamp's Career*, Aminta in *Lord Ormont*. It helped, admittedly, if the woman to be thus admired could be admired for her physical attractions too. Captain O'Donnell in *Celt and Saxon* grows eloquent in his praise of Adiante:

She's that fiery dragon, a beautiful woman with brains – which Helen of Troy hadn't, combustible as we know her to have been: but brains are bombshells in comparison with your old-fashioned pine-brands for kindling men and cities.

It was in *Diana of the Crossways* that Meredith made a 'beautiful woman with brains' the central character. Diana Warwick was modelled, with little disguise, on Caroline Norton, a woman whose life-story must have been familiar to all his readers. Irish by birth, and a granddaughter of the playwright Richard Brinsley Sheridan, she was married at the age of nineteen to the wealthy George Norton. He subjected her to acute unhappiness, to quarrels exacerbated by his heavy drinking, and sometimes to physical brutality. After nine years of marriage she left him, taking their two sons. By this time, because Norton was also mean and kept her short of money, she was writing popular, lightweight poems and plays. Since Norton was also an MP, Caroline's dinner-parties in Storey's Gate, a few minutes' walk from the Houses of Parliament, attracted visitors from the political as well as the literary world, including the Prime Minister, Lord Melbourne, who sometimes stayed late and was alone with her. Norton brought a lawsuit charging Melbourne with 'criminal conversation' (then the legal term for sex) with his wife. Though Melbourne was cleared, such an accusation against the Prime Minister was of course sensational and left Caroline with a reputation as a seductress. In 1845 she figured in another scandal: the decision by Sir Robert Peel, now the Tory Prime Minister, to repeal the Corn Laws and split his party was leaked to *The Times* – perhaps by Caroline, as a member of Peel's Cabinet was her lover. By producing a stream of pamphlets on controversial issues, as well as three novels, she stayed in the public eye until her death in 1877.

Meredith had been introduced to Caroline Norton by Lady Duff Gordon. Despite her literary ambitions and his taste for the company of women of strong personality, they did not make friends. She suspected him, rightly, of quarrying for information about her life for use in fiction; he thought that, though witty and charming, she had a shallow mind and her constant chatter could be tedious (an opinion shared by others). When Caroline Norton became Diana Warwick, Meredith confided to Robert Louis Stevenson: 'I have had to endow her with brains.'[7]

Though she lived in the period that saw the first wave of feminism in Britain, Caroline Norton cannot be defined as a feminist. She made a disclaimer in one of her pamphlets: 'The wild and stupid theories advanced by a few women, of "equal rights" and "equal intelligence", are not the opinions of their sex. I, for one (I, with millions more) believe in the natural superiority of man.' However, she was ready to do battle of two issues. One was the right to care for her children and keep them with her; a father, under the prevailing law, was free to whisk children away from their mother. The other issue was a wife's right to control money; marriage, at that time, gave a husband possession of any money that a wife might have, whether inherited from her parents or earned by her exertions. Caroline complained: 'God gave me the power of writing ... [but] my husband has a legal copyright of my works.'[8] The injustice was remedied, thanks in part to Caroline's campaigning, by the passage of a Married Women's Property Act in 1882.

Diana, as Meredith's heroine, is forthright in her protests and demands, defying the male sex in these words: 'Give us the means of independence, and we will gain it, and have a turn at judging you, my lords! You shall behold a world reversed.'

While Caroline Norton was concerned with a woman's right to the money gained by her talents, for instance as writer or artist, Diana broadens the issue to the entry of women in general to the world of work. She is heartened when she hears that a lawyer 'expects the day to come when women will be encouraged to work at crafts and professions for their independence'.

In Meredith's narrative, Diana's life closely follows Caroline's. Young and inexperienced, she marries Augustus Warwick with no knowledge of his real character. He is never presented to the reader – it is unusual for Meredith to keep an important character off-stage – and Diana's experience is outlined in brief summary: 'Her dissensions with her husband, their differences of opinion, and puny wranglings, hoistings of two standards, reconciliations for the sake of decency, breaches of the truce, and his detested meanness.' After the separation, she has to reflect that she is 'a wife and no wife, a prisoner in liberty' (then the official term for release on licence). Even the passage of the Divorce Act of 1857 brings no relief, since judgements are in the hands of all-male jurists. Diana interprets their attitudes:

Is it a suit for divorce? – Well, we have wives of our own, and we can lash, or we can spare; that's as it may be; but we'll keep the couple tied, let 'em hate as they like, if they can't furnish pork-butchers' reasons for sundering; because the man makes the money in this country.

Diana has an imprudent friendship with Lord Dannisborough (Melbourne), Warwick brings his vindictive lawsuit, and Diana is loved by Percy Dacier, Dannisborough's nephew, a rising star in the Tory Party. After the crisis over the newspaper leak – Dacier has confided the political secret to Diana – the relationship crashes. Meredith deepens the Caroline

Norton story by his analysis of Diana's character and her predicament. Like Emila growing into Vittoria, like Aminta, like Carinthia, Diana is a naïve girl moving towards self-realization as a woman. The key passage reads:

> The strong pure ecstasy was not a transient electrification; it came on waves on a continuous tide; looking was living, walking flying . . . To be a girl was magical. She could fancy her having risen from the dead. And to be a girl, with a woman's broader vision and receptiveness of soul, with knowledge of evil, and winging to ethereal happiness, this was a revelation of our human powers.

But the conflict is between Diana's pride in her independence and her possible commitment to Percy. Today, the successful popular novelist, estranged from her husband, and the noteworthy politician would be known as 'an item' and few eyebrows would be raised. It was very different in the nineteenth century; Diana does not have the bold carelessness of a Mrs Lawrence Finchley, let alone a Bella Mount. A feasible option for lovers is to go abroad – Meredith may have been thinking of his own wife and Henry Wallis – and Diana agrees to this course on Percy's urging, but does not carry it through. True, she has to change plans because of the sudden news of Emma Dunstane's illness, but this plot device masks a real reluctance on Diana's part. Earlier, a snatch of dialogue reveals that she recoils from Percy's demanding male sexuality:

> 'The woman I want, the only woman I could marry, I can't have.'
> 'You have her in soul.'
> 'Body and soul, it must be! I believe you were made without fire.'

In fact, Diana has been wounded – one might even say sexually anaesthetized – by her early experiences. Emma guesses accurately:

> Lady Dunstane conceived that the unprotected beautiful girl had suffered a persecution, it might be an insult. She spelt over the names of the guests at the houses. Lord Wroxeter was of evil report; Captain Rampan, a Turf captain, had the like notoriety . . . There were, one hears that there still are, remnants of the pristine male . . . whose 'passion for the charmer' is an instinct to pull down the standard of the sex, by a bully imposition of sheer physical ascendancy, whenever they see it flying with an air of gallant independence.

Though Emma does not know it, persecution also comes from her own husband, Sir Lukin. In search of safety, Diana marries Warwick, only to find that a wife can be subjected to worse brutalities than a girl. When she frees herself from Warwick, or at least becomes a 'prisoner in liberty', Percy comes on the scene. He is no brute, but she sees the insistent lover as a possessive male in another guise. It has become impossible for her to give herself 'body and soul' to him or to anyone else. The only emotional bond that presents no threat is with another woman – Emma.

Emma, a few years older than Diana, is taking shape as a character that Meredith drew with respect and affection: the wise, observant, sympathetic woman whose role is to supply reliable advice. This is the role of Lady Blandish in *Richard Feverel*, Lady Jocelyn in *Evan Harrington*, Aunt Dorothy in *Harry Richmond*, Rosamund in *Beauchamp's Career*, Baroness von Crefeldt in *The Tragic Comedians*. Sometimes, an older woman exerts her authority to put a stop to a love affair deemed to be unsuitable: the Margravine will not let Harry Richmond win Ottilia, Madame d'Auffray will not allow an illicit romance between Nevil and Renée. But (if we make an exception for the comically drawn aunts in *One of Our Conquerors*) Meredith does not portray the older woman as a dried-up prude with a horror of sexual emotion. Lady Blandish tries to allure Sir Austin Feverel and draw him out of his misogyny; Rosamund is happy to marry the Earl of Romfrey when she gets the chance; the Baroness is 'still good friends' with Alvan, her former lover.

Although Meredith could warn of the pitfalls of romantic love, he could also show the retreat from love as the most tragic of missed opportunities. For women as much as for men, the indispensable quality is courage. Constantia Durham, and then Clara Middleton, have the courage to break away from Sir Willoughby; Aminta has the courage to break away from her husband and commit herself to her lover. By contrast, Renée cannot make the break, and flinches from the appeal by Nevil that is also a challenge:

'Have you courage? that's the question . . . Own me, break the chains, come to me; say, Nevil Beauchamp or death! . . . No heart to dare is no heart to love! – answer that! Shall I see you cower away from me again?' . . .

Beauchamp might believe he had prevailed with her, but for her forlorn repetition of the question: 'Have I courage, Nevil?'

So Renée does not dare to commit herself irretrievably to Nevil, nor

Ottilia to Harry, nor Clothilde to Alvan. In each case, the woman is the aristocrat and the venturesome lover is unacceptable to the head of the titled family. In each case, too, the lover is seen as an alien. Nevil is English while Renée is French, Harry is English while Ottilia is German, Alvan (as a Jew) is not considered to be a true German. The courage that is lacking is the courage to defy the rigidity of prejudice.

Diana, however, cannot be fitted so clearly into this classification. Would it be more courageous for her to elope with Percy when she is legally Mrs Warwick, or to preserve her independence when tempted by love? Meredith leaves the question open.

Nataly in *One of Our Conquerors* throws a different light on the problem. As a young woman in love, she has agreed to live with Victor, knowing that he is a married man. But she has been drawn into this decision by Victor's forceful demand, rather than by her own courage. Aware that she is 'a woman little adapted for the post of rebel', Nataly plays a role for which she is quite unequipped. For the rest of her life, she is tormented by the consciousness of her transgression and the pretences required to cover it. As Alice Woods commented: 'In her worship of Victor she has been, as she herself acknowledges, slave not helper. She has given him her life, but it has not saved him.'[9] For Victor is no more 'adapted for the post of rebel' than Nataly; the irony (or, in the Meredithian sense, comedy) of the novel lies in the fact that these transgressors of convention are both conventional people.

Victor's legal wife, Mrs Burman Radnor, is also a 'slave of existing conventions' and refuses to agree to a divorce. Reading the novel as a young man, H. G. Wells was appalled by its depiction of 'terrible inflexibility'. Release for Victor and Nataly can come only from Mrs Burman's death – she is old and in fragile health – and Victor makes no secret of his 'wrath at the crippled woman who would not obey the dictate of her ailments instantly to perish and spare this dear one annoyance'. Victor's (and apparently Meredith's) lack of any compassion for Mrs Burman, whose life has after all been lonely and empty, can be called heartless, but it stems from his conviction that his love for Nataly is natural, while Mrs Burman's tenacity contravenes the 'laws of nature'. The 'terrible inflexibility' is really that of social convention, which Victor cannot overtly defy. His impatience for Mrs Burman to die contrasts with the calmness of Matthew and Aminta in *Lord Ormont*; as liberated lovers, they can wait contentedly for Aminta's husband to live out his span.

Throughout his creative life, all the way from *Evan Harrington* to *The Amazing Marriage*, Meredith reiterated that women were doomed to stunted

[163]

lives unless they could find and develop resources of strength. The point was grasped by a few critics; as early as 1864, the *Westminster Review*, published an article by Justin McCarthy headed 'Novels with a Purpose', which praised *Richard Feverel*, *Emilia* and Caroline Norton's *Lost and Saved*. He wrote:

> Women have especial need, as the world goes, to be shrewd, self-reliant and strong; and we do all we can in our literature to render them helpless, imbecile and idiotic. We [an authorial 'we'] are therefore disposed to give a friendly reception to George Meredith and Mrs Norton, were it for nothing but the mere fact that conventionality might be inclined to shriek against them.

Women were on the threshold of a revolt against male domination which was encouraged by the publication in 1869 of John Stuart Mill's *The Subjection of Women* – a book that Meredith read with enthusiasm – and which gradually gained force in the last quarter of the century. In the 1870s, Meredith was planning two challenging novels: *The Egoist*, published in 1879, and *The Amazing Marriage*, laid aside to be resumed later and eventually published in 1895. In 1876, he used the more direct literary form of poetry to write 'A Ballad of Fair Ladies in Revolt'. The poem is a dialogue in alternating verses between a group of women and a group of rather bewildered men who are trying to understand what the revolt is all about. One man warns a woman that, by promoting antagonism, she risks forfeiting 'much honour and much glory'. She retorts:

> Sir, was it glory, was it honour, pride,
> And not as cat and serpent and poor slave,
> Wherewith we walked in union by your side?
> Spare to false womanliness her delicacy,
> Or bid true manliness give ear, we crave:
> In our defence thus chained are we.

The man says dismissively:

> You are few,
> Scattered, ill-counselled, blinded: for a proof,
> I have lived, and have known none like you.

But the woman tells him:

[164]

We may be blind to men, sir: we embrace
A future now beyond the fowler's nets.
Though few, we hold a promise for the race
That was not at our rising: you are free
To win brave mates; you lose but marionettes.
    He who's for us, for him are we.

The novel that expands this trumpet-call to symphonic length, *The Egoist*, could have been called 'The Revolt of Clara Middleton'. The need to assert herself as an independent personality dawns on Clara when she finds herself critical of Willoughby over his treatment of the boy Crossjay Patterne. Willoughby perceives the seeds of revolt:

Was it possible he did not possess her utterly? He frowned up.
Clara saw the lift of his brows, and thought: 'My mind is my own, married or not.'
It was the point in dispute.

Realizing that she is trapped by her engagement, she does not yet hope to escape:

She was a captured woman, of whom it is absolutely expected that she must submit, and when she would rather be gazing at flowers. Clara had shame of her sex. They cannot take a step without becoming bondwomen; into what a slavery! For herself, her trial was over, she thought . . . She could hardly be said to complain. She did but criticise him and wonder that a man was unable to perceive, or was not arrested by perceiving, unwillingness, discordance, dull compliance; the bond-woman's due instead of the bride's consent.

It is through a casual conversation, in which Clara learns the word 'egoist', that she becomes aware of Willoughby's real character, of his breathtaking vanity and insensitivity, and hence of the disaster inherent in marriage to him. Willoughby himself says jocularly: 'Beware of marrying an Egoist, my dear!'

He bowed gallantly; and so blindly fatuous did he appear to her, that she could hardly believe him guilty of uttering the words she had heard from him . . . Sir Willoughby had positively said beware! Marrying him would be a deed committed in spite of his express warning.

[165]

From this time, she cannot bear to think of the approaching marriage, and reveals this to Colonel de Craye (they are out riding) when he asks who the bridesmaids will be. The cynical, experienced de Craye has his eye on Clara for himself, and is goading her into admitting what he has guessed. He asks:

'Do all the bridesmaids decline?'
'The scene is too ghastly.'
'A marriage?'
'Girls have grown sick of it.'
'Of weddings? We'll overcome the sickness' . . .
'Marriage!' exclaimed Clara, dashing into the ford, fearful of her ungovernable wildness and of what it might have kindled.

This is a crucial turning-point, not only in the narrative of *The Egoist*, but in Meredith's vision. Hitherto, he had protested against enforced, loveless marriages, such as Renée's marriage to the repulsive Marquis. Now, for the first time, he cast doubt on marriage in general. Clara does not fully realize what she has said, and it leaves her fearful; but Meredith has written it. As the novel goes on, we see Willoughby not only refusing to release Clara and determined to keep her as his 'captured woman', but also determined *to be married*, and thus to uphold this essential social institution. When Clara, mustering all her courage, does break free, he decides that he can at least marry Laetitia, only to find that she is not automatically available. Desperate, Willoughby no longer lays claim to love, as he did with Clara, and pleads with Laetitia: 'Love me or not, but marry me.' For the egoist, love is the desirable optional extra, but marriage – in effect, possession – is indispensable.

After *The Egoist*, Meredith's next novel was *The Tragic Comedians*. It can well be judged as the least successful of his novels, largely because it adhered too closely to events in real life. He had read the memoirs of Helene von Dönniges, an aristocratic German lady who had fallen in love with a Socialist leader, Ferdinand Lassalle. Lassalle was killed in a duel with another suitor of Helene's, Prince Racowitza, and she then married the Prince – a denouement more credible in reality (for in reality nothing is incredible) than in fiction, which has its own laws of probability. Still, Meredith was able to write another study in a young woman's self-realization, when it occurs to Clotilde (Helene) that she is not obliged to marry either the dominating Count Constantine or the weak, inadequate Prince Marko (Racowitza):

She caught a glorious image of the woman rejecting him [Marko] and his rival, and it informed her that she, dissatisfied with an Adonis, and more than a match for a famous conqueror, was a woman of decisive and independent, perhaps unexampled, force of character.

Clotilde overestimates herself; when she comes under pressure, her force of character does not suffice for her to defy prejudice and commit herself to Alvan (Lassalle), the man forbidden to her by her family. She ends up, after her bid for independence, as the wife of Prince Marko. Another would-be rebel has submitted to marriage. Yet we are left with the knowledge that Clotilde's love for Alvan has been the supreme experience of her life, and that marriage can only be a diminishing aftermath.

Five years later, Meredith wrote *Diana of the Crossways*. This novel is both more and less than an attack on marriage; Diana's marriage to Warwick is obviously a disaster, like Renée's marriage to the Marquis, but her years as 'wife and no wife' make it possible for her to evade a judgement on marriage as an institution. At the end of the novel, and directly after the collapse of her relationship with Percy, Warwick's sudden death leaves her free to marry Tom Redworth, who has loved her since her girlhood. Redworth, described as 'a right good unimpulsive gentleman' (unlike Percy), presents no threat of cruelty or domination, so the question of whether Diana should marry him is unavoidably a question of her attitude to marriage itself. Emma – an unambiguous believer in marriage, despite Sir Lukin's shortcomings – overcomes Diana's hesitations, though Diana exclaims in dismay: 'But marriage, dear Emmy! marriage! Is marriage to be the end of me?' Diana surrenders, but without illusions: 'I am going into slavery to make amends for presumption. Banality, thy name is marriage!' Meredith concludes: 'So, then, this union, the return to the wedding-yoke, received sanction of grey-toned reason.'

With *Lord Ormont*, Meredith's critique of marriage becomes more emphatic, though it is made through an irony. Aminta is concerned to establish the validity of her marriage, since the actual ceremony in the British Embassy in Madrid could be regarded as a fiction and Lord Ormont's sister, Lady Constance Eglett, insists on believing that Aminta is no more than a mistress; on the other hand, she is driven by Lord Ormont's refusal to take her seriously to the conclusion that the marriage has no real moral value. She has to reflect: 'Her title was Lady Ormont, her condition actually slave.' Married as a girl, and viewing her husband – a military hero – with respect and admiration, she comes with emotional maturity to see the deprivation inherent in this marriage:

She had not known love; she was in her five-and-twentieth year, and love was not only unknown to her, it was shut away from her by the lock of a key that opened on no estimable worldly advantage in exchange, but opened on a dreary, clouded round, such as she had used to fancy it must be to the beautiful creamy circus-horse of the tossing mane and flowing tail and superb step. She was admired; she was just as much doomed to a round of paces, denied the glorious fling afield, her nature's food.

What is desolating, Meredith points out, is that conventional society, while perhaps condemning the monstrous egotism of a Willoughby Patterne or the brutality of an Augustus Warwick, sees nothing wrong with the subjection of the average wife:

We forget her having been conceived in the fear of men, shaped to gratify them. She is their fiction of the state they would fain beguile themselves to suppose her sex has reached, for their benefit; where she may be queen of it in a corner, certain of a loyal support, if she will only give men her half-the-world's assistance to uplift the fabric comfortable to them; together with assurance of paternity, ease of mind in absence, exclusive possession, enormous and minutest, etc; not by any means omitting a regimental orderliness, from which men are privately exempt, because they are men, or because they are grown boys — the brisker at lessons after a vacation or a truancy, says the fiction.

The observation that men are 'grown boys' recalls the explanation of Willoughby Patterne's immaturity — 'he had been once a young Prince in popularity' in *The Egoist*. It recalls, too, Meredith's criticism of the separate upbringing of boys and girls: young men are taught to assume that they are entitled to domination, young women that they are destined to submission.

Pampered but also despised by her husband, imprisoned in luxurious idleness, conscious of the absence of love, and harried by would-be seducers, Aminta ponders on marriage, which — so she was led to believe as a girl — was supposed to bring happiness:

That institution of Marriage was eyed. Is it not a halting step to happiness? It is the step of a cripple . . . The conditions are denied to women by Marriage – denied to the luckless of women, who are many, very many.

By conventional standards, Aminta would be considered lucky, not luckless; an orphan without prospects, she has been married to a distinguished man who protects and indulges her. But she thinks of her sisters and echoes Clara Middleton's question: 'What of wives miserably wedded?' She moves towards a rejection of the whole 'institution', as Diana did in reflecting: 'It was her marriage; it was marriage in the abstract: her own mistake and the world's clumsy machinery of civilisation.'

Aminta wins through when she finds that Matthew Weyburn can give her, not only love and sexual fulfilment, but also a partnership (without marriage) based on equality and respect for her personality. She leaves Ormont with dignity and without bitterness, telling him in her farewell letter: 'The release is yours.' But she lets him know clearly: 'I, too, am sensible of the release. My confession of a change of feeling to you as a wife, writes the close of all relations between us.'

We have to imagine ourselves living in the nineteenth century to realize how many women wished to write such a letter and were unable to. By comparison with Clara, Aminta has got away easily; she has not suffered as Renée suffered. In fact, *Lord Ormont* is a relatively painless book. Meredith's last indictment of marriage as an institution and as a human experience, *The Amazing Marriage*, is much more painful and – since it describes an extreme case of male cruelty and egoism – much more dramatic. But, like *Lord Ormont*, it works through an irony. Carinthia, in her naïveté, begins by idealizing marriage, while Fleetwood attaches no value to his marriage until he is losing it. Just as much as Aminta – more so, indeed, since she is 'a plain girl' – Carinthia, another orphan without prospects, is lucky to find herself the bride of the richest man in England. In the first moments after the wedding, she is deliriously happy:

This Carinthia, suddenly wedded, passionately grateful for humbleness exalted, virginly sensible of treasures of love to give, resembled the inanimate and most inspiring . . . Her blood rather than recollection revived their exchanges during the dance at Baden, for assurance that their likings were one, their aims rapturously one; that he was she, she he, the two hearts making one soul.

A few pages later, Meredith writes: 'Marriage is our incubus now.' The statement summarizes the realization arrived at by one Meredith heroine

after another: Clara, Renée, Diana, Aminta. But here it is Fleetwood
who groans under the incubus: 'The spiteful hag of power ties a wife to
us . . . Wives are just as inexplicable curses, just as ineradicable and
astonishing as humps imposed on shapely backs.'

As viewed by conventional society, Carinthia is so unfitted to be Fleetwood's wife that there can be no rational explanation for her success in
ensnaring him:

> She is not a person of society, lineage? Nor of beauty. She is a witch;
> ordinarily petticoated and not squeaking like a shrew-mouse in her
> flights, but not a whit less a moon-shade witch . . . She is the created
> among women armed with the deadly instinct for the motive force in
> men, and shameless to attract it . . . Her infinitesimal spells are seen;
> yet, despite experience, the magnetism in their repulsive display is
> barely apprehended by sedate observers until the astounding capture
> is proclaimed.

From the morrow of the wedding, Fleetwood acts to shatter Carinthia's
illusions, to show that their likings and aims are opposed, and to prevent
the marriage from becoming a reality. The title of the novel embodies
another irony: the marriage is amazing because it has so improbably
happened, but also because – with Carinthia discarded and reduced to
find shelter in the poverty of Whitechapel – the situation is glaringly
inappropriate for the woman who is, after all, Lady Fleetwood. Of course,
it is a sensation:

> So talked, so twittered, piped and croaked the London world over the
> early rumours of the marriage, this Amazing Marriage; which it got
> to be called, from the number of items flocking to swell the wonder.

Then Carinthia changes. Other Meredith heroines grow into self-
realization; Carinthia is driven into it as the price of survival. When
Fleetwood meets her again, he can barely recognize the adoring bride
who was willing to submit to a brutal rape with the incantation: 'It is my
husband.'

> By singular transformation since . . . she had become a personage . . .
> Her aspect was entirely different; her attitude toward him as well:
> insomuch that he had to chain her to her original features by the

conjuring of recollected phrases memorable for the vivid portraiture of her foregone simplicity and her devotion to 'my husband.'

For some time, Carinthia's wish is to regain the marriage – to be granted a home with her husband and a money allowance in the proper manner. But when this is refused her, she echoes Aminta in claiming her release and asserting 'the close of all relations'. The tables are turned, and Fleetwood is the one pleading for concessions. After she is given a home in one of his country mansions, she grants him entry as a guest and refuses to sleep with him, confronting him with the resolute phrase: 'I guard my rooms.' Fleetwood is forced to admit that he must respect her. 'The very word "respect" pitched him upon her character; to see it a character that emerged beneath obstacles, and overcame ridicule, won suffrages, won a reluctant husband's admiration.'

Pressed by Woodseer, he confesses: 'I did her a wrong.' But she is in no hurry to forgive him:

> She, with no idea of benignness, might speak pardon's word to him, on a late autumn evening years hence, perhaps, or to his friends tomorrow, if he would considerately keep distant.

The marriage is over. Carinthia's only remaining ties are with her child (the legacy of the rape) and her brother, Chillon. Chillon is going to fight in a civil war in Spain and Carinthia decides to go with him as a wartime nurse (like Georgiana Powys in Italy). She tells Fleetwood:

> 'I have my freedom, and am thankful for it, to follow my brother, to share his dangers with him. That is more to me than luxury and the married state. I take only my freedom.'

While Aminta was on centre-stage more often than Lord Ormont, in *The Amazing Marriage* the character most carefully analysed is Fleetwood. The novel could perhaps have been called 'The Education of Lord Fleetwood'. Step by step, Meredith describes his arrogance and brutality, his painful progress towards repentance under the influence of Woodseer, his eventual redemption, and his final incarnation as 'Brother Russett' in a monastery. By the end, he is able not only to bow in admiration to Carinthia, but even to grasp the wider implications – 'This woman protected her whole sex,' he reflects. And: 'Women, then, are really half the world in power as much as in their number, if men pretend to a step above the savage.' Perhaps, in this last novel, Meredith was reckoning the liberation of women as an ensured prospect for the twentieth century, and turning his attention to the effect on men.

Read as they must have been by many women, Meredith's novels offer a sustained and formidable attack on marriage. Yet, for all their bitter experiences and clear insights, the heroines do end up at the altar. Rhoda Fleming, who has been strongly critical of Robert and accepted him, at best, as a useful friend, finally marries him – a fact that Meredith notes tersely and casually on the last page. Clara, forgetting her scornful declaration that 'girls have grown sick of it', marries Vernon Whitford. Diana marries Redworth. Clotilde marries Prince Marko. Carinthia, after stating firmly that the only man who can have any importance in her life is her brother, marries Owain Wythan, as we learn from another summary note on the last page.

Not surprisingly, Meredith has been posthumously reproached by the feminist Alice Woods and the Marxist Jack Lindsay. On Carinthia's marriage to Wythan, Woods commented: 'It is difficult to reconcile the action with the character of our brave, fearless, firm-willed Carinthia Jane.'[10] Lindsay wrote more sharply: 'What spoils *Diana* is . . . the final abandonment of any struggle against the society that has twisted her; she merely succumbs to a conventional marriage . . . A conclusion acceptable to the middle-class public.'[11]

Defences can be found. With his retiring nature and his total lack of egoism, Whitford is a man whom Clara has no need to fear, and she pursues him rather than the other way round. Diana recognizes Redworth as the man she ought to have married, had he asked her, in the first place; she has cause to be grateful to him, since he has helped her at crucial moments and secured her beloved home, Crossways, for her; and the scale is turned by Emma's affectionate pressure. In *The Tragic Comedians*, Meredith boxed himself into a corner by his fidelity to real events (the novel is subtitled 'A Study in a Well-Known Story'). Carinthia yields to 'the beseeching applicant for her hand', Wythan, 'in compassion', remembering the frustration of his childless, practically sexless, first marriage. We have to bear in mind Carinthia's suitability for motherhood on Darwinian principles. Still, her surrender to Wythan contradicts the lessons that we are entitled to find in *The Amazing Marriage*, as well as being a clumsy and unconvincing last-minute twist to the plot. Despite his contempt for 'library fiction', Meredith laid himself open to the charge of adopting that most hackneyed device, the artificial happy ending. The reason must be sought in an ambiguity in his view of marriage which he never quite resolved. Marriage as he observed it, and indeed described it, was often atrocious, hypocritical, and grossly unjust to women – yet he could not relinquish the belief that it could be a mutually rewarding partnership of equals. The ambiguity was rooted, probably, in his memories of his first marriage, which turned out to be a miserable failure but might have been a brilliant success.

Meredith was merciless in dissecting the tyrannical, egotistical man who dominated the scene (and so many unhappy homes) in his time: Sir Austin Feverel, Sir Willoughby Patterne, Lord Ormont, Lord Fleetwood. The balance was redressed by portraits of men like Major Waring in *Rhoda Fleming*, Merthyr Powys in *Vittoria*, Vernon Whitford, Tom Redworth, Matthew Weyburn, Gower Woodseer; men who are understanding and considerate towards women, emancipated from the prevailing crudities and prejudices, and (in today's language) non-sexist. Midway between the extremes is Percy Dacier; he is aggressive in his sexuality and self-centred in his career ambitions, but makes an effort to respect Diana's autonomy and admires her achievement as a writer. The most interestingly developed of these portraits is that of Dartrey Fenellan, who makes the right impression on the 1890s 'new woman', Nesta Radnor, after she has contemptuously rejected her conventional suitors. Fenellan, whose wife has died after a successful marriage, is scornful of promiscuity and casual seduction, though aware that he is attractive to women. It is Judith Marsett, the 'fallen woman' victimized by men, who perceives that she can respect and trust him:

> She liked his manner with her. Not a doubt was there, that he read her position. She could impose upon some: not upon masculine eyes like these. They did not scrutinize, nor ruffle a smooth surface with a snap at petty impressions; and they were not cynically intimate or dominating or tentatively amorous; clear good fellowship was in them. And it was a blessedness (whatever might be her feeling later, when she came to thank him at heart) to be in the presence of a man whose appearance breathed of offering her common ground, whereon to meet and speak together, unburdened by the hunting world, and by the stoning world.

While Meredith stigmatized the evil in sexist men, he was not blind to the failings or inadequacies of his non-sexist men. Major Waring and Tom Redworth are thoroughly decent, honourable men, but it is hard not to find them uninspiring, even boring; we can see why the good

Major did not excite the lively Margaret Lovell. Vernon Whitford's cautiousness in relations with women, which puzzles Clara and provokes her impatience, reveals an inhibited personality. Although Woodseer is courageous in confronting Fleetwood and his insights are perceptive, he is also sententious and priggish. When Meredith sought to portray men who were fully worthy of his women, he succeeded best with Dartrey Fenellan and Matthew Weyburn.

In the end, it is the women in the novels who can truly be defined as heroines, while the men are heroes, at most, in the literary sense of being central characters. Women in Victorian fiction were often shown as pathetic victims, and it is remarkable that only one of Meredith's women, Dahlia Fleming, is in that class. His protagonists are the women – Clara, Vittoria, Aminta, Carinthia – who fight their battles against all the odds and all the powerful forces arrayed against them. It is the courage of women which Meredith celebrates, and it is in this sense that he can be called their champion.

9

Money Is Power

'MONEY is power, they say. I see the means it is to damn the soul.' The words are Lord Fleetwood's, torn from him in the throes of his repentance for his treatment of Carinthia. Fleetwood is, as we are reminded several times in *The Amazing Marriage*, the richest man in England; his wealth is described as 'enormous' or 'immense'. It is literally true that his money is equivalent to power, for he owns coal-mines in South Wales employing thousands of men, whom he regards as subjects without rights, much as serfs and peasants were regarded in remoter centuries by feudal barons.

Fleetwood's status is that of the big mine-owners – outstandingly, the Guest and Crawshay families – whose fortunes derived from the booming coal and iron industries. The founders of these dynasties in the late eighteenth century, John Guest from Shropshire and Richard Crawshay from Yorkshire, were men without aristocratic pretensions; but well before Meredith's time their successors had acquired estates in the pleasant countryside of southern England, the Guests in Dorset and the Crawshays in Berkshire. Fleetwood's residences in Kent are even more distant from the rugged, smoky sources of his wealth. However, he has a castle in the Welsh mining valleys where he stays occasionally and briefly – as, in reality, the Crawshays had Cyfartha Castle, on a hill dominating Merthyr Tydfil. Visiting Wales in 1888, before he wrote (or, precisely, before he completed) *The Amazing Marriage*, Meredith may well have gazed at Cyfartha Castle, built in 1825 by a Crawshay who was named by one authority as 'the richest man in Britain'. An impressive edifice in pseudo-baronial style, the castle had seventy-two rooms and the cost of construction was £30,000, a vast sum at the money-values of the period.

Fleetwood is an Earl (as the third Guest of the dynasty was Lord Wimborne), but he owes his peerage to his ascendancy as a capitalist, not to any descent from ancient lineage. We recall Louisa Harrington's irreverent question: 'What does anybody's birth matter who's well off?' By the nineteenth century, the borderlines between the capitalist class and the traditional upper class had become blurred to the point of being virtually erased. While the former had taken to aristocratic habits and snobberies, the latter had accepted the bourgeois financial pattern: earls and dukes invested in securities, borrowed from the banks and mortgaged their stately homes. Writing to Maxse in 1868, Meredith remarked: 'The aristocracy has long since sold itself to the middle class; that has done its best to corrupt the class under it.'[1] Frederick Engels, a little later, made the point in a letter to Marx – England, not content with having a bourgeoisie, required a bourgeois aristocracy and a bourgeois proletariat.

Meredith was acutely aware that he was living under a plutocracy, and saw little hope for England's future unless the money-power was broken or at least curbed. As usual, he set out his beliefs most directly in poems. In 1867, John Morley made an extended visit to America and Meredith filled his place as editor of the *Fortnightly Review* during his three months' absence. He wrote a poem, 'Lines to a Friend Visiting America', published in the *Review*. Despite his championship of the South in the Civil War (or forgetting it), he voiced a hope that democratic America would avoid the evils to which England had fallen prey. About these evils, he was categorical:

> A false majority, by stealth,
> Have got her fast, and sway the rod:
> A headless tyrant, built of wealth,
> The hypocrite, the belly-God.

Nor did he miss the opportunity to attack Tennyson, the Poet Laureate who, with *Idylls of the King*, had clearly emerged as worshipper of an élite:

> A poet, half a prophet, rose
> In recent days, and called for power.
> I love him; but his mountain prose –
> His Alp and valley and wild flower –

Proclaimed our weakness, not its source.
What medicine for disease had he?
Whom summoned for a show of force?
Our titular aristocracy!

Why, these are great at City feasts;
From City riches mainly rise:
'Tis well to hear them, when the beasts
That die for us they eulogize!

But these, of all the liveried crew
Obeisant in Mammon's walk,
Most deferent ply the facial screw,
The spinal bend, submissive talk.

(Presumably, the 'beasts that die for us' were the soldiers sacrificed at Balaclava, eulogized by Tennyson in *The Charge of the Light Brigade*.)

Meredith struck the same note in a long poem, 'The Empty Purse', based on the parable of the prodigal son. It was published only in 1892, but a partial early draft has been found in a notebook of the 1850s – an example of how a theme could preoccupy him throughout his life. The stress is on the accumulated wealth of the father, rather than the prodigality of the son, which is indeed praised as healthy repudiation:

This wealth was a fortress-wall,
Under which grew our little beast-god stout;
Self-worshipped, the foe, in division from all;
With crowds of illogical Christians, no doubt . . .

Till they see, with the gape of a startled surprise,
Their adored tyrant-monster a brute to abhor,
The sun of their system a father of flies!
So, for such good hope, take their scourge unashamed;
'Tis the portion of those who civilize,
    Who speak the word novel and true:
How the brutish antique of our springs may be tamed,
Without loss of the strength that should push us to flower.

Hope breaks through in the concluding section, with the line: 'By my faith, there is feasting to come' and the promise:

[177]

When our Earth we have seen, and have linked
With the home of the Spirit to whom we unfold,
Imprisoned humanity open will throw
Its fortress gates, and the rivers of gold
    For the congregate friendliness flow.

The dating of the first draft of this poem reveals an association in Meredith's mind with *The Shaving of Shagpat* and the overthrow of the 'tyrant-monster', Shagpat, by the brave young Shibli Bagarag. But the attack on money-power is renewed in almost all (or, if we take note of what are sometimes secondary themes, all) of Meredith's novels. Because the novels deal with individual experiences in a realistically described contemporary world, they trace the crippling, corrupting influence of money on men and women – 'the means to damn the soul'.

If the nineteenth-century novel can be seen as the reflection in literature of nineteenth-century England, then it was natural for writers to grapple with the contrast between, on the one hand, human emotions and desires and, on the other, the dominating compulsions of money. We have only to think, in *Middlemarch*, of the agonies of Lydgate, the idealistic young doctor whose career and marriage are wrecked by his failure to make an income. We see money damn the soul of Pip in *Great Expectations*, Dombey in *Dombey and Son*, the 'golden dustman' in *Our Mutual Friend*. Trollope was almost obsessively concerned with lovers who cannot marry because of lack of money. No writer of the period, however, confronted his readers with the power of money more persistently, or more harshly, than Meredith.

Evan's poverty and the apparent hopelessness of his love for Rose is the mainspring of *Evan Harrington*. In *Emilia*, the theme spins three interweaving threads: the millionaire Pericles uses his wealth to manipulate Emilia's life; Mr Pole has to speculate with Mrs Chump's money to avoid bankruptcy; Purcell Barrett, the disinherited son of a baronet, cannot marry Cornelia and shoots himself when he thinks he has lost her. In *Harry Richmond*, Richmond Roy swings wildly between ostentatious wealth and the debtors' prison, while Harry is committed by his grandfather's bequest to marry Janet. In *Beauchamp's Career*, Cecilia loves Nevil but, being an heiress, knows that he will be too scrupulous to seek her in marriage. In *The Egoist*, it is assumed that either Clara or Laetitia would be glad to marry Sir Willoughby for his money and social position. In *Diana of the Crossways*, lack of money prevents Redworth from marrying Diana at the outset, acquisition of money enables him to marry her eventually, and need for money is her motive for leaking the political secret and thus alienating her lover. In *One of Our Conquerors*, it was money that impelled Victor to make his loveless marriage with Mrs Burman, the shadow on his subsequent life. In *Lord Ormont*, Aminta's penniless state is her aunt's justification for disposing of her to an old husband. So, finally, we come to *The Amazing Marriage* and Lord Fleetwood – not forgetting that Carinthia's troubles stem partly from the meanness of her uncle, Lord Levellier.

But the novel most mercilessly concentrated on the money theme is *Rhoda Fleming*. The chapter headings alone tell their story: Chapter III, 'Suggests the Might of the Money-Demon'; Chapter XXXIII, 'La Question d'Argent'; Chapter XL, 'A Freak of the Money-Demon'. Meredith was writing this novel at the time when he was hoping to marry Marie and was obliged to give her father a humiliating account of his barely adequate financial position. After his marriage, he finished *Rhoda Fleming* in a rush – he would have preferred to get on with *Vittoria* – only to find that Chapman and Hall could not publish it quickly. In urgent need of money, he sold it cheaply to a new firm which aimed at big sales to the libraries; these big sales did not materialize and *Rhoda Fleming* did not earn its advance.

As a picture of England, *Rhoda Fleming* presents contrasting scenes of city and country. In Kent (then authentically rural) we are shown two traditional figures, Squire Blancove and Farmer Fleming. They are free from the avarice and cunning of the urban world, and the farmer especially is a man of sturdy integrity and a simplicity amounting to naïveté. But he cannot stand out against the money-power; faced with losing his farm, which has ceased to be viable, he can save it only by trying to force his daughter Rhoda into a marriage with the squire's worthless son, Algernon.

In alternating scenes, we are taken to the up-to-date, bustling, sophisticated world of London. Here, the significant institution is the bank. In Meredith's time there were no giants like today's NatWest or Barclays, but banks were already solid, impregnable strongholds of capitalism, equipped to function with smooth efficiency. If they had possessed computers and fax machines, Meredith would surely have included these devices in his description; as it was, they could safely depend on a staff of well-trained, loyal clerks and messengers. A Victorian bank was headed by a single, dominant figure, 'the banker', impressive by virtue of his experience, his professional knowledge and judgement, his dignity and his power of decision. This figure is Sir William Blancove, the squire's

[179]

brother. He is a man immune to any kind of emotion, seen by Meredith less as a human being than as an embodiment of his social and economic importance. A widower without any indiscreet entanglements, he needs to make no effort to succeed in marrying the attractive Mrs Lovell, not by pursuing her but simply by being there.

The quality that Blancove respects is competence, and he has nothing but contempt for those who lack it. Lacking in a high degree is his nephew Algernon (the squire's son), an idle, self-indulgent young man who is in trouble with debts and gambling losses. When entrusted with £1,000, Algernon – to whom Meredith refers derisively as 'the fool' – fritters it away in the course of a comic chapter headed 'The Melting of the Thousand'. But Edward, the banker's son, although he is a far more mature and serious young man and views Algernon with a contempt worthy of Sir William, also falls short of his father's standards; he falls in love with the socially insignificant Dahlia Fleming and, after a period of maintaining her as a mistress in the approved manner, decides to marry her. Sir William, too calm and dignified to react with anger, expresses his disapproval. A young man capable of such neglect of prudent calculation or advantage is clearly unfitted to be 'the banker', and Sir William advises Edward to emigrate. Sir William himself plans to marry Margaret Lovell, as he can afford to pay her debts, which her faithful lover, Major Waring, cannot. At every turn, we are reminded of the cold, commercial values that dominate society.

The essential statement of *Rhoda Fleming* is that the money-power has its victims. The pathetic Dahlia is the obvious victim; Edward, surviving but lastingly seared by his experience, is a victim too. In the most direct sense, the victim is the trusted bank messenger, Anthony Hackbut. Being in temporary charge of large amounts of money, in tangible gold sovereigns, is his pride as well as his duty; this, and nothing else, gives meaning to his life. He confides to his brother-in-law, Fleming: 'It's an emotion when you've got bags of thousands of pounds in your arms.' The surprising word 'emotion' and the phrase 'in your arms' reveal that for this solitary bachelor money has supplied the passion that other men would find in love or sex. Eventually, the passion brings about Hackbutt's downfall when he cannot bear to deliver the money to its proper destination and keeps it in his own hands (or arms). By Blancove standards, the lifelong servant of the bank has become a thief. Rhoda urges him to give her the money to replace the £1,000 that Algernon has wasted, and thus to save Dahlia. If he keeps it, she warns him, 'It will be a curse to you.' Hackbut by now is feeling ill and on the verge of mental and physical collapse.

When Rhoda says that the money-bags are 'poison to you', it is almost literally true. There is only one way for him to get rid of them:

> He seized them, and dashed them to the ground with the force of madness. Kneeling, he drew out his penknife, and slit the sides of the bags, and held them aloft, and let the gold pour out in torrents, insufferable to the sight; and uttering laughter that clamoured fierily in her ears for long minutes afterwards, the old man brandished the empty bags, and sprang out of the room. She sat dismayed in the centre of a heap of gold.

Rhoda's hope that the money can be put to good use is an illusion; it is a poison to her as well as to Hackbut. She has to confess: 'I was like a fiend for money. I must have been acting wrongly. Such a craving as that is a sign of evil.'

Except by implication, *Rhoda Fleming* is not a political novel. Indeed, its analysis of a society ruled by money is all the more powerful because it is worked out at a personal level; the Flemings and the Blancoves imagine that they are free to act from untrammelled individual motives, when in truth they are not. Meredith had yet to write his directly political novels – *Vittoria*, *Beauchamp's Career*, *The Tragic Comedians*. But, from his early manhood if not his boyhood, he held a political position to which he was willing to give a name; he was a Radical. A letter, undated but obviously belonging to the 1850s, refers to 'such Radicals as my brother-in-law and myself' – the brother-in-law being Edward Peacock. In 1868 he was working for the Radical candidate for Southampton, Frederick Maxse, and it is clear that this was a political commitment as well as an act of friendship. In 1880, writing to Maxse, he criticized the vacillations of the Liberal Party and concluded: 'The only hope, it seems to me, is that Radicalism should be avowed.'[2] Almost at the end of his life, when reporters clustered at his house on his eightieth birthday, he told them: 'Say that I am well, and that you found me sitting in my chair, delivering myself freely of very Radical sentiments.'[3]

So far as it goes, this is unambiguous; but it is less easy to define what Meredith, or anyone else in his time, meant by Radicalism. There was never a Radical Party to which one could belong, and people who called themselves Radicals constituted a wing – to use French terminology, a *tendance* – within the Liberal Party. Their central idea, like that of the Chartists before 1848, was that political action should be directed towards social objectives, primarily towards remedying the poverty in which the

majority of the population lived. George Eliot used the word in this sense
when she wrote *Felix Holt, the Radical,* published in 1866. So far as the
objectives were social and economic, and could even imply a thorough
reconstruction of society, Radicalism could shade into Socialism – an
identifiable political force in France and Germany from mid-century, and
in Britain after the founding of the Social-Democratic Federation by
Meredith's friend Hyndman in 1881. The development is reflected in the
ruminations of Victor Radnor in *One of Our Conquerors*:

> To back a native pugnacity, is morality, humanity, fraternity . . . And
> that lands me in Red Republicanism, a hop and a skip from Socialism!
> said Mr Radnor, and chuckled ironically at the natural declivity he
> had come to.

The problem for Radicals was that they did not really belong in the
Liberal Party, or belonged in it only if they could transform it and take
it over. The precursors of the Liberals were the Whigs, who derived
their traditions from the so-called Glorious Revolution of 1688. Opposed
to absolute monarchy, and upholding parliamentary (but by no means
democratic) government, the Whigs ruled Britain as an oligarchy through
most of the eighteenth century. In the first part of the nineteenth century,
their great achievement was the Reform Act of 1832, which gave the vote
to a limited number of middle-class men on a property basis and secured
representation in the Commons for industrial towns such as Manchester.
The Liberal Party was the political vehicle of the new capitalism; the typical
Liberal stalwart, especially in the north of England, was a factory-owner,
merchant or banker. Thus, it served the interests of just that money-power
which Meredith detested. Liberalism stood for free trade, low taxation,
economy in public spending, and strictly limited governmental functions.

While the party held together, under the revered leadership of Gladstone, Radicals grumbled. Meredith expressed their frustration in an 1880
letter:

> There is no other real party than the Tory. The rest is but a fractional
> party constantly flying to shreds, sewn together by a popular cry, and
> rent again when that is exhausted. The one comfort of the Radical is that
> Sham Liberalism will not for some time be able to take the lead of him.[4]

He must have been encouraged when Joseph Chamberlain, in 1885,
produced what was significantly called the Unauthorized Programme, a

call for free education, social services, compulsory purchase of land for community purposes, and graduated taxation. It was, as G. D. H. Cole wrote later, a 'bid to win over the Liberal Party and to check the rise of Socialism as a separate political force'. With the electorate now enlarged to include a majority of the male population, the Liberals faced at least a potential threat. Hyndman's SDF and William Morris's Socialist League paved the way for Keir Hardie's Independent Labour Party, and ultimately for the Labour Party.

Although Chamberlain himself ended up as a Tory, his Radicalism lived on. Before his death, Meredith witnessed the battles over Lloyd George's 'People's Budget' of 1909. Thereafter, Radicalism found expression through the Labour Party, with a Liberal ancestry. To carry the story on: the standard-bearers of the Left, Michael Foot and Tony Benn, both had Liberal fathers (Benn's joined the Labour Party, Foot's did not).

The contest – or race – between Radical Liberalism and Socialism was a drama that had already been played in the 1860s, but on the German stage. With his knowledge of the German language and his visits to Germany every few years, Meredith was better placed to follow it than most Englishmen. The protagonist was the charismatic Ferdinand Lassalle, killed in a duel a year after launching his General German Workers' Association, which was virtually a political party and had an explicitly Socialist programme. Lassalle was well remembered when, in 1879, Helene von Racowitza published her frank (if not entirely truthful) book, *My Relations with Ferdinand Lassalle*. Meredith was able to read it in German and plunged into writing *The Tragic Comedians*, assuring readers in a preface that he had invented nothing. It was of course the love story and its tragic dénouement which seized the novelist's imagination, but Alvan (Lassalle) was given long speeches expounding his ideas and strategy, actually expounded by Lassalle in four-hour speeches, or lectures, which were then published in pamphlet form.

Germany in the 1860s was not yet united as an empire, but the dominant state, Prussia, contained the booming industrial regions of the Rhineland and Ruhrland, as well as the city of Berlin. Though Germany's industrial revolution had not quite caught up with Britain's, and the population was predominantly rural, there was a cohesive working class and a thrusting, confident middle class. The political instrument of this middle class was the Progressist Party, corresponding to Britain's Liberal Party. But whereas in Britain the Liberals competed for power with the Tories, and the parties won elections more or less alternately, Germany had no Tory Party; conservatism relied on the authority of the King of Prussia and on his very forceful Chancellor (Prime Minister), Bismarck. In fact, the Progressists had a huge majority in the Landtag (the Prussian Parliament). They owed this to the franchise system which operated, as in Britain after the 1832 Reform Act, to favour the property-owning middle class. As one might expect in Germany, the system was constructed with scientific precision. Under the constitution, drawn up in 1849 as a response to the upheavals of 1848, there were three classes of voters, each electing the same number of Landtag members; there were 153,000 voters in Class I and nearly three million in Class III. So, when Lassalle formed his party, his first demand – as in Britain it had been the first demand of the Chartists – was for universal suffrage.

Ironically, this demand appealed to the arch-conservative Bismarck, for it offered the best chance of depriving the Progressists of their Landtag majority. The Progressists and Lassalle's Socialists were on extremely hostile terms, breaking up each other's meetings and fighting in the streets, like Communists and Social-Democrats when Hitler was at the gates of power. Lassalle sent a telegram of complaint to Bismarck when one of his meetings was closed down by a Progressist mayor. 'Progress – pooh! That is a middle-class invention to effect a compromise,' Alvan says to Clotilde in *The Tragic Comedians*. Bismarck and Lassalle exchanged letters (which came to light only in 1927, after the fall of the Empire) and met for private talks. The outcome was that Bismarck introduced universal suffrage. Almost at the same time, Disraeli was outflanking the Liberals with his broadening of the franchise in the Second Reform Act.

Alvan's account of his negotiations with 'old Ironsides', as he calls the Chancellor, shows how well Meredith understood the relationship. Alvan tells Clotilde:

> We agreed that we were on neutral ground for the moment: that he might ultimately have to decapitate me, or I to banish him, but temporarily we could compare our plans for government. He showed me his hand. I showed him mine ... Enough that we parted with mutual respect. He is a fine fellow ... Had he been born with the gifts of patience and a fluent tongue, and not a petty noble, he might have been for the people, as knowing them the great power.

Lassalle, in fact, could not conceal his admiration for Bismarck, although their meetings and deals were secret and his public role was that of Bismarck's irreconcilable opponent. In one speech, he declared that Bismarck was at least a man, whereas the Progressists were old women.

Whether Lassalle could have triumphed over Bismarck if he had lived beyond 1864 is an unanswerable question. He certainly thought so; he was inspired by his Messianic belief in his own powers and his conviction that the future belonged to him (or to his movement, but for him they were indistinguishable). Eduard Bernstein, in a biography published in 1891, pointed to his 'huge self-confidence and vanity' but also to 'legitimate pride – legitimate because founded on principle'. In Bernstein's view: 'This cult for the personality of Lassalle did, for a long time, greatly help on the movement.' Lassalle himself claimed, in a letter to a young woman whom he sought to marry before he met Helene, that the people regarded him as 'a man of the greatest genius and of almost superhuman character, of whom they expect the greatest deeds'.[5] Actually, the people did not respond quite as he hoped, membership of the Workers' Association grew slowly, and just before his death he complained of 'the horrible disappointment and annoyance that the apathy and indifference of the working classes caused me' – the words of a man in a hurry, who could not see why he was not instantly irresistible.

Meredith's Alvan tells Clotilde:

> Politically also we know that strength is the one reality; the rest is shadow. Behind the veil of our human conventions power is constant as ever, and to perceive the fact is to have the divining rod – to walk clear of shams. He is the teacher who shows where power exists; he is the leader who wakens and forms it.

The German word for leader is *Führer*, and *Lassalle der Führer* was the title of a psychological study of Lassalle (which Freud had in his library). Lassalle was certainly no democrat, even within the sphere of the Workers' Association. 'Whoever is President,' he stated firmly (of course, the President was Ferdinand Lassalle), 'his powers must be dictatorial.' He was creating a model for the so-called democratic centralism of later Communist parties. As Bernstein commented, in his attitude to the emerging party 'he could only regard it from the point of view of his own personality, and treated it accordingly'.[6]

Unlike most other Socialist theorists, Lassalle had a clear doctrine of the organization of a future Socialist society. He proposed that control of industry should be exercised by the workers with financial support from the State. The assumption is of a central government using the mechanism of graduated taxation. This was the policy of social democracy in the twentieth century, notably of the British Labour government from 1945, with its nationalized, subsidized National Coal Board, British Railways and so forth. Meredith made a favourable comment in 1887 when, as reader for Chapman and Hall, he reported on a book of essays:

> They are tersely written, tending to enlarged modern views in politics: so far Socialistic that he is for the Nationalization of Land; the putting of much into the hands of the State – which is opposed to English feeling, although there are signs of English reason awakening to some idea of the necessity.[7]

But Lassalle was also influenced by the concept – developed by Hegel and Fichte, and dominant in Prussia – of the State as an ideal embodiment of the national spirit (*Volksgeist*). This concept was to be stigmatized by Karl Popper, in *The Open Society and Its Enemies*, as the progenitor of totalitarianism. Lassalle's State Socialism is at the opposite pole from the English utopia sketched in William Morris's *News from Nowhere*. In the future of which Morris dreamed, all official authority is a thing of the past; liberated men and women rely on voluntary agreements, guided by rational common sense and innate altruism.

When the German Social-Democratic Party was founded in 1875 at a congress held at Gotha, representatives of the Workers' Association succeeded in getting most of Lassalle's policies into the programme adopted there. This angered Marx and Engels, who had detested Lassalle in his lifetime, and they voiced their disagreements in a *Critique of the Gotha Programme*. To read this document is to see that the idea that Socialism as conceived by Marx was based on state power (a belief held by people ignorant of history) is completely fallacious. In a letter following up the *Critique*, Engels urged: 'The whole talk about the state should be dropped, especially since the [Paris] Commune, which was no longer a state in the proper sense of the word.' He suggested that the word 'state', everywhere in the programme, should be replaced by *Gemeinwesen*, for which the closest equivalent in English is 'community'. Marx and Engels looked forward to 'the withering away of the state', which – after a transitional period, as short as possible – would surrender its powers to the community. As Engels wrote: 'As soon as it becomes possible to speak of freedom, the state as such ceases to exist.'[8] Such was the theory of Marx and Engels, who should not be blamed for the practice of Stalin.

However, Meredith was not a Socialist and these arguments between Socialists were not his province. For an English Radical, Chamberlain's

Unauthorized Programme contained sufficient objectives. Before *The Tragic Comedians*, Meredith had written a novel with a Radical hero, *Beauchamp's Career*.

Beauchamp is a name with an aristocratic ring, and Nevil is of aristocratic descent since his mother was a daughter of the Earl of Romfrey. Nevil's uncle, the Hon. Everard Romfrey, who eventually succeeds to the earldom, is 'in mind a medieval baron, in politics a crotchety unintelligible Whig'. Meredith draws a portrait resembling his portrait of Squire Beltham in *Harry Richmond*; Beltham is a Tory while Romfrey is a Whig, but both are deeply conservative and traditionalist in outlook, and would be more at home in the England of the eighteenth century.

While Meredith does not take Romfrey and Beltham as seriously as they take themselves, and makes gentle fun of their prejudices, his portraits are sympathetic. Harry comments on the Squire: 'He was a curious study to me of the Tory mind, in its attachment to solidity, fixity, certainty, its unmatched generosity within a limit, its devotion to the family, and its family eye for the country.' In *Beauchamp's Career*, a conversation among a group of Tory gentleman, who are deploring the extension of the franchise, catches the tone of their nostalgia:

A domination of the Intellect in England would at once and entirely alter the face of the country . . . Do you not hear in imagination the land's regrets for that amiable nobility whose pretensions were comically built on birth, acres, tailoring, style, and an air?

The passage is ironical, and in the course of the novel Meredith shows that the nobility, when its position is challenged, can be far from amiable. Romfrey's horsewhip attack on Dr Shrapnel is an act of crude brutality. Baskelett, the Tory candidate in the Bevisham election, resorts to the lowest kind of dirty tricks, though these are repudiated by his fellow-candidate, a decent Tory. It is Nevil, the Radical, who always behaves honourably both in his political career and in personal life. But whether he does so because of his Radical principles, or because he has inherited the traditional gentlemanly code, is an open question.

Meredith is exceptional among the major Victorian novelists (though Trollope is comparable) in that many of his characters belong to the aristocracy or at least the landed gentry. We have only to mention Sir Austin Feverel, Sir Francks Jocelyn, the Earl of Romfrey, Sir Lukin Dunstane, the Hon. Percy Dacier, the Earl of Fleetwood, Lord Ormont; or, among the women, Lady Blandish, Lady Charlotte Chillingworth, Lady

Constance Eglett, the heiresses Cecilia Halkett and Constance Asper. The scene is set in the ample acres of Sir Austin's Raynham Abbey, the Jocelyns' Beckley Court, Sir Willoughby's Patterne Hall, the Dunstanes' Copsley or Lord Ormont's Steignton. When he looks abroad, Meredith seems equally at home in Prince Ernest von Sarkeld's castle, the Marquis de Rouaillout's château, or Countess Ammiani's villa on Lago Maggiore. All this is the more remarkable in that, in real life, Meredith was never a figure on the country-house circuit and his friends were middle-class intellectuals and journalists. The social territory of the aristocracy is a country of the imagination, but a country that held a seductive fascination for him.

Meredith never equalled Dickens's extraordinary range of characters in every corner of nineteenth-century society, nor George Eliot's familiarity with the provincial middle class, nor Hardy's rural landscape. Still less did he attempt to depict the life of the working class in an industrial town, as Dickens did in *Hard Times* and even Disraeli did in *Sybil*. Meredith does give us farmers and farm labourers, reproducing the accent and vocabulary of talk at the village inn with painstaking accuracy; white-collar cogs in the capitalist machine, such as Braintop in *Emilia*, Hackbut in *Rhoda Fleming* and Skepsey in *One of Our Conquerors*; middle-class people who are outside the world of fashion and gentility and are generally introduced for comic effect, like Tom Cogglesby in *Evan Harrington* or Mrs Chump in *Emilia*; and occasionally (but less often than one might expect) an intellectual, like Gower Woodseer, whose independence casts a critical light on the social structure. But these characters, while they enrich the canvas of a Meredith novel, are peripheral to the main narrative.

Meredith's aristocrats are generally castigated for their arrogance and egotism. His merciless dissection of Sir Austin and Sir Willoughby (and indeed secondary characters such as Lord Laxley in *Evan Harrington* or Lord Brailstone in *Lord Ormont*) and finally of Lord Fleetwood – these amount to a formidable indictment of the privileged class. But the mine-owning Fleetwood, we must bear in mind, represents the plutocracy, not the nobility with its ancient traditions. Romfrey may have the mind of a medieval baron, but it is filled with revulsion at conditions in industry. Nevil, as a boy, is told by his uncle:

'You shall have a glance at the manufacturing district some day . . . They work young children in their factories from morning to night. Their manufactures are spreading like the web of the devil to suck the blood of the country . . . On the top of it all they sing Sunday tunes!'

Nevil asks: 'Don't they belong to the Liberal party?' As we have seen, that party had the allegiance of the middle class – the owners of the 'manufactures'. In resistance to exploitation, the workers often mustered under Radical and Chartist banners; but sometimes they turned to Tory aristocrats, who had no responsibility for their sufferings and could perhaps offer some protection in the name of older values, hierarchical no doubt but more humane. Benjamin Disraeli, a brilliant opportunist throughout his life, caught the tide of the 1840s with his novels *Coningsby* and *Sybil*. In *Sybil* – subtitled 'The Two Nations' to stress the gulf between rich and poor – the aristocratic Charles Egremont falls in love with penniless Sybil, daughter of a Chartist, who reassuringly turns out to be heiress to a castle and its estate. Disraeli's message was that social justice and a reconciliation of opposing classes could be achieved by an alliance of generous aristocrats and the masses oppressed by the money-power. Young Nevil imbibes the idea: 'The nobles, he felt sure, might resume their natural alliance with the people, and lead them, as they did of old, to the battle-field.'

In 1847, two years after the publication of *Sybil*, Meredith was introduced by Richard Charnock, the Radical solicitor to whom he was articled, to a discussion group called the Arundel Club. One of its members was Lord John Manners, the leading figure in the Young England Movement, inspired by Disraeli's doctrines. Lord John, a recognizable character in *Coningsby*, was in the line of descent of the highly placed Manners family (whose motto was 'Manners Makyth Man') and became the seventh Earl of Rutland. Meredith almost certainly heard him speak at club meetings. After Meredith ceased to work in Charnock's office and moved out of London, it is unlikely that he ever saw Lord John Manners again, and indeed the Young England Movement was short-lived. But, twenty years later, the memory is discernible in *Beauchamp's Career*.

This is a novel comparable in its richness and complexity to *Richard Feverel*. It is a political novel, and at the same time it is a love story: indeed, its emotional power depends on the intensity of feeling that Nevil brings both to his political idealism and to his love for Renée. As a character, too, Nevil recalls Richard Feverel; they are alike in their romantic temperament, their sincerity amounting to naïveté, and their impulsiveness. Fred Maxse, on whom Nevil was based, was known – and loved, though also teased, by his friends – for his impulsive nature. Nevil is moved by impulse at every turning-point: when he first falls in love with Renée and tries to carry her off; when he suddenly decides, having just met Dr Shrapnel, to contest the Bevisham election; when he responds to Renée's appeal on her unexpected reappearance; and, finally, in the sacrifice of his life. Above all, Nevil is an idealist, capable of making a dedication – to Renée and, with just as much emotional intensity, to the Radical cause – without reservation and without calculation.

Sadly for Nevil, the one dedication is in conflict with the other. At a crucial moment, Rosamund Culling observes: 'He was trying to be two men at once.' He does not speak of his political ideals when he is with Renée, and they can have no meaning for her. When she is at last willing to commit herself to him, she wants him to leave England and go to Italy with her, and has no conception of what it would cost him to abandon his campaigning plans. But for his devotion to Renée, he could have married the intelligent, thoughtful Cecilia, who, despite her Tory upbringing, is coming round to an understanding of his Radicalism. By the time he realizes this, it is too late. When he marries Jenny Denham, whom he does not love, it can be said that Meredith opted for a weak resolution (as we have seen, Meredith characters generally end up married, by no means always ideally) but it is also a choice. Freed from Renée, Nevil for the first time in his life is no longer torn between the two kinds of dedication.

The novel concludes with Nevil's death; he rescues a boy who has fallen out of a boat, but is drowned trying to save another boy. The same thought occurs to Nevil's two father-figures, Romfrey and Shrapnel: 'This is what we have in exchange for Beauchamp!' Most commentators have read this conclusion as a bitter irony, or an admission that chance rules in a cruelly meaningless world. However, that would be more like Hardy than Meredith. The comment, and the dismissal of the rescued boy as an 'insignificant bit of mudbank', may reveal the inhumanity of the older men. It is Nevil who has given the ultimate proof that every human life has value (the boys are the sons of a poor fisherman). Read thus, Nevil's sacrifice is a dramatic illustration of the Young England doctrine that the generous idealism of the aristocracy can come to the rescue of the common people.

The doctrine is illustrated again in *The Amazing Marriage*, against a background of strikes and riots. Carinthia's beloved brother, Chillon, is a cavalry officer:

Heading a squadron in a riotous Midland town, he stopped a charge, after fire of a shot from the mob, and galloped up the street to catch a staggering urchin to his saddle-bow, and place the mite in safety.

When Carinthia hears of this, she is at Fleetwood's castle in Wales. The miners are on strike to resist a wage cut. (A strike on this issue had occurred in 1867.) Fleetwood delays going to the coalfield to deal with the situation, and when he does go he rejects his manager's advice to be flexible. As he sees it:

These fellows fixed to the spot are for compromise too much. An owner of mines has no steady reckoning of income if the rate of wage is perpetually to shift according to current, mostly ignorant, versions of the prosperity of the times.

This is the attitude of a plutocrat, not an aristocrat of the type eulogized by Disraeli. Carinthia contrasts it with the outlook of her father, who had owned a mine in the province for which she was named, Carinthia. 'How would her father have acted by these men? He would have been among them. Dissensions in his mine were vapours of a day.' She feels at home in the mining village, though unhappy in the castle. 'She was gathering the people's language; many of their songs she could sing, and please them by singing to them. They were not suspicious of her.' But they are suspicious of her husband, as she can well understand, having been treated by him with the same arrogant callousness. Carinthia places herself firmly on the side of the miners:

'He speaks to command. The men ask to be heard. He will have submission first. They do not trust him . . . I am with the men because I am so like them. I beg to be heard. He commands obedience. He is a great nobleman, but I am the daughter of a greater man, and I have to say, that if these poor miners do harm, I will not stand by and see an anger against injustice punished.'

Fleetwood arrives in Wales to be present when Carinthia confronts a rabid dog, warning people (in Welsh) to get their children indoors. She is in imminent danger, for the dog seizes her gown. Unlike Nevil, Carinthia will survive, but she too is risking her life to save children whom Fleetwood would class as 'insignificant'. Her courage is contrasted with his helplessness:

[191]

Right and left, the fury of the slavering fangs shook her loose droop of gown . . . Fleetwood hovered helpless as a leaf on a bough. 'Back, I pray', she said to him, and motioned it, her arms at high stretch . . . And she waved him behind her, beckoned to the crowd to keep wide way, used her lifted hands as flappers; she had all her wits.

She is still in danger (for the dog is still at large) when she volunteers to burn the wound of a child who has been bitten. 'This young woman is a very sword in the hand of her idea of duty,' Fleetwood has to concede after trying in vain to dissuade her. His own reaction is selfish – 'I shall be bitten if I stop here a minute longer; I'm gone; I can neither command nor influence.' And he jumps into his carriage, to rejoin his yacht at Cardiff. On the way, he reflects uneasily: 'He had done as much as a man could do in such a situation. At the same time he had done less than the woman.'

Meredith's attack on the money-power, and on the moral corruption that it brought to men like Fleetwood, was always uncompromising. His political position, however, was never so extreme (or, a critic would say, so consistent) as that of Morris, who – as he expressed it – 'crossed the river of fire' to become a campaigning Socialist. Meredith's allegiance was to democracy, which in the mid-nineteenth century was not yet the sanctified ideal to which men of all parties professed to subscribe; influential voices were raised to warn that democracy could be dangerous if carried too far. Meredith wrote in a letter to Maxse:

> Democracy must come and the sooner it overflows rulers who are *cowardly*, the better for all. We say – Democracy, as if it were some deadly evil; whereas it is almost synonymous with Change. Democracy never rests. The worst of it is that it *can* be violent in its motion.[9]

The last sentence is significant. Meredith put his faith in change by democratic process, not in revolution. True, he once told Maxse: 'I see no hope but in a big convulsion to bring a worthy people forth.' But too much should not be built on a phrase that may have been generated by impatience and frustration. There was an element of moderation, even of caution, in Meredith's outlook, which restrained him from going along with Maxse's impetuous enthusiasms. In an affectionately bantering tone, yet with underlying seriousness, Meredith wrote to his friend:

> My precept is ever Moderation. You hold Moderation in contempt. So consequently my wisdom is foolishness to you . . . You must have

the world moving in your own fashion. Drench the political world with pure water. Attack us all from your new point of view. Combative as you are, for you to see a truth and not insist on it universally, will be impossible. I, meantime, will stand by and mark.[10]

In the early 1870s, there was an estrangement between Meredith and John Morley, the editor of the *Fortnightly Review*. Evidently there were arguments, which provoked Morley to write a letter breaking off their friendship. He felt, he said, that Meredith had not shown proper respect for his 'opinions, ideas, and likings'. In his later memoirs, he referred to Meredith's 'too downright and imperious speech'.

Meredith replied to Morley's letter:

I cannot but be shocked and grieved . . . I chose to blame myself, as the safer way of closing a slight wound . . . It may be too often my manner. I might well think my friend would not let it live with him, and that he knew my mind better than to allow a sense of variance to spring from such differences in open talk . . . We will see one another as little as we can for two or three years, and by and by may come together again naturally.[11]

Meredith's conciliatory tone can be explained partly by the fact that he was starting work on a big novel, *Beauchamp's Career*, and hoped to offer it to the *Fortnightly* for serialization. When the novel was finished, after 'two or three years', it was first submitted to the *Cornhill Magazine*, turned down, and then offered to the *Fortnightly*. Morley accepted it subject to the author's agreement to make cuts, and Meredith promised to do so. He proposed cuts in 'the heavier of the electioneering passages' and 'a host of my own reflections', while assuring Morley that he would retain 'a noble devotion to politics from the roots up'. Thus, their former good relationship was restored.

The letters do not tell us what the arguments were about, nor why Morley took offence so severely. Norman Kelvin, who has discussed the episode in his book *A Troubled Eden*, suggested that the novelist annoyed the editor – whose interests were primarily political, and who was hoping to get into Parliament, as he finally did in 1883 – by insisting that a novel must be a work of art, not a political statement, with the implication that this concept was beyond Morley's range. This does not quite hit the nail on the head, since Meredith always maintained that fiction should be 'the vehicle of philosophy' (or, as we should say now, of ideology). Another guess may be hazarded. It is possible that Morley, a stalwart of the Radical wing of the Liberal Party, resented criticisms by Meredith of Radicals whose personal qualities were at odds with their proclaimed beliefs.

In *Beauchamp's Career*, the novel on which Meredith was embarking, a major character is the Radical Dr Shrapnel. Nevil, in his all-or-nothing way, is uncritically devoted to this guide and mentor. For Nevil, he is 'the humanest, the best of men, tender-hearted as a child; the most benevolent, simple-minded, admirable old man – the man I am proudest to think of as an Englishman and a man living in my time, of all men existing'. At another point, Nevil declares: 'I reverence him.' One might expect Meredith to draw an admiring portrait of a man who can be reverenced, as he did of 'the Chief' (Mazzini) in *Vittoria*. Instead, the portrait of Shrapnel is as derisive as the portrait of Sir Willoughby Patterne, although Meredith was hostile to Sir Willoughby's social and political outlook but was sympathetic to Shrapnel's Radicalism. It is easy to see why Shrapnel should be loathed by the local Establishment figures, such as Romfrey and Colonel Halkett, who calls him 'that old rascal'. It is more surprising that Rosamund and Cecilia, who are both so fond of Nevil that they would excuse his infatuation if they could, are equally repelled.

It is indeed impossible to like or respect the character that Meredith created. For Hannah Lynch, he was 'that unmitigated old bore'. A Marxist critic, Arnold Kettle, described him as 'a crank and a bit of a bore'. Shrapnel seems to have been based on a Dr Edwin Hearne, who was a supporter of Maxse in Southampton and author of a pamphlet that attempted to prove that cholera was not contagious (there had been a raging epidemic in England in 1832). When Rosamund first encounters Shrapnel, he inflicts three rambling, eccentric speeches on her in quick succession. An example of his rhetoric is:

Sound the conscience, and sink the family! ... No man ever did brave work who held counsel with his family ... The family view is everlastingly the shopkeeper's! Purse, pence, ease, increase of worldly goods, personal importance – the pound, the English pound! ... Lord, Lord, is it the region inside a man, or out, that gives him peace? *Out*, they say; for they have lost faith in the existence of an inner. They haven't it. Air-sucker, blood-pump, cooking machinery, and a battery of trained instincts, aptitudes, fill up their vacuum.

Later, he tells a Liberal (and perfectly pleasant) friend of Jenny:

Your Liberals are the band of Pyrrhus, an army of bastards, mercenaries professing the practicable for pay . . . What are they? Stranded Whigs, crotchetty manufacturers; dissentient religionists; the half-minded, the hare-hearted; the I would and I would not – shifty creatures, with youth's enthusiasm decaying in them, and a purse beginning to jingle . . . Once let them leave sucking the teats of compromise, yea, once put on the air of men who fight and die for a cause, they fly to pieces.

Rosamund is relieved when Jenny starts playing the piano to interrupt Shrapnel's 'fanatical nonsense' (Shrapnel denounces the piano as a bourgeois instrument). Her comment as she leaves the house is 'Silly old man!' Meredith observes that Shrapnel is pouring out lectures all day, regardless of who may be within earshot, 'for his private spiritual solace'. In fact, everything about Shrapnel is ridiculous. Even his handwriting is a 'really abominable scrawl, which was like a child's drawing of ocean with here and there a sail capsized'. Jenny tries to keep him out of the election campaign, but he insists on indulging in 'the canvass and the harangue in person; by which conduct, as Jenny had foreseen, many temperate electors were alienated from Commander Beauchamp'. After Nevil predictably loses, Shrapnel cannot even offer sympathy: 'Not one syllable of personal consolation did he vouchsafe to Beauchamp.' And this Radical is sternly conservative in sexual matters. When Nevil contemplates running off with Renée, he knows that he will offend against 'Dr Shrapnel's heavy puritanism'.

It is, moreover, hard to decipher Meredith's treatment of the horse-whipping episode. The scene itself is off-stage, though Meredith normally delighted in vividly presented action. Apparently, Shrapnel fails to defend himself, though Romfrey makes the attack without assistance and it is noted that Shrapnel is taller and younger. 'It was no joke holding him tight,' Romfrey remarks complacently. Although Romfrey is ultimately forced to recognize that the whole affair was caused by Baskelett's dishonest machinations, and offers Shrapnel a reluctant apology, he evidently feels no guilt; and nobody is outraged except, of course, Nevil. The implication seems to be that Shrapnel deserves whatever is coming to him.

Beneath Shrapnel's eccentricity there is a real strain of fanaticism and intolerance; this is what causes Rosamund to feel an instinctive repugnance. Nevil too is intolerant and absolutist in his political outlook, but he can be excused (like Maxse in real life) by his sincerity and simplicity, and in any case he is under the influence of Shrapnel, described by Rosamund as 'our evil genius'. True, Shrapnel is an absurd figure and in no sense menacing, since there is no chance of his being in a position to do any harm in peaceful Hampshire. A much more sinister threat is presented by Barto Rizzo, the dedicated and ruthless conspirator in *Vittoria*.

Rizzo – poor, and a shoemaker by trade – is a man of total and incorruptible integrity, and the cause that inspires him, the liberation of Italy, is one for which Meredith felt passionate sympathy. Nevertheless, Meredith's first description of him conveys a warning to the reader:

> This man regarded himself as the mainspring of the conspiracy; especially its guardian, its wakeful Argus. He had conspired sleeplessly for thirty years; so long that, having no ideal reserve in his nature, conspiracy had become his professional occupation . . . He was prepared to suspect everyone of insincerity and of faithlessness . . . His arrangements had always been perfect; hence the deduction was a denunciation of some one particular person. He pointed out the traitor here, the traitor there.

Rizzo points out Vittoria as a traitor and orders her liquidation. She is stabbed by Rizzo's wife, but survives. With an intuition of Rizzo's paranoia, she says to Carlo: 'Here is a madman; a mild one, I trust' (but she is wrong about that). When Rizzo is given proof that he has accused her unjustly, it is beyond his comprehension. He can only say: 'I had lived in virtuous fidelity to my principles. None can accuse me. Why were my senses false, if my principles were true?'

It is left to Merthyr Powys, equally devoted to the Italian cause but a sane and balanced personality, to draw the lesson: 'The Fates are within us. Those which are the forces of the outer world are as shadows to the power we have created within us . . . Our destiny is of our own weaving.' As Meredith had written in 'Modern Love': 'We are betrayed by what is false within.'

Meredith's insight is both psychological and political. Rizzo's world – the dark side of dedicated idealism – is the closed, cruel world of conspiracy; the world of Dostoyevsky's *The Possessed* and Conrad's *Under Western Eyes*. Today, the validity of the insight needs no emphasis. We enter this world again in Kate O'Riordan's novel *Involved*, set in Belfast and published in 1995.

10

European and Cosmopolitan

'I AM European and Cosmopolitan – for humanity!' Meredith made this declaration in a letter to Maxse on 27 February 1871. The precise date is significant. It was the day set by Bismarck for the entry of German troops into Paris, sealing their victory in the Franco-Prussian War (so it was generally called, though Prussia had the aid of other German states, such as Bavaria). Emotionally, the conflict tore Meredith apart. His memories of Germany went back to the happiest years of his boyhood; France was the homeland of his wife.

France had been regarded by the majority of English people as the most culpable disturber of the peace. For twenty years, Napoleon III had been seeking to revive the military glories of his uncle, the great Emperor. While Britain and France shared responsibility for the Crimean War of 1854–56, it was English opinion – primarily English liberal opinion – which recognized the war with hindsight as a pointless adventure. In 1859 French armies were sent into Italy. Meredith passionately supported the cause of Italian liberation, but he knew that Napoleon was demanding a pay-off in the annexation of Nice and Savoy; worse, he protected the Pope and, for a time, prevented the Italians from securing Rome as their capital. Then, in 1870, Napoleon recklessly provoked war with Prussia. In his letter, Meredith reminded Maxse of this record:

Can you pretend to believe that France was not in need of the bitterest of lessons? Her philosophers said one thing, but military glory stuck to the passions of her people . . . I cannot forget that she appealed to the *droit du plus fort*. Nor can I forget that she has always been the perturbation of Europe.

The war began with a crushing German victory at Sedan (witnessed by the American General Sherman as invited guest of the King of Prussia). Napoleon, like 800,000 of his soldiers, became a prisoner, to end his days as an exile at Chislehurst. The Germans advanced to Paris and besieged it. But the French declared a republic, headed by Jules Favre, who struck a new note: 'It is for the King of Prussia, who has declared that he is making war on the Empire and not on France, to stay his hand.' The hand was not stayed. Léon Gambetta, who escaped from Paris in a balloon, emerged in the role of De Gaulle, refused to accept defeat, and raised fresh volunteer armies. With the recapture of Orleans and Chartres, there were hopes of the relief of Paris. It was only at the end of January 1871 that the Republic was forced to sign an armistice, the prelude to a punitive peace treaty.

Favre and Gambetta were Radicals, who had been in consistent opposition to Napoleon's rule and had protested against his declaration of war. The new spirit of France was incarnated in the *francs-tireurs*, fighters without uniforms, who harried the Germans by resistance activities such as blowing up bridges, which met with merciless reprisals. Consequently, the sympathies of Radicals in England swung rapidly and emphatically toward France. Maxse, going the whole hog as usual, spoke at a London meeting on 10 January 1871 to urge that Britain should enter the war on the French side. Meredith, taking a cool view as usual, discounted this suggestion, and so did John Morley. Meredith told Maxse:

> He [Morley] agrees with me that it would have been a silly madness to create a terrible and a justly wrathful enemy for ourselves (looking to the origin of this war) on the chance of securing a frenzied fantastical ally. So will you in time. Generous sympathies hold you spell-bound.[1]

The moment marked a turning-point not only in perceptions of France, which became a victim instead of a perennial aggressor, but also – and more important for the future – in perceptions of Germany. Persistence in the war after Sedan, it was quickly seen, could turn the emerging German Empire into a repressive, authoritarian regime. Karl Marx had presciently written in July 1870:

> On the German side, the war is a war of defence ... [But if] the German working-class allow the present war to lose its strictly defensive character and to degenerate into a war against the French people, victory or defeat will prove alike disastrous.[2]

Suddenly, Germany was perceived – in visible reality for France, and potentially for Britain – as a 'menace'. Several factors converged to form this perception: German arrogance and conviction of superiority, German social discipline, the growing German effectiveness in industry and technology, the traditions of the *Junker* class as personified by Bismarck, and of course the overwhelming Prussian victories in three wars (against Denmark, Austria and then France) since 1864. From the march through Paris and the proclamation of the German Empire at Versailles, only two months elapsed before *Blackwood's Magazine* published a startling futuristic story, entitled 'Reminiscences of a Volunteer', in May 1871.

The story is told, fifty years after the event, by an old man to his grandson. Attacking without warning, the Germans sink the British fleet with torpedoes, then a new weapon. German troops land at Worthing and take Horsham within two days. The British fall back to the North Downs and the decisive battle is fought at Box Hill, described as 'made for a battlefield'. The British effort is marked by 'vacillation of purpose', 'great confusion', 'hopeless disorder'. Refugees clog the roads; volunteers get no orders or conflicting orders; when a supply train reaches Leatherhead, there are wagons but no horses. When captured, volunteers are condemned to be shot as *francs-tireurs* but contemptuously released. Soon, London is occupied and the war is over. In the aftermath, the Germans impose an indemnity (as they did on France) and the inevitable heavy taxes, the narrator explains, 'keep us paupers to this day'. India is lost, the USA takes over Canada, Ireland is 'independent and in perpetual anarchy and revolution'. The outcome is a Britain with 'its trade gone, its factories silent, its harbours empty, a prey to pauperism and decay'.

With the more catchy title of 'The Battle of Dorking', the story was republished as a pamphlet and went into seven editions. Nor was it forgotten, at least in Germany. A translation entitled *Was England Erwartet* – 'What England Awaits' – was published in Berlin in May 1940.

The author of the story was anonymous, like those of most magazine contributions at the time, but the author was later identified in the Dictionary of National Biography as a British general, Sir George Chesney. The editor of the DNB was Meredith's friend Leslie Stephen, who was scrupulous about his facts. Chesney was a man of varied abilities who wrote two novels and became an MP after retiring from the Army. However, he might have had difficulty in getting his details right in the time at this disposal. He made his career in India and was in England only on temporary duty – to set up the College of Military Engineering – in 1871.

If we did not know about Chesney, internal evidence would point abundantly to George Meredith as the author. Box Hill is not the only imaginable location for the key battle, but it is directly in front of Flint Cottage. The successive stages in the British retreat – Epsom, Esher, Kingston – are places that Meredith knew well. The narrator, wounded and exhausted, takes shelter in a friend's house in Kingston, where Meredith's friend William Hardman lived. A child who is pathetically killed by a shell is called Arthur, the name of Meredith's son. There is dialogue in colloquial German, which Meredith had at his command. It is hard not to conclude that Meredith had, at the least, an advisory hand in the 'Reminiscences'.

What matters more is that the German threat and British military unpreparedness were linked subjects that preoccupied – one can almost say obsessed – Meredith from the time of the Franco-Prussian War to the end of his life. Nevil Beauchamp, as a by-election candidate, puzzles his Radical supporters by refusing to advocate cutting down the Army and Navy. Matthew Weyburn and Aminta, in their youth, worship Lord Ormont as a military hero, and respect him even after they adopt other values. A similar character, in *The Amazing Marriage*, is Carinthia's father, Captain Kirby, who 'never forgave the Admiralty for striking him off the list of English naval captains' – presumably in an economy drive. In *One of Our Conquerors*, Skepsey's worries about national fitness and the failing supply of potential soldiers are meant to be taken seriously. The thoughtful Dartrey Fenellah, who had been an Army captain, makes the 'sad admission that England had certainly lost something of the great nation's proper conception of Force: the meaning of it, virtue of it, and need for it'. England, he warns, 'bleats for a lesson, and will get her lesson'.

Meredith used one of his interpolated essays, in *Celt and Saxon*, to tilt at an English habit that particularly irritated him: the swing between excessive, complacent optimism and excessive, even panicky, pessimism. In the press and at dinner-tables, there is alarm at 'the awakening energy of the foreigner – a prodigious apparition on our horizon'. Unsatisfactory trade figures are cited: 'They led invariably to the question of our decadence. Carthage was named: a great mercantile community absolutely obliterated!' But the alarm yields to reassurance: 'Laudatory articles upon the soldierly "march past" of our volunteers permit of a spell of soft repose, deeper than prudent, at the end of it, India and Ireland consenting.'

In Meredith's view – and it is a view rammed home in 'Reminiscences of a Volunteer' – a part-time, inadequately trained volunteer force could never compete effectively in a serious war. What was needed, he insisted time and again, was conscription. This was a highly controversial question, and one that divided opinion among Radicals as well as more conventional Liberals. The idea of wrenching men from their innocent occupations and forcing them to fight was abhorrent to Radical standard-bearers such as John Bright or Henry Richard, the Welshman honoured as 'the Apostle of Peace'. On the other hand, some were influenced by the arguments of the French Left, which saw conscription as an egalitarian institution and a professional army as a threat to democracy. One fervent advocate of conscription was the pioneer Socialist, Robert Blatchford.

Remembering the Crimean War in the 1870s, Meredith used it as the occasion for Nevil Beauchamp's personal heroism. That war was almost fought again in 1878, when a Russian advance in the Balkans seemed to threaten Constantinople. Music-hall audiences chorused: 'We don't want to fight but by jingo if we do . . . The Russians shall not have Constantinople.' Supporters of Disraeli's anti-Russian policy were mostly Tories (or, as William Morris put it, 'greedy gamblers on the Stock Exchange [and] idle officers of the army and navy') but they also included Marx, on the grounds that Czarism was the world's most reactionary force, and Hyndman, founder a few years later of the Social-Democratic Federation. With Morris in opposition were the campaigning editor W. T. Stead, Dante Gabriel Rossetti, Browning, Trollope, and incidentally Mary Meredith's one-time lover, Henry Wallis.

Meredith was strongly in favour of resistance to Russia, and his anxiety was that lethargic Britain was reacting too slowly. (In the event, Disraeli secured an agreement that averted war and kept the Russians out of Constantinople; his claim of 'peace with honour' provided Neville Chamberlain with a useful precedent in 1938.) In a letter to his Tory friend Hardman, with whom he was in full agreement, Meredith wrote:

. . . the sentimental, or party ridden, or funky English have spoiled the hour. It is now too late to oust the Russians . . . Meanwhile press for an army. Ultimately it will come to a conscription, and the sooner the better. The volunteering system gives us a scum of men no match for countries that bring their best into the field, and in overpowering hosts.[3]

By 1891 Meredith was expressing relief that the British Army did not have to fight Bulgaria or Serbia. He was writing to another Tory friend, Frederick Greenwood, who had started a weekly called *The Anti-Jacobin* (it died a year later). After making it clear that 'my domestic political views are on t'other side', Meredith went on: 'I share your feeling for the country, and am with you in your watchful outlook.' He invited Greenwood for a visit and a talk about 'the clash coming, and our military inefficiency, etc.'.[4]

Up to 1898 (the year of an Anglo-French quarrel over territory in Africa) France was still a possible enemy, but with the turn of the century it was clear that the antagonist was Germany. Meredith, who seldom wrote 'letters to the editor', now wrote to the *Daily Telegraph*:

> [The Germans] stir a somnolent people, and, without stopping to regard them as enemies, we can accept them as urgently stimulating rivals, whose aim is to be the first of the world powers, chiefly at our expense . . . we have only to take the warning they give us, and be armed, stationed, and alert.[5]

In 1905 he wrote to Seymour Trower, chairman of the Navy League, pointing out that even predominance in naval power might not ensure Britain's safety:

> You have a patriot's heart in your Blue Water bosom. Join, then, with others of your kind in urging your countrymen to the cause of Compulsory Service. All the present muddle about our Army comes from the cowardly endeavour to shirk this main question.[6]

However, in his advocacy of military strength Meredith was concerned solely with the dangers of war in Europe. He was never an enthusiast for the British Empire, which was in a state of continual expansion through the last quarter of the nineteenth century – unlike Joseph Chamberlain, who transformed himself from Britain's leading Radical into the leading Imperialist. The proclamation of Queen Victoria as Empress of India in 1877 left him cold, and he wrote to Maxse:

> These English are so astonishing to my ideas of dignity and valour. Their present hugging of their India, which they are ruining for the sake of giving a lucrative post to younger sons of their middle class, is a picture for mankind. They and the Russians are matched.[7]

The dissociation, as though he was himself in no sense English, reads strangely. Perhaps he was in a mood of identifying himself as Welsh – or perhaps as cosmopolitan and 'for humanity'.

Almost every year during this period, English (and Welsh, Scots and Irish) lives were being sacrificed in Burma, Afghanistan, Sudan or some-where else around the globe. In *Celt and Saxon*, an Irishman levels the accusation: 'There's hardly a day in the year when your scarlet mercen-aries are not popping at niggers . . . You fight to subjugate, to enslave.' Expressing his own attitude in a letter, Meredith wrote on the Zulu war of 1879: 'Here is a strange war, in which the best of our nation are heartily with the enemy!'[8]

The biggest of these far-flung wars was the South African war of 1899–1902. Always hostile to imperialism, Meredith might have been expected to identify himself as a 'pro-Boer'. Actually, he described himself – in a letter to the *Daily News* protesting against a death sentence on a Boer guerrilla leader – as 'one who is neither for the Boer nor against him'. He did indeed write to congratulate Hyndman on his anti-war stand in the SDF journal, *Justice*, but the letter is less partisan than reminiscent of Meredith's agonized feelings in the Franco-Prussian War:

This hateful war tears me in two. I have to wish for the success of our men in the cause that I condemn. The Demon is in that mount of Gold. I had always the dread that the first steps of Imperialism would be bloody.[9]

In fact, Meredith was not so pro-Boer as he had been pro-Zulu, for in the Zulu war he had not felt obliged to 'wish for the success of our men'. The reason was a perception rare among the Radicals of the time: that the Afrikaners were harsher than the British in their treatment of the native African population. For the typical Liberal or Radical pro-Boer, the Afrikaners were a victimized community like Italians, subjected to the Austrian Empire, or Poles, oppressed by Russia. Inconvenient aspects of the South African scene were ignored, to be discovered only decades later in the era of apartheid. Meredith was able to cut across both the simplistic imperialist and the simplistic pro-Boer vision, pointing to the need to take account of 'the inferior civilisation of that people [the Afrikaners]'. He wrote: 'They were sons of the wilds, masters of slaves, Christians to whom the life and the agonies of a fractious black count for about as little as the end of a disabled horse.'[10]

Meredith was a humane man, alert to the suffering inherent in warfare. He regarded most of the wars that he witnessed in his lifetime – the Crimean War, the Franco-Prussian War, the South African war – as disasters that should never have been allowed to occur. The only war in which he was ardently partisan was the Italian war of liberation. But it is also true that he was fascinated by warfare and military affairs and fancied himself as an authority, or at least knowledgeable. Devotion to the cause was not the only reason why he was delighted to go to Italy as a war reporter; and his reports, while dramatically vivid, also comment with confidence on strategic problems and decisions. An anecdote from 1903 shows him correcting the judgement of a prestigious general, Sir John French. More curious is his obituary of Leslie Stephen. According to Meredith, Stephen 'had in him the making of a great military captain'[11] – a view that would not have occurred to other friends of the scholarly editor, who never put on uniform.

It is revealing, too, to observe how often military metaphors came to Meredith's mind and his pen. A dinner-table argument in *The Egoist* sounds like 'the sharp snap of rifles and the interval rejoinder of a cannon'. In a letter of advice to an advocate of Irish Home Rule, Meredith urged: 'Having blazed on the English lines with the artillery of agitation, you ought to charge them with the cavalry of facts.'

Then, the novels are full of men who are, or have been, in the Army or Navy. An incomplete list would include Major Strike in *Evan Harrington*; Robert Eccles and Major Waring in *Rhoda Fleming*; a whole array of characters in *Vittoria*; Nevil and his friend Roland in *Beauchamp's Career*; Lieutenant Patterne and Colonel de Craye in *The Egoist*; General Ople; Lord Ormont; Captain Fenellan in *One of Our Conquerors*; Chillon Kirby in *The Amazing Marriage*. And, though Meredith stressed the factual authenticity of *The Tragic Comedians*, he made Clotilde's father a general, whereas Helene's real father had been a professor.

War, it appears, inspired in Meredith the same contradictory mixture of attraction and repulsion as duelling. If duelling had meant nothing to him, he would not have introduced so many duels into the novels; but he repeatedly disclaimed any approval and indeed denounced the ugly and absurd custom. Similarly, experience in battle reflects credit on Carlo Ammiani, Nevil Beauchamp, Chillon Kirby and Lord Ormont, but when Meredith speaks in his own voice war is abhorrent. In a poem entitled 'On the Danger of War', he appeals:

Avert, High Wisdom, never vainly wooed,
This threat of war, that shows a land brain-sick.

In a letter evoked by a disarmament conference, he wrote:

We may hope that a time is at hand when without further bloodshed
the energies of men will be directed to a more complete conquest of
the elements, for the common weal. Battle enough for them in that
region.[12]

No doubt, this is what Meredith did hope, like most other reasonable and
compassionate people. Yet the thought is unoriginal and the expression is
stilted; one does not feel that his whole heart is in it.

Ambivalent feelings about war should not cause astonishment, when
we consider what war was like in the nineteenth century. There was still
(as Meredith reported from Italy) plenty of scope for individual combat,
for the sword and the pistol, for skill, initiative and courage. However,
changes in technology – heavier guns firing shells with greater frequency
and greater range, land-mines, machine-guns – meant that soldiers could
be killed in large numbers without getting a chance to display these
admirable qualities. In the Crimea, the American Civil War and the
Franco-Prussian War, the battlefield was a scene of mass slaughter. Meredith did not live to see the horrors of 1914–18, but they were in fact the
culmination of earlier developments. In principle, there was no limit to
what might be invented, and Meredith once wrote what reads uncannily
like a forecast of nuclear weapons:

... scientific men in all countries have been busying themselves with
the invention of destructive engines that shall annihilate armies and
fleets, and represent a fight of brains rather than animal force. We
have heard philosophers of the old school declare that the end of all
science was to polish man off the face of the globe! Perhaps there
cannot be much doubt that with man's consent the thing might be
accomplished.

His next sentence attempted reassurance: 'With the rapid advance of the
principle of destruction we are entitled to look forward all the more
confidently to the advent of the millennium of peace.'[13] But he cannot
have felt altogether sure about it.

Meredith had a right to claim that he was 'for humanity'; no nation
and no race was excluded from his visions of a better future under the
benevolent guidance of Nature. When he called himself a European, he
was stating an affinity with three countries that he knew well: France,
Germany and Italy. He travelled often and enjoyably in all three; he
spoke the languages; as a writer, he considered himself the inheritor of

a common culture, in which the names of Dante, Molière and Goethe meant as much to him as Shakespeare. As a citizen, however, he was English (or British, but in his time the adjectives were used interchangeably). On his doorstep, there were three minorities that figured recurrently in his novels. These were the Jews, the Welsh and the Irish (the Scots are surprisingly absent, though he had some Scottish friends).

Victorian attitudes, reflected in literature, produced two very different pictures of the Jew. There is the Jew as intellectual, full of learning and wisdom, representing a cultural tradition that demands respect. Such figures are Sidonia in Disraeli's *Coningsby* and George Eliot's Daniel Deronda. Generally, this Jew is Sephardic and brings to English eyes a fascinating touch of the exotic. When Clotilde in *The Tragic Comedians* imagines Alvan, before meeting him but expecting to admire him, she muses: 'Perchance a Jew of the Spanish branch of the exodus, not the Polish.' (Lassalle was actually an Ashkenazi Jew from Breslau, as Meredith knew.) On the other hand, there is the Jew as money-lender – mean, grasping, vulgar and altogether despicable. On a larger scale, he can be a financier in the Rothschild or Montefiore mould. Meredith could even imply that most financiers were Jews, describing Mattock in *Celt and Saxon* as 'one of the few Christians that can hold up their heads beside the banking Jew as magnates in the lists of gold'.

Meredith regarded anti-Semitism – along with other forms of xenophobia and stereotyping – as a vice of the narrow-minded English middle class, from which real aristocrats are exempt. Lady Constance Eglett in *Lord Ormont* says of her Jewish lawyer and adviser, Arthur Abner: 'Not many Christians have the good sense and the good heart of Arthur Abner.' Later, she declares:

> As for the Jews, I don't go by their history, but now they're down I don't side with the Philistines, or Christians. They're good citizens . . . They beat the world by counting in the head.

A rambling talker and not a very clear thinker, Lady Constance may be confusing Philistines in the Old Testament and philistines in the sense of the word originated by Matthew Arnold. Either way, she rises above bourgeois Christian society.

Algernon Blancove ('the fool') in *Rhoda Fleming* defrauds Mr Samuels, the jeweller, by pawning pieces of jewellery for which he has not paid. Meredith is attacking the assumption that gentlemen are not obliged to behave honestly towards Jews. Samuels, by employing a detective to investigate and confront Algernon, shows shrewdness and a proper concern for his own business interests, but also comes out above Algernon on the moral scale. When Algernon says: 'Mr Samuels is a very tolerable Jew; but he doesn't seem to understand dealing with gentlemen', the detective answers with a rebuke: 'I assure you, sir, Mr Samuels does know how to deal with gentlemen.' Nor is Mr Samuels a Shylock, for Algernon is let off with paying £300 out of the £500 that he owes.

The fullest treatment of anti-Semitism is, of course, in *The Tragic Comedians*. As soon as Clotilde shows interest in Alvan, she comes up against a horrified aunt: 'What on earth can you want to know about a creature who is the worst of demagogues, a disreputable person, and a Jew!' By upbringing, Clotilde herself is imbued with prejudice:

> The Jew was to Clotilde as flesh of swine to the Jew. Her parents had the same abhorrence of Jewry. One of the favourite similes of the family for whatsoever grunted in grossness, wriggled with meanness, was Jew.

The irony is that Clotilde too is Jewish, at least by Jewish law. In real life, Helene von Dönniges proudly recorded in her memoirs: 'My mother belonged to one of the old and highly cultured Jewish families in Berlin.' In the novel, Meredith notes: 'A streak of the blood was in the veins of the latest generation and might have been traced on the maternal side.'

Unimpressed by the aunt, Clotilde finds that Count Kollin, 'a dashing officer of social besides military rank', is a whole-hearted admirer of Alvan. Then she sees Alvan and is relieved to find that he does not, in the stereotypical sense, 'look Jewish'. This enables her to turn prejudice on its head, and she decides:

> There is the noble Jew as well as the bestial Gentile. There is not in the sublimest of Gentiles a majesty comparable to that of the Jew elect. He may well think his race favoured of heaven, though heaven chastise them still. The noble Jew is grave in age, but in his youth he is the arrow to the bow of his fiery eastern blood, and in his manhood he is – ay, what you see there! a figure of easy and superb preponderance, whose fire has mounted to inspirit and be tempered by the intellect.

Clotilde's father reacts violently when he learns that she is in love with Alvan: 'The General chattered and shouted of the desperate lawlessness and larcenies of that Jew.' Losing control, he drags Clotilde by her hair and threatens her with an axe (this scene too was taken from Helene's memoirs). Meredith draws a parallel between anti-Semitism and anti-feminism, for the General is acting from

> practical observance of two or three maxims quite equal to the fullest knowledge of women for rightly managing them: preferable inasmuch as they are simpler, and, by merely cracking a whip, bring her back to the post, instead of wasting time by hunting her as she likes to run.

What he fails to grasp is that Clotilde's romantic worship of 'the noble Jew' is matched by – and fed by – Alvan's pride and assertion of Jewish superiority in everything from sex to politics:

> 'We Jews have a lusty blood. We are strong of the earth. We serve you, but you must minister to us. Sensual? We have truly excellent appetites. And why not? Heroical too! Soldiers, poets, musicians; the Gentile's master in mental arithmetic – keenest of weapons: surpassing him in common sense and capacity for brotherhood . . . Already we have the money-bags. Soon we shall hold the chief offices. And when the popular election is as unimpeded as the coursing of the blood in a healthy body, the Jew shall be foremost and topmost, for he is pre-eminently by comparison the brain of these latter-day communities.'

From his reading and his knowledge of Germany, Meredith knew about blinkered anti-Semitism, but also knew about Lassalle's 'huge self-confidence and vanity'. Another irony: anti-Semites believed all Alvan's claims – that Jewish men were lusting for sexual conquest of Gentile women, that the Jewish plan was to move on from financial to political power, and that ultimately the Jew would be 'foremost and topmost' in Germany. Had they read Meredith, Alvan's speech might have been quoted by Hitler and Streicher.

However, in Meredith's time the threat to civilized values came unequivocally from anti-Semitism, not so much in Germany as in France and Russia. France, from the fraudulent conviction of Captain Dreyfus for spying in 1895, was swept by a wave of virulent anti-Semitism that captured most of the press and considerable sections of society, whether aristocratic, bourgeois or working-class. English admirers of the Voltairean tradition were astonished and shocked. Emile Zola's statement in defence of Dreyfus, remembered as *J'accuse*, was made at real risk; he was sentenced to prison and had to take refuge in England. Meredith, who detested Zola as a novelist and considered him a harmful literary influence, paid tribute to his political courage.

Russia, in the same period, was the scene of pogroms (a Russian word) in which thousands of Jews were slaughtered by armed gangs encouraged or at least tolerated by the authorities. In England, a journalist named Lucien Wolf wrote a book, *The Russian Government and the Massacres*, to nail this responsibility, and sent a copy to Meredith. Reading the book in 1906, Meredith wrote to Wolf:

> The story of this persecution of the Jews in Russia sweeps us back to the Middle Ages. It is hard to write of with composure after going through the pages . . . What a confused idea the Christian still has of the Jew. Russian and Polish Jews may be hard to bear with, but they are the fruit of the rigours they had to endure for centuries; and from the lowest depths of poverty they produced a Maimonides.[14]

Despite his sympathy with the Jews, Meredith was not attracted by Zionism, which was making progress (thanks to the pogroms) among Jewish communities in Europe and was supported in England by, among others, Israel Zangwill. For Meredith, the Jews were a valuable element in a nation such as Britain. He concluded his letter to Wolf:

> You are against Mr Zangwill's Palestine scheme, and I, for a different reason I fancy. For I would have the strong Jew blood mix with ours. Meanwhile it runs and soaks in this Russian red pit, to blacken our outlook on a future.[15]

He could extend sympathy to the Jews; with the Welsh he could feel empathy, from his belief in his Welsh descent. As we have seen (Chapter 1), he often introduced Welsh characters into his novels and made observations on the distinctive 'Welsh nature'. The characters were always admirable, the observations favourable. One might therefore have expected him to make regular visits to Wales, probably to Powys, the part of Wales associated with the shadowy Welsh princes who bore the name of Maredudd or Meredith. The strange fact is that he went to Wales only once in his life, and then with great reluctance.

Meredith's younger son, William, qualified as an electrical engineer and took a job with a company that was replacing steam-driven by electrical equipment in the steel mills and coal-mines of South Wales. He went to live in Llanelli, a flourishing centre of the steel industry. In 1888, he invited his father and his sister Mariette for a summer visit. Meredith had planned to stay with a friend, George Stevenson, in Scotland, and then to take Mariette for a tour of Germany and Austria. Mariette chose to go to Wales, so Meredith agreed and wrote accordingly to Will, asking him to rent a house by the sea. Apologizing to Stevenson, Meredith explained: 'It is not a prospect of pleasure to me, but I have learned to shut my eyes.'[16] To another friend, he complained that Mariette 'preferred *Wales* to *Bayreuth* and *Tyrol*'.[17] The italics (or rather underlinings) are eloquent.

For whatever reason, there was no rented house, so Meredith and Mariette stayed at a hotel in Tenby. The Welsh, he reported to Maxse, 'know no better than the English how to cook'.[18] They went on to Llandeilo, Llandovery and Brecon. 'Drives to castles and waterfalls,' Meredith noted without enthusiasm.[19] Mariette twisted an ankle walking on the Brecon Beacons, and it rained incessantly. There was nothing to do in the evenings: 'imagine the desperation of a man who has to strip for bed at half past nine o'clock! Up at six, to gaze on the same wet pavement!' Before thankfully reaching Cardiff and the train home, they stopped at Ferndale in the Rhondda valley, where Will suggested going down a pit. 'Blindly I consented,' Meredith wrote after getting his face black. However, he was impressed by the electrically powered lift and timed the descent of a quarter of a mile at fourteen seconds – 'rather magical'.[20] The visit yielded material for scenes in *The Amazing Marriage* and Meredith learned a little Welsh (then the spoken language in the valleys) or, more likely, got someone to supply him with the phrases he needed. The mining community is portrayed sympathetically in *The Amazing Marriage*, but without the insight and authenticity that Zola achieved in *Germinal*.

The only Welshman mentioned personally in Meredith's letters was Will's boss, Mr Howells, whom he described as 'a supremely energetic Welshman – worth twenty Saxons, for the work he does'. Howell Edwards is the name given to the colliery manager who opposes Lord Fleetwood in the strike. Other than that, Meredith merely noted: 'People were kind, polite as the Welsh are always.'[21] The comment is favourable, but based on scanty experience. He returned to compare notes with a friend, Louisa Lawrence, who had been to Stuttgart, where he recalled the cafés, the opera and the vineyards. 'I contrast your tour with mine,'[22] he told her enviously.

Meredith continued to enthuse over the qualities of the Welsh whom he did not know – 'they have poetry in them, they are valiant, they are hospitable', he declared in *Celt and Saxon*. Encountered in reality, they were merely kind and polite. One sees why he had to be dragged to Wales by Mariette and, when he got there, went to bed at half past nine. He had no need of the real Wales; the Wales that he loved was a country of the imagination.

Meredith never went to Ireland and wrote no Irish scenes in his novels, except the glittering Dublin ball at the beginning of *Diana of the Crossways*. He considered himself half-Irish because his mother's maiden name had been Macnamara, but this meant less to him than his romantic identification with the Wales of the ancient princes. In the novels, Diana's glamour is enhanced by her Irishness, but some Irish characters are introduced for comic effect: Mrs Chump in *Emilia*, the wildly quarrelsome Sullivan Smith in *Diana*, and Con O'Donnell, with his cloudy flights of rhetoric, in *Celt and Saxon*. Mrs Chump speaks in a phonetically spelt Irish brogue, which – like Cockney – was a comic effect in itself, for instance in *Punch* cartoons. Meredith himself found the brogue funny and teased his friend Bonaparte Wyse about his accent. There seems to be no reason why the vulgar, tactless Mrs Chump should be Irish; she might be more convincing as a Cockney. Certainly, Meredith would not have created a Welsh Mrs Chump.

But, unlike Wales, Ireland presented a political problem which was greatly to the fore in the nineteenth century. The Fenian Brotherhood – forerunner of the IRA – raised the banner of an independent Irish Republic and went into battle with bombings, assassinations and, once, an attempt at guerrilla war. Charles Stewart Parnell forged the Irish Nationalist Party into a formidable political weapon with the demand for Home Rule. The precise shape of Home Rule was negotiable; it did not imply rejection of the British Crown, but it did mean the establishment of an Irish parliament and government with power over Irish affairs. Gladstone, as leader of the Liberal Party, was a convert to Home Rule and in 1886 it became the policy of his Liberal government. The Cabinet post of Chief Secretary for Ireland, and the responsibility of trying to get a Home Rule Bill through the Commons, went to Meredith's friend John Morley. Justin McCarthy, who had written enthusiastically about Meredith's novels in his role as literary critic, was now an MP supporting Home Rule. Through him, Meredith met other prominent Nationalists, such as John Dillon and Barry O'Brien. But Frederick Maxse, fast moving away from his old Radicalism, was fiercely opposed to Home Rule.

Not only did Meredith support Home Rule, but he recognized that British politicians would not have yielded to it without the Fenian campaign of violence. He wrote to George Stevenson in 1887:

... consider what they have had to do even to rouse drowsy Bull! Petards discharged between his knees merely fretted him. They had to be exploded under his chin. Think of the French, Russians, Poles and Socialist Germans, you will own that the Irish are by comparison a docile and a patient people.

Nevertheless, the same letter shows that he was repelled by the thought of a complete separation of Ireland from England, and discounted the idea of an Irish Republic:

Dillon would not at first visit an English house, but since he came to know the English he has humanized to real brotherhood ... I have friends who conceive that the Irish are scheming for a Republic. They have their wits; they are not the people to put the hand to the throat. They cannot exist without England or in opposition – and they know it ... I would rather have the simple form of a central Government, only that England at the close of eighty odd years has proved herself unfit for the task.[23]

It was, in fact, 'eighty odd years' since Pitt's Act of Union, in 1800, had abolished the autonomous Dublin parliament and established a centralized United Kingdom. The blunder was to treat Irish (and Scots and Welsh) people simply as though they were English. Yet Meredith did attach a precious value to the idea of an association without oppression. He was torn (how often he was torn!) between nationalism and internationalism, as he showed in another context. An ardent sympathizer with Italian nationalism, he was also able to respect the ideal of the multi-national Austro-Hungarian Empire. Count Serabiglione, the collaborator in *Vittoria*, is a cowardly and pitiable character, but his belief in an Italy peacefully making the best of Austrian supremacy is not indefensible. Anna von Lenkenstein, the Austrian lady who loves Italian civilization and wants to live happily in Italy, is portrayed sympathetically.

There is ambivalence in a description of a march through Milan by troops under Austrian command. It is led by Italians wearing, Meredith writes disapprovingly, 'the livery of servitude'. Then:

Following the Italians came a regiment of Hungarian grenadiers, tall, swart-faced, and particularly clean-limbed men, looking brilliant in the clean tight military array of Austria. Then a squadron of hussars, and a Croat regiment; after which, in the midst of Czech dragoons and

German Uhlans and blue Magyar light horsemen, with General officers and aides about him, the veteran Austrian Field-Marshal rode, his easy hand and erect figure and good-humoured smile belying both his age and his reputation among Italians. Artillery, and some bravely-clad horse of the Eastern frontier, possibly Serb, wound up the procession.

This is an admiring picture of the Austrian Army, which Meredith rated as the best in Europe. But what is stressed is the welding of men from diverse ethnic groups into a common allegiance, symbolized by the commander, Field Marshal Radetzky, who was of Hungarian descent and had his home in the Czech lands. The British Army, similarly, had its Irish and Scots and Welsh regiments.

Meredith set *Celt and Saxon* in the 1850s, when British power was challenged both in Ireland and in India; Philip O'Donnell is wounded in India, presumably in the repression of the 1857 Mutiny. In his outlook, Philip is placed midway between the English arrogance of Adister and the defiant Irish nationalism of his cousin, Con. At a dinner-party, Con provokes the English by making fun of their national emblems – the lion is a beer-drinker while the unicorn is 'a consumer of doctor's drugs'. But he fails to get a rise out of Mr Rumford, who merely replies: 'One loves the banner of one's country – that is all.'

Meredith was probably satirizing some of the Irish Nationalists he had met when he gave Con a long, rambling speech, inspired by whisky, ranging over 'the empty glories of our Isle of Saints', Ferkelné the bard, Craftiné the harper, Cuchullin, and the charge of the Enniskillen Dragoons at the Battle of Fontenoy (as a contingent of a British force, a point that Con overlooks). Coming to present times, he reproaches Philip for his moderation:

'Will Philip O'Donnell tell me that Ireland should lie down with England on the terms of a traveller obliged to take a bedfellow? . . . Thousands of us are in a starving state at home this winter . . . We don't want half and half doctoring, and it's too late in the day for half and half oratory. We want freedom, and we'll have it, and we won't leave it to the Saxon to think about giving it . . . They tell us over here we ought to be satisfied. Fall upon our list of wrongs, and they set to work yawning. You can only move them by popping at them over hedges and roaring on platforms . . . Ay, the time for the Celt is dawning: I see it, and I don't often spy a spark where there isn't soon a blaze . . . Off with our shackles! We've only to determine to be free, and we'll bloom again; and I'll be the first to speak the word and mount the colours.'

But when Con declares: 'The Englishman has an island mind, and when he's out of it he's at sea', Philip retorts: 'The Irishman too has an island mind, and when he's out of it he's at sea, and unable to manage his craft.' Meredith has two targets: the ungenerous callousness of the dominant power, and the parochial obsessions of the oppressed.

After Con has stumbled off to bed, leaving the brothers Philip and Patrick to talk over the scene, Philip remarks: 'Rhetoric is the fire-water of our country.' Con is planning to get into Parliament for an Irish constituency and wants Philip to do the same. Philip sees that Con would 'become the burlesque Irishman of the House'. As Meredith could have gathered from McCarthy or Dillon, flights of rhetoric by unsophisticated Nationalists, delivered in a brogue, gave the English an excuse to dismiss the serious reality of their case. 'Once there, I should be boiling with the rest,' Philip admits.

As an officer in a British regiment, Philip has found that he gets on well with Englishmen. He explains to Patrick:

'I burn to live in brotherhood with them, not a rift of division at heart! I never show them that there is one. But our early training has us; it comes on us again . . . These tales of starvation and shootings, all the old work just as when I left, act on me like a smell of powder. I was dipped in "Ireland for the Irish"; and a contented Irishman scarcely seems my countryman.'

The problem, as Philip sees it, is the inability of the stolid, unimaginative English to build co-operation on a basis of tolerance:

'Friendship, as far as possible; union, if the terms are fair. It's only the name of union now; supposing it a concession that is asked of them; say, sacrifice; it might be made for the sake of what our people would do to strengthen the nation. But they won't try to understand our people. Their laws, and their rules, their system are forced on a race of an opposite temper, who would get on well enough, and thrive, if they were properly consulted. Ireland's the sore place of England, and I'm sorry for it. We ought to be a solid square, with Europe in this pickle.'

In the figure of Philip O'Donnell, we see the most attractive side of Meredith: the reasonable man, the liberal with a small 'l', making a plea for understanding and harmony above the opposing forces of fanaticism and intolerance. But, after Gladstone had twice failed to bring Home Rule to fruition, Meredith never completed *Celt and Saxon*. Perhaps he foresaw the furious and bloody conflicts that blazed up after his death.

11

Forgotten and Discovered

'GRIEF and Fame' is the apt heading for a chapter in Lionel Stevenson's biography. It deals with the year 1885: the year of Marie's death and also of the publication of *Diana of the Crossways*, Meredith's most successful novel in both critical and commercial terms. He had reached the age of fifty-six, and had become a senior figure in the literary world.

Marie was buried in the Dorking cemetery, where Meredith had bought a plot. No one outside the family was invited to the funeral except John Morley, to whom Meredith wrote: 'If your engagements and state of mind permit, you would be very welcome by my side to back me on this forlorn march of dust.'[1] Fourteen-year-old Mariette, acutely distressed, went the day after her mother's death to stay with Jim and Alice Gordon, and then spent some weeks with the Morleys. Will, now twenty, went to stay with a Vulliamy uncle in France. Meredith wrote a dozen or so letters to friends. In one letter, Marie was 'the best of wives, truest among human creatures';[2] in another, 'the most unpretending, brave and stead-fast friend ever given for a mate'.[3]

Meredith's status as an important writer had been established in 1879 by *The Egoist*. A supporter, James Thomson, noted sardonically: 'A man of wonderful genius and a splendid writer may hope to obtain something like recognition after working hard for thirty years.' The critics were puzzled or disappointed by *The Tragic Comedians*, but enthusiastic about *Diana*. The influential W. E. Henley had already (when reviewing *The Egoist*) hailed Meredith as 'a companion for Balzac and Richardson, an intimate for Fielding and Cervantes', and he wrote in his review of *Diana* for the *Athenaeum*: 'Every touch is to the purpose, every sentence packed with significance and luminous with insight.' For the *Saturday Review*, *Diana* was 'a singularly vivid conception, worked out with great literary power'. The *Illustrated London News* wrote: 'Seldom is it the privilege of the reader of modern novels to take up one so fresh, so vivid, so strong in its incidents as is *Diana of the Crossways*.' The *Spectator*, hostile to Meredith throughout his career, conceded that *Diana* was 'decidedly his best'. Arthur Symons in *Time* declared that it was 'purely a work of genius'.

Public interest was heightened when it was realized that *Diana* was transparently based on the life of Caroline Norton, who had died in 1877 but was well remembered. She was remembered for her campaigns for women's rights, and the growing recognition of the courageous 'new woman' was a major factor in the success first of *The Egoist* and then of *Diana*, especially with women readers, who were important customers of the bookshops and libraries. Caroline was remembered, too, as the central figure in two big scandals: the 'criminal conversation' lawsuit against Lord Melbourne and the leak to *The Times* of Peel's decision to repeal the Corn Laws. Both episodes were described in detail in *Diana*.

Caroline Norton's responsibility for the leak has never been proved and is regarded as doubtful by her modern biographer, Alan Chedzoy. In 1885 it was accepted by reviewers of *Diana* as 'historic fact' (*Saturday Review*) or 'a matter of history' (*Illustrated London News*). But her family, whether motivated by loyalty or conviction, upheld her innocence. An Irish peer and prominent Establishment figure, Lord Dufferin, was her nephew. At the time when *Diana* was published, he was Viceroy of India and was busy with the conquest of Upper Burma. It took him ten years to give his attention to Meredith's novel, but in 1895 – he was then ambassador in Paris – he issued this statement: 'I am in a position to prove that neither Mrs Norton nor Mr Herbert were in any way concerned in the transaction.' Meredith agreed to include a note in new editions of *Diana*:

A lady of high distinction for wit and beauty, the daughter of an illustrious Irish House, came under the shadow of a calumny. It has been examined and exposed as baseless. The story of *Diana of the Crossways* is to be read as fiction.

Clearly, Meredith had no wish to get involved in a wearisome wrangle. Readers either went on believing that Caroline had leaked the secret and the retraction was a matter of form, or (more likely) had lost interest in the scandal, now fifty years in the past, and were content that *Diana* should be 'read as fiction'. If anything, Lord Dufferin's belated action may have been good for sales.

The success of *Diana* in 1885 owed much, of course, to its quality, something to the Caroline Norton story and the feminist readership, something to the reviews, and a good deal to Edward Chapman of Chapman and Hall. He had a treble relationship with Meredith: as publisher, as employer – for Meredith was still devotedly working as reader for the firm and going to the office once a week – and as a friend. Having persevered with Meredith ever since he had published *The Shaving of Shagpat* in 1856, he was determined to push *Diana* as hard as he could and reprinted it twice during the year. More than this: he reprinted all Meredith's novels in a uniform edition at lower prices. This was the accepted accolade for a writer admitted to the literary canon, and might have given Meredith the inexhaustible sales of Dickens, Thackeray, George Eliot and Trollope – but never did.

Up to this time, Meredith was virtually unknown in the United States, though *Evan Harrington* had been published there. Now, however, the Boston firm of Roberts Brothers published all his novels up to and including *Diana*. Sales were reasonable, considering that Meredith was a new writer to the American public and Roberts was not a leading firm; reviews were highly favourable and in the author's opinion more intelligent than in British papers. In 1889 he wrote to Jessopp:

> To the Americans I am indebted for their having bent a serious examination to my works, instead of the jeer and round shoulder of the Lout. Consequently I feel that I am an American writer; and it is for the money simply that I publish here.[4]

Later, in 1893, the more prominent firm of Scribners brought out a new American edition, paying an advance of £1,200 and royalties at the rate of 15 percent, instead of the 10 per cent that was the rule in Britain. Meredith became still more pro-American. In one letter to an American admirer, he wrote: 'I have looked on them as the hope of our civilisation.'

After Marie's death, Mariette went on living at Flint Cottage and a governess moved in to see to her education. Though Meredith was quite an authoritarian father, Will and Mariette were fond of him and the relationships were harmonious. But Meredith's elder son, Arthur, kept his distance and was on affectionate terms with only one person, his half-sister Edith. Even though he had felt himself exiled by being sent to schools on the Continent, he chose not to live in the same country as his father and stepmother. After leaving school, he had taken a job in a warehouse at Lille. He had vague ambitions to be a writer and Meredith offered to help – 'I am allowed the reputation of a tolerable guide in writing and style'[5] – but he produced only a few magazine articles. In 1881 he became seriously ill with tuberculosis, perhaps caused by the dust in the warehouse. He went to live in Italy, had a relapse, was brought to a hospital in London, and was then cared for by Edith and her husband. A sea journey to Australia was suggested and Arthur agreed to go, but refused a first-class cabin; he probably guessed that his father would be paying for it. After returning, he was nursed by Edith until he died in September 1890. Meredith wrote to her: 'I am relieved by your report of Arthur's end. To him it was, one has to say in the grief of things, a release.'[6] Arthur was buried at Woking, where Edith lived. It was not far from Box Hill, but Meredith did not attend the funeral; he was advised by Will, he explained to Edith, that standing through the ceremony would be tiring for him.

This year of 1890 was a sad one for Meredith. Two of his closest friends, Fred Maxse and William Hardman, died – Hardman a week after Arthur. Bonaparte Wyse died in 1892. Leslie Stephen, four years younger than Meredith, survived until 1904. Even for people who lived comfortably and had the best of medical care, it was unusual to pass the age of seventy.

But, as Meredith often asserted in his poems and his letters, life went on. In 1892 Will married an attractive and musically gifted young woman, Margaret Elliot ('Daisy' to the family). Two years later, Mariette married a wealthy City man with American origins, Henry Parkman Sturgis. Their home was in Leatherhead, within easy reach of Box Hill. Within a few years, both these couples became parents and Meredith was a grandfather.

He had long ago given up writing for the *Ipswich Journal*, and had nothing but contempt for newspaper journalism. He made Alvan tell Clotilde in *The Tragic Comedians*: 'Journalism for money is Egyptian bondage. No slavery is comparable to the chains of hired journalism.' He proved himself a good journalist when he covered the Italian war for the *Morning Post*, but it is clear that he took on the assignment out of enthusiasm for the cause, not from interest in the work. Hyndman, who was with him in Italy, recalled: 'Meredith positively hated writing as a daily task, and could not bear to think of the whole thing as a mere matter of business.'[7] The editor, Sir Algernon Borthwick, later tried several times to enlist Meredith as a contributor, but in vain. Eventually, Borthwick (or the accounts department) removed him from the list of people who received the paper free. Meredith exploded to Maxse: 'Does the great Sir Algernon imagine I shall take in of my own free will and exhaust my funds by paying one penny for his journal? He cannot be so insulting to my taste, my opinions, my economy and my intelligence.[8]

By contrast, Meredith stuck to his chore as publisher's reader for Chapman and Hall until 1895. He had to read and report on a great deal of rubbish, but he seems to have enjoyed making acid comments, sometimes in the course of recommending publication on commercial grounds. On a novel by one prolific lightweight of the age, Annie Thomas (a pseudonym), he commented: 'It is written for the market and will suit the market. There is no fire or genius in the book, and no pretension . . . She is certainly very clever, and quite shallow enough for common readers.'[9]

Occasionally, he wrote to the author to convey his view that she (more often than he) was writing below her powers. He complimented Anna Steele, author of *So Runs the World Away*, on her 'cleverness, literary faculty, glimpses of a power of humour, at present rather hard, and the capacity for simple pathos, as well as a trained observation superior to that of many reputed good writers' – but then advised her to study Stendhal and told her: 'I have a residue of hostility to the enchantress who *could* be of the true sort and preferred to attire herself in the conventional garb to tickle the English ear and captivate the English eye to the sacrifice of her art.'[10]

Believing that women could and should write as seriously as men, Meredith was angrily scornful of women who churned out artificial, sentimental romances. He rejected *East Lynne*, the first novel by Mrs Henry Wood, and years later he rejected a novel by Ouida (another pseudonym). Harrison Ainsworth, himself a best-selling novelist, championed them both and obliged Chapman to make Meredith give *East Lynne* a second reading, which did not alter his opinion. In market terms, Ainsworth was absolutely right and Meredith crashingly wrong. *East Lynne* sold a million copies, stayed in print for decades, and was eventually dramatized and filmed. Mrs Wood wrote forty successful novels, while Ouida wrote forty-five.

On the other hand, Meredith took a favourable view of Olive Schreiner's *The Story of an African Farm*, recognizing its quality while reporting that it needed some rewriting. A Chapman and Hall employee recalled that Meredith 'took unusual pains to give Miss Schreiner his help and advice, and she readily and graciously accepted them'. Schreiner herself, however, denied that she ever let Meredith or anyone else touch her work.

By literary standards, Meredith's worst mistake was his rejection of Samuel Butler's *Erewhon*. 'Will not do,' he told Chapman tersely. Butler's comment (years later and not for publication) was that if he had occupied

Meredith's position he would have rejected *Diana of the Crossways* – 'No wonder if his work repels me that mine should repel him.'[11]

In 1869, a young man from Dorset named Thomas Hardy submitted a novel entitled *The Poor Man and the Lady* – a curious echo of the theme of *Evan Harrington*. Meredith advised rejection, but spotted talent and invited Hardy to the office for a talk. It was his custom to withhold his name, introducing himself simply as 'the reader', and Hardy identified him only when, as established writers, they met again. Hardy's first effort was never published, nor did he become a Chapman and Hall author, but his career was well launched during the 1870s. He recalled after Meredith's death: 'Meredith was very kind and most enthusiastic. He gave me no end of good advice, most of which, I am bound to say, he did not follow himself.' This was true enough; the novice writer was advised to concentrate on his plot and tone down his social criticism.

Chapman was paying Meredith £250 a year, and it was seriously needed up to the success of *Diana* and the American deal. In 1867 Marie admitted to her father: 'Money is horribly scarce. We can't get any from any body.' Over the years, Meredith's position improved and he was able to save. Conspicuous expenditure and big parties were no part of his way of life; but he was hospitable to friends and even to comparative strangers, he kept a good wine-cellar, and he took long holidays abroad (though not every year). Doctors' bills and nursing, in Marie's terminal illness and later when his own health declined, must have been a considerable expense. When he died, his estate was valued at £33,701. It is hard to explain how he accumulated this amount, even with back royalties from the uniform edition and his American earnings. Profitable investment is the only possible answer; the capable Will Meredith was acting as his father's financial adviser.

The long relationship between Meredith and Chapman broke down in 1893. The contract for the uniform edition had given the firm the copyright for five years, but Meredith discovered that they had been retaining the copyright and marketing the books for two years longer. He told a friend, Louisa Lawrence:

I have been occupied in a conflict with my publishers, who have been nefariously issuing my books after expiry of the lease of my copyright ... You will be glad to hear that on inspection of the accounts we find that the sale of the books doubles every year. So they are regarded as 'a property'. But where I should claim £600 per annum, the publishers, relying on my ignorance, proposed the half.[12]

To Chapman, he wrote angrily: 'You have not behaved openly and honourably . . . I must own that I am outwearied by your shifty dealings.'[13] Chapman, who was near to retirement, may not have been personally responsible, but Meredith now had a literary agent – it was a fairly new profession – and was in a position to look for another publisher. The last Meredith book published by Chapman and Hall was *Lord Ormont* in 1894. Will had given up his profession as an electrical engineer and joined the publishing firm of Constable. Confident that his son would prevent any 'shifty dealings', Meredith became a Constable author. The firm published *The Amazing Marriage* and also his last book of poems, *A Reading of Life*. After his death, they brought out a Memorial Edition, very handsomely produced.

As he grew older, Meredith became an elder brother, or even a father-figure, to younger writers. Hardy was only twelve years younger, so the gap was less than a generation. They had a good deal in common; both were novelists, both were poets, and both believed that philosophy should be at the heart of literature. But reflection, as well as a difference in temperament, drew Meredith to belief in the beneficence of Nature, and Hardy to the disillusioned conclusion that the world was cruel and meaningless. Edmund Gosse recorded a meeting between Meredith and Hardy, after which the former felt that he had been grieved by Hardy's pessimism. Gosse commented to Hardy, 'I wonder whether you were not saddened by his optimism?'[14]

In what was really the younger generation, one can compile a remarkable list of writers who were welcomed at Flint Cottage or left memories of Meredith on record: Robert Louis Stevenson (twenty-two years younger), Oscar Wilde (twenty-six years younger), Bernard Shaw (twenty-eight years younger), George Gissing (twenty-nine years younger), Arthur Conan Doyle (thirty-one years younger), James Barrie (thirty-two years younger), H. G. Wells (thirty-eight years younger). For Meredith, they were all fellow-craftsmen. Stevenson, spending a week at the Burford Bridge Inn, was introduced to Meredith by Leslie Stephen. Alice Gordon, Meredith's neighbour, observed that he 'had the art of drawing out the best of Mr Meredith's brilliant powers of conversation'; but Meredith was impressed as well as flattered and 'prophesied success and fame for him'. Stevenson had not yet published his first book.

Gissing was a Chapman and Hall writer and received advice from Meredith about his early novels, *The Unclassed* and *Isabel Clarendon*. Coming from a poor background, he found his material in the insecure life of the 'unclassed' – hack journalists, shop assistants, prostitutes. When he worried that this might alienate potential readers, Meredith reassured him. He recorded: 'Meredith tells me I am making a great mistake in leaving the low-life scenes; says I might take a foremost place in fiction if I pursued that.'[15]

Barrie, at first, was not a pupil but a pilgrim. He went to gaze at Flint Cottage from the hillside across the road, and when Meredith walked down from the house to the gate, he took fright and ran away. Later, he was introduced to the great man by his employer – Meredith's friend Frederick Greenwood, editor of the *St James' Gazette* – and was often a guest.

Oscar Wilde was also a guest, and Meredith, with his taste for epigrammatic wit and paradox, wrote that he was 'good company'. This, however, was before the disaster. When Frank Harris tried to get Meredith's signature to a petition pleading for Wilde to be released on parole, he met with no sympathy. Meredith replied that 'Abnormal sensuality in a leader of men . . .' was 'a crime, and should be punished'.[16]

When Wells leaped to fame with *The Time Machine*, the new genre of science fiction caught Meredith's interest. He felt, however, that younger writers were better fitted to develop it. He urged G. K. Chesterton to write a novel about the threat of a comet that might destroy the earth, and then the story of 'a man who wanted to improve humanity and was for ever getting into quarrels in endeavouring to do so'. Meredith's proposed title was *The Knight of Perfectibility*, and in 1904 he invited Wells to Box Hill for a day and offered the subject to him. The 'knight of perfectibility' does indeed sound Wellsian, but the book remains unwritten.

These young writers were fervent admirers. Stevenson, popular enough by 1888 to be interviewed in San Francisco, declared: 'I think George Meredith out and away the greatest force in English letters . . . No other living writer of English fiction can be compared to Meredith.'[17] Gissing, in a letter to his brother, went even further: 'It is incomprehensible that Meredith is so neglected. George Eliot never did such work, and Thackeray is shallow in comparison.'[18]

But in the chorus of admiration, the voice of Henry James is conspicuously absent, despite (or perhaps because of) the similarities that can be listed. Both Meredith and James explored the subtleties of character analysis; both excelled in portraits of women; both were given to complexities of style and structure and addicted to abstruse words that readers found baffling. It is a fine point whether *One of Our Conquerors* or *The Golden Bowl* is more difficult to read. Yet James was infuriated by Meredith. In a letter to Gosse, he claimed that he could not read more than ten pages a day of 'the unspeakable *Lord Ormont*', which is surely the most accessible and straightforward of Meredith's novels. It was, he complained, full of 'extravagant verbiage, of airs and graces, of phrases and attitudes, of obscurities and alembications'. The Oxford Dictionary does not list 'alembication', though it defines 'alembic' as 'an apparatus formerly used in distilling'.

While enjoying the adulation of young (male) writers, Meredith made ventures into emotional relationships with young women. He was not looking for another wife; of the four women with whom he thus became involved, two were married and he was on good terms with their husbands. However, what he offered and sought was certainly love. He wrote that it was permissible for a man to love another man's wife 'if he has long adored her, and known himself to be preferred by her in innocency of heart; if he has solved the problem of being her bosom's lord, without basely seeking to degrade her to being his mistress'. This passage occurs in an unfinished novel or novella entitled *The Gentleman of Fifty and the Damsel of Nineteen*, published in the posthumous Memorial Edition with no indication of when it was written. The gentleman, Gilbert Pollingray, has been devoted for years to an unhappily married French woman, strongly reminiscent of Renée in *Beauchamp's Career*, but is now attracted by young Alice Amble, who is charming and strong-minded, with a passion for riding which recalls Janet Duff Gordon, or Rose Jocelyn. She admires Pollingray, but he makes her feel gauche and immature – 'Mr Pollingray must and does think me a goose.' He reflects:

> What are fifty years? They mark the prime of a healthy man's existence. He has by that time seen the world, can decide, and settle, and is virtually more eligible – to use the cant phrase of gossips – than a young man, even for a young girl. And may not some fair and fresh reward be justly claimed as the crown of a virtuous career?

In 1886, the year after Marie's death, twenty-four-year-old Hilda de Longueuil came to stay with Meredith's neighbour Grant Allen and his wife. She was a French-Canadian, but evidently she had friends or relatives in France and Meredith regarded her as French. She had gone to live in France, in the south-western town of Pau, to recover from a love affair that had ended disastrously. A period of calm was presumably what she wanted, but during her stay in Surrey she received attentions from a distinguished 'gentleman of fifty' (actually fifty-eight) which provided fuel for gossip. Will Meredith was worried and wrote to his father, who replied tersely: 'The report has no truth in it . . . Gossip must be strangely in want of immediate provision for her jaws to be gabbling about a man of my years. I charitably suppose that your poverty of language causes you to address me on such a subject so bluntly.'[19]

Hilda left England at the end of the year, pursued by a long letter from Meredith which began:

My dear friend and best,

The solitude of the Chalet presses on me now that you have quitted England. I followed you step by step with the hours . . . when that same Mlle de L. is out of her shyness, and conventionally animated, I would back her for true illumination of beauty against the field of enchantresses – and I think I am something of a judge . . . I remember too at one moment taking a dive into an eye that sparkled pure light and still detains me.[20]

Hilda inspired two poems, of which one was sent to her soon after her departure:

> Can another love be born
> In heart that love has left outworn;
> Appearing dead to sweet desire,
> Its mouths of earth once mounts of fire? . . .
>
> Give life to Life; in turn it gives.
> Believe thy heart alive; it lives.
> Know Love more heavenly than of old
> Revealed, and Love will not be cold.
> The Past is dust; thy heart is blood;
> It bears thy fate upon its flood,
> Set it on nobleness, and soon
> A nobler love will crown thy noon.

This lyric was followed by a long poem, 'The Sage Enamoured and the Honest Lady', which was published in 1892 with a new edition of 'Modern Love'. The lady, wounded by her unhappy experiences with men, is wary of the Sage's advances, but responds to his appeal to a love justified by equality of the sexes:

For us the double conscience and its war,
The serving of two masters, false to both,
Until those twain, who spring the root and are
The knowledge in division, plight a troth
Of equal hands: nor longer circulate
A pious token for their current coin,
To growl at the exchange; they, mate and mate,
Fair feminine and masculine shall join . . .

And the Sage can rejoice:

A new land in an old beneath her lay;
And forth to meet it did her spirit rush,
As bride who without shame has come to say,
Husband, in his dear face that caused her blush.

Meredith envisaged an intellectual as well as an emotional relationship, writing: 'I am sure she has reserves of thought to throw off an impression on the senses, however strong the stamp, whatever the causes. She has mind, and a friend to point the mind . . . Perceive that I embrace your whole existence . . .'[21] He proposed an exchange of letters, which could be published with the title 'Letters to a Lady, on the Art of Fiction'. The letters could be impersonal – 'nothing in relation to your dear wounded heart, save when it has imperious voice for its friend'. This project never came to fruition. In June 1887, Hilda seems to have yielded to his declarations of love, but now he was cautious:

It seemed to me my duty the other day to destroy a pencilled letter, that might, if anything happened to me, be read by others not so well able to judge of the heroism of the writing. I did so with the sense of suffering a heavy loss. I had in it palpably the dearest of women's hearts open and gushing on mine. It has gone and had to go.[22]

So the romance dwindled. While Hilda moved to St Jean de Luz, Meredith spent the summer with Leslie Stephen and his family in Cornwall. In September he apologized for delay in writing to her, giving various reasons: arrears of work, finding a new governess for Mariette and a new cook, and 'digestive struggles'. He ended the letter: 'Your faithful and devoted George M.' – but it was his last.

[226]

Hilda's successor was Jean, the young and attractive wife of Walter Palmer, of the biscuit-making company Huntley and Palmer. He was a rich man, and she was able to create a fashionable salon in their Mayfair house. The French writer Léon Daudet was a guest in 1894 and his wife recorded: 'She [Jean] paid great attention to Meredith, in a way that showed she was in full sympathy with this great man of genius.' His letters to her, written in a sentimental tone not intended to be taken seriously, were addressed to 'Queen Jean', 'Adorable Sovereign', or 'Sweetest and Dearest of the Powers of Earth'; but he was generally careful to slip in: 'My love to Walter'. When she made a journey to South Africa, he told her: 'I shall not be sure of you until again I see the dear eyes I love.'[23] Mrs Palmer never inspired a poem like 'The Sage Enamoured', but she received a light-hearted verse:

> I would I were with Jean,
> A-tripping on a green,
> And she to call me her true knight,
> And I to crown her queen.

In 1895, the *Illustrated London News* published an enthusiastic review of *The Amazing Marriage*: 'Intellect, beauty, drama, hesitating narrative, turns and returns of thought – all pass into the springing and beating flame.' It was signed by Alice Meynell, a woman in her forties with a high reputation as a poet and critic. Her husband, Wilfrid Meynell, was editor of the *Weekly Register*, and they belonged to a cultured and rather earnest literary circle. Meredith immediately invited her to Flint Cottage, where she paid many visits up to the time of his death. Her manner was reserved (or perhaps cautious) and she was more of a listener than a talker. He reassured her:

> I can find the substance I want in your silences, and can converse with them . . . I am well disposed either to listen or to worship the modest lips that have such golden reserves.

To please her, he started to grow violets, her favourite flower, in his garden, and to send them to her from time to time. A species of blue iris was dedicated to her with the name of Alicia Caerulia. In a sonnet headed 'To A. M.', she read:

> For reasons known to us we give the name
> Alicia Caerulia to that flower,
> Sweet as the Sea-born borne on the sea-wave;
> That Innocent in shame where is no shame,
> That proud Reluctant; that fair slave of power,
> Who conquers most when she is most the slave.[24]

Meredith's last object of adoration, appearing on the scene in 1899, was Lady Ulrica Duncombe, daughter of the Earl of Faversham. Unusually for a young woman of her class, she had been a student at Girton College. When they became friendly, he knew that, like Hilda, she had been through an unhappy love affair. He wrote to her:

> I read on your brows that the young heart had gone through torment. You have done me the honour to open it to me, and I may help to comfort you.

Sentimental letters began to reach her in London or follow her to the Yorkshire moors: 'I speak to the pearliest of ears . . . and if in such cases the heart is a galloper, it is not to be distrusted when a veteran is at the reins' . . . 'You know you are sunshine to my sight – not only to mine! You are a shedder of warm gold.'[25] Bunches of violets also arrived, announcing themselves poetically:

> Our joy is unsurpassed
> By those among the Blest,
> May we but breathe our last
> Beside Ulrica's breast.

But Meredith was now over seventy and in ruined health, so he could do no more than lecture her on the value of love:

> The whole mystery of love is in the phrase. It means that we have perpetually the presence of the beloved; that whatever may befall her is shared by us; that we are inseparable, though our mortal destinies be entirely different, so that there is joy in pain, or rather the joy conquers pain. That is love, and I want you to know what it is; for at present I think you hold it in some disesteem.[26]

He wrote that, when he was too ill to work: 'I conjured up a transparent image of Ulrica, with her decisive ways, her intrepidity, that may be recklessness by fits . . . One thought of her drew me to regions where wings have play and bosoms are bare.' As he imagined her, or wished to shape her, she was once again the intrepid Rose Jocelyn. But the real Ulrica was a serious-minded product of Girton, far from any recklessness, and did indeed hold romantic love in disesteem. She felt that his attitude to her was patronizing, and he had to defend himself:

Ulrica has been fancying that I dilute her pretensions to join in the greater questions of the world, treat her with a pat-patting bonhomie, am probably attracted to her more by her personal charm (it counts for something, I being man and poetic) than by her mental calibre . . . I am glad it has been stated; it shows her sensitive in the wish to be taken seriously as one whose mind is alert and abroad, which was known to me from the beginning; or would even the personal charm have controlled me and directed me to think of her so constantly?[27]

He had sent her a complete set of his novels, only to find that she preferred to read philosophy or history. Admiration for Goethe (she read German) gave them a link. He was pained to learn that Ulrica disapproved of Diana, a character whom he loved. He protested:

Yet Ulrica says of herself, that she has imagination. Then she ought to be able to enter the breast of a passionate woman . . . subject in crisis to a swoon of the mind – mark that, O imaginative lady! for there are women and noble women, who stand unpractised and alone in the world, liable to these attacks, driven for the moment back on their instincts: – cannot Ulrica compassionately, if not sisterly, realise the position?[28]

As an Earl's daughter, Ulrica was expected to choose a husband from her own caste, in which 'bluestockings' or intellectual women were not valued. Meredith sympathized:

Ulrica's misfortune lies in her having tastes out of the ken of her class – the 'barbarians' of M. Arnold. So that she exacts too much of the men around her . . . such are our English still that a titled young woman, however beautiful, must expect to be worshipped half for the aureole gilding her name.[29]

His prediction was: 'Ulrica will at some period hence astonish the world with the exhibition of an eccentric choice that she has made.' Had she been Rose Jocelyn, he could have been right, but by 1902 she was showing signs of yielding to convention, which he recognized by starting his letters with 'Dear Lady Ulrica'. The relationship was fraying; she was slow in answering letters, forgot to thank him for violets, and cut down both the frequency and the duration of her visits. He reacted sadly:

> I am resigned to take what my Heavens bestow, though I prayed for more, and this that I am to get seems doled out parsimoniously to the starving wretch, just to keep him alive. You shall be met at the station on Saturday at 4.15 ... Your return to town is evidently intended to be early, alas! – Some cloud is on Ulrica's mind, I know it by being chilled.[30]

In September, she left to spend the winter in India. She returned in the spring of 1903, but there was no real revival of the letters and visits. In 1904 she married Everard Baring, an Army officer whom she had met in Calcutta, where he was Military Secretary to the Viceroy. The immense wealth of the Baring family, based on the famous bank, may have compensated her for the afternoons she had devoted to discussing Goethe at Flint Cottage.

Meredith had always been an exceptionally handsome man, and was reluctant to admit to any change as the years went by. In *The Gentleman of Fifty*, young Alice thinks that Gilbert looks twenty years younger than he really is: 'His moustache and beard are of the colour of a corn sheaf, and his blue eyes shining over them remind me of summer.' The real Meredith, at the age of sixty-seven, made a striking impression on Léon Daudet:

> Meredith was beautiful, with a strange, high-strung, painful beauty, the result of sorrow and thought. Long curling hair, a high, white, open brow, a pointed white beard, frosty blue eyes glowing with a watchful flame, a straight nose, a deep strong voice, nervous hands, and ataxic legs, gave him the appearance and the fascination of a modern sorceror, a Celtic Mephistopheles.[31]

But another visitor, Edith Cooper, had drawn a more ruthless picture four years earlier. For her, his eyes did not glow:

There is a little nervous difference in their focus – about them something of that piteous old-dog decrepitude one sees in portraits of Carlyle. The hair is in tint stone colour, what there is of it curls. The mouth is gaunt with suffering, the nose fierce and withered, the brow rather narrow, much lined, the laugh a brilliant contradiction to the features – Tragic life written over them . . .[32]

'Gaunt with suffering' was no idle phrase, for Meredith's physical condition was lamentable. The dyspepsia that had plagued him even as a young man never left him; in 1883 he adopted a strict diet of milk and fruit, but he found that he lost energy and reverted with relief to meat and wine. Later, he told a visitor: 'The brain never gets tired. It is the stomach that conquers one. And I was born with a bad stomach.'[33]

More seriously,he was attacked by gallstones. In 1892 he was operated on by a leading surgeon, Buckston Browne, who was an admiring Meredith reader and offered to forgo his fee. Mariette wrote to a friend a month after the operation: 'Thanks to Mr Buckston Browne's great skill and care, he is able to walk about again, and he hopes soon to set to work again, and he seems to begin once more to enjoy life.'[23] But the problem recurred and Browne had to perform two more operations, in 1896 and 1899.

From about 1890, Meredith grew increasingly deaf. Visitors found that he preferred monologue to conversation, as to a considerable extent he always had. John Morley described him in 1894 as 'very deaf'. Desmond MacCarthy, a young man who was received at Flint Cottage in 1901, noted: 'He was almost stone-deaf, which accounted for the exaggerated loudness of his voice, and the continuity of his discourse, which rolled elaborately along.' In fact, Meredith talked and MacCarthy listened for two hours, until a nurse appeared with a dose of 'some dismal fluid'. As MacCarthy left, Meredith was talking to his dog.

He had two attacks of ulcerated eyelids, an irritating interruption to work, in the 1890s. MacCarthy observed that 'his eyes, once blue, were faded'; but another pilgrim, Chesterton, found as late as 1905 that 'his eyes were startlingly young'. Those eyes had served him through decades of longhand writing, proof-reading and reading manuscripts for Chapman and Hall (from the 1870s there were typewriters in offices, but seldom in the homes of aspiring writers). Meredith never used spectacles, just as he adamantly refused to use an ear-trumpet.

From 1881, he began to have difficulty in walking. This condition is described as locomotor ataxia, but that is a description of the symptom rather than a diagnosis. The most obvious explanation is osteo-arthritis, but this is normally accompanied by severe pain, of which there is no mention either in Meredith's letters or in accounts by Will, Mariette or any of his visitors and friends. In 1881 he told Maxse: 'the malady seems to be nervous, affecting the spine, and I begin to feel my legs labouring after an hour of motion'.[35] Two years later, he told Jessopp: 'My doctor attributes the malady, which is of many apparitions, to a congestion of the lower spinal cord.'[36] And he wrote to Cotter Morison: 'Burney Yeo [the doctor] is positive as to the spinal cord as the seat of the malady.'[37] In 1884 he told Stevenson bluntly: 'I am a cripple.' Yeo's diagnosis is borne out by the fact that a lesion of the spinal cord often leads to bladder and bowel problems, which were repeatedly affecting Meredith.

It was a depressing affliction for a man who had once been a thirty-mile-a-day walker. He had to tell Stevenson in 1884 that he could walk 'not much more than a mile'.[38] As time passed, he even found it difficult to walk from the chalet to the house. A friend, James Sully, recalled: 'As he moved awkwardly down the steep grassy slope of the hill, I instinctively stretched out my hand to help him. He gently but firmly put away the proffered aid.'[39] In 1890 an American visitor, David Bispham, was invited to meet Meredith for dinner at a house half a mile from Flint Cottage. The great writer arrived late and had to support himself by holding on to 'a chair, a table, the mantelpiece, or whatever he chanced to be near' – which made Bispham suspect that he was drunk.[40] In 1902 he wrote to Leslie Stephen: 'I remember how when you last left the cottage a pang of envy seized my legs at sight of your power to walk without leaning on an arm, as I must.' In February 1904 he wrote to Stephen sadly: 'We, who have loved the motion of legs and the sweep of the winds, must come to this.'[41] Stephen died soon after receiving this letter. Meredith lived for five more years, immobilized, cared for by a resident nurse, and seated in his armchair to greet visitors. He went out in a donkey-cart, with his dog Sandie running alongside. Mercifully, all his disabilities were physical, with no effect on his mental capacity or his speech. He was able to say in 1903: 'I still look on life with a young man's eye. I have always hoped I should not grow old as some do – with a palsied intellect, living backwards.'[42]

Meredith had come to hold a unique position in literature. The uniqueness lay in the contrast between his high reputation, from which there were few dissenters, and his failure to attract a mass readership. Other writers hailed as 'great' – Fielding in the eighteenth century; Scott early in the nineteenth; then Dickens, the Brontës and George Eliot; and Hardy in Meredith's own time – had been admired by the discerning and had also found widespread acceptance in the bookshops and the lending libraries. Meredith's public was confined, as he put it himself, to 'an acute and honourable minority'. In 1896 a leading article in the *Daily Chronicle* made an unequivocal judgement: 'By general consent of the English-speaking world . . . Mr Meredith is accepted as our foremost living novelist, with Thomas Hardy by his side.' Half a dozen eulogistic books were published; there were honorary degrees, and then the Order of Merit; in 1895 the Burford Bridge Inn was the scene of a celebratory dinner, attended by forty writers or critics including Hardy and Gissing, both repaying Meredith's early encouragement in their own careers. Nothing was lacking – except the sales.

Talking or writing to friends, Meredith was bitter – though he tried to sound resigned or even amused – about the lack of appreciation. In 1871 he complained: 'I publish and find my head in the pillory, am battered with bad eggs, and am suffered to withdraw promptly.'[43] In a digression that suddenly interrupts the narrative in *Beauchamp's Career*, he wrote: 'My way is like a Rhone island in the summer drought, stony, unattractive and difficult . . . back I go to my wilderness.' In 1881 he told Arthur: 'the better the work the worse the pay, and also, it seems, the lower the esteem'.[44] He denounced reviewers as 'Sunday parsons, children of pay, slaves of the multitude, leaders of the blind'.[45] Writing in 1882 to Mrs Wyse, he exclaimed: 'Who can help laughing to see an old fellow still stitching books that nobody buys!'[46] Stevenson was told in 1884: 'I have for five and thirty years addressed unwilling listeners.'[47] In 1898 he wrote to Janet Ross that he was always described as 'obscure, eccentric, and the like' – 'I never see my name in print without displeasure.'[48] He discouraged Walter Jerrold from writing a book about him – 'an unpopular author should be held from exhibition'.[49] (Jerrold wrote the book, all the same.) In 1902 he declined a request for an interview with: 'The opinion of an ex-practitioner in Light Literature is of small value, and my name counts for nothing with the public.'[50] According to Ellis, one of his last statements was: 'no-one reads my books'.[51] In 1908 he discouraged a French admirer, René Galland, in the same terms as he had Jerrold: 'why give your time to the pushing me forth as a prominent author, when I have no claim to popularity in England!'[52]

Meredith was complaining both about his small readership – which, after *Diana*, was larger than he conceded – and about adverse criticism. After his death, Galland not only wrote two books about Meredith but also studied the reviews 'to ascertain the real truth of the matter'. This led him to declare with some irritation:

> Who is the writer who has never been misunderstood? Keats and Shelley fared much worse at the hands of reviewers. The legend of a Meredith reviled by British criticism must go. What gave birth to it were the words of Meredith himself . . . making the critics responsible for public disdain.[53]

Galland was right. The highly favourable reviews of *Diana* have been quoted earlier; here are some of other novels:

> The wealth of imagination and thought which is lavished upon this large company [of characters] is something wonderful. (The *Westminster Review* on *Emilia in England*)

> He has shown as much power of thought and style as would fit out a dozen writers of sensation novels. There is scarcely a page in which there is not evidence of originality, and, what is much rarer, of conscientious labour, often skilfully applied. (The *Saturday Review* on *Vittoria*)

> Mr Meredith has long since won a recognised position in literature. Whatever he writes, and he has written much, is distinctively marked by real genius . . . We know no one with whom to compare him for the purposes of criticism. (The *Westminster Review* on *Harry Richmond*)

> Even while we are not sure that we thoroughly comprehend all the purpose of this novel, it is impossible not to be struck with its merits. There is intellectual wealth in it enough to set up half a dozen writers of fiction. (The *Examiner* on *Beauchamp's Career*)

> He has this sure mark of lofty genius, that he always rises with his theme, growing more strenuous, more self-contained, more magistral, as the demands on his thought and imagination increase. (The *Secularist* on *Beauchamp's Career*)

> There is no question but *The Egoist* is a piece of imaginative work as solid and rich as any that the century has seen, and that it is, with

Richard Feverel, not only one of its author's masterpieces, but one of the strongest and most individual productions of modern literature. (Henley in the *Athenaeum*)

The gentleness, the mastery, and the perfect beauty of expression are a gift and a possession for ever, for which we would do homage on our knees . . . Mr Meredith is easily first of our living English authors, and among the highest of all time his rank is high. He stands towering above his contemporaries. (The *Saturday Review* on *Lord Ormont*)

Indeed, a feeling grew that adulation had gone too far. The *Spectator* protested in 1894: 'We have barely a dozen works of imagination in the English language which would justify the piled-up epithets of panegyric applied during the past five or six years to the novels of Mr George Meredith.' He benefited, this article suggested, from 'an artificially imposed vogue'. Was Meredith, in fact, promoted by 'people who are supposed to know much better than the multitude'? That was the view of Margaret Oliphant who, in a bilious review of *The Egoist*, described him as 'the favourite of the clever, the pet of the superior classes, *goûté* above all by those who confer fame'. She was the author of more than a hundred books, identified in the *Oxford Companion to English Literature* as 'undemanding romances'. For those in her intellectual bracket, the word 'clever' was enough to dismiss both Meredith and his admirers.

While there was a consensus (with a few dissenting voices) that Meredith was an important writer, there was also a consensus that he was a minority writer. The sympathetic Arthur Symons echoed the hostile Margaret Oliphant: 'Mr Meredith's latest novel [*Diana*] is the event of the day to a small, but very select and very devoted, circle of admirers.' 'It is not probable that Mr Meredith will ever be a popular author' was the opening sentence of the *Athenaeum* review of *Beauchamp's Career*. In 1893, a long and respectful article in the journal *Temple Bar* summed up: 'Popular, in the sense in which Dickens and Walter Scott on the one hand were popular, or on the other in which Miss Braddon and Mr Rider Haggard are popular, he is not and never will be. But it is impossible to imagine Mr Meredith ever bending for a moment to catch the vulgar ear.' Mary Braddon wrote seventy-four successful novels, including the sensational *Lady Audley's Secret*. Rider Haggard wrote thirty-four adventure novels, including *She* and *King Solomon's Mines*.

Why was it that Meredith was not and never could be popular? Justin McCarthy, who was an admirer and also a personal friend, gave an explanation: Meredith lacked the essential gift of telling a story, and 'the power of holding firmly the attention and interest of his readers'. Alexandre Dumas, in McCarthy's opinion, was an 'inspired idiot', but he was also 'the best story-teller our age has seen'. McCarthy went on:

> In our own literature Mr Wilkie Collins . . . is not to be compared for a moment with Mr Meredith in intellect, and fancy, and true perception of human feeling; but he is a good story-teller, and his books are read everywhere, while Mr Meredith's novels only extort the half-reluctant admiration of some rare groups of intellectual readers.

For the reader who was happy with Dumas and Collins, Meredith presented all kinds of problems. The story did not move along. It was interrupted by commentaries and digressions. Some happenings were highly improbable – the 'statue' episode in *Harry Richmond*, the marriage itself in *The Amazing Marriage*. Some were out of character – could Diana have been foolish enough to betray the political secret and lose Percy? There were always, except in *Richard Feverel* and *The Egoist*, too many sub-plots and minor characters. Worst of all, the novels were over-complicated and confusing. Margaret Oliphant found in *Harry Richmond* 'such a thicket of incidents and emotions, as it is very difficult for the reader to force his way through'. Geraldine Jewsbury (another novelist) gave up on *Vittoria*: 'No mortal memory can keep in mind the Lauras, the Amalias, the Leckensteins, the Violettas, the Austrians pure and simple, the Austrianized Italians, the prudent Italians, the patriots, the conspirators . . . How are human beings with limited faculties to understand all the distressing threads of this unmerciful novel?'

Some critics felt that Meredith was not cut out to be a novelist at all – not, anyway, a novelist convincingly presenting the life of his time and place. The (regrettably anonymous) writer of a study in *Temple Bar* commented on *Rhoda Fleming*:

> As we close the volume we feel less that we have been assisting at a tragedy of actual life, than that we have been watching a drama of absorbing interest, in which the veracious and masterly presentation by two or three great actors of the shock of passions has made us indifferent to the want of reality in their surroundings.

Meredith's novels do, indeed, have a strong affinity to drama – perhaps to dramas that were originally written to be read rather than staged, such as *Faust* or *Peer Gynt*. 'We feel', said the writer in *Temple Bar*, 'that he has less in common with the modern novelist than with the Elizabethan dramatist.' The same thought occurred later to Virginia Woolf; she suggested that Meredith was born out of his time, and should have been an Elizabethan or Jacobean dramatist. In fact, Meredith named Shakespeare and Molière, rather than any novelists, as the masters to whom he was most indebted.

If readers had trouble with his narrative method, and with his principle that narrative was 'the vehicle of philosophy', they had still more trouble with his style: the complexity of his syntax, his elaborate metaphors, his rich but strange vocabulary. Again and again, they were brought up short by words that seemed to make no sense in the context, or were so unfamiliar as to be incomprehensible. 'Difficult' and 'obscure' were the labels that became attached to him, and still cling to him today. He was defiant, but not surprised, when he found that his last book of poems 'has caused everybody to take up the old cudgel "Obscurity" for my incorrigible nob'.

Reviewers sighed over the task of deciphering his meaning – often sympathetically, but they sighed, and warned readers of the difficulties. The *Athenaeum* quoted a passage in *Harry Richmond* as 'a fair sample of the meaningless sententiousness with which Mr Meredith writes'. The *Times* reviewer of *Beauchamp's Career* complained: 'It is often very difficult to follow his meaning . . . He not only writes high over the head of the average reader, but he credits him with his own quickness of apprehension, and, glancing from point to point, indulges recklessly in elision . . . We are sometimes inclined to suspect that he is mocking our dullness.' The *Examiner*, finding the same faults in *The Egoist*, reproved him: 'Obscurity, we can assure Mr Meredith, is not necessarily interesting.' Also with reference to *The Egoist*, the *New Quarterly Magazine* judged: 'He is so artificial as to seem to have lost the power of using straightforward language.' Edmund Gosse, reviewing *The Amazing Marriage* for the *St James's Gazette*, declared: 'the Alexandrian extravagance of Mr Meredith's style has now reached such a pitch that it is difficult to enjoy and sometimes impossible to understand what he writes'. Only one review – of *Emilia* in the *Examiner* – credited him with writing 'clear, accurate English, individual yet unaffected'.

However, some critics noticed that Meredith was capable of varying his style in accordance with the mood he was seeking to evoke. The novelist Arabella Shore wrote in the *British Quarterly Review*:

His ordinary style, especially that of his vivid dialogue, is terse, abrupt, full of force, point and colour, in brief, strong sentences, like the waves of a short chopping sea. But in his most reflective and most touching passages he has that grave sustained tone which seems to dominate the situation, using its restrained pathos, its musical suggestions, and its deep inquiring murmur, according to a law of his own.

Lionel Johnson, reviewing *Lord Ormont* in *Academy*, picked out 'two perfect passages': Aminta's journey to Steignton and her marathon swim in the sea with Matthew. Johnson wrote:

His style in such places has the brilliance of rippling and sparkling waves, laughing and dancing shoreward, with a kind of delighted way-wardness, a grace upon their strength. It is joyous writing, cordial and entrancing; it clears the air to an exulting serenity.

It is easy to find examples – and, alas, there are too many – of the 'difficult', 'obscure' Meredith. Harry Richmond, in his first-person narration, is made to say:

The stains on me (a modern man writing his history is fugitive and crepuscular in alluding to them, as a woman kneeling at the ear-guichet) burnt like the blood-spots on the criminal compelled to touch his victim by savage ordinance, which knew the savage and how to search him.

This is equalled by a sentence in *The Tragic Comedians*:

Were the spot revealed in the man the whole man, then, so unerring is the eyeshot at him, we should have only to transform ourselves into cowards fronting a crisis to read him through and topple over the Sphinx of life by presenting her as the sum of her most mysterious creature in an epigram.

On the other hand, if we are looking for evocative, deliberately simple writing, we can find this in *Harry Richmond*:

I lifted my face to the sky; it was just sunrise, beautiful; bits of long and curling cloud brushed any way close on the blue, deliciously cool; the grass was all grey, our dell in shadow, and the tops of the trees burning, a few birds twittering.

Or this, from the 'statue' scene:

> I knew it was my father, but my father with death and strangeness, earth, metal, about him . . . I saw him descend. I dismounted. We met at the ropes and embraced. My arms slid on him. Each time he spoke I thought it an unnatural thing; I myself had not spoken once.

Even when Meredith was conveying thought, not action, he could choose directness and simplicity, as in this passage from *The Egoist*:

> It would be madness to let her go. She affected him like an outlook on the great Patterne estate after an absence, when his welcoming flag wept for pride above Patterne Hall. It would be treason to let her go. It would be cruelty to her. He was bound to reflect that she was of tender age, and the foolishness of the wretch was excusable to extreme youth. We toss away a flower that we are tired of smelling and do not wish to carry. But the rose – young woman – is not cast off with impunity.

In dialogue, too, Meredith suited his style to the character, in this case Robert Eccles in *Rhoda Fleming*:

> 'One kiss, my girl,' he said. 'Don't keep me jealous as fire. One! and I'm a plighted man. One! – or I shall swear you know what kisses are. Why did you go out to meet that fellow? Do you think there's no danger in it? Doesn't he go about boasting of it now, and saying – that girl! But kiss me and I'll forget it.'

Accounts of Meredith's way of talking also show a variation between easy clarity and mannered complexity. Hyndman recalled that one day in 1863, when Meredith was talking 'without effort or artifice', Frank Burnand exclaimed: 'Damn you, George, why won't you write as you talk?' But at other times, Hyndman observed, Meredith 'deliberately cultivated artificiality'.[54] Especially in later years, he was seen as giving 'a performance' or 'an exhibition'. An American visitor, Julian Hawthorne, made the perceptive judgement: 'He would have been happier as a beautiful and brilliant woman, the queen of a salon.'[55] As Flaubert is remembered to have said '*Madame Bovary, c'est moi*', Meredith might have said 'Diana is me'.

In any consideration of Meredith's style, we must bear in mind that he wished in his heart to be valued and remembered as a poet. 'Only a few read my verse, and yet it is that for which I care most,' he told his friend Edward Clodd. Little of Meredith's poetry is now remembered, except for 'Modern Love', which holds classic status and was republished in 1996 in a 60p Penguin edition. However, the only poet who wrote a biography of Meredith, Siegfried Sassoon, rated him very highly. For Sassoon, 'Love in the Valley' was 'one of the very greatest sustained love lyrics in English poetry', and 'Lucifer in Starlight' was 'among the greatest sonnets in the language'. Sassoon even thought that some of the poems in Meredith's 1887 collection would live when *The Egoist* had become 'a museum piece'.

Meredith, with Scott and Hardy, was a writer with a large output of both poetry and prose. Literary historians have trouble in placing such a writer: is he a novelist who also wrote poems or a poet who also wrote novels? Sassoon regarded 'The Woods of Westermain' as 'a Meredithian masterpiece', but when he reached its third section he found that 'the thinker and the novelist are getting the upper hand of the poet'.[56] Priestley judged: 'When we read his novels we are constantly reminded of the poet. But then when we turn to the poetry we find ourselves back in the company of the novelist and philosopher.'[57] Gillian Beer's analysis was: 'Typically his manner in his novels is condensed and associative, close to much poetry and close also to unstructured thought-processes.'[58] In the end, Priestley rated Meredith as 'the master of a medium that is somewhere between poetry and prose'.[59]

Most critics found, both in the poetry and in the novels, that Meredith was pressing on too fast for readers to follow him. Pritchett remarked on 'his passion for compressing, for crystallising, for the economy of telescoping his ideas and for the abrupt transition from image to image'.[60] G. M. Trevelyan made the point: 'Sometimes they [Meredith's metaphors] are mixed, because, before the reader has finished with the first, the poet's mind has rushed on to a new image, and the result is a sort of composite photograph, the imposition of one picture on another. His pen has too little control over the pace at which his brain works.'[61] Priestley commented: 'His imagination pours out images while his thought presses forward, and we see him leaping from metaphor to metaphor like a man leaping from log to log across a river' (an image that Meredith might have appreciated).[62] As Sassoon put it: 'His brain works so rapidly that the words themselves seem bustled along at a rate which does not allow them to permeate one's mind with full effect. Words resent being run off their legs; Meredith often forgot this, and denied them the slowness which enables them to do their proper service.'[63] We can meet this effect time and again in Meredith; here is one example:

> But still may they who sowed behind the plough
> True seed fix in the mind an unborn Now
> To make the plagues affecting us things past.

But obscurity in Meredith – or, to view it more sympathetically, the difficulty of reading Meredith – has another cause. The novel as a literary form was undergoing a profound change, to which Meredith himself powerfully contributed. In a novel like *The Heart of Midlothian* or *Jane Eyre* (to name two that are unquestionably great) the reader could clearly follow what was happening, both in the outer world of events and in the feelings and motives of the characters. After *Richard Feverel*, and increasingly in the modern novel, these feelings and motives were not presented to the reader as data, but explored as they developed. At the same time, in the post-Darwinian age of intellectual and philosophical uncertainty, the efforts of the characters to understand the world in which they found themselves, and shape their conduct accordingly, became in large part the subject-matter of, at least, the serious novel. Not accidentally, the novel generally considered to be Meredith's most difficult and forbidding, *One of Our Conquerors*, is concerned with two problems which the central character, Victor Radnor, cannot resolve. The moral problem of his life with Nataly is enough of an anxiety for one man to bear, and might well be the whole content of, say, a Trollope novel. But equal weight is given to Victor's search for 'the Idea' which could make sense of the world if only he could find it. An American critic, Donald David Stone, writing in 1972, observed:

> ... the Meredithian obscurity often perfectly suits the theme of the novel. Meredith's occasional inability to articulate curiously parallels Victor's inability to comprehend ... it is obscurity which vanquishes both hero and novelist, although in a strangely functional, often compelling manner.[64]

It could be said that the accusation of obscurity was the price paid by Meredith for being ahead of his time, and for writing a twentieth-century intellectual novel about a struggle to interpret the world, like Mann's *The Magic Mountain* or Sartre's *The Age of Reason*.

Certainly, it was his misfortune that the 'obscure' tag injured him in a way it did not injure Henry James, nor Proust, nor even James Joyce. Joyce, in fact, was an admirer of Meredith and quoted him in *Portrait of the Artist as a Young Man.* Today, there are readers who have considerable trouble in working their way through Salman Rushdie, or Italo Calvino, or Gabriel García Márquez; but 'difficulty' has not debarred any of these writers from mass popularity. In literary or artistic matters, it is useless to ask for justice.

'There is nothing saddening about death to a man of my age,' Meredith wrote in 1881. His age then was fifty-two. He was writing to Arthur, who was recognized to be tubercular and was going to the Swiss Alps in the hope of benefiting from the mountain air. 'But the thought of a child of mine having the prospect of life extinguished in youth, is a cruel anguish,' Meredith continued.[65] He may have felt guilty about surviving Arthur, to whom he had been of little help as a father. He was himself in a bad state of health; he had been unable to work for some months because of stomach trouble, now he had whooping-cough, and the 'spinal malady' had begun to limit his walking. He cannot have expected to live to be an old man, and evidently he did not greatly want to. In 1890, when Arthur died, Meredith wrote to his friend John Morley: 'I am ready for my day of darkness.'[66]

His feelings about death stemmed from a blend of stoicism and optimism. Taking his stance with Greek and Roman stoics, and rejecting the consolations of Christianity, and certainly any illusion of personal immortality, he was resigned to bidding farewell to the world with his last heartbeat. Yet his faith in Nature gave him cheering, if vague, thoughts of being merged into an everlasting unity. He drew confidence, moreover, from thoughts of the younger generation. Arthur was dead, but Will and Mariette were flourishing, and the company of young writers gave assurance of continuity. In the collection of poems published in 1892, this spirit is voiced with confidence in a poem entitled 'Youth in Memory':

> Yet have we glad companionship of Youth,
> Elysian meadows for the mind,
> Dare we to face deeds done, and in our tomb
> Filled with the part-coloured bloom
> Of loved and hated, grasp all human truth
> Sowed by us down the mazy paths behind.

The poem rises to a climax of prophetic optimism:

Despite our feeble hold on this green home,
And the vast outer strangeness void of dome,
Shall we be with them, of them, taught to feel,
Up to the moment of our prostrate fall,
The life they deem voluptuously real,
Is more than empty echo of a call,
Or shadow of a shade, or swing of tides;
As brooding upon age, when veins congeal,
Grey palsy nods to think. With us for guides,
Another step above the animal,
To views in Alpine thought are they helped on.
Good if so far we live in them when gone!

'I take as keen an interest in the movement of life as ever, and I enter into the passions of youth,'[67] Meredith told W. T. Stead, the crusading editor of the *Pall Mall Gazette*, in 1904. It was a defiant statement, perhaps intended to dispel any idea that his mind was failing as his body weakened; for he was now aware that he was living on borrowed time. In September 1903 he had been, as Ellis recorded, 'Very ill, and near to dying'. One newspaper reported that he had 'periods of partial consciousness'. His heart almost failed, but was, as he put it in a letter to Leslie Stephen, 'roused to resume its labours'.[68] Poignantly, Stephen himself was on his deathbed when he received this letter. For four months during the winter of 1903/4, Meredith moved out of Flint Cottage to live with Mariette and her husband in their house at Leatherhead. Mariette wrote letters from his dictation; one was to Theodore Watts-Dunton, who was caring for Swinburne (a chronic invalid and recovered alcoholic), to ask after Swinburne's health. Meredith told Watts-Dunton: 'I have myself just come from a point where, as the doctor said, the end could be seen. They pulled me back and thereby did a man of 75 small service.'[69]

He was convalescing when Stead saw him. Meredith's remarks on this occasion were not meant for publication, and he was annoyed when he found them reported in March 1904. He had said: 'People talk about me as if I were an old man. I do not feel old in the least. On the contrary, I do not believe in growing old, and I do not see any reason why we should ever die.'[70] Meredith had said, or written, several times that he was resigned to dying when he had lived a full term of life, and that it was in the course of nature for the old to cede their place in the world to the young, so his words to Stead are in direct contradiction to his philosophy. He may have been joking, or rambling, or he may have been misquoted by Stead, who was not taking notes in an informal conversation.

He lived for another five years after the critical illness. So far as we can tell, he was happy in this final phase of his life. He no longer wrote novels, but he had always attached more importance to his poetry and taken more pleasure in it. His last collection of poems, *A Reading of Life*, was published in 1901; more poems after that date appeared occasionally in magazines, or were left in manuscript. In general, the late poems are fairly turgid and uninspired, and add nothing to his achievement, unless it is an achievement to write poetry at all in old age. (Hardy, however, published three volumes of poems after he was eighty.)

Swinburne died on 10 April 1909. Meredith wrote to Watts-Dunton: 'The blow was heavy on me. I had such confidence in his powers of recovery. The end has come! That brain of the vivid illumination is extinct.' He added that Swinburne was 'the greatest of our lyrical poets'.[71] They had quarrelled when they tried to share a house as young men, and had rarely met in later years, but they had much in common. Both rejected orthodox religion and relished the heritage of Greek paganism; both were denounced by rigorous moralists; both were dedicated poets.

It was also in April 1909 that Meredith saw Lady Ulrica – now Lady Ulrica Baring – for the last time. When she promised to come to Box Hill in her motor, he told her: 'You will give me the pleasure of a fine day in Winter.'[72]

On 8 May, Meredith wrote to his grandson, Jack Sturgis, to reassure him about Sandie, the dog. It seems that Sandie, though living at Flint Cottage, had been given to Jack. Meredith wrote: 'The vet has been to see Sandie. He says that your old dog is not too fat for his age . . . He sleeps well, has appetite, and is ever ready for the ball.'[73] Meredith's last letter, on 13 May, was to a journalist, Ella Dixon, agreeing to receive a visit from her but declining to give an interview. The letter is in clear, coherent English and, according to the editor of Meredith's correspondence, the handwriting is as legible as usual. But Ella Dixon never made her visit. On 14 May, Meredith went out for his usual drive in the donkey-cart and caught a chill. The doctor found heart weakness, and a Harley Street physician called in for consultation took a grave view. By the night of 17 May Meredith was unable to speak; Mariette, she said afterwards, could see in his eyes that he knew he was dying. He died early the next morning as the summer dawn came up over Box Hill.

The Society of Authors, of which Meredith was President, made plans to have him buried in Poets' Corner in Westminster Abbey. It is doubtful whether Meredith would have approved; he had regretted that Watts-Dunton arranged a church funeral for Swinburne. However, when Browning in 1889 and Tennyson in 1892 were buried in the Abbey, he had attended the funerals. Unexpectedly, the Dean of Westminster refused to admit Meredith to the Abbey. Newspapers supported or attacked the Dean's decision; Meredith had aroused his last controversy. Hardy remarked that what the Abbey needed was 'a heathen annexe'. Hardy himself was buried in the Abbey when he died in 1928 and the pall-bearers included Edmund Gosse and Bernard Shaw, both non-believers. But the Dean was not the same as in 1909. Meredith was cremated and his ashes were buried, beside Marie's body, in the Dorking cemetery.

But by one account he was never cremated or buried. Constable published a sixteen-page booklet, written by J. M. Barrie and entitled *George Meredith 1909*. It begins with a gathering of Meredith characters outside the door of Flint Cottage:

They were the mighty company, his children, Lucy and Clara and Rhoda and Diana and Rose and old Mel and Roy Richmond and Adrian and Sir Willoughby and a hundred others, and they stood in line against the box-wood, waiting for him to come out. Each of his proud women carried a flower, and the hands of all his men were ready for the salute.

Meredith rises from his chair, rejuvenated:

His eyes became again those of the eagle, and his hair was brown, and the lustiness of youth was in his frame, but still he wore the red tie. He rose, and not a moment did he remain within the house . . . He flung open the door, as they knew he would do who were awaiting him, and he stood there looking at them, a general reviewing his troops . . . He took their offerings and passed on. They did not go with him, these, his splendid progeny, the ladies of the future, they went their ways to tell the whole earth of the new world for women which he had been the first to foresee.

Then Meredith walks up to 'a little house of two rooms':

It is the Chalet, where he worked, and good and brave men will for ever bow proudly before it, but good and brave women will bow more proudly still. He went there only because he had gone so often, and this time the door was locked; he did not know why nor care. He came swinging down the path, singing lustily, and calling to his dogs, his dogs of the present and the past; and they yelped with joy, for they knew they were once more to breast the hill with him.

He strode up the hill whirling his staff, for which he had no longer any other use. His hearing was again so acute that from far away on the Dorking road he could hear the rumbling of a coach. It had been disputed whether he should be buried in Westminster Abbey or in a quiet churchyard, and there came to him somehow a knowledge (it was the last he ever knew of little things) that people had been at variance as to whether a casket of dust should be laid away in one hole or in another, and he flung back his head with the old glorious action, and laughed a laugh 'broad as a thousand beeves at pasture.'

Box Hill was no longer deserted. When a great man dies – and this was one of the greatest since Shakespeare – the immortals await him at the top of the nearest hill. He looked up and saw his peers. They were all young, like himself. He waved the staff in greeting.

Of those awaiting Meredith, the most recently immortalized is Robert Louis Stevenson, who runs down the hill 'to be the first to take his Master's hand'. Barrie added a neat concluding sentence: 'In the meanwhile an empty coach was rolling on to Dorking.'

It is appropriate that this flight of imagination should have been produced by the man who had given the world the phrase 'Death must be an awfully big adventure'. Gissing as well as Stevenson was waiting at the top of the hill; Barrie stayed below until 1937.

Five years after Meredith's death, Britain was plunged into the First World War (in which his grandson and namesake, young George Meredith, won the Military Cross). That war made sweeping changes in accepted attitudes in every sphere: social, political, cultural and literary. 'Pre-war', an epithet much in use in the 1920s, meant 'outdated and irrelevant'. 'Victorian' was even more dismissive. Lytton Strachey's book of iconoclastic biographies, *Eminent Victorians*, published in 1918, set the tone for a disrespectful view not only of men and women who had been revered, but of the values of the Victorian age.

The reputations of the novelists and poets most esteemed in the nineteenth century – Dickens, Thackeray, Trollope, Tennyson, Browning – went into eclipse. Reading Dickens aloud had once been an enjoyment in many a home; in the young Evelyn Waugh's *A Handful of Dust* (1934) it was a torment, used for comic effect. Since undeniable chronology made Meredith a Victorian, he was swept away with the rest. He had attacked the most sacrosanct Victorian assumptions on everything from commercial prosperity to the institution of marriage and from the Christian religion to the British Empire, but that gave him no exemption.

In 1930 Somerset Maugham published an entertaining novel, *Cakes and Ale*, whose central character, a writer named Edward Driffield, was an idol of the Victorian period, revealed after his death to have both literary and personal feet of clay. The narrator of the novel explains that 'what the critics wrote about Edward Driffield was eye-wash', since his real merit was neither his realism nor his style, but simply his longevity. Readers assumed that Driffield was a thinly disguised portrait of Hardy, who had recently died at the age of eighty-eight. In a preface to a later edition, however, Maugham denied that Driffield was modelled on Hardy, remarking: 'I was never so much interested in him as I was at one time in George Meredith.'

The literary pantheon was embodied in short books published by Macmillan as the 'English Men of Letters' series (a few women, however, were included). Leslie Stephen had written the books on Pope, Swift, Dr Johnson and George Eliot. By the 1920s there was still no book on Hardy, perhaps because of his longevity, but books were commissioned on Meredith, Swinburne, Stevenson and Conrad (who died in 1924). A young literary journalist, J. B. Priestley, was commissioned to write on Meredith, and his book appeared in 1926. His tone was far from debunking and may have been inspired by a desire to rescue Meredith from neglect:

> Of his genius, and the breadth and fullness of that genius, there can be no question. He had genius, all the fertility of imagination and unresting vigour of intellect claimed for him by his most enthusiastic critics.

Priestley admitted, however, that Meredith was difficult to read. His poetry, especially, was like 'a very rich pudding, containing the most varied and delightful ingredients, that does not make friends with the palate because it has not been properly mixed and cooked'.[75] Many years later, V. S. Pritchett too expressed his criticism in culinary terms: 'To read some stretches of Meredith is like living on a continuous diet of lobster and champagne: lobster done in every known sauce and champagne only too knowingly addressed as the Veuve.'[76]

Indeed, Meredith's ornateness and complexity ran counter to the taste of the 1920s and particularly of the Bloomsbury group, who could not tolerate anything that might be suspected of posturing or insincerity. E. M. Forster, in his 1927 book *Aspects of the Novel*, was merciless toward Meredith:

> What with the faking, what with the preaching, which was never agreeable and is now said to be hollow, and what with the home counties posing as the universe, it is no wonder Meredith now lies in the trough.[77]

Katherine Mansfield, too, found *Richard Feverel* 'so false, so preposterous – one could only groan for it – and it's so odious'. Yet the letter in which she voiced this condemnation ends with a reluctant tribute: 'But he is a big man, and he *can* write wonders.'[78]

One can imagine the Bloomsbury group arguing endlessly about Meredith, doubtless with contributions from Virginia Woolf and Vanessa Bell – the Stephen sisters – who remembered him from their childhood and youth. Woolf, like Mansfield, disliked *Richard Feverel* and refused to believe in its characters: 'We at once exclaim how unreal they are, how artificial, how impossible,' she wrote in one of her two essays on Meredith in *The Common Reader*. But, like Mansfield again, she was driven to reluctant admiration. On *Harry Richmond*, she commented: 'Just as we are about to drop the book, the rocket roars into the air; the whole scene flashes into light; and the book, years after, is recalled by that sudden splendour.'

She agreed with Forster that: 'His teaching now seems too strident and too optimistic and too shallow.' The Bloomsbury outlook was antipathetic to the didactic element in Meredith and his concept of the novel as 'the vehicle of philosophy'. But this was outweighed by the qualities that impressed her: 'his English power of imagination, with its immense audacity and fertility, his superb mastery of the great emotions of courage and love, his power of summoning nature into sympathy with man'.

And Virginia Woolf concluded her consideration of Meredith with a prophecy: 'He will be forgotten and discovered and again forgotten and discovered like Donne and Peacock and Gerard Hopkins.'[79]

Plot Summaries

THE ORDEAL OF RICHARD FEVEREL

Sir Austin Feverel, 'a man of wealth and honour', lives on his estate at Raynham Abbey, not far from London. After five years of marriage, his wife has eloped with Denzil Somers, a friend whom Sir Austin employed as bailiff, who writes poetry under the name of Diaper Sandoe. Sir Austin devotes himself to the upbringing of his son, Richard, and to writing a book of moral aphorisms called 'The Pilgrim's Scrip.' In this book, he sets out his System, embodying the principles that should control Richard's development. Lady Feverel makes a secret visit to Raynham to gaze at her sleeping child, but does not hope to be forgiven by her husband. Lady Blandish, an attractive widow in the neighbourhood, has a close friendship with Sir Austin, but he holds her at arm's length emotionally.

Others living at Raynham Abbey are: Mrs Doria Forey, Sir Austin's widowed sister, and her daughter Clare. Sir Austin's brother Algernon, who had to leave the Guards after losing a leg in a cricketing accident. Another brother, Hippias, an ineffectual character constantly worried about his health. A nephew, Austin Wentworth, in disgrace because he married his mother's housemaid (he no longer lives with her). Another nephew, Adrian Harley, known as the Wise Youth, who has 'caused himself to be required by people who could serve him.'

Sir Austin has decided that Richard should not be married before the age of twenty-five and that he will select a suitable bride. He appoints Ripton Thompson, son of the family solicitor, to live at Raynham as a friend for Richard. On his fourteenth birthday, Richard feels humiliated when ordered to strip for a medical examination, so he absents himself from the celebration party and goes off into the woods with Ripton. They take their guns and Richard shoots a pheasant on land belonging to Farmer Blaize, a tenant of Sir Miles Papworth. Blaize sees them, accuses them of poaching, and horsewhips both boys. To take revenge, Richard pays Tom Bakewell, a ploughman, a guinea to set fire to Blaize's ricks and supplies him with matches at night. After they return home, Sir Austin overhears the boys boasting of what they have done. Adrian Harley and Austin Wentworth also find out what has happened.

Tom Bakewell is arrested on suspicion and is to appear before Papworth, the local magistrate, a stern enforcer of game laws; if convicted, he faces a sentence of transportation. Richard makes a plan to help Bakewell to escape by smuggling a rope and file into the jail, but it proves impossible. Adrian thinks it advisable to sacrifice Bakewell, but Wentworth persuades Richard to go to Blaize and confess. Blaize demands a full apology and compensation of £300, which Sir Austin is willing to pay. Reluctantly, Richard swallows his pride and makes the apology. This arouses admiration in Lucy Desborough, Blaize's young niece, but Richard takes no notice of her. Bakewell is acquitted for lack of evidence and becomes a devoted servant to Richard.

Growing up, Richard has to give his father a daily account of his studies and his 'moral experiences.' When he is detected in writing poems, he is ordered to burn them. As Clare is becoming too fond of him, Mrs Forey removes her for a long stay at the seaside. It is really Ralph Morton, a friend of Richard's, who is attracted to Clare, and Richard forwards a letter for him. Then Richard meets Lucy again and they fall in love. Adrian finds out and informs Sir Austin, but Richard denies that anything is going on. However, Blaize decides that she should be sent to a convent for a while (she is a Catholic) and should then marry his son, Tom Blaize. Richard goes to see Blaize and refuses to give up Lucy. He hurries off to follow her, but collapses and falls ill when about to catch the train.

After recovering, Richard goes to London, accompanied by Ripton, to stay with his uncle Hippias at the Feverel town house. Tom Blaize is on the same train, going to meet Lucy. Richard misdirects Tom, meets Lucy himself, and tells Ripton to find lodgings for her. The landlady whom Ripton finds is Mrs Berry, formerly a servant at Raynham and wife of Sir Austin's valet. Richard persuades Lucy to marry him and succeeds, though both are under age, in getting a license. When he is about to go to the church for the wedding, he runs into Mrs Doria, Clare and Adrian. Flustered, he drops the wedding-ring and Clare picks it up. There is an embarrassing moment in the ceremony, but Mrs Berry gives

Richard her own ring, and Lucy insists on keeping it. Once again, it is Adrian who finds out what has happened, this time by questioning Bakewell. Sir Austin is appalled when he learns that Richard has married without his consent, and rebuffs Lady Blandish's attempts to console him. Mrs Doria suggests that the marriage could be contested and declared illegal, but Sir Austin declines to do this and continues to give Richard an allowance.

Richard and Lucy go for their honeymoon to the Isle of Wight, where the yachting season is at its height and they meet the wealthy Lord Mountfalcon. Adrian goes to see them and finds that he likes Lucy, but advises Richard to stay until he hears from his father. Clare, meanwhile, is to marry John Todhunter, a middle-aged man selected by her mother, who once had an affair with him. Richard tries to dissuade Clare, who is by no means in love with Todhunter, but she fatalistically consents to the marriage; Richard does not realise that she is hopelessly in love with him.

Leaving Lucy on the Isle of Wight, Richard goes to stay with Hippias in London in the hope of meeting his father there, but Sir Austin does not appear. Richard meets Peter Brayder, a friend of Mountfalcon, who invites him to a dinner-party attended by a number of obviously loose women, including the fascinating Bella Mount. Richard becomes gripped by the idea of reclaiming women who have had unhappy experiences; he finds his mother, who is disillusioned with her lover, and takes her to live with Mrs Berry. He also hopes to rescue Bella, who tells him that she was seduced as a girl by a nobleman. In fact this nobleman was Lord Mountfalcon and 'Mrs Mount' has been his mistress. Mountfalcon now has designs on Lucy and Brayder is offering money to Bella to detain Richard in London. Lucy, who is pregnant, is getting worried as Richard's absence stretches to three months, but Adrian visits her and advises her to be patient.

Lady Blandish and Mrs Doria hear about Richard's involvement with Bella and are horrified, but he insists that he is only seeking to befriend her. However, he is at her house for a night of champagne and kisses and the reader can presume that they make love. Richard goes to the Sussex coast and writes to Bella to join him there. Brayder, snooping at her house, sees the letter.

Mrs Berry goes to the Isle of Wight and tells Lucy, who is concerned because Richard's letters have ceased, that he is no longer in London. Sir Austin, finally prepared for a reconciliation, goes to London, but Richard he is not there, and he cannot bring himself to invite Lucy to

Raynham, as Lady Blandish advises. Another month passes. Then Richard returns to London and comes to terms with his father, while Lucy is also in London staying with Mrs Berry, who has warned her against Mountfalcon. Because of his indidelity and guilt, Richard cannot contemplate seeing Lucy, and when their paths cross in Kensington Gardens he pushes Mrs Berry away so that Lucy doesn't see him. That evening, Mrs Doria is called away because Clare is ill. She finds that Clare has taken poison and is dead, leaving a note asking to be buried wearing Richard's ring.

Shattered, Richard goes to Germany to stay indefinitely. Lucy gives birth to a son, but Richard does not know. Austin Wentworth, who has been for some years in Africa, returns and meets Adrian, who brings him up to date with events. Wentworth finds Lucy and escorts her to Raynham, where Sir Austin gives her a friendly welcome; he decides that she is a perfectly acceptable wife for Richard and is delighted that she has produced an heir. Mrs Berry, too, is back at Raynham and reunited with Berry.

EVAN HARRINGTON

The novel opens with the death of Melchisedec Harrington, a tailor with a business in Lymport-on-Sea, known as 'The Great Mel' because of his aristocratic manners and upper-class social connections. Characteristically, he has chosen to be buried in his uniform as an officer in the militia. While friends and neighbours gather for the funeral and the ensuing formal meal, his widow is visited by Lady Roseley, who was married to one of his customers, an Admiral. Sentimentally attached to the Great Mel, she expresses her grief and kisses the dead man's forehead. Learning that he died leaving large debts, and that the burden of repaying them will be incumbent on his son, Evan, she offers to help in finding Evan an occupation more gentlemanly than tailoring.

Melchisedec was the father of three daughters and a son. The eldest daughter, Caroline – the beauty of the family – is unhappily married to Major Strike of the Royal Marines, who is regarded in garrison society as 'a disgustingly jealous brute' and is ashamed of Caroline's origins. Harriet, the second sister has married Andrew Cogglesby, a brewer, a more likeable man who considers that being 'in trade' is nothing to be ashamed of. Louisa, the third sister, has married a Portuguese nobleman, Count Silva de Saldar, and gone to live in Lisbon. The Count, who speaks no English, has never been told that his wife was a tailor's daughter. Evan, the youngest of the family, has worked for two years in the office of the Cogglesby brewery, but has then been taken in tow by Louisa, who brought him to Lisbon to acquire the polish of high society and secured him a temporary job as secretary to Melville Jocelyn, a British diplomat. This enables him to meet Rose Jocelyn, sixteen-year-old daughter of a country gentleman, Sir Franks Jocelyn, who has been staying with her uncle Melville. Louisa decides that Rose would be an ideal match for Evan, and indeed the young people are strongly attracted to each other.

Louisa is now returning to England with her husband, who has run into political difficulties in Portugal, and with Evan. Melville Jocelyn, who is retiring from the diplomatic service and hopes to enter Parliament, is travelling on the same ship with his wife and Rose. They will be staying with Sir Franks at his Hampshire residence, Beckley Court. Evan would like to see more of Rose, but when the ship docks in London he is met by Mr Goren, a master-tailor working in London and a friend of the Great Mel. Goren tells Evan that his father has died. After one night with the Cogglesbys, Evan sets off for Lymport. Louisa declines to attend the funeral and persuades Caroline and Harriet not to go. Evan misses the coach and hires a carriage, but finds that he hasn't enough money to pay for it and has to walk most of the way.

In London, Andrew Cogglesby has a talk with his brother Tom, an eccentric man who likes to conceal his thoughts and feelings and haggles over small amounts of money though he is really wealthy. Andrew suggests that Evan should be given a place in the brewery business, but Tom is equivocal. Meanwhile, Evan's mother tells him sternly that he must work as a tailor to pay off the debts, and begin by learning the trade from Goren.

Louisa has managed to secure invitations to Beckley Court for herself and for Evan. When asked about her family, she pretends that her father was Sir Abraham Harrington, Baronet, who luckily has just died. Evan reluctantly refuses the invitation and sets out, again on foot, to return to London and start work with Goren. On the way, he meets a weeping girl who seems to be ill and is in fact heavily pregnant. He also meets an old friend, Jack Raikes, who was an usher, or junior teacher, at Evan's school and is now out of a job. They all stay the night at the Green Dragon at Fallowfield, where a gentleman named Drummond Forth gives up his room to the girl; she gives birth to a child during the night. A jolly drinking party is in progress at the expense of a person who wishes to be known only as Mr Tom (readers will recognize Tom Cogglesby). He is celebrating his sixtieth birthday and making himself popular with a view to pushing a candidate – not yet selected – for Parliament in opposition to the Tory, Melville Jocelyn.

A two-day cricket match between the villages of Fallowfield and Beckley is in progress, and three young men who have been playing for Beckley appear at the Green Dragon. They are clearly gentlemen; they are Harry Jocelyn, Rose's brother, and his friends, Ferdinand Laxley and William Harvey. The former is the heir to Lord Laxley and the latter is the son of the Chief Justice. These young men, especially Laxley, behave with great arrogance and pick a quarrel with Evan and Jack. Laxley challenges Evan to a duel, but Evan evades it by saying that he is the son of a tailor; Laxley recognizes that he cannot fight a man of inferior social position.

Next day, Evan goes to the cricket match and is greeted by Rose, who is among the spectators. She is delighted to see him, much to the displeasure of Laxley, who is hoping to marry her. Louisa has now reached Beckley Court. She is recognized by Lady Roseley and also by some local people, as the Harrington girls went to school in the neighbourhood. But Lady Roseley says nothing and the others decide that the Countess de Saldar, with exotic appearance and foreign accent, can't possibly be Melchisedec's daughter. Finding that Melville Jocelyn has gout and cannot hold a pen, Louisa arranges for Evan to resume working as his secretary, so Evan moves in at Beckley Court. Harry, who is fascinated by Louisa, is soon convinced that Evan must be a gentleman and pretended to be a tailor's son to smooth over an unpleasant incident, but Laxley is still suspicious.

Also present at Beckley Court are old Mrs Bonner, Lady Jocelyn's mother, and her granddaughter Juliana (Lady Jocelyn's niece). Louisa discovers that Rose is not really an heiress, since Beckley Court belongs to Mrs Bonner; she is likely to leave the estate and a great deal of money to Juliana rather than to Sir Franks. Thus, it would be preferable for Evan to court Juliana, not Rose. But Juliana is a cripple, is in generally poor health, and is not at all attractive, while Evan is now deeply in love with Rose. Louisa is still in favour at Beckley Court and brings her sister Caroline to stay, as a relief from Major Strike. Another guest is the widowed Duke of Belfield, who is attracted by beautiful Caroline and hopes to make her his mistress.

Rose is getting worried after Laxley insists that Evan is actually a tailor's son and demands: 'Let him unsay it.' Evan now reads an anonymous letter, signed 'A Friend', which was handed to him at the cricket match. The writer of the letter offers him £300 a year if he will give up his pretensions and carry on the tailoring shop. Evan decides that he must do so. First, he has to go to the Green Dragon to find Jack Raikes and let him know that he has been accepted, on Evan's suggestion, as a tutor to teach Juliana Latin. Riding back in a storm, he meets Polly Wheedle, a housemaid, and gives her a lift on his horse. Polly has been to see her sister, Susan, the mother of the illegitimate infant; it becomes clear that Harry was the seducer. Polly, who is under the impression that Evan is engaged to Juliana, tells him that Rose has been singing his praises and Laxley is furious. Evan changes his mind about leaving, seeing that he has hopes of Rose. When he returns to the house, Rose is about to go riding and shows that she wishes to go with him, not with Laxley. Evan tells Laxley that he will fight him and that he has a right to do so. (Later, he offers Laxley an apology and there is no duel.) Rose challenges the two young men to take a difficult jump. Laxley stops short of it, while Evan takes it. His horse falls and he is injured, but not gravely.

Evan now declares his love to Rose. She assures him that she loves him and will speak to her mother so that they can be engaged. But Evan has placed himself in a false position by lying to Laxley; Louisa has been recognized again and escaped only by staging a faint; Andrew Cogglesby has arrived at Beckley Court and Lady Jocelyn knows that he is the Great Mel's son-in-law. Faced with all these problems, Evan writes a letter of renunciation to Rose, to be delivered by Polly. Louisa gets hold of it, but when Rose tells Evan that she never received a letter, he tells her the full truth. Her reaction is: 'We have to fight a battle'; she is sorry to hear of his low birth, but is ready to marry him. She speaks to her mother, who has been putting two and two together and is not greatly surprised. Rose's aunt (Mrs Shorne, Sir Franks's widowed sister) is appalled and declares that the marriage must be stopped. However, Lady Jocelyn, though far from pleased, thinks it best merely to advise Rose against it and play for time. Tom Cogglesby, who was a boyfriend of Lady Jocelyn when they were young, goes to see her and promises to settle £1,000 a year on Evan and Rose, with the same on their first child.

While Laxley is resentful, Juliana is miserable, for she too is deeply in love with Evan. She agrees to lend Harry fifty pounds to repay a loan from Evan (Harry had needed the money to pay off Susan). Influenced by Laxley, Harry is strongly hostile to Evan, but still under Louisa's control. To put pressure on him, she orders Raikes to fetch Susan and the child and produce them during the forthcoming picnic, a big annual occasion at Beckley Court. At the picnic, this is not the only embarrassment. Two people who knew Sir Abraham Harrington condole with Louisa on the death of her 'father'. Then Evan's mother appears and announces sternly: 'I have come for my son.' The next event is the hasty departure of Mrs Evremonde, a woman who is having an affair with Drummond Forth. Her husband, Captain Evremonde, appears in pursuit of her, having received a letter telling him where she is. Apparently, the letter was written by Laxley. For betraying a lady in this manner, he is ordered to leave the house.

That night, Mrs Bonner has a dangerous attack and clearly has not long to live. Louisa admits to Evan that she wrote the letter to Evremonde, imitating Laxley's handwriting. Evan urges her to confess to Lady Jocelyn, but she refuses and is supported by Caroline; so he decides to take the guilt on himself. He makes a confession to Lady Jocelyn, who is baffled and asks if there is madness in his family, but of course he must leave Beckley Court and must not write to Rose. Rose, in great distress, goes to see Juliana, who says that people of low birth should not be expected to behave like gentlemen. But Juliana is herself sure that Evan is not guilty – she loves him and trusts him more than Rose can.

Caroline has decided not to run off with the Duke because Evan would despise her. Evan insists that Louisa and Caroline must leave Beckley Court with him, taking the coach from the village inn. Rose appears there and pleads with Evan to clear himself. He is silent; Laxley comes along and takes Rose away. Before Evan goes, he receives a note from Juliana – '*I* do not believe it.'

Evan goes to work with Goren, while also keeping accounts for a company in which Major Strike is involved. He discovers that Strike is embezzling and there is a nasty scene. Meanwhile, Mrs Bonner dies, leaving Beckley Court to Juliana, who writes to tell Caroline. The Duke, still pursuing Caroline, offers Evan a job as his estate bailiff.

Months pass. In the winter, Juliana falls ill, and goes to stay with Andrew and Harriet in London. She writes a letter to Rose, to be delivered after her death, saying that she has proof of Evan's innocence. She dies, and in her will she has left Beckley Court to Evan; however, he hands it back to Lady Jocelyn.

There is a comic interlude when the Cogglesby brothers pretend that the brewery is bankrupt. Evan returns to Lymport to carry on the shop. He goes to Beckley to see Susan, whose father is forcing Harry to marry her. Polly is there and tells him that Rose is engaged to Laxley (now Lord Laxley). Laxley and Harry waylay Evan on the road; Laxley demands that Evan must renounce any claim on Rose, and hits him with a whip. Rose appears and Evan makes the renunciation. Rose then reads Juliana's letter and goes to Lymport to seek Evan out. He tells her that he was indeed innocent. All ends happily. Married at last to Rose, Evan assumes the status of a gentleman in real earnest and takes his place in the diplomatic service with a post in Naples.

EMILIA IN ENGLAND

Samuel Pole is a City merchant working in partnership with Mr Pericles, a wealthy Greek who has a passion for music. Pole, a widower, lives at his Surrey house, Brookfield, with his three daughters and one son. Arabella, the eldest, is hesitating between two suitors, Edward Buxley and Freshfield Sumner. Cornelia is in love with Purcell Barrett, disinherited son of a baronet, a poorly paid organist at the local church, but her father wants her to marry Sir Twickenham Pryme, a middle-aged MP. Adela is flirting with Captain Gambier, a man about town. Wilfrid, an Army officer, is just back from India. His father is planning a marriage for him with Lady Charlotte Chillingworth. Pole himself is interested in Martha Chump, a widow with an Irish brogue and uncouth social manners, whom the daughters find appalling.

One summer night, the Pole girls, along with Wilfrid and Pericles, discover a young girl singing in the woods. Pericles is excited by her beautiful voice and decides to have her trained for the opera. Wilfrid makes enquiries and finds that she is Emilia Belloni, daughter of an exiled Italian patriot now playing the violin in a London theatre orchestra. The Pole sisters adopt her and bring her to live at Brookfield. They take her to a fashionable dinner-party where she meets Merthyr Powys, a Welshman strongly sympathetic to Italian liberation; another guest is Gambier, who has tried to pick up Emilia in a London park. Emilia sings and is admired, but then disappears because she has promised to sing for a village club. A fight breaks out between the men of two villages. Wilfrid rescues her and embraces her. She falls in love with him on the spot.

Much to his daughters' annoyance, Pole invites Mrs Chump to stay at Brookfield. He is speculating with her money in the hope of buying a grand house in the neighbourhood, Besworth. Wilfrid thinks that Charlotte will marry him if he can offer her the prospect of living at Besworth. He goes to stay at Stornley, Charlotte's home. Emilia follows him there, calls him 'my lover', and asks naively: 'When will you marry me?' She is willing to give up her chance of going to Italy and training at the Milan

Conservatorio; when she tells Pericles this, he is furious. Wilfrid, more or less committed to Charlotte though they are not definitely engaged, has to tell Emilia that he would like to marry her but cannot afford to displease his father. Pole suffers a stroke, but recovers enough to take Emilia to the theatre, where she sees her father in the orchestra. At the hotel where they stay, she tells Pole that Wilfrid is pledged to her, and reproaches him for bringing pressure on Wilfrid to marry Charlotte. Through Merthyr and his half-sister, Georgiana Ford, Charlotte hears that Wilfrid has compromised himself with Emilia. She sees Emilia and tries to persuade her to be sensible and give Wilfrid up. Wilfrid now tries to get out of marrying Charlotte, but she says that she will marry him even without the prospect of acquiring Besworth.

Three men are now in love with Emilia – Tracy Runningbrook, a poet who is writing the libretto for a projected opera, with Emilia as composer and singer; Merthyr; and Braintop, a clerk in Pole's office. Emilia regards Tracy and Merthyr as good friends, but believes that Wilfrid is her faithful lover. Pole, in serious financial trouble, collapses again. Wilfrid, backed by his sisters, expels Mrs Chump from Brookfield. He then goes off on a trip in his yacht, with Charlotte, Merthyr, Georgiana and Adela. He hopes to go to Dover and meet Emilia, but Charlotte directs the yacht to Devon, where Mrs Chump lives. She is to stay with Mrs Chump. Emilia has received a note from Wilfrid and goes to Devon, escorted by Braintop. Charlotte meets Emilia in the street.

Wilfrid goes to see Charlotte and tells her that his father is ruined. She replies that she already knew this, but is prepared to marry him and live cheaply abroad. She compels him to say explicitly that he loves her and has never loved Emilia. Unknown to Wilfrid, Charlotte has brought Emilia into the next room and told her to listen. Emilia, thrown into deep distress, is able to return to London as Braintop gives her his return ticket. Wilfrid goes to London, explaining that he must escort Mrs Chump to Brookfield, as his father needs her. Charlotte stays on the yacht.

Emilia consoles herself with the thought: 'I have my voice.' But when she goes to see Pericles, she finds that she cannot sing and he rejects her. Hungry and penniless, she wanders about London and contemplates suicide. Merthyr finds her and takes her to his home in Monmouth. She is shocked to hear that Wilfrid is to take a commission with the Austrian Army, arranged by his uncle, Colonel Pierson. Merthyr and Georgiana try to distract her by taking her to a ball at Penarvon Castle. Wilfrid, who has found out where she is, appears while she is alone in a coach, held up by a landslide. He again declares that he loves her, but Merthyr prevents her from going with him. Merthyr then hears that an uprising has begun in Italy and goes there to fight for Italian freedom.

Emilia, now in London and cared for by Georgiana, agrees to see Wilfrid. Impulsively, he begs her to marry him. She cannot trust him now, but she promises to stay in England if he will promise not to join the Austrians.

Barrett, now a baronet after his father's death, goes to Brookfield to find Cornelia, but he overhears servants talking of a forthcoming marriage. Thrown into depression, he shoots himself.

Emilia finds that she has regained her voice, and tells Georgiana that she will break her promise and go to Italy. Again, she sings in the woods near Brookfield. Her voice attracts Wilfrid, who is with Charlotte and Pericles. Pericles, delighted, says that he will ensure her training at the Conservatorio. Wilfrid once more declares that he loves her, but she is determined to go to Italy. Charlotte has been planning to arrange a job for Wilfrid as a diplomat; she now tells him calmly that he is on his own.

Merthyr returns from Italy, wounded; the uprising has been crushed. Mrs Chump is at Brookfield again. Pole has been saved from bankruptcy by Pericles, who is taking Emilia to Milan with him. She writes to Merthyr, telling him that she belongs to Italy but will never forget England. Merthyr hears that Wilfrid has joined the Austrians after all.

RHODA FLEMING

William Fleming, a Kent farmer, is a widower with two daughters, Dahlia and Rhoda. Dahlia goes to London as company for her bachelor uncle, Anthony Hackbut, a trusted messenger at Boyne's Bank. On a visit to London, Rhoda sees that Dahlia has a lover. This is Edward Blancove, son of the head of the bank, Sir William Blancove, whose brother is the squire of Wrexby, the village near the Fleming farm. Rhoda is courted by two men: the squire's son Algernon and Robert Eccles, who has been a soldier but is now helping Fleming and learning farm work. But Rhoda's emotions are concentrated on her sister's troubles.

Dahlia suddenly leaves London and spends some months with Edward in Italy. She writes home saying that she is married, but her father and Rhoda are sceptical. She returns to London and gives an address; when Fleming and Rhoda go to the house, they are told that she has moved. Edward is now tired of Dahlia and will be leaving her alone to spend Christmas with a house-party at Fairly Hall, Hampshire. However, accompanied by his cousin Algernon, he takes her to the theatre. Her father and Rhoda are also at the theatre and catch a glimpse of her. They see Algernon but not Edward and thus believe that Algernon is the seducer.

Edward and Algernon are both at Fairly Hall, and so is Mrs Margaret Lovell, a fascinating young widow. Robert, on Algernon's trail, goes to nearby Warbeach, which is his native village, and where he meets his friend Major Waring, who had an affair with Margaret in India and is still in love with her. Robert attacks Algernon and pulls him off his horse. One night, he is waylaid and savagely beaten up by a local man of bad reputation, Nicodemus Sedgett, an attack instigated by Edward. Margaret secures Dahlia's London address and, through Algernon, gives it to Robert. When he goes there he finds that she has moved on again. Margaret devises a plan to extricate Edward from his embarrassing situation by finding a husband for Dahlia. Edward agrees to pay Sedgett £1,000 to marry Dahlia.

Edward goes to Paris and sends a draft for £1,000 to Algernon to be paid to Sedgett directly after the marriage. Dahlia stops Hackbut in the street and he is shocked by her appearance; she has been gravely ill, is plunged in guilt and unhappiness, and is penniless. Sedgett is put in contact with her and, though repelled, she agrees to marry him so that her father will be reconciled to her as an honest woman. Rhoda favours the marriage, unaware of the bribe and believing Sedgett to be a decent young man.

Algernon cashes the draft, but uses most of the money to repay his debts and gambling losses. Edward, in Paris, has a crisis of conscience and realizes that he loves Dahlia after all and must marry her whatever the consequences. He comes to London and confesses the whole story to his father, who advises him to emigrate. He hurries to Dahlia's lodgings but is intercepted by Rhoda, who refuses to let him see Dahlia. Next day, Sedgett duly marries Dahlia, but when he fails to get the money he abandons her at the church door. Robert tells Rhoda of Sedgett's real character. Rhoda then comes across Hackbut, who has undergone a mental collapse and is wandering about London with a bag of gold sovereigns that he is supposed to deliver. He pours them into Rhoda's lap.

Dahlia returns to the farm with her father, Rhoda, Robert and Anthony, whom they will have to shelter. Sedgett, having changed his mind and decided to accept as much money as he can get, appears at the farm and demands to take Dahlia away. Her father orders her to go with her husband, despite Rhoda's pleas. But Major Waring, who has been making enquiries at Warbeach, arrives with evidence that Sedgett is already married; he tricked his wife into boarding a ship for America, but thanks to bad weather she came ashore at another port and made her way to Warbeach. Sedgett hastily makes his escape. Edward now appears and declares that he loves Dahlia. They find that she has taken poison. Although she recovers, she no longer has the strength to remake her life with Edward.

Algernon's father has died and he is now the squire. Fleming is keen that Rhoda should marry him and thus solve the family's financial problems, but she decides to marry Robert. It is also for money reasons that Margaret Lovell declines to marry Major Waring and marries Sir William Blancove, the banker. In the aftermath, Edward is never married. Dahlia stays at the farm with Rhoda and Robert and their children, but dies seven years later.

VITTORIA

Italian patriots are meeting on a mountainside not far from Milan. Among them are the veteran Agostino Balderini; young Carlo Ammiani, a Count but nevertheless an ardent republican; and Vittoria Campa, a singer about to make her opera debut, who has changed her name since living in England as Emilia Belloni. Agostino has written an opera, *Camilla*, in which Vittoria is to sing the lead, and it is agreed that she will sing a song, 'Italia shall be free', not included in the text passed by the Austrian censor, which will be the signal for an uprising. Beppo, Vittoria's devoted servant, catches a man who has been following her. This man, Luigi Saracco, denies that he is an Austrian spy; he is employed by Vittoria's patron, Pericles.

They are disturbed by a party of English tourists, including Adela Pole, now Mrs Sedley, who knew Vittoria in England. Adela intends to meet her brother Wilfrid, once in love with Vittoria, now in the Austrian Army as Lieutenant Pierson and engaged to an Austrian lady, Lena von Lenkenstein. Captain Gambier, who also knew Vittoria in England, comes to meet Adela and recognizes Vittoria, who drops a note warning Adela to avoid Milan. Luigi picks up this note and takes it to Barto Rizzo, leader of the underground in Milan. Then Vittoria writes to Wilfrid appealing to him to change sides. Rizzo, by mustering a crowd to attack Wilfrid as he rides into Verona, gets hold of this letter and sends a copy to General Pierson, Wilfrid's uncle. Wilfrid tells the General that he has only had a letter from Adela. The Austrians realize that a revolt is likely and send reinforcements from Verona to Milan. Rizzo overhears Adela arranging to meet the General at the opera, and cancels the uprising. Convinced that Vittoria is betraying the cause, Rizzo draws a black circle round her name on a La Scala poster. Carlo, now in love with Vittoria, is furious when he hears that she is suspected, but Agostino is doubtful.

Vittoria goes to see her friend Laura Piaveni, widow of a patriot executed by the Austrians. A note, 'You are suspect', has been pinned to Vittoria's dress. Laura advises Vittoria not to sing, but she says that she will go ahead unless instructed otherwise by the Chief (Mazzini). Laura finds that her friend Amalia – an Austrian duchess, but sympathetic to Italians – knows about the plot. Pericles tells Amalia that he plans to take Vittoria to Meran, in Austrian territory, for her own safety.

Carlo escorts Vittoria to a rehearsal at the house of Rocco Ricci, the conductor. Another singer, Irma di Karski, is singing the second role and is jealous of Vittoria. As they leave, Irma is hustled into a carriage; she has been mistaken for Vittoria. Vittoria is determined to give the signal unless instructed otherwise by the Chief, who writes to her: 'No backward step.' Carlo sees that the revolt is hopeless, but is told by Gambier that Vittoria has gone to Meran. When he hears that this is not true, he goes to La Scala and bets Pericles that Vittoria will sing. Countess Ammiani, Carlo's mother, has General Pierson and Wilfrid in her box. She is concealing Angelo Guidascarpi, who has killed Paul von Lenkenstein, Lena's brother, who was his sister's lover. When her house was raided, the Countess said that Angelo was her son, Carlo. Captain Weisspriess, an Austrian who is hoping to marry Lena's sister Anna, has pursued the carriage hired by Pericles and brought Irma back to Milan. Irma sings the second role, but Vittoria appears to sing the lead and triumphs: at the interval, she receives a cheque for a thousand guineas from Pericles. The General, sensing the danger, orders Wilfrid to surround the opera house with troops and gives orders that the curtain must fall at the end of the permitted libretto, but Carlo jumps on to the stage and holds the curtain up while Vittoria sings 'Italia shall be free'. Wilfrid begs De Pyrmont, a French friend of Laura, to fetch a carriage to take Vittoria to safety and goes to the stage to rescue her from the threat of arrest. She makes her escape with Carlo, not with Wilfrid, but as the carriage drives away Carlo is arrested because he is identified as Angelo. Angelo gets away from Milan by jumping on the box-seat of the carriage, like a servant.

Vittoria and Angelo stop at an inn but find that Captain Weisspriess, disguised as a civilian, Herr Johannes, is there too. They give him the slip by leaving at two in the morning, leave the carriage behind and walk for two days. Angelo then heads for Switzerland, taking an innkeeper, Jacopo, as a reluctant guide. He meets Austrian soldiers who are searching for Vittoria. Weisspriess catches up with Vittoria, but Angelo suddenly appears. The men fight and both are wounded; Jacopo fetches help to take Weisspriess to the nearest inn on a stretcher. Vittoria pushes on to Sonnenberg, Amalia's castle, where she is coldly received by Anna. Laura is there, also Wilfrid, and Merthyr Powys, Vittoria's friend from English days, who is going to meet his sister Georgiana in Switzerland. Angelo is in hiding in Meran, near the castle. Vittoria tells Wilfrid that Carlo is her lover and they expect to be married. Wilfrid is in disgrace with General Pierson and under orders not to leave the neighbourhood. Laura persuades Vittoria to hint to Wilfrid that he can win her back if he helps Angelo to escape. With Wilfrid's help, Angelo gets away in Adela's carriage, pretending to be her husband, Mr Sedley. Lena breaks off her engagement to Wilfrid.

No uprising occurred at the time originally planned, but three months later Milan is on the verge of revolt. Carlo is in prison, while Vittoria is in Turin, a star at the opera, financially supported by Pericles. In a Milan street riot, Wilfrid is seized and hidden in Rizzo's house together with Rinaldo Guidascarpi, Angelo's brother and also involved in the killing of Paul von Lenkenstein. They are released by Rizzo's wife who is in love with Rinaldo. Milan bursts into rebellion and Carlo is freed from prison by a mob led by Rizzo. In five days of street fighting, the Austrians are expelled from the city. Carlo rescues Lena and Anna and their brother, Count von Lenkenstein. He goes to the home of Violetta, Countess d'Isorella, a woman he had been in love with in younger days. Now that Carlo is free, his mother sends for Vittoria, but she decides to stay in Turin where she can earn money for the patriotic cause, or go to sing in London as Pericles is urging. Carlo is angry, the more so as Vittoria admires the King of Piedmont, whom he distrusts. Piedmontese troops advance to liberate Lombardy; Merthyr Powys and Gambier are fighting with them and Gambier is wounded. Vittoria and Laura go with the army as nurses. Pericles traps Vittoria into a carriage which takes them to Austrian-held territory. Rinaldo is captured and shot on the orders of Count von Lenkenstein. Wilfrid, as a civilian, is travelling with Vittoria and Laura. The Italians make a counter-attack and Carlo is reunited with Vittoria; he assures her that he loves her and tells her to go to his mother, who is at

Brescia, while he goes to Vicenza, in liberated territory. However, Vicenza is retaken by the Austrians and the King retreats to Piedmont. Vittoria and Laura return to Milan with Merthyr, who is wounded, and the city is again occupied by the Austrians.

Vittoria goes to Countess Ammiani's villa at Pallanza, in Piedmont. Carlo goes there too, but only for one night; he is being influenced by Violetta, who advises him not to marry Vittoria. Vittoria receives a letter of accusation from Rizzo and is also abandoned by Pericles, who has taken up Irma again. But Carlo and Laura come to Pallanza and take Vittoria in a boat to Pericles' villa along the lake; she sings and he is again enraptured with her.

In Milan, Weisspriess has killed a friend of Carlo's in a duel. Carlo challenges him; Weisspriess replies, naming a time and place for a duel but advising Carlo to drop the challenge and go to Venice. The letter is given to Vittoria's servant Beppo, who gets into a fight with Austrian soldiers and loses it, so Carlo does not keep the rendezvous. The letter reaches the Austrian generals and is seen by Anna, who is angry with Weisspriess for letting Carlo off the hook. She gets her friend Major Nagen to send another challenge, forging Weisspriess's name, but Countess Ammiani intercepts it. Carlo and Vittoria are quietly married. Wilfrid recognizes that he has lost Vittoria for ever, but has broken up with Lena. Rizzo is arrested on the instigation of Pericles, who knows that he is Vittoria's enemy. Vittoria is stabbed by Rizzo's wife, but not badly injured.

Merthyr arrives from Rome, where Mazzini is heading a republic; he urges that it represents the only hope for Italian liberation. There are plans for a new rising in the north, and Vittoria advises Carlo to keep out of it. He knows she is right, but is committed to take part. Merthyr finds out that the plan has been betrayed by Violetta. Nevertheless, Carlo goes to Bergamo, where the hopeless rising has begun. Vittoria writes warning him to be careful of Nagen, who has been put on his track by Anna.

The rising is crushed at Brescia. Carlo and Angelo, with a handful of men, try to get across the Swiss frontier. Anna has now given up her hatred of Italian patriots, wants Lena to marry Weisspriess, and urges Weisspriess to save Carlo from Nagen. Vittoria, with Merthyr, reaches Jacopo's inn in search of news. Going ahead, Merthyr finds that the fugitives have been captured half a mile from the frontier. Weisspriess, in an argument with Nagen, insists that Carlo's life should be spared, though Angelo must be executed as a murderer. Carlo demands the right to fight the overdue duel with Weisspriess and kills him. Rizzo and a few other men burst out of an ambush to effect a rescue, but they have no change against Nagen's force. Carlo is killed, as well as Rizzo and all the remaining Italians.

THE ADVENTURES OF HARRY RICHMOND

Augustus Fitz-George Roy Richmond is a man of mysterious origins, who is preparing a lawsuit to prove that his parents, a member of the royal family and an actress, were actually married. As a penniless singing teacher, he has eloped with and married Marian Beltham; Harry is their son. Marian has returned to live with her father, the wealthy Squire Beltham of Riversley Grange, and her sister Dorothy. Before the novel opens, Marian has become insane and Dorothy looks after Harry. Richmond suddenly appears at Riversley in the middle of a winter night and insists on taking Harry away. Living in London with Richmond and a housekeeper, Mrs Waddy, the child Harry is dazzled by a round of treats, outings and parties, but this enjoyable life comes to an abrupt close when he is sent to live at Dipwell Farm with Mrs Waddy's sister and her husband, John Thresher. His playfellow is the miller's daughter, Mabel Sweetwinter. Meanwhile, his mother dies. He is again fetched by his father for another period of affluent life in a grand London house and a tour of Europe. In Venice, they meet Clara Goodwin, daughter of a Colonel.

But Harry's life changes once more when he is sent to a boarding-school run by the brutal Rippenger, who humiliates and mistreats him because his father fails to pay the fees. Harry hero-worships the head boy, Walter Heriot, who is in love with Rippenger's daughter, Julia. In trouble for striking an assistant teacher, Heriot leaves the school, saying farewell to Julia by climbing a ladder to her window. With £5 sent by Heriot, Harry organizes a feast in the nearby woods. The boys are traced by Rippenger, so Harry runs away, is hidden in a tent by a gipsy girl, Kiomi, and walks with her to the neighbourhood of Riversley. He meets his aunt Dorothy on the road. Riversley becomes Harry's home, he grows into his teens, and his grandfather, the Squire, decides that he should marry Janet Ilchester, the Squire's grand-niece. Temple, a schoolfellow of Harry's, comes to stay and falls in love with Janet.

Through an overheard conversation, Harry learns that his father is 'in the Bench'. He goes to London with Temple and they try to find 'the Bench', gradually realizing that it is the King's Bench, a prison for debtors.

They get drunk and are taken aboard a ship by a helpful sailor. After sleeping all day, they find that the ship has sailed down the Thames. Captain Welsh, a religious fanatic, proposes to keep the boys with him to save them from dissipation. They reach a German port, evade Welsh, and meet Colonel Goodwin and Clara. Goodwin tells Harry that his father is at Sarkeld, a small German principality, but that Harry would be wiser to return to his grandfather. However, Harry and Temple travel to Sarkeld. In a forest hut, they meet a twelve-year-old girl who tells them of a celebration next day and the unveiling of a statue to a former prince. The girl is Princess Ottilia, daughter of Prince Ernest.

Richmond, who is in the service of the Prince, has undertaken to provide a statue in record time. The unveiling reveals the statue, which is really a bronze casing with Richmond inside it. Astonished to see his son, Richmond calls out 'Harry, my boy!' and thus gives the game away. The princely family are annoyed, so Richmond leaves Sarkeld with Harry and Temple. They go to Paris, run out of money, and manage to borrow enough to reach England. Living at Riversley again, Harry renews his friendship with Heriot, now an Army officer. They go to the Epsom races and Heriot smuggles Kiomi, the gipsy girl, into the select enclosure. Richmond is in the debtors' prison again, but Harry gets him released with Heriot's help. Soon, Richmond is in Bath, entertaining lavishly and incurring more debts. Captain Bulsted, a Navy man who lives near Riversley when not at sea, has married Julia Rippenger after being rejected by Dorothy Beltham.

On his twenty-first birthday, Harry inherits £70,000 from his grandfather, who promises another £20,000 when he marries Janet. He visits Dipwell Farm with Heriot. Mabel, the local beauty, catches Heriot's eye and Richmond warns him not to seduce her. Then Richmond takes Harry on another European trip, with a tutor, the Rev. Ambrose Peterborough. At Ostend, they meet Ottilia, who is with her aunt, the Margravine, and is convalescing after a fall from a horse. Richmond hires a yacht and takes them on a cruise. They all go to Sarkeld, but Richmond refuses to apologize for his trick with the statue and is still *persona non grata*. Richmond and Harry go to the Austrian Alps, where they find Ottilia again. Harry becomes a student at a university near Sarkeld, while Richmond is accepted by the Prince as manager of a coal-mine. Harry meets Ottilia, gets rid of her cousin, Prince Otto, by giving him a horse to ride back to the castle, and tells Ottilia that he loves her; she says that she returns his love, and commits herself in a letter. Her father, Prince Ernest, tells Harry that it is impossible for Ottilia to marry a man who is not a German aristocrat. Prince Otto, who has taken offence, challenges Harry to a duel. Both are wounded, and Ottilia comes secretly to nurse Harry. It is arranged that she is to marry the scholarly, forty-year-old Prince Hermann.

Richmond is determined to help Harry to marry Ottilia. He arranges for them to meet at midnight in the palace library, where they will pledge themselves and be heard by the Rev. Peterborough. Ottilia is followed by Baroness Turckems, who rings a bell. Richmond sets fire to the curtains to provide an explanation for the alarm bell.

Harry returns to Riversley, where Janet is now living. Beltham, when told about Ottilia, is hostile to the idea of Harry marrying a foreign princess, but is persuaded by Janet to accept it. Mabel Sweetwinter has disappeared, and Heriot is going around with Julia when her husband is away. Beltham demands to see Harry's bank-book and finds that he has written cheques for a total of £57,000; the money has been spent by Richmond. Richmond has told many people in London that his son is to marry Princess Ottilia, and it has got into the newspapers. Harry arranges a meeting between Beltham and Richmond, who promises to repay the money within two months. But Richmond is now mentally unstable and makes a disastrous speech at a dinner, thanks to a deception for which the fashionable Lord Edbury is responsible. Richmond is compelled to issue a denial of the alleged marriage plans.

A sudden death causes a by-election and Richmond persuades Harry to contest it, in the hope that Prince Ernest will be impressed by hearing that his daughter's lover is an MP. Richmond finances the campaign and Harry wins, but Richmond is almost bankrupt again and is saved by a mysterious gift of £25,000.

Walking to Captain Bulsted's house, Harry is attacked by gipsies who have mistaken him for Heriot. He is unconscious for several days and wakes up to find that Kiomi is caring for him. She sends for his father, who takes him to the Isle of Wight to convalesce. Harry meets Clara Goodwin, who tells him that Ottilia is on her way, having been told in a letter from Richmond that Harry is dying. Ottilia arrives, coming on the same boat from Portsmouth as Janet and Dorothy. In a short talk with Harry, Ottilia says: 'We must not be impatient.' Janet and Ottilia soon become friends. Prince Ernest comes to England and is taken on a boat trip by Richmond, who claims that the Prince now approves of the marriage and informs the newspapers accordingly. But Ottilia confides to Janet that she cannot marry Harry, and Prince Hermann appears on the Isle of Wight.

In a tense interview with Beltham, Richmond admits that he brought Ottilia to England by a deception. Highly suspicious, Beltham forces Dorothy to admit that she gave Richmond the £25,000; she has been in love with him ever since he married her sister. Richmond was unaware of this and it is a shattering blow to him. Ottilia agrees to marry Hermann, and the Germans go home.

Eight months later, Beltham dies, leaving Riversley and his money to Janet. She decides to give the house to Harry on condition that Richmond is not invited there. After hearing that Ottilia has married Hermann, Harry goes abroad for a while. He returns to find that Richmond has lost his lawsuit and is 'raving', and that Janet is engaged to Lord Edbury. Mabel has been Edbury's mistress and been dismissed by him; Welsh has taken her on his ship. Harry makes a long journey, travelling to Asia on an Austrian ship. A letter from Ottilia, asking him to come to Sarkeld, reaches him. He finds Janet at Sarkeld. The day before he was due to marry Janet, Edbury went on to Welsh's ship to see Mabel and was trapped there. The ship sank in a storm; everyone on board was drowned. Janet agrees, with Ottilia's blessing, to marry Harry.

They return to find Riversley on fire. Richmond has arranged a fire-work display as a welcome home. When the house catches fire, he rushes inside to rescue Dorothy, who in fact is away on a visit. Richmond is never seen again.

THE EGOIST

Sir Willoughby Patterne is rich, handsome and much admired, especially by his mother and his aunts Eleanor and Isabel, who live with him at Patterne Hall. Choosing a future wife, he considers beautiful Constantia Durham and pretty, clever Laetitia Dale. Constantia is the daughter of another landowner, while Laetitia's father is an impoverished army surgeon, a tenant on the Patterne estate, so Willoughby chooses Constantia and they are engaged. He refuses to receive a visit from a relative, a Marine officer called Crossjay Patterne, because he is badly dressed; this incident makes a bad impression on Constantia. Ten days before the wedding, she goes to London and marries another suitor, Captain Oxford. Willoughby's reaction is to take a walk with Laetitia, raising her hopes, but he cools off. He goes for a three-year world tour with his cousin, Vernon Whitford, who had made a socially unsuitable marriage. Since his wife's death, Vernon is a loner, cautious towards women. He has ambitions as a writer, but accepts a job as estate manager and comes to live at the Hall. Vernon is also tutor to twelve-year-old Crossjay Patterne, the Marine's son, who boards with Mr Dale and Laetitia and hopes to get into the Navy.

Willoughby makes another approach to Laetitia, who idolizes him, but again cools off. He proposes to eighteen-year-old Clara, daughter of a scholarly clergyman, Dr Middleton, who has come to live in the neighbourhood. Clara accepts but asks for a six-month engagement. She is puzzled by a conversation in which Willoughby wants her to promise not to remarry if he dies; he is seeking total devotion. At this time his mother dies.

Clara meets and likes both Vernon and Laetitia; she knows that Willoughby wants to get them married. Clara herself becomes more and more dubious. She is fond of young Crossjay and agrees with Vernon that he should go to a cram-school to pass the Navy entry exam, but Willoughby opposes this plan. Crossjay tells Clara how his father was snubbed by Willoughby. Also, she tries in vain to intercede with Willoughby for Flitch, a coachman dismissed for being drunk. She decides that she has made a mistake and asks Willoughby to release her from the engagement, but he refuses. When she suggests that he would do better by marrying Laetitia, he replies: 'Never!'

Colonel Horace de Craye, a middle-aged bachelor with a record of affairs with women, arrives for a visit. He is attracted by Clara and thinks that Willoughby is a fool to risk losing her. Clara asks her father to take her away (they are now guests at the Hall) and at first he agrees, but after enjoying Willoughby's old port he finds it impossible to leave. Clara writes to a London friend, Lucy Darleton, asking to come and stay, and Lucy replies extending a welcome. One rainy morning, she disappears from the Hall, leaving a letter for Willoughby. Vernon finds her at the station, takes her to the Railway Inn for a change of stockings and a brandy, and advises her not to go to London. Mrs Mountstuart Jenkinson comes to the station to meet a guest, Professor Crooklyn, but he seems not to have arrived. To prevent her from seeing Clara, Vernon talks with her and goes off with her in her carriage. De Craye appears at the station. Clara cannot take the risk of travelling to London with him, so she returns to the Hall in a cab driven by Flitch. She makes up a story about paying visits in the neighbourhood and is supported by Crossjay. De Craye helps by rescuing the letter before Willoughby can read it.

They go to dinner with Mrs Mountstuart. Crooklyn, who did in fact arrive, gives an account of how he had to wait at the Railway Inn because no cab was available, and how he was told about a lady and a gentleman drinking brandy. Willoughby assumes that Clara was at the inn with De Craye. In a talk with Laetitia, he declares emotionally that he cannot bear deceit. Crossjay is to be expelled from the Hall for lying; he runs off. Laetitia gets the impression that Willoughby will now release Clara, and tells Clara so. But her own view of Willoughby has changed; she sees him as like other men, 'one of them'. Flitch comes to the Hall with Clara's purse and ticket to London, which she dropped in the cab.

Mrs Mountstuart tells Clara that she must in the end marry Willoughby, but Clara says that she simply cannot. Mrs Mountstuart asks if there is a man she could marry. Clara admits that there is; she is thinking of Vernon but Mrs Mountstuart guesses that she means De Craye. Willoughby is now revising his plans – he will marry Laetitia and Clara can marry Vernon; Laetitia will be grateful and he will be praised for his generosity.

He locks the door of Crossjay's room as a punishment. Crossjay returns and, unable to get into his room, goes to spend the night on a sofa in the drawing-room. Willoughby brings Laetitia to the room and, while Crossjay listens unobserved, proposes to her. To his astonishment, she rejects him. In the morning, he tries to patch things up with Clara, saying that there has been a misunderstanding. Dr Middleton grasps for the first time that Clara really wants to break the engagement. He is furious, and gives her one hour to recognize her duty or find a good reason against it. Dr Corney, the local doctor, finds Crossjay on the road and takes him to Dale's house. There, De Craye discovers him and, though he doesn't want to talk to anyone but Vernon, successfully guesses what happened in the night. He meets Clara and tells her. She confronts Willoughby and her father with her knowledge. Willoughby pretends that he was proposing to Laetitia on Vernon's behalf.

People gather at the Hall: Mr Dale, Mrs Mountstuart, other ladies in search of gossip. Everyone is mystified. The aunts are sent to fetch Laetitia. Realizing at last that he cannot have Clara, Willoughby feels that the worst humiliation for him will be if she attaches herself to De Craye; it would be better for her to marry Vernon. Clara and Dr Middleton are to leave the Hall the following day. In a farewell talk with Laetitia, Clara urges her to marry Willoughby. Vernon now recognizes that he is in love with Clara and she loves him. In a somewhat unemotional way, he proposes to her and invites her on a tour of the Alps.

Willoughby desperately begs Laetitia to marry him. She makes it clear that she will never love him, and if she marries him it will be mainly for the sake of her father, now in very poor health. As she remarks to the aunts, she has become as much of an egoist as Willoughby. She states her terms: he must forgive Crossjay and let him go to the cram-school for the Navy, and he must forgive and reinstate Flitch. After all that he has been through, Willoughby is ready to agree to anything.

BEAUCHAMP'S CAREER

Nevil Beauchamp, whose parents are dead, has been brought up by his uncle, the Hon. Everard Romfrey. Owner of an estate at Steynham, Sussex, and a traditional Tory in his outlook, Romfrey is a younger son of the Earl of Romfrey. He employs a housekeeper, Rosamund Culling, widow of an Army officer and still quite young, who is devoted to Nevil. There are other members of the Beauchamp family: an old and very rich great-aunt; Cecil Baskelett, a cousin of Nevil's; and another relative, Blackburn Tuckham, a lawyer.

Though he would prefer to study, Nevil is sent into the Navy as a midshipman. Feeling that England has been insulted in French newspapers, he challenges any member of the French Imperial Guard to a duel. There is no answer, perhaps because Rosamund did not post the letter. A few years later, Britain and France are allies in the Crimean War. Nevil saves the life of a French officer, Roland de Croisnel. Both ill with fever, they become friends, and at the end of the war they go to Venice to convalesce. There, Roland is joined by his beautiful young sister Renée, their father, the Comte de Croisnel, and the Marquis de Rouaillout, who is to marry Renée thanks to an arrangement with the Comte, though he is an unattractive middle-aged man. Nevil falls in love with Renée and, one night in a gondola, she gives him her hand, which he interprets as a pledge. Roland, though sympathetic to Nevil, tells him that the arranged marriage must go through. Nevil hires a boat to see the sunrise over Venice from the sea, going with Renée, Roland and Rosamund, who has come to Venice. He orders the boat crew to head for Trieste, hoping to marry Renée, but she lacks the courage to consent to this rebellion and they return to Venice, where she ultimately marries the Marquis.

Nevil, promoted to Commander, makes a voyage to the African coast chasing slave-ships. Back home, he listens to a speech by an extreme Radical, Dr Shrapnel, is converted to Shrapnel's ideas, and decides to stand as Radical candidate for Bevisham in the forthcoming election.

Staying in Shrapnel's cottage, he meets Shrapnel's ward, a serious young woman, Jenny Denham. Rosamund goes there to visit Nevil, but he is out and she is so offended by Shrapnel's eccentric speeches that she leaves without seeing Nevil, and tells Romfrey that she was glad to escape. Romfrey jumps to the conclusion that Shrapnel insulted her. Rosamund is worried because she hopes that Nevil will forget Renée and marry Cecilia Halkett – a very suitable match since Cecilia is beautiful, is already fond of Nevil, is an heiress, and is the daughter of Colonel Halkett, a good friend of Romfrey.

Bevisham elects two MPs. Nevil is uneasily paired with Cougham, a moderate Liberal. Seymour Austin is standing as a Tory and no second Tory candidate has yet been found. It is normally a safe Tory seat and much depends on bribery, but Nevil makes headway with energetic canvassing. Lord Palmet, who has no political ideas and is interested only in women, goes around with Nevil and is attracted by Jenny. A lampoon linking Nevil with 'a French Marquees' circulates and is seen to be damaging. Nevil visits the home of an old Whig gentleman, now a Tory, Grancey Lespel, and finds himself in the midst of a Tory house-party. There is to be a drive, with a procession of carriages, into Bevisham next morning. Unknown to Nevil, this is to show off Cecil Baskelett, a surprise Tory candidate. The plan, devised by Romfrey, is to make Nevil ridiculous by placing him on Baskelett's carriage. Cecilia warns him just in time.

Nevil gets a letter from Renée with the short message: 'Come at once.' He crosses to France and goes to her château. Her husband, the Marquis, is away, but Agnes d'Auffray, sister of the Marquis, is there, and it transpires that she has promoted the invitation in order to foil the intentions of Comte d'Henriel, who is chasing Renée, and has summoned the Marquis to return. Nevil at first restrains himself but then pleads passionately with Renée to commit herself to him. Again, she cannot find the courage. Henriel challenges Nevil to a duel, but Nevil declines, as it is not an English custom, and Roland fights the duel on his behalf. However, the rumour spreads in Bevisham that he has paid a romantic visit to his 'French Marquees' and fought a duel for her. Shrapnel, a figure of ridicule in the town, has been disastrously taking over the campaign in Nevil's absence, so when polling day comes the Tories win easily. Meanwhile, Cecilia has rejected a proposal from Tuckham. Despite her Tory background, she is impressed by the sincerity and idealism she sees in Nevil and by this time is in love with him.

Nevil loses a coat and, with it, a packet of letters, including a long political letter from Shrapnel. Baskelett gets hold of it and amuses Romfrey by reading it aloud. They both detest Shrapnel and Baskelett goes to his cottage to provoke him. He hints that Jenny is Shrapnel's mistress, and Shrapnel retorts by pointing out that Romfrey too has a lady who is no relation, Rosamund, living in his house. Baskelett informs Romfrey of this imputation, so Romfrey goes to Shrapnel's home and beats him with a horsewhip. Nevil, who is at Steynham, demands that Rosamund should tell him if she has ever been insulted by Shrapnel; she answers evasively. Nevil wants Romfrey to apologize, he refuses, and this causes a breach between uncle and nephew. Nevil gets Shrapnel's letter back and tries to read it to Cecilia, but she refuses to listen. Later, however, she is surprised to find that Austin, a thinking Tory, has read it and finds it worthy of consideration.

Nevil asks Cecilia for a ride on the Downs and she hopes for a proposal. Instead, he takes her to visit Shrapnel, who is ill as a result of the beating. Having seen a photograph of Renée, Cecilia is very unhappy. Nevil's rich great-aunt has died. As she was shocked by his Radical ideas, he expects to get nothing under her will, but Tuckham has persuaded her to share out the legacy and Nevil gets £80,000. He is hoping to start a Radical paper called *The Dawn*. The legacy is enough for a weekly, but not for a daily which could reach the masses of working men.

Romfrey is now the Earl, as his brother has died. Nevil is not welcome at Steynham, but goes to the Romfrey house in London to stay there for the last time. He meets Baskelett coming out and is told that a French lady is there – Renée. He wires Rosamund to come in order to protect Renée's reputation. Renée has finally decided that she can no longer bear her marriage to the Marquis, who has a mistress, and she is willing to live with Nevil, not in England but in Italy or Greece. Rosamund arrives and Nevil stays the night at a hotel. In the morning, before Nevil and Renée can go off together, Agnes arrives, soon followed by the Marquis. Romfrey, alerted by Baskelett, also comes to London. Rosamund, feeling that she has been to blame by failing to persuade Romfrey to apologize to Shrapnel, resigns from her job, but Romfrey has decided to marry her and make her the Countess.

Having lost Renée, Nevil now wants to marry Cecilia. Though she loves him, she is not happy about this because it is her money which would finance the newspaper, and also because she hears from the gossipy Mrs Lespel a distorted account of what appears to be Nevil's rendezvous with Renée in the empty London house. Colonel Halkett credits this version and Nevil has scrupulously forbidden Rosamund to tell Cecilia the truth, so Cecilia, in great distress, agrees to a long yacht trip in the

Mediterranean with her father, Austin, and Tuckham. When they return, Tuckham proposes to her and, without love, she accepts him. Nevil then appears and proposes, but she has to tell him that he is too late.

On account of visiting the home of a poor man dying of fever, Nevil becomes dangerously ill. Jenny is caring for him at Shrapnel's cottage. Rosamund now tells Romfrey that she was never insulted by Shrapnel and he reluctantly agrees to make the apology. He goes to the cottage and finds Cecilia sharing the task of nursing Nevil with Jenny. After being delirious and almost dying, Nevil is recovering. Romfrey makes a formal apology to Shrapnel and they shake hands.

Nevil and Jenny are to be married, though without love. Nevil sees Renée for the last time when, with Roland, she pays a friendly visit to Bevisham. Cecilia lends the Halkett yacht so that Nevil, with Jenny and Shrapnel, can make a convalescent trip. Nevil and Jenny are married in Venice. Romfrey is delighted that his wife is pregnant and there will be an heir to the earldom, but Rosamund is still guilty and distressed and the baby, a boy, dies an hour after birth. Jenny, however, has a son.

On the day when Nevil returns to England and gives back the yacht, he rescues two small boys who have overturned a boat and fallen into the sea, but he himself is drowned. Romfrey and Shrapnel, hurrying to the scene, are united in their grief.

DIANA OF THE CROSSWAYS

Diana Merion – beautiful, witty, Irish, eighteen years old – is the star of a grand ball in Dublin. A visitor from England, Thomas Redworth, prevents a quarrel and a possible duel between two of her admirers; he is himself fascinated by her, but lacks the money needed to court her. Diana has no living parents and her childhood home, Crossways in the south of England, is let to tenants, Mr and Mrs Warwick. Her closest friend, Emma, is married to Sir Lukin Dunstane, owner of an estate, Copsley, in Surrey.

While Diana is staying at Copsley, Sir Lukin makes a sexual advance to her. Her reaction is that, since all men are predatory, she needs to get married as soon as possible. By marrying Augustus Warwick, nephew of the tenants of Crossways, she can hope to regain her old home, and accordingly she marries him, but without love. Redworth by now has become rich through investment in new railways, but when he is in a position to marry Diana he learns from Emma that she has just accepted Warwick.

Warwick gets a Government job thanks to the elderly politician, Lord Dannisborough. Diana enjoys Dannisborough's company, receives late-evening visits from him, and takes him to Copsley for a day while her husband is abroad. This imprudence leads to paragraphs in scandal sheets and Warwick brings a lawsuit alleging adultery, and insists on pursuing it despite a plea from Sir Lukin. Diana decides to go abroad, but Emma sees that this would be a fatal evasion and sends Redworth to Crossways just in time to stop her. Diana is determined never to live with Warwick again and to make a career as a writer, and Redworth finds her a house in London. In London society she meets Percy Dacier, Dannisborough's nephew, an MP tipped for a big future in politics. Redworth too has entered the House of Commons. Diana is cleared by the jury and goes with friends for a leisurely journey abroad. In Italy she again meets Dacier, who is also travelling, and both realize that they are strongly attracted, though he is half-engaged to a rich heiress, Constance Asper. Dacier hears that his uncle is ill and returns at once to England.

Diana's first novel appears and is a success; Redworth uses his press connections to get it well reviewed. Diana is now at the centre of a social circle including various editors and journalists and an aspiring young poet, Arthur Rhodes. When she is staying at Copsley, Rhodes comes with a message from Dacier that Dannisborough is dying. She hurries to see him for the last time and this occasions another intimate meeting with Dacier. Dacier is rightly identified as the hero of Diana's new novel, *The Young Minister of State*. Lady Wathin, a rigidly conventional woman and wife of a judge, emerges as Diana's enemy and a sympathizer with Constance, who is pining for Dacier. There is a prospect that Diana may become free, as Warwick has heart disease. When she goes for a holiday alone in France, Dacier follows her and makes it clear that he loves her, but she responds cautiously, while denying that she will ever be reconciled to Warwick.

Problems accumulate for Diana. She is spending too much on dinner-parties and is making no progress with her current novel. Emma, now in bad health, dislikes what Diana has written and there is coolness between them. Lady Wathin comes to see Diana with a request from Warwick for a meeting, which Diana refuses.

Dacier now declares: 'I can't live without you.' He persuades her to go abroad with him and they agree to meet the following evening at the station to take the night train and boat to Paris. Just as she is about to leave her house, Redworth appears with an urgent message that Emma is about to undergo an operation at Copsley. She goes there with

Redworth, while Dacier waits at the station in vain. Sir Lukin, who loves his wife deeply despite his repeated affairs with other women, is agonizing. The operation is successful and Diana goes with Emma for a convalescent stay on the Isle of Wight. The two women are close again and Diana admits to Emma that she is in love with Dacier.

Back in London, Diana sees Dacier again but they are discreet and he doesn't again suggest going abroad. Warwick, in any case, is not expected to live much longer. Diana has lost money through a rash investment and is in debt. She is forced to sell Crossways and Redworth promises to look for a buyer. Tonans, a newspaper editor, has been offering to pay her for any inside political information.

Dacier comes to her house late at night with the news that his party chief has decided on the repeal of the Corn Laws, the great political issue of the period. In a state of excitement, he puts emotional pressure on her – they must be lovers. She puts him off until the next day. Then she goes to Tonans's office and gives him the news. Dacier reads the paper at breakfast, is astonished and baffled, and hastens to see Diana. On the way to her house, he is invited to lunch by Quintin Manx, Constance's rich uncle, and has to accept. Diana admits that she gave Tonans the information, pleading that she did not realize it was a secret. Dacier accuses her of betrayal and says an icy goodbye. When he goes to lunch, Constance is there. He proposes to her and she is happy to agree to an early marriage. At home, he receives a long letter from Diana but burns it without reading it. A few days later, Warwick is knocked down in the street and dies, but Dacier and Constance are already married.

Emma finds Diana in a state of collapse, refusing to eat and hoping for death. With Emma's support, she slowly recovers. She gets a cheque from Tonans, but burns it. Now that she is a widow, she can choose a husband – Redworth, Rhodes, or any of several other men. Emma is a persuasive supporter of Redworth. Diana learns that he has bought Crossways for her and that he has taken action to refute a slanderous allegation against her. She will never love Redworth as she loved Dacier, but recognizes that he is an utterly decent man and has watched over her interests since he first saw her. After calm consideration, she marries him.

THE TRAGIC COMEDIANS

Clotilde, daughter of General von Rüdiger, is young, beautiful and independent-minded. She is courted by Prince Marko Romaris, likes him,
but finds him immature. Seeking a man worthy of dominating her, she
is fascinated by what she hears of the Socialist leader Sigismund Alvan,
and contrives to meet him. In a long night of talking, they decide that
their ideas and personalities coincide and they must spend their lives
together. She warns him, however, that her deeply conservative parents
will be a problem, for conventional Prussian society hates Alvan as an
outsider, a demagogue and a Jew. Clotilde is also sorry to disappoint
Marko, but he accepts her preference.

On Alvan's side, Baroness Lucie von Crefeldt, with whom he had a
love affair twenty years ago, dismisses Clotilde as 'a shallow girl', and his
friend Colonel Tresten thinks the same.

Alvan wants to marry Clotilde in the socially correct manner with the
approval of her parents. When the lovers meet in the Alps, he impulsively
suggests a runaway match, but she declines and he reverts to his first
plan. She joins her parents in Geneva and he comes to that city a day
later. She goes to his hotel to tell him that there is no hope of parental
consent. He advises her to take refuge with a sympathetic friend, Madame
Emerly. Her mother pursues her and refuses to listen to a word from
Alvan, whom she calls 'a thief'. Clotilde is now prepared to elope to Italy
with Alvan, but he is confident of his ability to persuade the Rüdigers
and tells her to return to them. She does so with great reluctance and,
as she feared, is shut up in their villa and forbidden all outside contact.
She sends a letter to Alvan renouncing him; he guesses that it was dictated
by her father but begins to feel uncertain. Marko pleads with Clotilde to
come to him; her reply is that she belongs to Alvan. She writes to the
Baroness asking for sympathy. The Baroness tells her that she ought to
give Alvan up.

Now Clotilde is compelled to return the letters and gifts she has received
from Alvan, and to write informing him that she is engaged to Marko.
Alvan replies, but she has to give the letter unopened to Marko. However,
her father allows her to see two emissaries – Colonel Trestan and a
lawyer, Dr Störchel – who bring a request for a meeting between her
and Alvan. Alvan is confident that this procedure will work in his favour
and makes plans to take Clotilde to Paris, but Clotilde refuses to see him,
because she feels that Tresten is hostile to her. She intends to write to

Störchel, whom she finds more sympathetic, but he leaves Geneva before she can do so.

Infuriated by these setbacks, Alvan challenges the General to a duel. The General declines the challenge because of his advanced age, but it is taken up by Marko. As Marko is quite inexperienced with weapons, Clotilde is sure that he will be killed and pities him. She decides to escape and join Alvan as soon as she hears of Marko's death. To her astonishment, Marko returns unhurt. Alvan is badly wounded, and three days later Clotilde hears that he is dead. She marries Marko, without love, but as the only way to free herself from her parents. A few months later, Marko dies. Clotilde has no future, but her heart is always Alvan's.

ONE OF OUR CONQUERORS

When he was twenty-one years old, Victor Radnor made a loveless marriage with a rich widow. Then he fell in love with his wife's companion, Nataly Dreighton. When the novel opens, Victor and Nataly have been living together for twenty years – happily, but under the shadow of exposure by his legal wife, Mrs Burman Radnor. Victor has built up a successful investment business and become a millionaire. His secret is known only to a few friends, including the loyal Simeon Fenellan and the tolerant, cynical Colney Durance. To establish himself socially, he has twice bought houses in the country, only to be forced to abandon them because of rumours leading to ostracism. He is now building a palatial residence in Surrey, Lakelands. Nataly feels that this project is unwise, and unfortunately Mrs Burman has learned of it through her butler, Jarniman, who spies on Victor.

Time is running out because Victor and Nataly have a daughter, Nesta, who has never been told that her parents are not married, and who is now old enough to be married herself. She has two suitors: the Hon. Dudley Sowerby, who has prospects of inheriting an earldom, and a clergyman, the Rev. Septimus Barmby. Fenellan hears from Mrs Burman's lawyer, Carling, that she may agree to a divorce, but nothing comes of this. However, she is in bad health and her death is another possibility. Skepsey, a clerk in Victor's office, strikes up a chance friendship with Jarniman – both are boxing enthusiasts – who says that he is employed by an elderly lady who has not long to live. Victor shows off Lakelands to a group of friends, including Dudley and Barmby, and takes them on a trip to Paris at his expense. Both Dudley and Barmby have shown their interest in Nesta; Victor tells them that they are free to speak to her and the choice will be hers.

Victor gives a big party, combined with a concert for charity, to inaugurate Lakelands. An unexpected guest is Simeon Fenellan's half-brother Dartrey, who has just come home from Africa and left the army, Dartrey's wife has recently died, ending an unhappy marriage. During the day, Jarniman appears – a warning sign that Mrs Burman knows about Lakelands and may cause trouble. Dudley proposes to Nesta and she accepts him, but Nataly perceives that she does not love him and is only trying to please her father. Because of the threat of unpleasantness from Mrs Burman, the parents send Nesta to stay for a month at Tunbridge Wells with the Duvidney ladies, elderly sisters related to Victor. Dudley's family estate is in the neighbourhood. Nataly goes to see him and informs him that his prospective bride is illegitimate. Genuinely in love with Nesta, but concerned over his position in his socially prominent family, Dudley cannot decide what to do. The journey is an ordeal for Nataly, who is suffering from an illness of which she has told nobody.

The Duvidney sisters take Nesta to Brighton, where she sees Dartrey, a man whom she strongly admires. She also becomes friendly with a woman known as Mrs Marsett, a social pariah because it is widely known that she is not really married to the man she lives with, Captain Marsett. In an emotional scene, Mrs Marsett tells Nesta her story. A friend of Marsett's, Major Worrell, makes a pass at Nesta. Nataly goes to Brighton and requests Dartrey to keep a friendly eye on Nesta. Dartrey, meanwhile, has to deal with Mrs Blathenoy, the pretty young wife of a rich businessman, who flirted with him at the Lakelands party and now makes it clear that she wants an affair with him. Dartrey commands her to return to her husband. Mrs Marsett asks to see Dartrey and tells him that Nesta should be advised not to associate with her, and that Nesta has been insulted by Worrell. A friend of Dartrey's, Colonel Sudley, points out Worrell to him.

Nothing more has been heard of Dudley and it is assumed that he has withdrawn from the engagement. Barmby proposes to Nesta in a walk on Brighton pier, and tactlessly indicates that he will overlook the 'shadow' on her. Nesta turns Barmby down, but is getting close to guessing the secret.

Skepsey, though Victor trusts him and Nesta is fond of him, has a tendency to get into trouble and has been before the magistrate three times: first, for an illegal prizefight, then for hitting his wife, who is an alcoholic, and now because of a street fight in Brighton, when he defended a Salvation Army volunteer, Matilda Pridden, against roughs. In this incident, Dartrey came to Skepsey's aid, wielding a stout stick which he acquired to threaten Worrell.

Nesta returns to London and tells her parents that she has guessed the truth and loves them as much as ever. Rumours are spreading more widely and some respectable ladies boycott the Radnors' next musical evening, but Victor is planning to stand for Parliament, as a vacancy has occurred in a South London constituency. Dudley tells Nataly that he had made up his mind to marry Nesta, but her involvement with people like Mrs Marsett and Major Worrell has made it really impossible. Nataly by this time is aware that she is terminally ill, and takes this as a divine punishment. She sees Dartrey and asks him about the Brighton incidents; he says that Nesta has behaved bravely and generously and been a good influence on Mrs Marsett. When he next sees Nesta, they know that they are meant for each other. Nataly is apprehensive. In her eyes, Nesta and Dartrey are both rebels and will always be in conflict with social conventions. Nesta makes it clear that she will not marry Dudley even if he is willing to forgive her unsuitable behaviour. Victor goes to Brighton and ensures that Captain Marsett will enter into a legal marriage.

Mrs Burman sends a message that she wants to see Victor. Nataly insists on going with him. Mrs Burman, aware that she is near to death, requests them to kneel and pray with her, and says that she forgives them. Victor is then due to speak at a meeting to open his election campaign; Nataly does not feel equal to accompanying him. When he is about to make his speech, he is called away. Nataly is dead. Next morning, Jarniman comes to Victor's house – Mrs Burman is dead.

The disaster is too much for Victor, who undergoes a mental collapse and has to enter an institution. Dartrey and Nesta are married and spend a year abroad. They return in time to hear of Victor's death.

LORD ORMONT AND HIS AMINTA

Matthew Weyburn is head boy of Cuper's school; he is good at lessons, good at sports, respected and popular. He hero-worships Lord Ormont and defends him against criticism by a teacher. A cavalry general, Ormont made a surprise attack on an Indian prince suspected of conspiracy instead of having recourse to the law; he was therefore relieved of his command and his military career is over.

Matthew and Aminta Farrell – a girl at the nearby Miss Vincent's school, nicknamed 'Browny' by the boys because of her complexion –

feel a mutual attraction when they see each other on Sunday walks. They exchange letters, carried by Selina Collett, who is at Aminta's school while her brother is at Matthew's. Miss Vincent finds out and seizes Matthew's letters, and Aminta's aunt, Mrs Pagnell (her guardian, as she has no parents), takes her away from the school, and then on a journey to Spain. On the ship, they meet Lord Ormont, who has decided to live abroad because of his unfair treatment by the British authorities. Aminta, like Matthew, sympathizes with Ormont and sees him as a hero. Despite the age gap – Ormont is sixty – they are married without publicity at the British Embassy in Madrid. They continue to travel in Europe, with only occasional visits to England. Ormont's sister, Lady Constance Eglett, hears that he is living with a young woman but refuses to believe that they are married.

Seven years pass. Lady Constance needs a tutor for her grandson, Leo, and Matthew is recommended by the family lawyer, Abner, whose son was at Cuper's school and has kept up friendship with Matthew. Lady Constance likes Matthew and suggests him as a secretary for Ormont, who plans to write his memoirs. At Ormont's London house, Matthew is introduced to Lady Ormont and half-recognizes her as 'Browny'; she tells him that she remembers him from schooldays. He sees his future in running an international school and is waiting to acquire enough money. Aminta, inclined to admire military men, finds this ambition disappointing. She has become dissatisfied with her marriage, since Ormont is unwilling to present her publicly as his wife or let her reside at his country estate, Steignton. Adolphus Morsfield, a society man, is in love with Aminta, who knows from her friend Mrs Finchley – an independent-minded woman living apart from her husband – that affairs are feasible. She goes so far as to keep Morsfield's passionate letters. Meanwhile, she has long conversations with Matthew and comes round to appreciating his school project.

While Matthew is visiting Lady Constance at her country house, he receives a message, forwarded by Aminta, that his mother is ill. He hurries to her home, arriving after her death, and finds that Aminta has been caring for her. Ormont has been in Paris, but Lady Constance hears through Abner that he has gone to Steignton to refurbish the house. Herself much attached to Steignton, her childhood home, she goes there with Matthew as escort. But Aminta, believing her husband to be still in Paris, decides on impulse to go to Steignton with Mrs Pagnell. Morsfield, tipped off by Mrs Pagnell, who is antagonistic to Ormont, also sets out for Steignton.

Angered by Aminta's unexpected appearance, Ormont instructs Matthew to take her back to London. They are pursued by Morsfield, but give him the slip. Ormont has finally made up his mind to let Aminta take her place in society as Lady Ormont and requests Lady Charlotte to hand over the family jewels. She resists strongly, being still convinced that Aminta is a mistress, but has to give in. However, when Aminta gets the jewels she looks on them as 'emblems of subjection'. She has realized that her marriage was a fatal mistake.

Morsfield gets involved in a violent quarrel with Captain May at a fencing club to which they belong. They break the rules by fighting without foils and May kills Morsfield. Suspicion spreads that May was put up to it by Ormont, who had learned of Morsfield's letters to Aminta. By this time, Matthew is ready to start his school in Switzerland, together with friends of various nationalities. He says goodbye to Ormont and hopes to see Aminta once more. Aminta is staying with Selina Collett on the Suffolk coast and Selina sends Matthew an invitation. Arriving early in the morning, he goes for a swim and finds that Aminta is doing the same. After a marathon swim together, they declare their love for each other and she tells him that she has written a letter to Ormont stating that their marriage is at an end. She will go to Switzerland to live with Matthew and be joint head of the school. Lady Charlotte, who is with Ormont when he gets the letter, pursues the lovers but is just too late to catch the ship by which they leave England.

Another seven years pass. Ormont is in Switzerland with Lady Charlotte and her great-nephew Bobby, whose health is precarious. An Italian gentleman tells them about a school that will be the right place for Bobby. Ormont visits the school and comes face to face with Matthew. Declining to make a scandal or attempt to reclaim Aminta, he simply places Bobby in the school. Six months later, Lady Charlotte writes to inform Matthew that Ormont is dead and Aminta is free to marry.

THE AMAZING MARRIAGE

Chillon John and Carinthia Jane (named for their birthplaces) are the children of Captain John Kirby, who had romantically eloped with their mother and lived with her in Carinthia, where he owned a mine. The girl Carinthia has never left her homeland, though Chillon has become a British Army officer. When the parents die, brother and sister walk to a spa town where Chillon is to meet Henrietta Blakenham, whom he loves.

On the way, they meet the wandering philosopher Gower Woodseer, who has injured his leg in a fall. They find that Henrietta has gone on to Baden with her father, Admiral Blakenham, Lord Fleetwood, and the latter's young stepmother, Livia. Fleetwood, owner of Welsh coal-mines and immensely wealthy, counts on marrying the beautiful Henrietta. He too meets Gower on the journey to Baden and is told of Carinthia.

At Baden, Fleetwood introduces the austere Gower to drink and gambling. Dazzled by stylish Livia, who allows him to stake for her, Gower wins heavily but loses the next night. Fleetwood sees Carinthia climbing a tree and realizes that she is the 'child of nature' whom Gower described. Henrietta has decided to marry Chillon, incurring Livia's disapproval because he has no money. Fleetwood is made aware of this by seeing Henrietta dancing with Chillon. He reacts by asking Carinthia to marry him and she accepts. Chillon has encouraged her to marry a rich man and help him with his Army career. They have a rich uncle, Lord Levellier, but he is a miser.

Fleetwood soon regrets his impulse and Carinthia, after arriving in England, hears nothing from him for two months. He is then cornered by Levellier and forced to go ahead with the marriage, which takes place at the village church near Levellier's estate. Fleetwood takes her to a prizefight, won by Kit Ines, the man he backs. Then he goes on to a ball, leaving Carinthia at an inn with Madge Winch, Kit's girlfriend, as a maid. Late at night, he enters her room through the window (as the reader learns only much later).

Gower reaches London, where his father is a shoemaker and Dissenting preacher in Whitechapel. He knows Madge and her sister Sarah, who have a greengrocer shop. Carinthia, left at the inn in Kent with no news of her husband and no money, eventually walks to London with Madge and stays at Woodseer's. Gower discovers Fleetwood's London address but finds that he is at his castle in Wales. Gower then goes to see Admiral Blakenham, who had liked Carinthia at Baden, but he is ill. Livia, the Admiral's niece and thus Henrietta's cousin, is there. The Admiral dictates a letter to Lady Arpington, asking her to help Carinthia, but Livia seizes it, and then the Admiral dies. Gower goes to see Lady Arpington, who is sympathetic and tells Fleetwood that he must behave better, but he refuses to meet Carinthia.

Talk about the situation is spreading in London. When Fleetwood and a group of friends visit Vauxhall Gardens, they get involved in a fight. Carinthia, who is there with Madge, seizes a stick to defend Fleetwood. Next, Carinthia is ambushed and forced into a carriage. Alerted by Madge, Gower rescues her and takes her to Fleetwood's house. He accosts

Fleetwood in Hyde Park; Fleetwood says that Carinthia can stay in the house and goes to a hotel. Chillon, meanwhile, is in Vienna seeking compensation for the value of his father's mine. Fleetwood goes on a journey to the Near East with Lord Feltre, a Catholic who is gaining influence over him. He returns to hear that Carinthia has given birth to a son. Livia advises him to obtain release from his marriage by accusing Carinthia of adultery, but he replies that he accepts paternity.

Fleetwood suggests that Carinthia should live at Esslement, his house in Kent, but she goes to Wales. Until now she has aimed to win him back as her husband, but she realizes that she no longer loves him and feels no obligation to him. She becomes friendly with Owain Wythan, employed by Fleetwood in his mining business, and his invalid wife Rebecca. The mines are halted by a strike and she sympathizes with the workers. Kit Ines is in the district and she suspects him of intending to seize her baby, so she moves to Wythan's house, but in fact he was sent by Fleetwood to protect her in case of riots. Criticized for staying away from Wales during this crisis, Fleetwood goes there briefly but refuses to make concessions to the miners and also refuses to talk to Carinthia. She accosts him in the street, demanding that he should decide on a name for the child and give her money to live on; he won't agree unless she goes to Esslement. A rabid dog runs down the street and bites a child. Humiliated by her courage, Fleetwood goes to board his yacht at Cardiff. Rebecca Wythan dies. Carinthia travels to Esslement, with an escort of Welshmen headed by Owain.

Chillon has been forced to sell his Army commission. He and Carinthia go to see Lord Levellier, but fruitlessly. Chillon has been associated with Levellier in a project to produce a new type of gunpowder, so far without result. Fleetwood comes to Esslement and finds Carinthia there with Chillon and Wythan; he notes that she calls him Owain, and she says that it was his wife's wish. Fleetwood now tries to conciliate Carinthia and offers her an income, but she is hostile. He takes a room at the inn and remembers that it was her room on the wedding night; he is becoming remorseful. One of his friends, Ambrose Mallard, commits suicide because of his gambling losses and his hopeless love for Livia, and this too has an effect on Fleetwood. Through Gower, he tells Carinthia that he has undergone a change of heart and she can have whatever she wants. Gower is to marry Madge; with an allowance from Fleetwood, he will live in a cottage and write. Owain, presumably mistaken for Gower, is attacked by Kit. Livia marries the young Earl of Cressett.

Briefly, Fleetwood and Carinthia are both staying at Esslement and speak politely at meals, though she will not admit him to her rooms. Owain and Chillon are protecting Lord Levellier, who has failed to pay his workmen and received threats from them. Carinthia is adamant against pleas from Fleetwood. He meets Henrietta and remembers that she was the woman he loved.

Chillon plans to go to Spain with a British contingent in the Carlist civil war, and Carinthia decides to go with him, while Henrietta will care for her son and her own daughter. Levellier's gunpowder is set off by an explosion. It was meant as a warning, or even a joke, by the unpaid workers, but the shock causes his death. Chillon and Carinthia will inherit large sums of money, but Chillon still intends to go to Spain and increase his military experience. Carinthia is busy organizing the expedition and buying stores; she wants to go as a nurse.

Fleetwood holds a big party at another of his country houses. Henrietta is there and is approached by Lord Brailstone, who tells her that Fleetwood is pursuing her. It is not clear whether Fleetwood or Brailstone himself is the threat, but Henrietta runs away, trips and collides with an oil-lamp. She burns her face and knows that she has lost her beauty.

Carinthia, as a nurse, follows Chillon to Spain. He is on the losing side, is wounded and taken prisoner; she secures his release. Fleetwood has not only become a Catholic but entered a monastery. Three years later, he dies. Carinthia marries Owain.

CELT AND SAXON

Philip and Patrick O'Donnell are brothers. Philip, the elder, was engaged to the beautiful Adiante Adister, but she yielded to her father's opposition to marriage with an Irish Catholic. Four years later, Philip, an Army captain, has returned from service in Canada and is staying in London with his cousin Con O'Donnell, married to a sister of Mr Adister. Patrick goes to Earlsfont, Adister's residence in Wales, in the hope of tracing Adiante, who is believed to be on the Continent. Adister receives Patrick coldly, but he learns from Caroline, Adister's niece, that Adiante is married to Prince Nikolas Schinderhannes, an elderly libertine and gambler, now engaged in a dynastic quarrel with another member of his family. Adiante's maternal grandmother, a Welsh woman, has bequeathed two estates to her, to the exclusion of her two brothers, and she proposes to sell the estates and use the money to finance her husband's campaign. Strongly disapproving, Adister consults a lawyer, Camminy, to find ways of frustrating this plan. Caroline gives Patrick a miniature painting of Adiante, which he gives to Philip when the brothers meet again in London.

The next piece of news is that Adiante has given birth to a son. Patrick writes a careful letter to Caroline to inform her and her uncle. Friends of Con O'Donnell are John Mattock, a rich young businessman, and his sister Jane, a serious-minded young woman who is running a laundry on philanthropic lines to provide employment. She likes Patrick but is strongly attracted to Philip. Patrick offers to work as secretary at the laundry and spends seven months there. He is replaced by the capable Emma Colesworth. Philip, meanwhile, goes with his regiment to India.

Some time later, Kathleen, young sister of the O'Donnell brothers, arrives at Holyhead with her parish priest and mentor, Father Boyle. Travelling on the same boat is Colesworth, Emma's brother, who is English but very sympathetic to Irish people. They spend an evening at the Holyhead hotel with Con O'Donnell, who is going to Ireland to fight a by-election as an Irish nationalist, and in the view of Father Boyle is sure to win.

Adiante is now back at Earlsfont with her father. Patrick has been in Vienna and has embarked on a journey to the East. Philip has been invalided home from India because of a heat illness followed by a fall from his horse. He is convalescing at a farmhouse in Surrey. Jane goes there to help in caring for him; she is falling in love with him. At this stage, Meredith left the novel unfinished.

References

[Date] indicates those letters from the collection of George Meredith's correspondence for which the exact date, in whole or part, is questionable (according to C. L. Cline, the editor of *The Letters of George Meredith*, Volumes 1–3, 1970).

CHAPTER 1: A VEIL OF RETICENCE

1. S. M. Ellis, *George Meredith: His Life and Friends in Relation to His Work*, 1919, p. 13.
2. J. B. Priestley, *George Meredith*, 1926, p. 8.
3. Ellis, op. cit., p. 15.
4. George Meredith (GM) to Arthur G. Meredith, 27 July 1881 in C. L. Cline, ed., *The Letters of George Meredith*, 1970, vol. 2, no. 707, p. 632.
5. Lionel Stevenson, *The Ordeal of George Meredith*, 1954, p. 8.
6. Siegfried Sassoon, *Meredith*, 1948, p. 2.

CHAPTER 2: FOUNDATIONS

1. cit. Stevenson, op. cit., p. 13.
2. Dr Marianne Doerfel, 'British Pupils in a German Boarding School: Neuwied/Rhine 1820–1913', in *British Journal of Educational Studies*, vol. xxxiv, no. 1 (February 1986), Oxford, 1986, p. 89.
3. See Stevenson, op. cit., p. 14.
4. GM to R. M. Hill, 1 January 1844, in *Letters*, vol. 1, no. 1, p. 1.
5. A. Woods, *George Meredith as Champion of Women and Progressive Education*, 1937.
6. B. Batty and J. Pinder in Doerfel, op. cit., pp. 90, 95.
7. Woods, op. cit., p. 7.

8. GM to Dr H. R. D. Anders, 5 April 1906, in *Letters*, vol. 3. no. 2294, p. 1556.
9. GM to Miss Louise Lawrence, 8 September 1882, in *Letters*, vol. 2, no. 755, p. 671.
10. GM to the Editor of the *Daily Telegraph*, [16 February 1903], in *Letters*, vol. 3, no. 2147, p. 1479.

CHAPTER 3: BORN AGAIN

1. Sassoon, op. cit. p. 7.
2. cit. J. B. Priestley, *Thomas Love Peacock*, 1927, p. 185.
3. Diane Johnson, *The True History of the First Mrs Peacock and Other Lesser Lives*, 1972.
4. cit. Ellis, op. cit., p. 281.
5. V. S. Pritchett, *Meredith and English Comedy*, 1970, p. 24.
6. See Priestley, op. cit. (1926), p. 88.
7. GM to Edmund Ollier, [8 or 9 July 1851], in *Letters*, vol. 1, no. 23, pp. 15–16.
8. GM to A. J. Scott, [July–August 1851], in *Letters*, vol. 1, no. 25, p. 18.
9. GM to Alfred Tennyson, [July 1851], in *Letters*, vol. 1, no. 24, pp. 16–17.

CHAPTER 4: ATTEMPTS AND FAILURES

1. Janet Duff Gordon Ross, *The Fourth Generation*, 1912, p. 50.
2. Ellis, op. cit., pp. 62–3.
3. Ross, op. cit., p. 20.
4. Stevenson, op. cit., p. 49.
5. Jack Lindsay, *George Meredith: His Life and Work*, 1956, p. 68.
6. cit. Stevenson, op. cit., p. 46.
7. Mary Ellen Meredith to Charles Kent, 24 January [1856], in *Letters*, vol. 1, no. 34, p. 24.
8. GM to Mrs Bovill, 16 August 1892, in *Letters*, vol. 2, no. 1444, p. 1095.
9. GM to the Revd James McKechnie, 21 May 1906, in *Letters*, vol. 3, no. 2300, p. 1559.
10. GM to Captain Frederick A. Maxse, RN, 9 September 1859, in *Letters*, vol. 1, no. 49, p. 41.

CHAPTER 5: THROUGH THE ORDEAL

1. Ellis, op. cit., p. 90.
2. GM to Justin T. Vulliamy, 10 June 1864, in *Letters*, vol. 1, no. 292, p. 269n.
3. GM to William Hardman, 3 June 1864, in *Letters*, vol. 1, no. 286, p. 262.

4. Virginia Woolf, *The Common Reader*, 1932 (Second Series), p. 228.
5. Priestley, op. cit. (1926), p. 164.
6. Ibid.
7. cit. Mary Sturge Gretton, *George Meredith: Novelist, Poet, Reformer*, 1908, p. 8.
8. GM to Samuel Lucas, [7 July 1859], in *Letters*, vol. 1, no. 48, p. 39.
9. Ellis, op. cit., p. 91.
10. Mary Ellen Meredith to Edward Chapman, 4 July 1860, in *Letters*, vol. 1, no. 73, p. 60.
11. Ross, op. cit.
12. GM, report of a comment by Frederick Chapman in letter to Miss J. Duff Gordon, 29 November 1860, in *Letters*, vol. 1, no. 96, p. 78.
13. Ross, op. cit., p. 84.
14. GM to Miss Janet Duff Gordon, 23 and 30 November 1860, in *Letters*, vol. 1, nos. 81 and 83, pp. 66, 68–9.
15. GM to Mrs Janet Ross, 17 May 1861, in *Letters*, vol. 1, no. 96, p. 78.
16. GM to Mrs Janet Ross, 1 December 1863, in *Letters*, vol. 1, no. 256, p. 235.
17. Ross, op. cit., pp. 161, 381.
18. GM to William Hardman, [30] October 1861, in *Letters*, vol. 1, no. 122, pp. 107–8.

CHAPTER 6: THE BEST YEARS

1. GM to Frederick A. Maxse, 8 August 1865, in *Letters*, vol. 1, no. 342, pp. 313–14.
2. GM to Frederick A. Maxse, 'Christmas 1870 [actually 1866]', in *Letters*, vol. 1, no. 382, pp. 350, 351.
3. GM to W. C. Bonaparte Wyse, [?] January 1862, in *Letters*, vol. 1, no. 136, p. 124.
4. GM to Frederick A. Maxse, 19 October 1861, in *Letters*, vol. 1, no. 121, p. 105.
5. GM to W. C. Bonaparte Wyse, [27] April 1861, in *Letters*, vol. 1, no. 93, p. 76.
6. Ellis, op. cit., p. 120.
7. GM to Mrs N. E. S. A. Hamilton, [?] October 1863, in *Letters*, vol. 1, no. 249, p. 230.
8. GM to Augustus Jessopp, 18 May 1864, in *Letters*, vol. 1, no. 279, p. 254.
9. GM to Frederick A. Maxse, 1 June 1864, in *Letters*, vol. 1, no. 285, p. 261.
10. GM to W. C. Bonaparte Wyse, 23 July 1864, in *Letters*, vol. 1, no. 300, p. 276.
11. GM to Frederick A. Maxse, 29 August 1864, in *Letters*, vol. 1, no. 304, p. 279.
12. GM to William Hardman, 29 May 1864, in *Letters*, vol. 1, no. 281, p. 257.
13. GM to Frederick A. Maxse, 29 August 1864, in *Letters*, vol. 1, no. 304, p. 279.
14. GM to William Hardman, 5 and 11 August 1863, in *Letters*, vol. 1, nos. 243, 244, pp. 225, 226.

15. GM to Augustus Jessopp, 24 April 1865, in *Letters*, vol. 1, no. 334, p. 308.
16. GM to Augustus Jessopp, 23 October 1868, in *Letters*, vol. 1, no. 411, p. 375.
17. GM to Augustus Jessopp, 4 October 1871, in *Letters*, vol. 1, no. 483, p. 451.
18. GM to Arthur G. Meredith, 25 April 1872, in *Letters*, vol. 1, no. 500, pp. 465–6.
19. GM to Augustus Jessopp, 30 January 1865, in *Letters*, vol. 1, no. 328, p. 302.
20. GM to Frederick A. Maxse, 26 July 1861, in *Letters*, vol. 1, no. 111, p. 93.
21. GM to Frederick A. Maxse, 16 August 1861, in *Letters*, vol. 1, no. 115, p.98.
22. GM to W. B. Bonaparte Wyse, 7 January 1863, in *Letters*, vol. 1, no. 203, p. 184.
23. GM to Augustus Jessopp, [17/24] March 1863 and 13 January 1864, in *Letters*, vol. 1, nos. 215 and 261, pp. 194, 241.
24. cit. Stevenson, op. cit., p. 132.
25. GM to William Hardman, 13 July 1864, in *Letters*, vol. 1, no. 299, p. 275.
26. GM to Augustus Jessopp, 21 November 1864, in *Letters*, vol. 1, no. 320, p. 294.
27. GM to William Hardman, [?] September 1865 and [4 June 1866], in *Letters*, vol. 1, nos. 347 and 369, pp. 316, 338.
28. GM to Frederick A. Maxse, [30 April or 1 May] 1866, in *Letters*, vol. 1, no. 364, p. 334.
29. Lady Butcher, *Memories of George Meredith O.M.*, 1919, pp. 3, 5.
30. Ibid, p. 7.
31. GM to Algernon C. Swinburne, 2 March 1867, in *Letters*, vol. 1, no. 385, p. 354.
32. GM to Arthur G. Meredith, 8 February 1868, in *Letters*, vol. 1, no. 416, p. 379.
33. Ibid.

CHAPTER 7: THE FAITH OF GEORGE MEREDITH

1. Gretton, op. cit., p. 8.
2. GM to Augustus Jessopp, 20 September 1862, in *Letters*, vol. 1, no. 176, pp. 160–1.
3. GM to George Pierce Baker, 22 July 1887, in *Letters*, vol. 2, no. 1066, p. 876.
4. GM to the Revd George Bainton, 14 September 1887, in *Letters*, vol. 2, no. 1082, p. 888.
5. cit. Lindsay, op. cit., p. 369.
6. GM to Augustus Jessopp, 23 December 1862, in *Letters*, vol. 1, no. 200, p. 181.
7. GM to Miss Louisa Lawrence, 30 March 1881, in *Letters*, vol. 2, no. 692, pp. 618–19.
8. GM to Frederick A. Maxse, 3 September 1874, in *Letters*, vol. 1, no. 531, p. 493.
9. GM to Frederick A. Maxse, 15 January 1866, in *Letters*, vol. 1, no. 357, pp. 326–7.

10. GM to Frederick A. Maxse, 31 August 1884, in *Letters*, vol. 2, no. 860, p. 744.
11. GM to Lady Ulrica Duncombe, 16 July 1900, in *Letters*, vol. 3, no. 1940, p. 1353.
12. Beatrice Webb, *My Apprenticeship*, 1926, p. 130.
13. Priestley, op. cit. (1926), p. 67.
14. GM to John Morley, 'First ten minutes of 1878', in *Letters*, vol. 2, no. 612, p. 557.
15. GM to Mrs Anna C. Steele, 20 March 1888, in *Letters*, vol. 2, no. 1118, p. 911.

CHAPTER 8: CHAMPION OF WOMEN

1. Hannah Lynch, *George Meredith: A Study*, 1891, p. 168.
2. Lynch, op. cit., pp. 120, 126.
3. Woods, op. cit.
4. GM to Mrs Leslie Stephen, 13 June 1889, in *Letters*, vol. 2, no. 1206, p. 964.
5. GM to the Editor of *The Times*, [28 October 1906], in *Letters*, vol. 3, no. 2331, pp. 1576–7.
6. Ellis, op. cit., p. 258.
7. GM to Robert Louis Stevenson, 24 March 1884, in *Letters*, vol. 2, no. 839, p. 731.
8. cit. Alan Chedzoy, *A Scandalous Woman: The Story of Caroline Norton*, 1992, pp. 155, 250–1.
9. Woods, op. cit., p. 29.
10. Ibid., p. 72.
11. Lindsay, op. cit., p. 268.

CHAPTER 9: MONEY IS POWER

1. GM to Frederick A. Maxse, 28 January 1868, in *Letters*, vol. 1, no. 404, p. 368.
2. GM to Frederick A. Maxse, 2 March 1880, in *Letters*, vol. 2, no. 650, p. 588.
3. Stevenson, op. cit., p. 351.
4. GM to Miss Louisa Lawrence, 12 March 1880, in *Letters*, vol. 2, no. 652, p. 590.
5. Edward Bernstein, *Ferdinand Lassalle as a Social Reformer* (1893), New York, 1969, pp. 32, 68, 69, 188.
6. Bernstein, op. cit., p. 33.
7. GM to Frederic Chapman, 3 October 1887, in *Letters*, vol. 2, no. 1087, p. 892.
8. Frederick Engels, letter to August Bebel, 18–28 March 1875, in Marx, Engels, Lenin, *Critique of the Gotha Programme* (Text of 1891), New York, 1938, p. 31.
9. GM to Frederick A. Maxse, 25 April 1866, in *Letters*, vol. 1, no. 363, p. 333.

10. GM to Frederick A. Maxse, 28 January 1868 and 17 December 1866, in *Letters*, vol. 1, nos. 404 and 380, pp. 348, 368.
11. GM to John Morley, 23 March 1871, in *Letters*, vol. 1, no. 473, pp. 443–4.

CHAPTER 10: EUROPEAN AND COSMOPOLITAN

1. GM to Frederick A. Maxse, 27 February 1871, in *Letters*, vol. 1, no. 471, pp. 440–1.
2. Karl Marx, 'Address to the Members of the International Working Men's Association in Europe and the United States', 23 July 1870, in *The Civil War in France*, 1933, p. 69.
3. GM to William Hardman, 15 March 1878, in *Letters*, vol. 2, no. 613, p. 558.
4. GM to Frederick Greenwood, 'October first fog, 1891', in *Letters*, vol. 2, no. 1357, p. 1047.
5. GM to the Editor of the *Daily Telegraph*, 16 February 1903, in *Letters*, vol. 3, no. 2147, p. 1479.
6. GM to Seymour Trower, 2 August 1905, in *Letters*, vol. 3, no. 2262, p. 1538.
7. GM to Frederick A. Maxse, 14 October 1878, in *Letters*, vol. 2, no. 620, p. 564.
8. GM to J. Cotter Morison, 1 July 1879, in *Letters*, vol. 2, no. 635, p. 575.
9. GM to H. M. Hyndman, 31 October 1899, in *Letters*, vol. 3, no. 1909, p. 1338.
10. GM to the Editor of the *Daily Mail*, [3] March 1902, in *Letters*, vol. 3, no. 2061, p. 1427.
11. cit. Norman Kelvin, *A Troubled Eden*, 1961, p. 67.
12. Ibid, p. 70.
13. cit. Sassoon, op. cit., pp. 211–12.
14. GM to Lucien Wolf, 20 January 1906, in *Letters*, vol. 3, no. 2286, p. 1551.
15. Ibid.
16. GM to George Stevenson, 27 June 1888, in *Letters*, vol. 2, no. 1138, p. 922.
17. GM to Miss Louisa Macpherson, 10 July 1888, in *Letters*, vol. 2, no. 1143, p. 926.
18. GM to Frederick A. Maxse, 10 September 1888, in *Letters*, vol. 2, no. 1150, p. 929.
19. GM to Mrs Frederick Jones, 17 September 1888, in *Letters*, vol. 2, no. 1151, p. 930.
20. GM to Miss Louisa Lawrence, 21 September 1888, in *Letters*, vol. 2, no. 1152, pp. 931–2.
21. GM to Frederick A. Maxse, 10 September 1888, in *Letters*, vol. 2, no. 1150, p. 929.
22. GM to Miss Louisa Lawrence, 21 September 1888, in *Letters*, vol. 2, no. 1152, p. 931.
23. GM to George Stevenson, 30 April 1887, in *Letters*, vol. 2, no. 1045, p. 860.

CHAPTER II: FORGOTTEN AND DISCOVERED

1. GM to John Morley, 18 September 1885, in *Letters*, vol. 2, no. 924, p. 784.
2. GM to Mrs Christopher Wilson, 28 September 1885, in *Letters*, vol. 2, no. 936, p. 791.
3. GM to Mrs Frank Hill, 26 September 1885, in *Letters*, vol. 2, no. 933, p. 789.
4. GM to Augustus Jessopp, 1 July 1889, in *Letters*, vol. 3, no. 1214A, p. 1709.
5. GM to Arthur G. Meredith, 19 June 1881, in *Letters*, vol. 2, no. 701, p. 625.
6. GM to Mrs Edith Clarke, 5 September 1890, in *Letters*, vol. 2, no. 1277, p. 1004.
7. cit. Stevenson, op. cit., p. 157.
8. GM to Frederick A. Maxse, 21 July 1881, in *Letters*, vol. 2, no. 706, p. 631.
9. GM to Frederic Chapman, [early 1865], in *Letters*, vol. 1, no. 329, pp. 303–4.
10. GM to Mrs Anna C. Steele, [11 November 1869], in *Letters*, vol. 1, no. 434, pp. 403–4.
11. cit. Priestley, op. cit. (1926).
12. GM to Miss Louisa Lawrence, 3 March 1893, in *Letters*, vol. 2, no. 1496, p. 1125.
13. GM to Frederic Chapman, 20 February 1893, in *Letters*, vol. 2, no. 1492, p. 1122–3.
14. Ann Thwaite, *Edmund Gosse: A Literary Landscape 1849–1928*, 1984, p. 402.
15. cit. Stevenson, op. cit., p. 263.
16. Ibid, p. 348.
17. Ibid, p. 277.
18. Ibid, p. 264.
19. GM to W. M. Meredith, 27 January 1887, in *Letters*, vol. 2, no. 1031, p. 848.
20. GM to Mlle Hilda de Longueuil, 26 December 1886, in *Letters*, vol. 2, no. 1026, p. 844.
21. GM to Mlle Hilda de Longueuil, [1 March 1887], in *Letters*, vol. 2, no. 1040, p. 855.
22. GM to Mlle Hilda de Longueuil, 8 June 1887, in *Letters*, vol. 2, no. 1055, p. 869.
23. GM to Mrs Walter Palmer, 12 February [1894], in *Letters*, vol. 3, no. 1546, p. 1154.
24. GM to Mrs Alice Meynell, 28 April 1896 and 26 June 1896, in *Letters*, vol. 3, nos. 1690 and 1704, pp. 1228, 1237.
25. GM to Lady Ulrica Duncombe, 16 July 1900, 11 October 1900 and 7 December 1900, in *Letters*, vol. 3, nos. 1940, 1961 and 1973, pp. 1353, 1366, 1378.
26. GM to Lady Ulrica Duncombe, 18 April 1901 and 26 December 1901, in *Letters*, vol. 3, nos. 1992 and 2040, pp. 1388, 1412.

27. GM to Lady Ulrica Duncombe, 2 March 1902 and 10 March 1902, in *Letters*, vol. 3, nos. 2060 and 2063, pp. 1425, 1428.
28. GM to Lady Ulrica Duncombe, [10 June 1902], in *Letters*, vol. 3, no. 2096, pp. 1451–2.
29. GM to Lady Ulrica Duncombe, 26 December 1901, in *Letters*, vol. 3, no. 2040, p. 1412.
30. GM to Lady Ulrica Duncombe, 19 March 1902 and 28 May 1902, in *Letters*, vol. 3, nos. 2064 and 2092, pp. 1430, 1448.
31. cit. Stevenson, op. cit., p. 317.
32. Ibid, p, 301.
33. Ibid, p. 317.
34. Miss Marie Eveleen Meredith to Theodore Watts-Dunton, 26 July [1892], in *Letters*, vol. 2, no. 1438, p. 1092.
35. GM to Frederick A. Maxse, 27 December 1881, in *Letters*, vol. 2, no. 726, p. 648.
36. GM to Augustus Jessopp, 17 September 1883, in *Letters*, vol. 2, no. 814, p. 711.
37. GM to J. Cotter Morison, 30 October 1883, in *Letters*, vol. 2, no. 822, p. 719.
38. GM to Robert Louis Stevenson, 24 March 1884, in *Letters*, vol. 2, no. 839, p. 731.
39. cit. Stevenson, op. cit., p. 288.
40. Ibid, p. 289.
41. GM to Leslie Stephen, 14 February 1904, in *Letters*, vol. 3, no. 2167, p. 1491.
42. Lindsay, op. cit., p. 337.
43. GM to Richard H. Horne, 9 November 1871, in *Letters*, vol. 1, no. 487, p. 455.
44. GM to Arthur G. Meredith, 23 June 1881, in *Letters*, vol. 2, no. 702, p. 628.
45. GM to James Thomson, 4 July 1879, in *Letters*, vol. 2, no. 636, p. 576.
46. GM to Mrs W. C. Bonaparte Wyse, 23 January 1882, in *Letters*, vol. 2, no. 729, p. 651.
47. GM to Robert Louis Stevenson, 10 October 1884, in *Letters*, vol. 2, no. 866, p. 748.
48. GM to Mrs Janet Ross, 24 July 1898, in *Letters*, vol. 3, no. 1842, p. 1305.
49. GM to Walter C. Jerrold, 23 June 1899, in *Letters*, vol. 3, no. 1893, p. 1330.
50. GM to Norman MacColl, 9 February 1902, in *Letters*, vol. 3, no. 2054, p. 1422.
51. cit. Ellis, op. cit., p. 316.
52. GM to René Galland, 6 September 1908, in *Letters*, vol. 3, no. 2496, p. 1662.
53. René Galland, *George Meredith: Les cinquante premières années (1828–1878)*, Paris, 1923.
54. Ellis, op. cit., p. 163.
55. Stevenson, op. cit., p. 235.
56. Sassoon, op. cit., pp. 162, 173, 174.
57. Priestley, op. cit. (1926), p. 94.
58. Beer, op. cit.
59. Priestley, op. cit. (1926).

60. Pritchett, op. cit., p. 24.
61. G. M. Trevelyan, *The Poetry and Philosophy of George Meredith*, 1906, p. 78.
62. Priestley, op. cit. (1926), p. 104.
63. cit. Galland, op. cit.
64. Donald David Stone, *Novelists in a Changing World: Meredith, James and the Transformation of English Fiction in the 1880s*, 1972, pp. 159–160.
65. GM to Arthur G. Meredith, 23 June 1881, in *Letters*, vol. 2, no. 702, p. 627.
66. GM to John Morley, 9 September 1890, in *Letters*, vol. 2, no. 1279, p. 1005.
67. cit. Stevenson, op. cit., p. 342.
68. GM to Leslie Stephen, 14 February 1904, in *Letters*, vol. 3, no. 2167, p. 1490.
69. GM to Theodore Watts-Dunton, 27 November 1903, in *Letters*, vol. 3, no. 2166, pp. 1489–90.
70. Stevenson, op. cit., p. 342.
71. GM to Theodore Watts-Dunton, 13 April 1909, in *Letters*, vol. 3, no. 2552, p. 1691.
72. GM to Lady Ulrica Duncombe (Baring), 19 April 1909, in *Letters*, vol. 3, no. 2556, p. 1694.
73. GM to J. O. Sturgis, 8 May 1909, in *Letters*, vol. 3, p. 1697.
74. J. M. Barrie, *George Meredith*, 1909.
75. Priestley, op. cit. (1926), pp. 88, 94.
76. Pritchett, op. cit., p. 41.
77. E. M. Forster, *Aspects of the Novel*, 1927, p. 86.
78. cit. Priestley, op. cit. (1926).
79. Virginia Woolf, *The Common Reader*, 1932 (Second Series), pp. 228, 231, 236.

Select Bibliography

Dates are those of first publication.

The date of a subsequent imprint is given wherever direct reference is made in the text to a later edition.

Place of publication is London unless noted otherwise.

Barrie, J. M., *Meredith*, 1909.

Beer, Gillian, *Meredith: A Change of Masks. A Study of the Novels*, 1970.

Bernstein, Edward, *Ferdinand Lassalle as a Social Reformer* (1891), New York, 1969.

Butcher, Lady, *Memories of George Meredith O.M.*, 1919.

Chedzoy, Alan, *A Scandalous Woman: The Story of Caroline Norton*, 1992.

Chesney, Sir George Tomkyns, *The Battle of Dorking* (1871, first published as *Reminiscences of a Volunteer*), in *The Battle of Dorking/ When William Came*, Oxford, 1997.

Cline, C. L., ed., *The Letters of George Meredith*, Volumes 1–3, 1970.

Cole, G. D. H., *Socialist Thought: Marxism and Anarchism 1850–1890*, 1954.

Collie, M., *George Meredith: A Bibliography*, 1974.

Darwin, Charles, *The Origin of Species by Means of Natural Selection*, 1859.

——, *The Descent of Man and Selection in Relation to Sex*, 1871.

Ellis, S. M., *George Meredith: His Life and Friends in Relation to His Work*, 1919.

Fletcher, I., ed., *Meredith Now*, 1971.

Footman, D., *The Primrose Path: A Life of Ferdinand Lassalle*, 1946.

Forster, E. M., *Aspects of the Novel*, 1927.

Galland, R., *George Meredith: Les cinquante premières années (1828–1878)*, Paris, 1923.

Gretton, Mary Sturge, *George Meredith: Novelist, Poet, Reformer*, 1908.

Johnson, D., *The True History of the First Mrs Meredith and Other Lesser Lives*, 1972.

Kelvin, Norman, *A Troubled Eden: Nature and Society in the Works of George Meredith*, 1961.

LeGallienne, R., Lane, J., *George Meredith: Some Characteristics*, 1894.

Lindsay, Jack, *George Meredith, His Life and Work*, 1956.

Lynch, Hannah, *George Meredith: A Study*, 1891.

Marx, K., *The Civil War in France* (1871), 1933.

Marx, K., Engels, F., Lenin, V. I., *Critique of the Gothoa Programme* (Text of 1891), 1933.

Meredith, George, *The Shaving of Shagpat: An Arabian Entertainment* [1855/6]

— *Farina: A Legend of Cologne*, 1857

— *The Ordeal of Richard Feverel*, 1859

— *Evan Harrington*, 1861

— *Modern Love . . . With Poems and Ballads*, 1862

— *Emilia in England* (later renamed *Sandra Belloni*), 1864

— *Rhoda Fleming*, 1865

— *Vittoria*, 1867

— *The Adventures of Harry Richmond*, 1871

— *Beauchamp's Career* [1875/6]

— *Comedy and Uses of the Comic Spirit* (Lecture given 1877)

— *The House on the Beach* (previously *Van Diemen Smith*), 1877

— *The Case of General Opie and Lady Camper*, 1877

— *The Egoist*, 1879

— *The Tragic Comedians*, 1880

— *Poems and Lyrics of the Joy of Earth*, 1883

— *Diana of the Crossways*, 1885

— *Ballads and Poems of Tragic Life*, 1887

— *A Reading of Earth*, 1888

— *One of Our Conquerors*, 1891

— *Poems: The Empty Purse . . . and Verses*, 1892

— *Lord Ormont and His Aminta*, 1894

— *The Amazing Marriage*, 1895

— *Odes in Contribution to the Song of French History*, 1898

— *A Reading of Life*, 1901

— *Last Poems*, 1909

— *Celt and Saxon*, 1910

Morton, Peter, *The Vital Science: Biology and the Literary Imagination, 1860–1900*, 1984.

Photiades, C., *George Meredith, His Life, Genius and Teaching*, 1913.

Podmor, Colin, *Essays in Anglican and Moravian History*, 1996.

Priestley, J. B., *George Meredith*, 1926.

——, *Thomas Love Peacock*, 1927.

Pritchett, V. S., *Meredith and English Comedy* (The Clark Lectures for 1969), 1970.

Ross, Janet Duff Gordon, *The Fourth Generation*, 1912.

Sassoon, Siegfried, *Meredith*, 1948.

Stevenson, Lionel, *The Ordeal of George Meredith*, New York, 1954.

Stone, Donald David, *Novelists in a Changing World: Meredith, James and the Transformation of English Fiction in the 1880s*, Mass., U.S.A., 1972.

Thwaite, Ann, *Edmund Gosse: A Literary Landscape 1849–1928*, 1984.

Trevelyan, George Macaulay, *The Poetry and Philosophy of George Meredith*, 1906.

Webb, Beatrice, *My Apprenticeship*, 1926.

Wimsatt, W. K., ed., *The Idea of Comedy: Essays in Prose and Verse: Ben Jonson to George Meredith*, 1969.

Woods, Alice, *George Meredith as Champion of Women and of Progressive Education*, 1937.

Woolf, Virginia, *The Common Reader* (1925, First Series), 1968.

——, *The Common Reader* (1932, Second Series), 1965.

JOURNALS

British Journal of Educational Studies (Volume xxxiv, no. 1), 1986.

Index

Abbotsholme school, 35
Academy, journal, 238
Act of Union (1800), 212
The Adventures of Harry Richmond, 17, 18, 19, 25, 28, 33, 36, 37, 40, 49, 77, 83, 109, 116–17, 124, 138, 140, 141, 144, 145, 153, 155, 156, 162, 178, 187, 234, 236, 237, 238–40, 248; plot summary, 265–8
Afrikaners, 203
Albert, Prince Consort, 61
allegories, 72–4, 77
Allen, Grant, 128, 224; *The Woman Who Did*, 158
Allende, Isabel, 69
The Amazing Marriage, 20, 21, 31, 109, 118, 121, 124, 138, 142–3, 144, 149, 153, 163, 164, 169–72, 175–6, 179, 188–9, 190–2, 200, 204, 210, 222, 227, 236, 237; plot summary, 282–5
ambiguity, theme of, 12–13
American Civil War, 17, 84, 99, 176, 205
'Angelic Love' (poem), 54
The Anti-Jacobin, weekly, 201
anti-Semitism, 206–9
Arabian Nights, 68, 69, 143
d'Arblay, General, 103
archaisms, deliberate (in vocabulary and sentence structure), 70–1, 77

Arnold, Matthew, 100, 130, 137, 206, 229; *Culture and Anarchy*, 62
Arundel Club, 189
Athenaeum, 58, 77, 86, 96, 235, 237
Austin, John and Sarah, 64
Austro-Hungarian Empire, 42, 70; liberation of Italy from rule of, 109, 110, 111–13, 212–13

Bagehot, Walter, 100
'A Ballad of Fair Ladies in Revolt' (poem), 164–5
Balzac, Honoré de, 216; *La Femme de Trente Ans*, 51
banks, bankers, 179–80
Baring, Everard, 230
Baring, Ulrica *see* Duncombe
Barrie, James, 222, 223; *George Meredith, 1909*, 245–6
'The Battle of Dorking' (pamphlet), 199
Batty, Beatrice, 32
Beauchamp's Career, 19, 33, 66, 83, 99, 101, 104, 118, 131, 138, 142, 144, 149, 153, 158, 162, 178, 181, 187, 189–90, 193, 194–5, 200, 201, 204, 224, 233, 234, 235, 237; plot summary, 271–4
Bedales, school, 35
Beer, Gillian, 240
Bell, Vanessa, 248
Benn, Tony, 183

Bennett, Arthur, 85
Berkeley, Earl of, 99
Bernstein, Eduard, 185
Besant, Sir Walter, 46
Bhanavar the Beautiful (novella), 67
Bildungsroman, 33–4, 117
Birmingham Art Gallery, 81
Bismarck, Prince Otto von, 37, 42,
    184–5, 197, 199
Bispham, David, 232
Blackwood's Magazine, 'Reminiscences
    of a Volunteer', 199–200
Blake, William, 45
Blatchford, Robert, 201
Bloomsbury group, 248
Blunt, Wilfrid Scawen, 102
Bembo, King of Naples (Ferdinand
    III), 70
Bonaparte, Lucien, 101
Bonaparte, Marie, 101
Borthwick, Sir Algernon, 111–12,
    219–20
Box Hill *see* Flint Cottage
Bradbury and Evans, publishers,
    91
Braddon, Mary, 235; *Lady Audley's
    Secret*, 235
Brandreth, Alice (Mrs Gordon),
    115–16; *Memories of George Meredith*,
    115
Brecht, Bertholt, 35
Bright, John, 201
British Empire, 202–3
British Quarterly Review, 34, 237–8
Brontë, Charlotte, 74; *Jane Eyre*, 48,
    241
Brontë sisters, 233
Brothers, Robert, publishers, 218
Browne, Buckston, surgeon, 231
Browning, Robert, 73, 92, 99, 201,
    245, 246
Buckett, Matilda *see* Meredith
Bunyan, John, *Pilgrim's Progress*, 73
Burford Bridge Inn (Fox and
    Hounds), 103, 115, 222, 233
Burnand, Frank, 101, 239
Burney, Fanny, 47, 103

Butler, Samuel, *Erewhon*, 220–1
Byron, Lord, 54

'Can another love be born' (poem),
    225
Calvino, Italo, 242
Capri, Mary and Wallis in, 81
Carlyle, Thomas, 33, 70, 231; *Sartor
    Resartus*, 70
Caroline, Aunt, 12
*The Case of General Ople and Lady
    Camper*, 21, 151, 155
Catherine, Aunt *see* Ellis
Catholic Church, 124
Cavour, Count Camillo Benso di, 109
Celt and Saxon, 22, 109, 124, 143, 144,
    158, 200, 203, 206, 211, 213–15;
    plot summary, 285–6
Celtic peoples, 20–1
Cervantes, Miguel de, 120, 216; *Don
    Quixote*, 17
Chamberlain, Joseph, 183, 202;
    Unauthorized Programme of,
    182–3, 186–7
Chamberlain, Neville, 201
Chambers' Edinburgh Journal, 43
Chapman, Edward, 71, 74, 78, 87, 88,
    91, 105, 218, 221–2
Chapman and Hall, publishers, 71,
    82, 86, 87, 91, 99, 116, 186, 218,
    222, 231; Meredith as reader for,
    87, 99, 186, 220–1; Meredith's
    conflict with, 221–2
Charnock, Richard, solicitor, 41, 42,
    46, 51, 52, 189; Meredith articled
    to, 40
Chartism, 61, 181, 184, 189
Chatterton, Thomas, 80, 93
Chedzoy, Alan, 217
Chelsea: Meredith's lodgings at 7,
    Hobury St, 78, 88; and home at
    Tudor House, 16, Cheyne Walk,
    102
Chesney, Sir George, 199–200
Chesterton, G.K., 223, 231
Chillianwala, battle of (1849), 42–3
'Chillianwallah' (poem), 43, 65

Chislehurst, Napoleon III's exile in, 198

cholera, 62, 63; epidemic (1849), 62

Christianity, 30, 34, 84, 100, 101, 107, 122–4, 125, 135, 242

class relationships, 15, 61, 82

Clodd, Edward, 128, 240

Cobbett, William, 47

Cole, G.D.H., 183

Collins, Wilkie, 236

comedy, Meredith's views on, 143–4, 149–50

Comenius, Bishop, 26

Commune, (1871), 42

Communist Manifesto, 85

Communists, 184, 185

Comte, Auguste, 100

Conan Doyle, Arthur, 222

Congreve, William, 143

Conrad, Joseph, 247; *Under Western Eyes*, 196

conscription, 201

Conservative Party/Tories, 117, 182–3, 189, 190

Constable, publishers, 222, 245

Constantinople, Russian threat to, 201

Cooper, Edith, 230–1

Copsham Cottage, Esher (Meredith's home), 89, 102, 193, 105

Corelli, Marie, 115

Corn Laws, repeal of the, 217

Cornhill Magazine, 101, 103

Crawshay family, 175

Crawshay, Richard, 175

'Creed' (poem), 125

Crimean War (1853–6), 62–3, 99, 197, 201, 203, 205

The Critic, 58, 72, 86

Critique of the Gotha Programme (Marx and Engels), 186

Custozza, Battle of, 112–13

Cyfartha Castle, 175

Daily Chronicle, 233

Daily News, 64, 203

Daily Telegraph, 37, 202

Daniel, Austin, 42

Dante Alighieri, 206

'Daphne' (poem), 54–6, 58, 59

Darwin, Charles, 127–30, 136; *The Descent of Man*, 85, 125, 129, 130, 148; *The Origin of Species*, 84–5, 127, 129, 130

Daudet, Léon, 227, 230

'The Day of the Daughter of Hades' (poem), 133–4, 137

death, Meredith's attitude towards, 135–8, 242–4

Defoe, Daniel, 86

Dickens, Catherine, 79

Dickens, Charles, 14, 62, 64, 65, 71, 79, 86, 91, 99, 111, 188, 218, 233, 235, 246; *David Copperfield*, 33; *Dombey and Son*, 178; *Great Expectations*, 13, 178; *Hard Times*, 188; *Little Dorrit*, 74; *Our Mutual Friend*, 178

Dictionary of National Biography, 101

Diana of the Crossways, 15, 19–20, 22, 118, 120, 124, 148, 154, 159, 160–2, 163, 167, 172, 173, 178–9, 211, 216–18, 221, 229, 234, 235, 236, 239; plot summary, 274–6

Dillon, John, 211, 212

Disraeli, Benjamin, 184, 191, 201; *Coningsby*, 189, 206; *Sybil*, 188, 189

Divorce Act (1857), 160

Dixon, Ella, 244

Dönniges/Racowitza, Helene von, 166, 185, 207; *My Relations with Ferdinand Lassalle*, 183

Dorking cemetery, Meredith buried in, 245

Dostoyevsky, Fedor, *The Possessed*, 196

Dreyfus, Captain Alfred, 208–9

Dublin University Magazine, 74

duels, duelling, 18–20, 204

Duff Gordon, Sir Alexander, 64, 67, 88, 105

Duff Gordon, Janet (Mrs Ross), 64, 67, 105, 113, 233; Meredith's relationship with, 88, 89–90, 91,

93, 105; marriage to Henry Ross,
89–90
Duff Gordon, Lady Lucie (*née*
Austin), 64, 67, 88, 159
Dufferin, Lord, 217
Dumas, Alexandre, 236
Duncombe, Lady Ulrica, 125, 126,
244; Meredith's relationship with,
228–30; marriage to Everard
Baring, 230

Earth, Meredith's concept of, 126,
132, 133, 135, 136, 144
'Earth and a Wedded Woman'
(poem), 126
East India Company, 63, 66
East India House, London, 47, 66
eau de Cologne, 75
Edith *see* Nicholls
education, 24, 25–38, 82, 101, 107;
girls', 31–3; Pestalozzi, 107
Edwards, Howell, 210
Egg, Augustus, 80
egoism, theme of, 148–51, 153, 165,
168, 173
The Egoist, 46, 50, 121, 124, 128, 139,
140, 144, 148, 149, 150, 152, 155,
158, 164, 165–6, 168, 178, 204, 216,
217, 234–5, 236, 237, 239, 240; plot
summary, 268–71
Eliot, George (Mary Ann Evans), 36,
65, 71, 72, 77, 99, 123, 182, 188,
218, 223, 233, 247; *Adam Bede*, 84;
Daniel Deronda, 206; *Felix Holt, The
Radical*, 182; *Middlemarch*, 178
Ellis, Catherine (aunt), 12, 50
Ellis, Major, 50
Ellis, S.M., *George Meredith*, 11, 12, 23,
24, 50, 65, 79, 114, 139, 148–9, 233,
243
Eltham Lodge, Meredith reads aloud
to Mrs Wood at, 87–8
Emilia in England (retitled: *Sandra
Belloni*), 21, 49, 52, 108, 109, 110–11,
113–14, 119, 120, 131–2, 153, 161,
164, 178, 188, 211, 234, 235, 237;
plot summary, 257–9

'The Empty Purse' (poem), 177–8
Engels, Friedrich, 85, 176, 186
Esher, 99; Meredith's homes in, 88,
105; and Copsham Cottage, 89,
102, 103, 105
Essay on Comedy, 143, 149
*Evan Harrington or He Would be a
Gentleman*, 12–13, 14, 15, 16, 17–19,
22, 23, 24, 28, 39, 50, 51, 64, 89,
91–2, 108, 124, 138, 141, 144, 147,
153, 156, 162, 163, 178, 188, 204,
218, 221; plot summary, 252–7;
serialization in *Once a Week*, 91
Evangelical Alliance, 29
Evans, Mary Ann *see* Eliot, George
Evelyn, John, 103
evolution, 85, 123, 125, 127–8, 129,
131, 137
Examiner, 234, 237

fantasy, theme of, 16–18, 20, 22
Farina, Giovanni Maria, 75
Farina ('A Legend of Cologne'), 37,
74–8, 82, 109
Faversham, Earl of, 228
Favre, Jules, 198
feminism, 159–60, 218; *see also* women
fencing or 'swordsmanship', 20
Fenian Brotherhood, 62, 211
Fichte, Johann Gottlieb, 186
Fielding, Henry, 86, 216, 233
First World War (1914–18), 246
Fitzgerald, Edward, translation of
The Rubaiyat of Omar Khayyam, 84,
102
Flaubert, Gustave, *Madame Bovary*, 93,
239
Fleetwood, Lord, 210
Flint Cottage, Box Hill (Meredith's
home), 99, 114–16, 117, 218, 222,
223, 227, 230, 231, 232, 243, 245
Foakes, Thomas, 87
Foot, Michael, 183
Forster, E.M., 158; *Aspects of the Novel*,
248
Fortnightly Review, 100, 111, 128, 176,
193

France, 70, 84, 101, 109, 197–8, 202, 205, 224; Crimean War, 62; Dreyfus affair, 208–9
Franco-Prussian War (1970–1), 197–8, 200, 203, 205
Fraser's Magazine, 59, 65, 66
French, Sir John, 204
Freud, Sigmund, 17, 101, 185
Fun, magazine, 101

Galland, René, 233, 234
Gambetta, Léon, 198
Gandhi, Mahatma, 125
Garibaldi, Giuseppe, 41, 44, 109
Garrick Club, 65
general election (1868), 117–18
General German Workers' Association, 183, 184, 185
'The Gentleman of Fifty and the Damsel of Nineteen', 143, 224, 230
George IV, King (Prince Regent), 18
German Social-Democratic Party, 186
Germany, German culture, 26–38, 40, 42, 64, 68, 74–5, 77, 110, 183–6, 197–200, 205; English perceptions of, 198–9, 202; Franco-Prussian War (1870–1), 197–8, 200, 203, 205; Meredith's honeymoon in Rhineland, 52, 57; Neuwied school, 25, 26–38; *see also Farina*
Gibbon, Edward, 36
Gissing, George, 222–3, 233, 246; *Isabel Clarendon*, 222; *New Grub Street*, 108; *The Unclassed*, 222
Gladstone, W.E., 100, 182, 211, 215
Goethe, Johann Wolfgang von, 33, 36, 37, 120, 206, 229, 230; *Wilhelm Meister* novels, 33
Gordon, Alice, 216, 222
Gordon, Dr, 115
Gordon, Jim, 115–16, 216
Gosse, Edmund, 222, 237, 245
Gotha Congress (1875), 186
Gray, Thomas, 80

Great Exhibition, Crystal Palace (1851), 61
Greenwood, Frederick, 101, 201–2, 223
Gregory, St, 76
Gregory VII, Pope, 76
Grotto Cottage (Mary's home), 88
Guardian, religious weekly, 58, 59
Guest, Lady Charlotte, 68
Guest, John, 175
Guest family, 175

Haggard, Rider, 235; *King Solomon's Mines*, 235; *She*, 235
Hamilton, Mrs, 104
'Hard Weather' (poem), 131
Hardie, Keir, 183
Hardman, William, 101, 103, 104, 105, 106, 200, 201, 219
Hardy, Thomas, 11, 99, 121, 137, 188, 221, 222, 233, 240, 244, 245, 247; *Jude the Obscure*, 158; *The Poor Man and the Lady*, 221
Harriet, Aunt, 12
Harris, Frank, 223
Hawthorne, Julian, 239
Haxthausen, Monsieur de, 67
Haynau, General, 42
Hearne, Dr Edwin, 194
Hegel, Friedrich, 186
Heinrich III, Kaiser, 76
Henley, W.E., 216, 235
Henty, G.A., 113; *Beric, the Briton*, 113; *The Lion of St Mark's*, 113; *With Clive in India*, 113
History Today, 81
Hitler, Adolf, 184, 208
Hofwyl school, Switzerland, 107
Hogg, Jefferson, 64
homosexuality, Meredith's attitude towards, 223
Hong Kong, 40
Hopkins, Gerard Manley, 99, 248
Horne, Richard, 43, 65
The House on the Beach (novella), 16–17, 109, 131
Household Words, weekly, 65

Huxley, Thomas, 100, 124
Hyndman, H.M., 113, 182, 183, 201,
203, 219, 239

idealism and realism, Meredith's
concept of, 120, 122
Illustrated London News, 217, 227
Independent Labour Party, 183
India, 42–3, 63, 213, 230
Indian Mutiny (1857–8), 63
Individualism, social philosophy, 85
Ipswich Journal, 87, 105, 219
Ireland, Irish, 62, 211–12, 213–15;
famine in, 62; Fenian campaign,
62, 211; Home Rule for, 100, 204,
211, 212, 215
Irish Nationalist Party, 211
Italy, 41, 42, 101, 197, 205, 212–13,
219; liberation and unification of,
109–13, 114, 204; Meredith's trips
to, 109–13; Meredith as war
correspondent in, 111–13, 114, 204,
219

James, Henry, 99, 223–4, 242; *The
Golden Bowl*, 223
Jerrold, Walter, 233
Jessopp, Rev. Augustus, 101, 104, 105,
106, 107, 108, 120, 122, 218, 232
Jessopp family, 104
Jews/anti-Semitism, 206–9
Jewsbury, Geraldine, 236
Johnson, Diane, 49
Johnson, Lionel, 238
Johnson, Dr Samuel, 247
Joyce, James, 242; *Portrait of the Artist
as a Young Man*, 242
*Joys of Earth see Poems and Lyrics of the
Joy of Earth*
Justice, SDF journal, 203

Keats, John, 54, 234; *Endymion*, 103
Kelvin, Norman, 139; *A Troubled Eden*,
193
Kettle, Arnold, 194
King Edward VI School, Norwich,
101, 107, 122

Kingsley, Charles, 59; *Alton Locke*, 59;
Westward Ho!, 71; *Yeast*, 59
Kingston Lodge, Meredith's home,
105–6, 114, 116
Kipling, Rudyard, 43; 'Recessional',
62
Kossuth, Lajos, 41–2, 44, 46

Labour Party/Government, 183,
186
Lamb, Charles, 47
languages, teaching of, 29
'The Lark Ascending', 134
Lassalle, Ferdinand, 19, 166, 183,
184–6, 206, 208
Lawrence, D.H., 158; *Sons and Lovers*,
33
Lawrence, Louisa, 210, 221
The Leader, magazine, 58, 65, 71, 72
Leatherhead, Sturgis home in, 219,
243
lending libraries, 86–7, 108
Lermontov, Mikhail, 19
Lewes, G.H., 58, 65, 71, 111
Liberals, Liberal Party, 117, 118, 181,
182–3, 184, 189, 194–5, 201, 203,
211; *see also* Whigs
Light Brigade, charge of the, 63, 112
The Limes (Weybridge), Meredith
home, 52, 53, 63, 66
Lindsay, Jack, 69–70, 139, 172
'Lines to a Friend Visiting America'
(poem), 176–7
Lloyd George, David, 'People's
Budget' of, 183
'London by Lamplight' (poem), 56–7
Longueil, Hilda de, Meredith's
relationship with, 224–6
Lord Ormont and his Aminta, 20, 28–9,
31, 33, 35, 107, 138, 140, 143, 148,
153, 157, 158, 163, 167–9, 171, 173,
179, 188, 200, 206, 222, 224, 235,
238; plot summary, 280–2
Louis Philippe, King of France, 41
Louisa, Aunt, 12, 23
love, romantic, 147–7, 162; extra-
marital, 156–8, 224

'Love in the Valley' (poem), 40, 59, 77, 134, 240
Lower Halliford (Peacock's house), 50, 51, 52; Meredith and Mary stay at, 66–7; *see also* Vine Cottage
Lucas, Samuel, 91
'Lucifer in Starlight' (poem), 240
Lucknow, siege of, 63
Lynch, Hannah, *George Meredith: A Study*, 139–40, 149, 194

Mabinogion, 68
MacCarthy, Desmond, 231
McCarthy, Justin, 211, 235–6; 'Novels with a Purpose', 164
Macirone, Mrs Elizabeth, 52, 63
Macirone, Emilia, 52
Macirone, Giulia, 52
Mackay, Charles, 115
McKechnie, James, 73–4, 77
Macmillan, publishers, 'English Men of Letters' series, 247
Macnamara, Anna, 24–5
Mann, Thomas, 121; *The Magic Mountain*, 241
Manners, Lord John, 7th Earl of Rutland, 189
Mansfield, Katherine, 248
'Marian' (poem), 49–50
Márquez, Gabriel Garcia, 69, 242
marriage, theme of, 141–4, 147, 155, 165–73
Married Women's Property Act (1882), 160
Marx, Karl, 85, 176, 186, 198, 201; *Capital*, 85; *A Critique of Political Economy*, 85
Maugham, Somerset, *Cakes and Ale*, 247
Maxse, Frederick, 74, 99–100, 103, 104–5, 112, 117, 123, 125, 176, 181, 189, 192, 194, 197, 198, 202, 210, 211, 219, 232
Mazzini, Giuseppe, 41, 194
Melbourne, Lord, 159, 160, 217
mental illness, 48–9

Meredith family, Welsh origins of, 20–1, 22
Meredith, Arthur (son), 64, 78, 79, 88–9, 101, 104, 105, 118, 122, 126, 233; father's relationship with, 106–8, 218–19; education, 101, 107, 218; Italian trip with father, 109; ill with tuberculosis, and death of (1890), 219, 242
Meredith, Augustus Urmston (father), 12, 13, 18, 23, 24, 25, 41, 52
Meredith, George, birth and early years, 12, 13, 14, 23–5; education, 24, 25–38; and attends Neuwied school in Germany, 26–38, 40, 107; articled to Richard Charnock, 40, 46, 189; appearance and character, 40–1, 230–1; Mary Peacock's relationship with, 48, 49, 51, 64, 69, 78, 79; and marriage to Mary (1849), 52, 79; indigestion suffered by, 64–5, 231; lives in Lower Halliford, 66–7; and Vine Cottage, 67, 78; lodgings in Chelsea, 78; breakdown of marriage, 78, 79, 81–2, 92, 93, 94–5, 105; as writer for *Ipswich Journal*, 87; and publisher's reader for Chapman & Hall, 87, 99, 186, 220–1; and reads aloud to Mrs Wood, 87–8; bans Mary from seeing Arthur, 88–9; Janet Duff Gordon's relationship with, 88, 89–90, 91, 93; Italian trips, 90, 109–13; friendships, 98–102; second marriage to Marie Vulliamy, 104–6, 108; Arthur's relationship with, 106–8, 218–19; war correspondent in Italy, 111–13, 114, 204; move to Flint Cottage, Boxhill, 114–16; election campaigning for Maxse (1868), 117–18; philosophy/'faith' of, 119–38; illness and death of Marie (1885), 134–5; estrangement between John Morley and, 193–4; holiday in Wales to see son

Meredith, George – *contd.*
William, 209–10; American
publication of his novels, 218, 221;
death of Arthur (1890), 219, 242;
and death of his friends Maxse,
Hardman and Wyse, 219; quarrels
with Chapman & Hall, and moves
to Constable, 221–2; as father
figure to younger writers, 222–3,
224; his emotional relationships
with young women, 224–30; ill-
health of, 228, 231–2, 243–4;
operated on for gallstones, 231;
receives Order of Merit, 11, 233;
lack of appreciation for, and
criticism of his novels,
233–42, 247–8; death of (1909),
244–6
Meredith, George (grandson), 246
Meredith, Harold ('son'), 81, 88;
name changed to Felix Wallis, 91
Meredith, Jane (*née* Macnamara:
mother), 20, 21, 23, 24, 211
Meredith, Margaret (*née* Elliot:
'Daisy'; daughter-in-law), 219
Meredith, Marie (*née* Vulliamy: 2nd
wife), 106, 114, 115; Meredith's
marriage to, 104–6, 108, 179; ill
with throat cancer, and death of
(1885), 134–5, 179, 216
Meredith, Marie Eveleen (Mariette/
Riette: daughter), 106, 210, 211,
216, 218, 221, 226, 231, 232, 242,
243; marriage to Henry Parkman
Sturgis, 219; death of her father,
244
Meredith, Mary (*née* Peacock: wife),
48, 49, 50–2, 54, 64, 65–7, 72, 88,
105; first marriage to Edward
Nicolls, 50; Meredith's relationship
with and first marriage to (1849),
48, 51–2, 64, 69, 78, 79; children
of, 64, 81; poetry of, 65; 'The
Blackbird', 65; cookery book, 66;
'Gastronomy and Civilisation', 66;
Meredith's separation from, 78, 79,
81–2, 92, 93, 94–5, 105; her love

affair with Henry Wallis, 79–81,
93, 161; ill-health of (kidney
failure), 81, 88, 89, 91; unhappy life
of, 88; banned from seeing Arthur
by Meredith, 88–9; last illness and
death of (1861), 90–1, 92, 93, 106,
134–5
Meredith, Matilda (*née* Buckett), 24
Meredith, Melchizedek ('the Great
Mel': grandfather), 12, 13, 16, 18,
23
Meredith, William (Will: son), 100,
106, 116, 216, 218, 225, 232, 242;
father visits him in Wales, 209–10;
marriage to Margaret Elliot, 219;
acts as father's financial adviser,
221; joins Constable, publishers,
222
Metternich, Prince Clemens, 41, 70,
114
Meynell, Alice, Meredith's
relationship with, 227–8
Meynell, Wilfrid, 227
Mickleham village, 103–4, 114; Old
House, 104
Mickleham Church, Meredith's
wedding at, 105
Milan, 41, 110, 212
Mill, James, 47
Mill, John Stuart, 47; *The Subjection of
Women*, 164
Modern Love and Other Poems, 59, 65,
92–7, 102, 108, 225, 240
Molesey (near Esher), Maxse's
cottage at, 99
Molière, Jean-Baptiste Poquelin, 36,
120, 143, 149, 206, 237
money-power, Meredith's attack on,
175–81, 192
Montefiore family, 206
Monthly Observer, 42, 43, 46, 51, 65
Moravian Brotherhood, 26–7, 29–30,
32, 34
More, Sir Thomas, 102
Morison, James Cotter, 100, 101, 104,
232
Morley, Henry, 27, 28, 31, 38

Morley, John, 27, 98, 100–1, 131, 176, 193–4, 198, 211, 216, 231, 242

Morning Post, 101; Meredith's Italian trip as war correspondent for, 111–13, 219

Morris, William, 71, 183, 201; *News from Nowhere*, 186

Morton, Peter, The Vital Science, 137

Mother, Meredith's concept of, 126, 132, 133, 134, 135, 136

Mudie's lending library, 108; *Richard Feverel* banned by, 86–7

Mussolini, Benito, 70

Napoleon III, Emperor, 42, 62, 109, 113, 197, 198

Nature, Meredith's concept of, 126–7, 128, 130, 131–2, 134, 135, 136, 137, 138, 144, 242

Nelson, Admiral Lord, 13

Neuwied, Germany, 101; Meredith attends school at, 25, 26–8, 40, 68, 107, 122

New Quarterly Magazine, 237

New Quarterly Review, 71–2

newspaper journalism, Meredith's contempt for, 219–20

Nicholls, Edith (step-daughter), 49, 51, 64, 66, 78, 79, 88, 90, 218, 219

Nicolls, Edward, 50, 51

Nicolls, General ('Fighting Nicolls'), 50, 78

Nicolls, Lady, 78

Niebuhr, Barthold Georg, 36

Nightingale, Florence, 63

North London Collegiate School, 31

Norton, Caroline, 159–60, 217, 218; *Lost and Saved*, 164

Norton, George, 159

Norwich, King Edward VI School, 101, 107

novels, Meredith's, political, 181; as 'vehicle of philosophy', 119–20, 121–2, 138, 193, 237; American publication of, 218, 221; posthumous Memorial Edition,

222, 224; lack of appreciation for and criticisms of, 233–42, 247–8; narrative method, 236; affinity to drama, 236–7; style and obscurity of, 237–40, 241–2; plot summaries, 249–86

O'Brien, Barry, 211

'Ode to the Spirit of Earth in Autumn' (poem), 132

'The Old Chartist' (poem), 92

Oliphant, Margaret, 235, 236

'The Olive Branch' (poem), 44

Ollier, Edmond, 53

'On the Danger of War' (poem), 204

Once a Week, magazine, 91, 92

One of Our Conquerors, 20, 21, 22, 36, 51, 89, 116, 121, 124, 138, 152, 153, 158, 162, 163, 179, 182, 188, 200, 204, 223, 241; plot summary, 278–80

The Ordeal of Richard Feverel, 19, 22–3, 33–5, 37–8, 39, 40, 59, 67, 74, 76, 80, 82–3, 85–7, 91, 92, 93, 94, 96, 107, 108, 109, 121, 131, 141–2, 144, 146, 147–8, 151–2, 153, 157, 162, 164, 173, 189, 235, 236, 241, 248; plot summary, 249–52

O'Riordan, Kate, *Involved*, 196

O'Shea, Kitty, 87–8

Ouida (pseudonym of Louise Ramé), 220

Ovid, *Metamorphoses*, 58

Pall Mall Gazette, 243

Palmer, Jean, Meredith's relationship with, 227

Palmer, Walter, 227

Paris, entry of German troops into (1871), 197, 198

Parker, John, publisher, 53, 59

Parnell, Charles Stewart, 87–8, 211

'Pastoral' (poem), 39

Peacock, Edward (brother-in-law), 46, 48, 51, 66, 80, 181

Peacock, Jane (*née* Gryffydh: mother-in-law), 47, 48; 'madness' of, 48–9, 66; death of (1852), 66

Peacock, Margaret, 48
Peacock, Mary *see* Meredith, Mary
Peacock, Mary Ellen, 46
Peacock, Rosa, 49
Peacock, Thomas Love, 46–8, 49, 50, 51, 52, 53, 64, 66–7; *Crotchet Castle*, 46, 47; *Melincourt*, 47–8; *Memoirs of Shelley*, 46; *The Misfortunes of Elphin*, 47; *Nightmare Abbey*, 46
Peel, Sir Robert, 159, 217
pennillion, (traditional poetic song), 47
People's Charter, 41
Pestalozzi schools, 107
Petöfi, Sandor, 41
philosophy, narrative as the vehicle of, 119–20, 121–2, 138, 193, 217
Pinder, Jane, 32
Pitt, William, 212
Pius IX, pope, 124
Ploverfield House, Bursledon, Maxse's home, 99, 117
Poems, 53–9, 71
Poems and Lyrics of the Joy of Earth, 126, 132, 134
poetry, Meredith's, 39, 40, 42–5, 49–50, 52–60, 65, 92–7, 118, 119, 125, 126–7, 131, 132–8, 164–5, 176–8, 225–6, 227–8, 237, 240–1, 242–3, 244
Pope, Alexander, 247
Popper, Karl, *The Open Society and Its Enemies*, 186
Portsmouth, 41; Meredith's early years in, 12, 13, 14, 23–4
Portsmouth Literary and Philosophical Society, 23
Positivist Society, 100, 101
Pre-Raphaelite Brotherhood, 79–80, 102
Priestley, J.B., 240; *George Meredith*, 14, 49, 52–3, 85, 127–8, 131, 139, 247
Pritchett, V.S., 52, 240, 247
Progressist Party, German, 183–4, 185
Prussia, 183, 184, 186, 199; French war with, 197–8
Punch, 64, 101, 211

Proust, Marcel, 242
Pushkin, Aleksandr, 19

'Queen of the Serpents', 67
Queen's College, Harley Street, 31

Racowitza, Helene *see* Dönniges
Racowitza, Prince, 166
Radetzky, Field-Marshal, 213
Radicals, Radicalism, 100, 117, 181–3, 186–7, 189, 190, 194, 198, 200, 201, 203
Ranelagh Street (now Ebury Street), Meredith's rented rooms in, 45–6
'The Rape of Aurora' (poem), 58
Reade, Winwood, *The Martyrdom of Man*, 137
A Reading of Earth, 126, 137
A Reading of Life, 222, 244
Reform Act, First (1832), 182, 184
Reform Act, Second (1867), 117, 184
religion, Meredith's attitude towards, 122–6, 127
'Reminiscences of a Volunteer', 200
Rhoda Fleming, 19, 39, 40, 49, 108, 109, 114, 138, 142, 155, 172, 173, 179–81, 188, 204, 206–7, 236, 239; plot summary, 259–61
Richard, Henry, 201
Richardson, Samuel, 216
Robinson, Lionel, 101, 110
Ross, Henry, Janet Duff Gordon's marriage to, 89–90
Rossetti, Dante Gabriel, 58, 102, 201
Rossetti, William Michael, 58, 91, 97, 102
Rothschild family, 206
Royal Academy, 80, 81
The Rubaiyat of Omar Khayyam, 84, 102
Rushdie, Salman, 69, 242
Ruskin, John, 80, 81, 91
Russell, William Howard, 63
Russia: Crimean War, 62–3, 99, 197, 201; Constantinople threatened by, 201; anti-Semitism in, 209

'The Sage Enamoured and the Honest Lady', (poem), 225–6, 227

St George's, Hanover Square,
    Meredith's marriage at (1849), 52
St James's Gazette, 101, 223, 237
Sala, George Augustus, 113
'Sandie', Meredith's dog, 231, 232,
    244
Sartre, Jean-Paul, *The Age of Reason*,
    241
Sassoon, Siegfried, 43, 134, 139, 240
Saturday Review, 12, 71, 77–8, 216–17,
    234, 235
Schiller, Friedrich, 'An die Freude',
    134
Schreiner, Olive, *The Story of an
    African Farm*, 220
science fiction, 223
Scott, A. J., 53
Scott, Sir Walter, 36, 53, 233, 235,
    240; *The Heart of Midlothian*, 241
Scribners, publishers, 218
Seaford, Sussex, Meredith in, 74, 78,
    109
Sebastopol, siege of, 63
The Secularist, 234
Sedan, battle of (1870), 198
'Seed-Time' (poem), 137
Sentimentalism, 114, 146
Shakespeare, William, 49, 120, 140,
    206, 237; *King Lear*, 94; *Othello*, 93;
    Richard II, 18; *Romeo and Juliet*, 18
The Shaving of Shagpat, 67–74, 77, 95,
    109, 178, 218
Shaw, George Bernard, 222, 245
Shelley, Mary, 47, 48
Shelley, Percy Bysshe, 46, 54, 234
Sheridan, Richard Brinsley, 159
Sherman, General, 198
Shore, Arabella, 237–8
Siddal, Lizzie, 102
Sikhs, 42–3
'The Sleeping City' (poem), 45
Smith, Elder & Co., publishers, 74
Smollett, Tobias, *Adventures of Peregrine
    Pickle*, 117
Smythe, George, 19
Social Democratic Federation, 113,
    182, 183, 201

Socialism, 182, 183; German, 183–6
Socialist League, 183
Society of Authors, 244; Meredith
    elected President of, 11
South African War (1899–1902),
    203
'South-west Wind in the Woodland'
    (poem), 57–8, 126–7, 131
Spectator, 12, 58, 72, 78, 96, 97, 217,
    235
Spencer, Herbert, 34, 85
Stalin, Josef, 186
Stead, W.T., 201, 243
Steel, Cecilia, 99
Steele, Anna, *So Runs the World Away*,
    220
Stendhal (Marie Henri Beyle), 70, 220
Stephen family, 102
Stephen, Leslie, 101–2, 199, 204, 219,
    222, 226, 232, 243, 247
Stephen, Virginia, 102, 140
Stevenson, George, 210, 211
Stevenson, Lionel, 102; biography of
    Meredith by, 40, 69, 139, 216
Stevenson, Robert Louis, 21, 122, 159,
    222, 223, 232, 233, 246, 247; *The
    Black Arrow*, 71; *Kidnapped*, 122;
    Prince Otto, 122; *Treasure Island*,
    122
Stone, Donald David, 241
Strachey, Giles Lytton, *Eminent
    Victorians*, 246
Sturgis, Henry Parkman (son-in-law),
    219, 243
Sturgis, Jack (grandson), 244
Sturgis, Mariette *see* Meredith
Stuttgart Gymnasium, 107
suicide, theme of, 93, 95, 102
Sully, James, 232
Sun, 72
Sunday Tramps, 101
Surtees, R.S., *Jorrocks' Jaunts and
    Jollities*, 14–15
Survey of London, 46
survival of the fittest, theory of, 85,
    129–30, 138
Swift, Jonathan, 247

Swinburne, Algernon, 97, 102, 116, 244, 245, 247; 'Laus Veneris', 102; *Poems and Ballads*, 97
Symons, Arthur, 217, 235

A Tale of Chloe (novella), 21
Tate Gallery, 80
Taylor, Tom, 63–4
Temple Bar, journal, 235, 236, 237
Tennyson, Alfred Lord, 59, 63, 64, 90, 94, 99, 137, 176–7, 245, 246; *The Charge of the Light Brigade*, 177; *Idylls of the King*, 176; 'In Memoriam', 59, 129, 130; 'Locksley Hall', 59; 'Morte d'Arthur', 59
Ternan, Ellen, 79
Thackeray, William Makepeace, 14, 86, 99, 148, 218, 223, 246
Thomas, Annie, 220
Thomson, James, 216
'The Three Singers to Young Blood' (poem), 141
Time, 217
The Times, 63, 86, 141, 217, 237
'To A.M.', sonnet, 227–8
Tolstoy, Lev, 121; *War and Peace*, 108
Tolstoy, Sonia, 108
The Tragic Comedians, 19, 148, 149–50, 151, 162, 166–7, 172, 181, 183, 184, 185, 187, 204, 206, 207–8, 216, 219, 238; plot summary, 277–8
Trevelyan, G.M., 240
Trollope, Anthony, 14, 108, 117, 148, 187, 201, 218, 241, 246; *He Knew He was Right*, 88; *Lady Anna*, 15–16; *The Warden*, 74
Trower, Seymour, 202
Tyndall, Professor John, 123

Vatican, 109, 124
Venice, 90, 109, 110, 113, 114
Victoria, Queen, 27, 61, 63, 202
Vienna, 101
Vigny, Alfred de, 80
Vine Cottage, Lower Halliford (Meredith home), 67, 78
Vittoria, 19, 20, 21, 41, 108, 109, 111,

114, 116, 117, 138, 156, 161, 173, 181, 194, 196, 204, 212–13, 234, 236; plot summary, 261–5
Vulliamy, Betty, 104
Vulliamy, Justin, 82, 104, 105, 114
Vulliamy, Kitty, 104, 114
Vulliamy, Marie *see* Meredith, Marie

Wagner, Richard, 68
Wales, Welsh, 20–1, 22, 47, 68, 175, 191, 206, 209–11; coal mining, 61; Mary and Wallis in, 78, 80–1; Meredith's visit to, 210–11
Wallis, Felix (Harold Meredith), 91
Wallis, Henry, 90, 91, 201; Mary's love affair with, 79–81, 82, 93, 161; *Thomas Love Peacock*, 89; *The Death of Chatterton*, 80, 81; *The Dead Stone-Breaker*, 81
wars, warfare, 197–205
Watts-Dunton, Walter Theodore, 244, 245
Waugh, Evelyn, *A Handful of Dust*, 246
Webb, Beatrice, 127
Weekly Register, 227
Wells, H.G., 81, 158, 163, 222; *The New Macchiavelli*, 153; *The Time Machine*, 223
West, Rebecca, 81
Westminster Abbey, Meredith refused burial in, 244–5, 246
Westminster Review, 65, 71, 97, 164, 234
Whigs, 182
Wilde, Oscar, 122, 222, 223
Wilhelm II, Kaiser, 37
Willis and Sotheran, 90
Wolf, Lucien, *The Russian Government and the Massacres*, 209
Wollstonecraft, Mary, 47
women, 47–8, 83, 217; education of, 31–3, 140; 'mad', 48–9; Meredith's attitude to and understanding of, 94, 103, 114, 139–74; votes for, 140; and romantic love, 145–7; masculine contempt for, 150–1; seducers of, 152–4, 157; sisterhood

of, 155; extra-marital love and adultery, 156–8, 159, 163, 224; intelligent and independent, 158–61, 228–9; revolt against male domination, 164–6; and marriage, 141–4, 147, 155, 165–73; as writers, 220

Wood, Mrs Benjamin, 87–8

Wood, Mrs Henry, *East Lynne*, 220

Woods, Alice, *George Meredith as Champion of Women and of Progressive Education*, 31, 34, 140, 172

'The Woods of Westermain' (poem), 132–3, 240

Woolf, Virginia, 85, 102, 237, 248; *To the Lighthouse*, 102

Wordsworth, William, 59, 80, 126

Wyse, Mrs, 233

Wyse, William Charles Bonaparte, 101, 103, 104, 109, 110, 211, 219

Yeo, Dr Burney, 232

Young England Movement, 189

'Youth in Memory' (poem), 242–3

Zangwill, Israel, 209

Zinzendorf, Count, 26–7

Zionism, 209

Zola, Emile, 48, 208–9; *Germinal*, 210

Zulu war (1879), 203